THE FUN FACTORY

THE FUN FACTORY

A Life in the BBC

WILL WYATT

AURUM PRESS

First published in Great Britain
2003 by Aurum Press Ltd
25 Bedford Avenue, London WC1B 3AT

Design by Don McPherson

A catalogue record for this book is available from the British Library.

ISBN 1 85410 915 4

1 3 5 7 9 10 8 6 4 2
2003 2005 2007 2006 2004

Typeset by M Rules
Printed in Great Britain by MPG Books Ltd, Bodmin

CONTENTS

CREDITS

For most of the years I was in the BBC I kept diaries and notes, not with a book in mind, merely to help remember glimpses of the passing scene. Most of the quotations in the book come from these. Where not, I have put into my own mouth my recall of what I said at the time and of how a conversation went.

It was my agent Hilary Rubinstein who suggested that I try this book and provided invaluable advice and cheering encouragement since. Piers Burnett at Aurum Press was bold enough to commission it and offer helpful suggestions.

I owe a debt to all my colleagues in the BBC. For reasons of space, I am unable to mention many with whom I worked closely and happily, particularly when producing television programmes. I do remember what I owe them and thank them.

To some I owe specific thanks for guidance during the writing of the book. Eddie Mirzoeff read most of it, put me right on some important matters, corrected some blatant errors and pointed out boring bits to cut. Iain Johnstone jogged my memories of early days, read many chapters and was equally candid. John Reynolds shared recollections of the newsroom and provided a disinterested critique of several chapters. Mike Fentiman, Tim Slessor, Brian Elliott, Kate Smith, Nicholas Moss, John Smith and David Docherty all provided significant help with my colouring in. Roger Mills provided trenchant advice on early chapters. Jonathan Martin checked my thoughts and memories for the chapter on sport. Robin Foster did the same for the final years and Keith Samuel for some early chapters. Jim Moir braved many chapters and steered me to where scissors were required. Others tipped in a memory or two and words of advice, among them David Barlow, Peter Bell, Paul Bonner, Bill Cotton, Nicholas Kenyon, Roger Laughton, Ron Neil and Peter Pagnamenta.

Steven Barnett gave the whole thing the once over to protect me from embarrassing howlers on the politics of broadcasting. I had many occasions to consult *The Battle For The BBC*, the book he wrote with Andrew Curry.

If there are mistakes or you nod off, the blame is all mine. All the above have seriously reduced the risks.

BBC Archives provided assistance wherever I requested it, and my thanks go to Paul Fiander for opening the doors and to Jeff Walden at Caversham and Kay Green at Ariel Way for digging out files in such a willing and friendly manner. At my right hand for much of the time were Leslie Halliwell's *Television Companion* and Jeff Evans' indispensable *The Penguin TV Companion*. I turned also to memoirs by John Birt, Bill Cotton, Marmaduke Hussey and Alasdair Milne, and to Michael Leapman's *Last Days of the Beeb* (he got that wrong) and Chris Horrie and Steve Clarke's *Fuzzy Monsters*.

Both my daughters, Hannah and Rozzy, have helped me beef up my limited keyboard skills. The greatest thanks go to my wife Jane. She appeared to tolerate my mental absences. She read the text as I went along and encouraged me. She provided for the writing of the book, as through all the events recorded in it, her loving support, for which I am a very lucky man.

In memory of my parents.

A mighty maze of mystic magic rays,
Is all about us in the blue,
And in sight and sound we trace,
Living pictures out of space,
To bring a new wonder to you.

So there's joy in store,
The world is at your door,
It's here for everyone to view...
Conjured up in sound and sight,
By the magic rays of light,
That bring television to you.

(Song composed for and performed in the opening programme of BBC television 1936)

Cannot [the television industry] understand that the one hope we have against this shallow evil and all-pervading influence is satiety and boredom? Is there not one silent moment during its self-worshipping assemblies when at least some look round and see themselves for what they are?

When men and women and their children finally switch it off and walk out into the gardens and streets, and see life again as it really is, and all the exhibitionist riff-raff are reduced once more to their proper level, television will have justified itself. It had to happen, it had to be destroyed and it will have destroyed itself.

Bring on more channels, more rubbish, and to hell with pseudo 'seriousness' of the so-called 'quality' programmes. The difference in value between a clown and the most exhibitionistic 'intellectual' pontificating on a screen is conceit and an expensive suit.

(Letter in *The Times*, 1987)

INTRODUCTION

This is neither an autobiography nor a history of the BBC. It is an account of my thirty-four years in the Corporation, of whatever small or large corner I was occupying and the view from there. Much of it is culled from diaries and notes I kept at the time. I will have underplayed some mighty themes and events and played up some minor matters, but this is the way it was – for me.

Chapter one
THE LIKELY LADS

'Before we start, you should know that I was against you getting this job,' I said. 'In fact, I thought that you should not even be a candidate.' Greg Dyke's amiable expression didn't change. I looked hard at his smooth features for a sign of irritation or indifference. It was still difficult to get used to a clean-shaven Greg. He had been bearded ever since he had come to prominence in the *TV:AM* days, but had shaved his facial hair off earlier in the year, presumably believing that serious candidates for the top job at the BBC came beardless.

'I am sure that you know that already,' I continued, 'but I thought I should tell you myself so that it is not lying there between us like an unopened package.'

It was 21 July 1999, just a month after Greg had been named as the thirteenth director-general of the BBC. He would take over in April of the following year. He had come for a sandwich lunch in my office on the fourth floor of the modern extension at the very rear of Broadcasting House.

'My concerns were mainly because you were a public supporter of a political party, but, now that you have the job, I will do whatever I can to help you make it a success.'

'Except stay on, I understand?' Greg replied.

'Except that.'

I was due to retire from the BBC at the end of 1999, after more than thirty-four years in the organization. I had loved it. I still believed it to be one of the glories of life in the United Kingdom. I relished the company and stimulation of my immediate colleagues and of almost everyone I came across in the BBC. But it was time to move on and I had already accepted other commitments.

On the morning of the press conference at which Greg's appointment had been announced a few weeks earlier, John Birt, the director-general, had telephoned me to suggest I go along to the chairman's office. I went in order to welcome Greg but, just as I passed the lift, he was getting into it to go down for a photo-shoot in the street outside. We caught each other's eye and raised eyebrows in wordless greeting, as people do when trapped out of reach. As I went into the outer office, the chairman, Sir Christopher Bland, looked a little surprised when he saw me. 'Will,' he said, and came forward to put his hand on my shoulder. Was he holding me at length lest I strike him? Was he restraining himself from thumping me? Was this part of a new touchy-feely BBC? Or was he merely expressing a conciliatory warmth? I hoped it was the last of these.

'Greg brings a lot to the place and I'll do anything I can to make it work,' I said.

'Anything?' asked Christopher. 'Like staying on another eighteen months?'

'I exaggerated.'

I walked downstairs and caught up with Greg in the corridor outside the green room to the art deco radio concert hall where the press conference was to be held. 'Welcome and congratulations,' I said. 'This is an absolutely wonderful organization and I know that you'll give it everything you've got. You'll have a marvellous time and find the place stuffed with terrific people.'

He was clearly very tense and seemed rather emotional. Although we didn't know each other well, he actually stepped forward and gave me a hug.

Thus ended a year and a half of speculation and scheming, of auditioning and aspiring. At first this had been no more than the sound of an off-stage band as the business of the BBC went on, but over the first six months of 1999 both volume and tempo obscured much else.

Throughout this time John Birt, the current director-general, had kept his foot hard down on the accelerator. His time in office had been one of radical change, dramatic events and continuous controversy. Now he was determined that he would leave the BBC with a licence fee settlement sufficient for it to be as powerful a player in the digital broadcasting world as it had been in the analogue era, and with the full map of the BBC's future digital services devised and agreed.

John had first laid out his own timetable to me in November 1997. The BBC was celebrating its 75th anniversary in ways that, we hoped, would remind people of its uniqueness and underline its value to the United Kingdom. The Queen had paid a visit to Broadcasting House to open the BBC Experience, the new visitor attraction. There was to be a great show-off concert in St Paul's Cathedral, with the BBC Symphony Orchestra performing Elgar's *The Dream of Gerontius*.

It was on the morning of that concert that John had asked me to come and see him. Bob Phillis, the deputy director-general who was leaving to be chief executive of the Guardian Media Group, had been seen off with a drinks party in the council chamber two days earlier. John's first question was to ask if I would now deputize for him in his absence. I said yes. He had also wanted the World Service to report to me. 'Too much,' I said. I had enough on my plate already. As Chief Executive, Broadcast, I was responsible for our domestic television and radio services, including the regional services and education, for the plans for new television channels and for the development of our non-news internet services.

'Well, in any case,' said John, 'the governors insisted on World Service being represented on the executive committee, and I had to go along with it.'

He then talked about the succession. 'I will definitely go in March 2000, when my contract runs out. There will be an early advertisement for my successor, in the spring of 1999, with the aim of getting someone in place by the autumn for six months as deputy director-general before taking over. I know that we agreed with you that September 1999 would be when you leave. Would you think about staying on until December in order to help get your successor in place?'

I said that I didn't think that would be a problem. John continued, 'The time will be right then for the next generation to take over.' I said that I hoped that it would be someone from inside who followed him. So did he. The trouble was, I observed, that many of the best candidates were for the most part a step, or even two, off the pace. It was unlikely that the board of governors, who would make the appointment, would opt for an internal person who was not on the executive committee. In which case, it would be necessary to get the leading contenders into big jobs as soon as possible. John thought a change round was needed early in the following summer. During the conversation there was a half-hesitant moment when John didn't quite say that he hoped I wasn't expecting to be a candidate. He need not have worried. I did not expect to be and I did not wish to be, as those closest to me well knew.

I had better try to convince the reader about this. And try not to sound as if I protest too much. I had thought about the director-generalship some years back, not because I thought that I was likely to be a prime candidate, but because, given the unpredictabilities of life, I could well find myself invited to the start line at some point, if only to make up the numbers. The job is an incredibly onerous one, and has become more so over the years. The responsibilities are enormous.

It wasn't the breadth of the editorial and creative leadership that I shied from – I felt confident of my judgement and abilities there. It was the stewardship of the great institution in increasingly difficult and complicated times. It was the need to take on one's shoulders all of the organization's purposes, activities and needs, from broadcasting overseas to driving its commercial operations. It was deciding an institutional course and steering to it through the rough and tumble of the political world. I could go on. I didn't feel that this was for me or that I was right for it. I was sure that anyone who had such doubts should not be doing the job. Also, perhaps, I was just chicken.

When I was at Cambridge, I was a fair rugby player for my college, Emmanuel, which was one of the best at the game. I was secretary of the rugby club in my second year. We won the college league and the seven-a-side tournament, which replaced the usual knock-out cup in that winter of frost and snow. The form was that the secretary went on to be captain in the following year, but I said that, while I wished to go on playing, I did not wish to be captain. I gave myself and my team-mates reasons, some of which were the same: I had better do more work in my final year, I wanted to spend more time in London where a girlfriend was going to art school, I didn't want to dedicate my whole time to rugby on and off the field, I loved the game but a little of the social side went a long way, and so on. In retrospect, I can see that I was dodging the responsibility. So, I had clucked before. Perhaps there was a pattern. I think I would have been a first-rate rugby captain. I don't have the same confidence about me as candidate for director-general.

I had been obliged to think all this through in 1996 and 1997, when it was uncertain as to whether John Birt would stay on beyond his five-year contract, which was due to end at the beginning of 1998. A number of colleagues came to me (and, no doubt, to enough others to provide insurance that was fully comprehensive), saying that John would go, he would have 'had enough', he 'wanted to go off and make some money', and that I was the 'obvious' choice to succeed. I discussed the possibilities with Jane, my wife, who was horrified by the thought. All her worst fears would be confirmed: yet more pressure, an even more distracted husband, a diary with even fewer moments of calm, journalists . . .

A bad moment for Jane came the following March. It was a Sunday evening and we were catching up with a video of *Dalziel and Pascoe* when I had a phone call from an excited sounding friend.

'Will, I've been with New Labour people, people close to Tony and Mandy, weekends at Chequers and so on. They were saying they wouldn't have wanted John Birt renewed any further and were critical of how he had not arranged the succession properly. They said it would have to be Will. I said, "Well, my understanding from Will is that he is very happy doing what he is doing but that he'd like to go off and do some other things." "No," they said, "he's lying. We've looked outside and there is no one else and he has the experience to do it so it will be him."'

This was very flattering, if not very insightful. It sounded like the sort of conversation that susceptible and self-important acolytes of the new government might have. But it meant little; neither they, nor Tony and Mandy, would be making the decision.

I recounted the conversation to Jane, whose feelings about the matter were evident in her response: 'Bloody hell.' She thought for a while and said, 'You'd do it if they pressed, wouldn't you?'

'Probably not. But it isn't going to happen. The next director-general will not be someone who palpably has no appetite for it, doesn't apply and would be 58 on taking over.' I restarted the video.

By April 1998 John's plans to leave in March 2000 had become public, and soon after, Christopher Bland's term as chairman was extended until 2003, so he would have three years working with his appointee. The governors also made it known that they wanted a much more open process than last time. Then, there had been no advertisement, no outside candidates and just two inside candidates: the incumbent, Sir Michael Checkland, who wished to stay on for at least two years, and his deputy director-general, John Birt.

This time the internals were aplenty. There was Tony Hall, chief executive of news, dubbed 'the head prefect' because of his eager beaver style; he had done well in news and the demeanour of his immediate team revealed his ambition for the top job. Patricia Hodgson was the highly able director of policy and planning and formerly secretary to the board of governors; her antennae were ever sensitive to opportunity or threat. Alan Yentob, who was the director of television, after excitingly successful spells as controller of BBC2 and then BBC1. Matthew Bannister, director of radio, was best known as the controller of Radio 1 who cleared out the Smashey and Nicey old guard of disc jockeys. Mark Byford, the director of regional broadcasting, had little public profile but was a rising star. Mark Thompson, controller of BBC2, was very bright and had demonstrated his talent both in news and in general programming.

On most people's long list of externals were Greg Dyke, chief executive of Pearson Television and long-time friend and colleague of Christopher Bland's from London Weekend Television; David Elstein, chief executive of Channel 5, always said to be very clever; Michael Jackson, who the previous year had left the BBC, where he had been controller of BBC2 and briefly of BBC1, to become chief executive of Channel 4; Howard Stringer, the Oxford-educated Welshman who was now president of Sony Entertainment after running CBS; and a name that was to cause considerable confusion in the early grindings of the gossip mill, Richard Eyre, chief executive of ITV and before that of Capital Radio, confused by some with Sir Richard Eyre, director of the National Theatre and a BBC governor.

The early rumblings of troop movements began, camouflage gear was donned and reconnaissances made. One evening in April, after a late meeting in my office to discuss film deals, John Smith, the director of finance and a good friend, lingered to observe that Patricia Hodgson and Tony Hall were fastest off their blocks. 'So, is the view that it's between them?' I asked.

'Not in Patricia's mind,' replied John. 'She believes that she is locked in mortal combat with you over the succession.'

'I'd better disabuse her.'

A week or so later I went to see Patricia after navigating the chicane of her outer office. Ever since I had known her, Patricia's PAs, presumably at her instruction, would play the game of making sure that you came onto the telephone line before she did. 'Shall we go through now?' her PA would ask yours, the convention being, and one would say common courtesy, that both put their bosses through together. But no. Only yours would press the connect button so that you had to speak to the PA before you were allowed to speak to Patricia herself. It irritated other PAs, who were made to feel junior. I just smiled.

In her office I told Patricia that she might like to know that I was not in any way a candidate for DG. I did a 'do not seek, will not accept' routine and said that if she were to work it out, I would, in any event, be too old.

'Oh, I thought that you would not be going until 2002 or 2003.' No, I said, I was going when planned and thought that she ought to know that. This seemed to set her mind buzzing.

A few days later I called Tony Hall and told him the same. He was full of thanks and sounded relieved to know that at least one obstacle had definitely been cleared. I said that if he wanted to talk about it at all, I was happy to. But we did not talk about the competition again until it was all over. I nearly did with Patricia in August that year, when we had lunch together in Soho. She was just back from holiday and very relaxed. We shared a liking for the American West, which we had both recently visited, and for Doris Day, a cassette of whom Patricia had once kindly given me. With my being definitely on the Deadwood stagecoach out of the BBC, we talked in general terms about what I might be doing. We talked about holidays, about the licence fee plans and internet developments. It was only afterwards that I realized the conversation had slowed to a walk near the end of the meal and that she had looked a little crestfallen. She had sought to raise the subject of John's successor by expressing her amusement at, and disapproval of, his plan to write an autobiography and I had not risen to the bait. Had she hoped that I was going to declare for her? After my visit to her office, word had got back to me that she believed I was playing my candidate's hand very, very cleverly.

The external name that aroused most early interest within the BBC was that of Michael Jackson. He had been much admired by those working with him in the Corporation, if a distant and rather enigmatic figure to many. He had not long left; was he enjoying Channel 4? I did not think that he was a serious candidate. He had yet to prove himself in his new job and, although he had a natural aptitude for television programme making and commissioning, he had at the BBC avoided managerial chores whenever he could. Sensible enough, you might think, for someone concentrating on the creative needs of his job as channel controller, but he had not had the right preparation, at least not yet, for running the BBC.

I was fond of Michael, I admired him and had promoted him three times, and now wished to hear his thoughts. And there were other BBC–Channel 4 matters to discuss, so I invited him to dinner. I had asked Sally, my PA, to book somewhere special, as Michael, skinny and ascetic looking as he was, liked good restaurants and, in particular, good wine. I had once seen him take a mouthful of a perfectly decent, if rather rustic, Hungarian red, and splutter it out in shock and disgust. We went to the Oak Room at The Meridian in Piccadilly.

I had never been a big expenses man and I call various BBC directors of finance as my witnesses to this. I liked good but appropriate restaurants. The Oak Room was certainly good, but an inappropriate place to go on public money. Michael and I had a happy and useful conversation. He had obviously settled comfortably into his new role. He enjoyed the sense of flirtation with the BBC but I didn't think for a minute that he would move back as anything other than DG, and it was far too soon for that. The occasion was chiefly memorable for Michael asking the waiter if he could have his main course 'without the sauce'. He might as well have asked a cardinal for a contraceptive. The waiter could not believe what he had heard. But the dish came as requested. When I reminded Michael of this later, he said that his memories were the sommelier's face when I asked him to recommend a bottle for under £100 and my grimace when the bill arrived. I put in my expenses the following day with a note of apology and a plea for exculpation.

May was the time when the executive committee and the board of governors went away for their annual review of the BBC's performance. The twelve governors comprised a non-executive lay body that in law constituted the BBC and was responsible for its overall strategy and performance. It met monthly, made appointments to the senior raft of jobs and held management to account. The eleven-strong executive committee (formerly the board of management) attended the governors' meetings and once a year joined the governors for a two and a half day conference. I decided that I would use the occasion to concentrate hard on my colleagues and decide who I thought was the best candidate for the succession. I favoured an internal appointment. Insiders usually do, especially lifers like myself. Only a fellow knight of the holy order, we like to think, could appreciate and understand the mystical complexity of our church, could be entrusted with its stewardship. But it was not blinkers alone that influenced me. The outside field was not strong, and there was a clutch of talented and energetic executives taking the BBC forward.

The venue was Wood Norton, a BBC owned and operated hotel and conference centre in a converted country house, near Evesham. It was a property the Corporation would have been happy to sell, but in its grounds was the bunker for emergency broadcasting in the event of war, so it could not be flogged off. BBC resources had made a virtue of this necessity and did a good job running it. The food was good, the rooms were comfortable and it was said to make a profit. The conference room was a bit of a squash for the governors and executives together. That, no doubt, helped the bonding. We sat in a rectangle, elbows touching, in front of us a pile of papers, a new A4 pad and a little block of yellow Wood Norton post-its on which was printed the endearingly old-fashioned house motto, '...You'll be impressed'.

The mood of the two days endorsed the sense that there were good people in position. We assembled the day after the British Academy of Film and Television Arts' awards ceremony, at which we had been spectacularly successful, achieving, among other things, a clean sweep of the drama awards. As the different parts of the BBC were reviewed, the governors were warm in their praise. When we broke up, Sir David Scholey, the distinguished banker and one of the most respected members of the board, offered his congratulations on both performance and the quality of papers and discussion: 'I have been to many such gatherings, but I shall never attend a better conference at any company.'

As my colleagues had made their presentations, responded to questions, dealt with criticisms and contributed to the debates, I had sized them up against the requirements of the top job. To my mind, the director-general had to be passionate about the importance of public service broadcasting, to understand and believe in the purposes and values of the BBC, its creative, democratic and educational roles. He or she had to be able to offer strong leadership to sustain this vision and the managerial capability to run the place effectively, providing licence fee payers with outstanding programmes and services and value for money.

The director-general would also need the energy and skill to drive through and achieve the BBC's emerging strategy for the world of digital broadcasting. A new license fee settlement would most likely be secured before the new person took over, but then the task would be to set a course through the political and competitive mountain ranges ahead in order to renew the BBC's charter, which ran until 2006. The right candidate would also have to command the respect of difficult constituencies within and without the organization. Over the following months, as I thought more about what the BBC had in front of it, I also came to believe that it needed someone who had the ability to change the culture of the BBC, to make it more collaborative and less internally competitive.

By the time I left Wood Norton Hall, I knew my favoured candidate. It was not my good friend Alan Yentob, the best known of BBC executives other than John Birt. Alan was the most exhilarating of all the colleagues that I worked with at the BBC. He had true brilliance and originality in devising programmes, in spotting talent and in developing ideas. He was tireless in forging relationships with the artistes, writers and producers he wanted for his programme or channel. He was indefatigable in his determination to get the best programmes and resolute in his refusal to put up with crap. He was a powerful and convincing advocate of the BBC's case. He was terrific fun to have around.

But he could be maddening in his procrastination. He was accused of being indecisive but that missed the point. He was often very decisive but he would not make a decision until he absolutely had to, until he was sure that he could not get something better, that all possible improvements had been made. But he was not well organized, was easily distracted and, because of his lack of administrative skills and chaotic time management, often left a trail of confusion and upset people in his wake. I loved him but he was not a director-general.

I had told Alan not to expect to get the job some months earlier. 'Alan, don't set your heart on getting it. It is a job that doesn't play to your strengths. I just don't think they will give it to you.' Whether he realized that or not intellectually, he could certainly not accommodate any such conclusion emotionally. Alan is a star. If the curtain rises, he has to perform.

My candidate was Mark Byford, the director of regional broadcasting. He was young, just coming up to his 40th birthday, and while his experience had been almost all in journalism, he was imbued with a deep belief in what the BBC stood for and had a natural ease and confidence in command. He was clever, dead straight, tough and determined and led from the front. He had been reporting to me for two years and I had watched him in action at close quarters. Apart from admiring his effectiveness as a journalist and manager, I liked his way with people. I had visited BBC staff in different parts of the country with him. He seemed to know everyone and they appeared genuinely pleased to see him. For some he was too much the no-frills Yorkshireman, but he exuded great warmth and demonstrated a punctilious courtesy to people at every level. I did not reveal my thoughts to him then, but shortly afterwards, when he and I were in Glasgow to visit the site at Pacific Quay, earmarked for a new home for BBC Scotland. I told him over a drink that he should see himself as a leading candidate, if he didn't already, and prepare accordingly. He must have heard this from others, too.

John Birt had begun a senior management succession plan a couple of years earlier. It was less a plan than a twice-yearly audit of the strengths, weaknesses and development needs of the rising talent, matched loosely against the likely opportunities. He now arranged several meetings with Margaret Salmon, the director of personnel, Ron Neil, the chief executive of production, who was due to retire at the end of 1998, and me.

It was essential to get at least two of the younger candidates for the director-generalship onto the executive committee to give them experience at the top level. It was already late. There would be barely six months for newcomers to make their mark. Ron's departure would create space for a new head of all the radio and television programme producing departments. Other positions were all filled, though it soon became evident that, off-stage, the cerebral Sam Younger, doing a competent if unspectacular job at World Service, was seen as expendable if room had to be made.

The pace was quickening. At their next meeting the governors wanted a briefing from Ron and me, as two disinterested parties, on the promotables, all of whom were working to one or other of us. As I had had to be around in August when John was away, Jane and I had taken a week's holiday in the Lake District, a place we had visited every year for thirty years, to clear the head and stretch the limbs. So, on 2 September, Jane and I rose at 4.30 so she could drive me to Penrith for the train to London. There was a full turnout of the board.

We gave our views of the runners and riders and some other ascending executives. The board, probably hard pushed by the chairman, were up for changes. 'How old is he?' he asked more than once, 'I'm ageist.' Sir Richard Eyre, director of the National Theatre, expressed concern that there was no one, other than Alan, who had experience of drama, entertainment or the arts. Michael Jackson was mentioned as if he might be the answer. Toughness was in the air.

Afterwards, John told me that the board favoured an outside appointment for DG, 'but let them go along that path and see who emerges', adding, 'inside will probably be the answer'. I caught an afternoon train back to Cumbria, where Ron rang me the following day. His news was that the board were gung-ho for easing out Sam Younger and moving Mark Byford to World Service. I thought that Mark's best bet would be production, as it would give him wider experience of the mainstream programme output across radio and television. A call at the weekend confirmed what Ron had told me and that it was Matthew who would take over the large and difficult production job. Sam Younger did not wish to go quietly, but in the event a deal was done and the new appointments announced on 22 September. (Sam fell on his feet as chairman of the Electoral Commission.)

I now had to fill the radio and regional broadcasting jobs. I rang Mark Thompson to urge him to apply for the regions. As controller of BBC2, he was in the best job in the whole of the BBC, the one job that I had aspired to and had twice been passed over for, but he couldn't do it for ever. If he wanted to succeed me, say, he needed to be on the board of management.

'Do you really think that I have a chance?' he asked.

'Put it this way, if you don't make a move now, you won't.'

We met for breakfast at Maison Blanc in Chiswick. I pointed out that the regions job had a huge managerial span. 'You will learn a lot about yourself and about managing, and the BBC will learn more about you. It will mean close relations with some of the governors and with the party political world. It will be hard graft but interesting and important. You will also get around the country and pick up more about what is going on in the United Kingdom than most others in the BBC. This will be fun. You would enjoy it.'

The interviews were on 18 November. The chairman, John and the four governors for the regions made up the panel. I opened with a briefing about the job and the candidates, then we interviewed three good people. Mark Thompson didn't let me down. After a nervous start, he shone, his breadth of experience and clarity of thought putting him well ahead. The governors and management were able to preen themselves upon the quality of all three candidates.

For Radio, the regional governors were replaced by three others. We saw Jenny Abramsky, head of continuous news, who'd launched Radio 5 Live, and James Boyle, the controversial controller of Radio 4. James had just had some more encouraging figures for his new schedule but Jenny was the person I wanted. She was more convincing in interview, full of good sense and with a deep understanding of, and love for, radio, and my recommendation was accepted.

As the year ended, there was a sense that the new cohort was beginning to take over. It just remained for the stalls to open and the race proper to get under way. Notice of this came with a confidential memo to members of the executive committee in January 1999. It laid out the timetable the governors intended to follow: headhunters appointed in mid-January, advertisements in March, leading to a decision in June.

The following day *Broadcast* magazine, the industry weekly, reported that Ladbroke's was taking bets on who would succeed John Birt. They had Greg Dyke and Michael Jackson joint favourites at 3–1; Matthew Bannister, now chief executive of BBC Production, at 5–1; Richard Eyre, chief executive of ITV, and me at 6–1; Alan Yentob at 7–1; Michael Grade, now running First Leisure, 8–1; Tony Hall, 10–1; Mark Byford, now chief executive BBC world service, 12–1; and David Elstein, 20–1. I spotted an opportunity, or so I thought. I knew that least one of the joint fourth favourites wasn't running, that Alan and Michael Grade were 'the rags' in betting terms, that Christopher Bland had been heard to say 'over my dead body' when Elstein's name was mentioned. Surely I had an edge here? I reckoned that Greg, a public and current supporter of the Labour party, had to be disqualified for that reason, so I decided to oppose him. It is easy to convince yourself that things can't happen just because you think that they shouldn't.

I didn't have an account with Ladbroke's and, in any case, I thought vainly, they might cramp the odds if I called them. I rang Sir Peter O'Sullevan and explained the position. 'Peter I think I know this field. Can you get on for me?' That most urbane and beautifully modulated of all broadcasting voices replied,

'Of course, Will, I might even have a little myself. Let me take this down.' I plunged.

'I want £100 on Mark Byford at twelves and £50 each on Richard Eyre and Matthew Bannister.'

As it happened, Peter and I were both guests at a small lunch given by Ladbroke's the following day. When we got up to leave, Peter came round the table conspiratorially. 'You're on. And I managed to get you £1250 to 100 on Byford.' I sensed that he was shrewd enough to keep his own money for the horses.

The chattering was everywhere one went over the next few months. 'Can we talk DG?' Matthew Freud, with whom I had barely a nodding acquaintanceship, took a moment off from moving and shaking to pose the question before a dinner at the Canadian High Commission. He was keen to talk up the case for some people in the music business. Then, 'What about Greg?' I was casting myself as a bit of an old wiseacre, beyond ambition, bags of inside track, scrutinizing the auguries with a furrowed brow.

'It's very difficult to see how such a prominent funder of the Labour party could take the job,' I replied.

'I think he might like it,' said Freud, 'after all, he's got nothing much to do.'

At a big reception at Buckingham Palace to mark Sir Robert Fellowes' retirement as private secretary to the Queen, Elspeth Howe, chairman of the Broadcasting Standards Commission, came charging over to ask what was happening. After a brief exchange of gossip, she slid off and Geoffrey, her husband, arrived. 'Do you know where she is, because we were just about to leave?'

'She may be next door looking at some videos,' I suggested. Geoffrey smiled.

'Do you know, I can tell you that the sex scenes look just the same on fast reverse as they do on fast forward.' Before there was time to pursue this insight further, he melted into the throng in search of his wife.

I had evidence that at least two of the putative outside candidates were indeed serious at a cosy dinner that Bob Phillis gave for Chris Smith at the Garrick club. Among the other guests was David Elstein, renowned in the industry for taking on the case for each new employer as would a junior barrister assigned to the next accused. He had been a noisy critic of the licence fee and here he was now, offering warm support for the Corporation. Another guest was ITV's Richard Eyre, who was strong on the value and distinctiveness of Radio 1. No commercial broadcaster could take the risk of programming it with such a range of new and specialist music, he said.

On Monday, 15 February I had a rare routine meeting with John Birt. 'Routines' are a longstanding part of the BBC's conduct of affairs, diaried meetings with an ad hoc agenda. They tended to be squeezed out by the pace and intensity of other business. John would have a typed list of matters he wanted to raise but always allowed me to go down my list first. The inevitable outcome was that there was never time to reach his agenda unless I had talked about some of the same things.

On this occasion we quickly began talking about the succession. For the first time he asked me, 'Who do you think it should be?' I said that I'd thought about it long and carefully and my choice was Mark Byford. For the first time he gave me his view. 'I agree,' he said. 'But I'm keeping it to myself at the moment. I think that we have got to play it long while the governors go through the search. They're very keen to have the right process and do it in the proper manner. The chairman,' he continued, 'is absolutely adamant that a strong managerial capacity is necessary. The BBC is a large and complex place to manage and it will need a considerable talent to do so. Christopher will be looking for clear evidence that the person can cope with the task.' He paused and pursed his lips. 'Of course, they could go for a big creature from outside.'

Thinking about the discussion afterwards, it came home to me how important it was to John that he achieve an orderly transition. He had revolutionized the way in which the BBC was run, had won the confidence of government, and many other external constituencies, obtained one good licence fee settlement and was moving towards another, had moved swiftly to take advantage of the new technologies and was drawing up the chart for the journeys ahead. We were working flat out on the grand digital strategy that would be his lasting legacy, to be implemented by his successor. John wanted endorsement of his success, which would come with continuity, with the crowning of an internal candidate, one of his team, someone who had learned and developed in his time. 'I will be closely involved with the process,' he had told me. 'The governors have had one meeting without me, so they had the opportunity to rubbish me if they wanted to. But I know from several accounts that they didn't. They want the place to continue on broadly the same lines.'

But did they? Or was John deceiving himself, even whistling to keep his spirits up? With hindsight it is evident that the governors did wish the BBC to travel in the same strategic direction, one they had approved and supported, but that they wanted a change of style and atmosphere. For some

governors that would only come with an outside appointment; for
Christopher Bland that meant Greg Dyke.

Looking back it seems so obvious that Christopher's fingers were on the
scales. Many observers saw it at the time. Yet I was able to convince myself
otherwise. Just because Christopher had once famously said, 'Every organization needs a Greg Dyke,' didn't mean he believed that the BBC needed one
as director-general. Because Christopher was close to Greg from working
with him in a successful partnership at London Weekend Television, it meant
that he would know his weaknesses as well as his strengths, weaknesses that
could hobble a DG. I would unload these self-deluding thoughts on anyone
who would listen. 'The fool doth think he is wise, but the wise man knows
himself to be a fool.'

The next time I discussed all this at length with John was towards the end
of April when he had asked me to come along 'for a little plot'. The morning was a sad one. Jill Dando had been murdered the previous day and the
whole of the BBC was reeling from, puzzling at and grieving over her death.
We had both known her, John better than I, and he was downcast. We
talked about the press coverage and speculated on the possible reasons for
the killing. Something to do with *Crimewatch*? Something in her past? A
crazy stalker? A Serbian connection? Everybody had loved Jill. It seemed
impossible that she could be shot so openly.

We moved on to the purpose of the meeting, a review of where the contest had got to and of what we could do to bring about the desired outcome.
We went over the internal candidates again. Matthew Bannister was able,
resilient as the Radio 1 saga had shown, had dash and presence but was
impetuous and inclined to bump into the furniture. Alan Yentob was not
right for the job but it was essential that the BBC kept him and that he
remained buoyant and motivated. John's chief worry was Patricia Hodgson.
She had a masterly grip of the political needs of the BBC and was a con-
summate operator but was completely wrong for the job. His concern was
that she knew well how to play the governors and would be convincing in
interview.

Mark Thompson was possibly the ablest of all but just did not have the
right experience yet. Worth a big ante-post wager, I thought, for the next running of this race. Tony Hall deserved a place near the head of the market this
time. He had done a big job well at news, was a good manager, believed in the
place, but did he have the stature for the job? Byford was definitely our man.

We swept quickly through the outside candidates, dismissing Richard
Eyre, who had only run tiny organizations, and settled on Greg. I rehearsed
his virtues. He would bring bounce, oomph, knowledge of the commercial
world. He was experienced editorially, knew about both television production and broadcasting. 'He is also very impetuous,' I said. 'When we did the
Premier League deal in 1992, I got a strong message that some of the football people were fed up with being told what to do by him.' And he had been
noisily dismissive of independent producers in a way that helped propel the
campaign for the 25 per cent quota for BBC and ITV. 'He's a free-booter, a

bit of a buccaneer. Very attractive qualities in many ways, but they could be a liability running the BBC.'

John was chuckling by now. 'He was my candidate to be my successor at LWT but I absolutely don't think that he is right to be director-general. What do you think about the politics?' I said that they disqualified him.

'But what about the chairman? He was a Tory.'

'It's quite different,' I said. 'Several chairmen of the BBC have been political figures. They are appointed by the government of the day. Everyone understands that. And there's usually a balance on the board. The director-general is quite different. He's the editor-in-chief, appointed by the board, not the government. We have never known the director-general's politics.'

'What about Ian Trethowan?' asked John. 'We knew his.'

'We could guess them,' I replied, 'but they were never declared publicly. We could guess the politics of other directors-general but they were never a matter of public record. That is a very important defence for the BBC and a matter of principle in my view. Under Mrs Thatcher the board of governors became increasingly politicized. It was less so under Major, but it is clear that we are going back to it in a big way under the current government.'

'You're quite right,' said John. 'I've been talking to people in government recently and saying how dangerous it was.'

'Too true.' I said. We then went through the governors and apportioned lobbying duties if they were required.

I went back to my office where Patricia came to see me about things digital. 'Have you seen the head-hunters yet?' I asked. She sighed in a way that said she had. 'Things will be difficult in the autumn when Greg is in place and waiting to take over,' she said. 'Robin Young, the permanent secretary at DCMS [Department of Culture Media and Sport], is going round telling everyone that Christopher came to see him to say that he was going to have Greg by hook or by crook.' I couldn't talk more, as I had to hurry down to Wimbledon to lead our presentation for renewal of the television rights. I didn't want to believe what Patricia had told me and found arguments to convince myself that it was not true.

Humility was given leave of absence and an epidemic of showing off broke out. At a board of governors meeting, when the executive was to give a presentation on our plans for future services, I was thrown when after only a couple of words of introduction, John came straight to me, much earlier than planned. He apologized afterwards. 'I discovered that the paper was going to be delivered entirely by Patricia and had to prevent that. She bullies the secretariat to make sure that her name is on as many papers as possible.'

Things were getting silly. Matthew Bannister's contribution to a seminar that he and other colleagues were giving to assembled worthies was a video of which he was the star. In fact, Matthew was becoming a bit of a joke, rushing around speaking, volunteering for tasks, being interviewed. Never was a young man in such an obvious hurry. I rang him.

'Matthew, is your hat in the ring?'

'Might be,' he replied.

'Come on, it must be.'

'Yes, it is.'

'A word of friendly advice, which you can ignore if you choose. Don't look so damned eager.'

Alan had become very assiduous about attendance and punctuality, never his foremost virtue, and he had grown terribly attentive of radio. His support was genuine and he waved it. 'I agree, radio is terribly important.' 'Jenny is absolutely right.' 'We mustn't forget radio.'

The newspapers were following the tournament with some excitement. They had a shrewd feel for what the eventual outcome would be. Greg Dyke was the favoured name throughout, yet they were often hopelessly wrong about the chances of internal candidates. They were generally blinded by their view of John Birt, who, for many in the press, could do little right. The *Telegraph* concluded a review of the form, 'Some say the fact that no one BBC name immediately springs to mind shows how ruthlessly Sir John has eliminated all internal challenges.' What it actually revealed was that John, who had sought to grow strong candidates to succeed him, had brought on the next cohort two years too late.

The *Telegraph* assessed the field according to the latest Ladbroke's odds. Bookmakers are usually well informed about contests on which they take bets. For them it is not just fun or speculation, but business. At the end of April, Greg Dyke was 9–4 favourite, followed by Richard Eyre at 4–1 and Mark Byford at 9–2, three candidates who, to the best of my knowledge, were among the last four standing when the choice was made.

Several papers were firmly against Greg, most notably *The Times*, which ran a sustained offensive. It revealed that he had given £50,000 to Labour, and followed up with other stories of his support for the party. It was not so much the donations that disqualified Greg for me, but the fact, of which the money was but a telling affirmation, that he was a Labour cheerleader. At the end of May, in the final days of the contest, someone gave me a copy of a letter that Greg had written to the *Independent* in 1996, in which he confirmed that he had funded the back offices of successive shadow ministers, including Chris Smith, and urged people to follow his example in giving money to Blair for the forthcoming election. I am not that proud to say that I found a way, unknown to colleagues in the BBC, of passing it to *The Times* without fingerprints. The paper duly splashed it, adding quotes from two members of the committee on standards in public life, Peter Shore of Labour and John MacGregor of the Tories, both saying that this had to rule out Greg as a candidate.

The Times' motives were not necessarily my own; indeed, they were probably reasons why I might have shouted for Greg in other circumstances. He was a firm opponent of the attempt by Sky to take over Manchester United (I had given evidence to the Monopolies and Mergers Commission opposing the deal) and he had been a vociferous critic of Murdoch at various times. But Greg's application to be director-general was, for me, like Peter Cook and Dudley Moore's 'One Leg Too Few' sketch, in which a one-legged man applies for the role of Tarzan.

'Now, Mr Dyke, I couldn't help noticing at once that you are a very public supporter of a political party.'

'You noticed that?'

'I noticed that, Mr Dyke. When you have been in the business as long as I have you come to notice these little things almost instinctively. Now, Mr Dyke, you, a political partisan, are applying for the role of editor in chief of the BBC – a role for which the absence of any known political stance would seem to be the minimum requirement . . .'

Much other fuel for the 'Stop Dyke' movement came from within the BBC. According to the feedback from the press, the chief source was the news division, and that was certainly the view in the Dyke camp. There were also nasty little stories about some of the BBC contenders: that Alan Yentob was so disorganized that he had turned up to a meeting in odd shoes; that Mark Byford had been a failure when he had worked in news; that one candidate, it was hinted, might not be unacquainted with illegal substances.

There was one interesting insight into how the press works. I took a party of people to see the Grand National at Aintree, among them Ross Kemp, one of the stars of *EastEnders*, with his girlfriend Rebekah Wade, then deputy editor of the *Sun*, and Mark and Hilary Byford. It was a jolly group. Everyone got on well, Mark his usual positive and chatty self. Ross had £20 on Bobbyjo, which won the National at 20–1, so he and Rebekah left even happier than the rest of us. A short time afterwards, the *Sun* devoted a leader to the BBC appointment. Howard Stringer, head of Sony Entertainment, would be a good choice, it concluded, but if he were unavailable, there was a good internal man in Mark Byford.

When the newspapers declared their hand in leaders, *The Times*, owned like Sky by Rupert Murdoch, along with the *Telegraph, Independent, Guardian, Standard* and *Mail on Sunday*, said that Greg should be ruled out of contention because of his active support of Labour. The only national to declare for him was the *Express*, at that time owned by Lord Hollick and still viewed as the house newspaper for Labour. Columnists Polly Toynbee and Peter Preston were for him; Hugo Young and Donald McIntyre against. Much quoted was support from Barrie Cox, ex-LWT, Melvyn Bragg and Clive Jones of Carlton, in effect Greg's campaign team and fellow Labour flag wavers.

It was time for the joint boards conference at Wood Norton once again. Just before the kick-off, John Birt took me aside. 'Let's think what we want to come out of this conference,' he said. 'We want the board of governors to believe and understand that the BBC is a very complicated place to manage.'

The first afternoon went well. Chris Smith arrived by helicopter for his session, after which he had dinner with the governors upstairs while the executive committee had a laughter-filled dinner below. During this, Patricia described how she once had a dish of live fish put in front of her in Finland when she had been a student. This was after she and her companions had all been for a sauna. 'Was it a naked sauna, Patricia?' asked John, to which she only giggled. Sauna stories all round, before Tony led off into great Nationwide cock-ups, a regular topic for these gatherings.

The conference ended on the Thursday with a bit of a love-in, both John and Christopher Bland saying how unified the two boards were, Christopher adding, 'These two boards comprise the strongest group of people that I have worked with, though not always the easiest.' It was tempting to feel that he admired the existing executives enough to select one.

A few days later I went to 100 Piccadilly, the offices of Heidrick and Struggles, the company handling the search and appointment process, to have a sandwich lunch with the selection panel. This, I discovered, was Christopher, Baroness Young, the vice-chairman, Roger Jones, the governor for Wales, Richard Eyre and Pauline Neville-Jones, the ex-Foreign Office governor who took particular responsibility for the World Service

Once the sandwich servers were out of the room, Christopher began, 'Thank you for coming, Will. We'd like to hear your views on the internal candidates we will be recommending to go forward to the final stage with the full board, of which there will be two.' He listed those who'd missed the cut. 'What do you think about that?'

I said that I would have made the division in the same place.

'Ah well, we've got it right so far then,' said Christopher, flattering my conceit a little, I fancied. 'Let's take them one at a time. Mark Byford first.'

I said that I had first come across Mark in 1991. I had been struck by his confidence, vigour and range, as well as his warmth and presence, even though he was then only 32. He'd worked to me for two years, during which he had demonstrated an impressive grip of his command. He mastered subjects quickly and comprehensively. I knew that he had originally wanted to be a barrister and he had those sorts of skills: a terrific memory, grasp of detail and a strong understanding of finance. He saw BBC issues in the context of the wider broadcasting industry. He had good judgement, was honest, had a strong news background and was politically very savvy. He had used his time in the regions to make good political contacts and learn how to play issues to them, He had great personal integrity, a good family life, was a practising Catholic – a man who knew who he was in the world.

Possibly he appeared a bit obedient, he was the son of a chief constable. Creativity wasn't his long suit. His background was journalism, but he got on well enough with creative people. He could be a bit prosaic, a bit long-winded in the way he spoke and wrote. I'd talked to him about this some time back, encouraging him to work on it. Also, he was young, 40. 'On the other hand,' I said, 'he is, as you know, older than his years in many ways and, frankly, when he was working for me, I had learned things from him. He has great self-discipline and pushes himself hard. He gets up at 7.00 on a Sunday morning in order to get through his weekend work in time to go to mass and spend the rest of the day with his five children.'

I concluded: 'Altogether, I think he is a genuine leader. He is the kind of general who would always care more about his troops than himself. Almost unique, that, I think, in the media world.'

Richard Eyre asked, 'Can't he be a bit pious when talking about the BBC?'

I said, 'Well, he does believe in the place.'

'What about the obedient bit?'

'He does seem very much the fully paid up bloke who's applying the policies. But then, aren't we all? In my view he's carrying out what's been agreed rather than being obedient. I've seen him make his own changes and push them through.'

'Tony Hall?'

I said I thought he was a decent man and a funny man. He was knowledgeable and fluent about the issues. He had very strong editorial judgement and experience. He was a good advocate for the BBC, a good and experienced manager who had learned to extend his skills. He had only worked in news, which might be a drawback, but he knew the BBC well. Again, was he seen as a bit obedient? Did he have the command, the presence?

'But,' said Christopher, 'he wouldn't be a disaster?'

'No,' I replied, 'and I think people would work for him because they would like and respect him'

I was asked to put them in order and did so. Then Richard asked, 'If we put through none of the internal candidates, what sort of message would that send?'

'A completely lousy one.'

'Well, we're not going to do that,' said Christopher.

'I know, but I wanted to put the question,' was Richard's response. I've wondered since if this were his signal that the governors were seeking a complete change of style which they felt would be impossible, save through an outsider. They might well be content with the overall direction of the place, but they did not like being governors of an organization which, in the press at least and however unfairly, had become a byword for unhappy people and bureaucracy.

When the chairman had first asked me if I would talk to the selection panel, he had said 'about the internal candidates and one external, Michael Jackson'. But there had been no mention of Michael, so he had either not stepped up or had been ruled out. There had been no chance to talk about what, for me, was the matter of most concern, so I wrote a note to the chairman and copied it to the other panel members:

> Christopher,
> Thank you for giving me the opportunity to offer my views on internal candidates. I hope that they were of use. I did not expect to be asked my views on the strengths and weaknesses of external candidates and will not offer them now.
>
> However, there is one matter on which I wish to make my views known to you, both because they may be of value and as a matter of record.
>
> There has never to my knowledge been a director-general of

the BBC whose political views were overt and publicly known. This has been crucial to the independence of the corporation and to the integrity, real and perceived, of the decisions that the director-general and his lieutenants have to make.

I believe that it is essential to the long term independence of the BBC that this position is continued.

Of the candidates I am aware of there is one, Greg Dyke, who is publicly associated with a political party. He is a known supporter and funder of the Labour party. I can't see how this can be discounted in any way and it is something which will not be forgotten. He may or may not be a candidate who would find favour with you, but in the event of his selection the cloud of political suitability would henceforth hang over the office.

The fact that Greg is a strong minded fellow who would not shrink from telling the Labour party where to get off is not the point. The real difficulties arise, of course, when – as he would surely have to at some point – he tells the Tories where to get off.

Under Mrs Thatcher it began to appear that political fit was a leading concern when appointments were made to the board of governors. The danger with this was that sooner or later, one felt, a different political party would come to power and want its stamp on the board.

Politics appeared less of an issue under Major, but now a different political party is in power and it does appear that it wants at least its share of board appointments.

Within reason this can be coped with. But if it should ever look as though the director-general's politics were also a relevant issue then I don't think it is too dramatic to say that sooner or later the game would be up on the political independence of the BBC. And if a candidate's politics are known, how can they be irrelevant?

A future Conservative government would need to be more saintly than we have a right to expect not to wish to see a fair share of sympathetic governors, and not to consider the politics of the director-general as a matter for its attention.

All this may be quite superfluous to your deliberations. But then it may not be. Good luck.

I was very wound up at the time, as my 92-year-old Dad was dying, and reading this now it gives off more than a whiff of self-importance. I still hold with its argument, however. There were other reasons for questioning whether Greg was right. Would he be a genuine and convincing believer in and advocate for the BBC? Was he a strategic thinker? Would the combination of him and Christopher Bland be too commercial a brew? Was he too much Christopher's man? These were pushed aside by the politics. Not that any of them were doing much damage. It was going Greg's way. Before the next governors' meeting John came round to my office: 'I think we need another council of war . . . We're going to have to work hard . . . I haven't tried to blow Greg out of the water, but I will have to do so.'

I flew up to Scotland at the weekend to host a pre-concert reception for BBC Music Live and to see the team producing the week's output from Glasgow. I turned things over in my mind on the plane. I worried that John would be seen to be manoeuvring too hard to manipulate his chosen successor into position. That would alienate some governors. And was my fixation about the politics becoming an obsession, was I simply an old native out of touch with the modern world? On return, I rang David Attenborough to engage his assistance. He didn't think Greg was right but was loath to write to the chairman. 'I just get the sense that he thinks I'm part of the old soldiers polishing their medals, as he puts it.' I asked him to write to Barbara Young, whom he knew well as chief executive of the Royal Society for the Protection of Birds.

I rang Roger Jones, the Welsh governor. He was one of the governors who had told me that I should be standing and might listen to me. 'Roger, I have a lot to do with other public service broadcasters in Europe and it has always been a proud boast, when they complain about the politicized nature of their organizations, that no one even knows the politics of the DG, let alone make them a consideration when appointing.'

'Well, it's all to play for, Will,' said Roger. 'I've been watching this like a hawk, looking for signs that the chairman is biased. Either he's playing a very clever game or it's wide open. My own criterion is who would deal with Murdoch best. Murdoch is a very dangerous man, a very sinister man and a great threat to the BBC. Greg would have to have a chance of being that person, but I've by no means come to my conclusion yet.'

I was due to go on holiday and fixed to see Christopher before I went. He thanked me for my letter and we went over the politics. 'Well, I can see it's practical difficulty and it may cause trouble, but I can't agree that it's an absolute principle,' said Christopher. We were not going to agree. He moved on to Greg's qualities. Did he think strategically, I asked?

'John thinks strategically, more than anyone I think I've ever met,' said Christopher. 'Of course there'll be good strategic ability in the organization, but I think the question about Greg is that he changes his mind quite a lot, unlike the current director-general, who never changes his mind.'

He talked about Mark, who was seen by some of the governors as a bit deferential and po-faced about public service broadcasting. I argued that he had many other sides to his personality. Such qualities were not so evident to the rest of the board, said Christopher. I left to go to speak at the launch of BBC Knowledge, a new digital channel, after which I rang Mark. 'I think they are going to see you again, Mark. Show some humour and that you are not always serious. Don't go on too much. Make it clear that you would want to make the place feel different and more fun. Remember, if you got the job, you'd be the boss. You don't have to defer. And show that you could deal with the outside world. Good luck.'

The following day, the day of my father's funeral, began with the news that William Hague had written to the chairman saying that Greg, as a political funder, should not be appointed. At first, this appeared to demonstrate exactly the kind of partisan row the BBC was opening up for itself. In fact, it was a clumsy intervention that allowed governors to close ranks against external pressure, smoothing the waters as Greg approached harbour.

I arrived back from holiday on Friday, 18 June, by which time the final candidates had been seen again. I rang John Birt, who said, 'I don't have very good news I'm afraid. There's probably a majority for Greg.' Over the weekend I rang four governors. They ranged from the tight-lipped: 'It's a tactical issue. Do I need to say more right now?' to the agonized: 'There will not be a unanimous view, it will have to be forced through if it's Greg . . . I'm afraid of what we could be saddling our successors with.' There was also the wobbly: 'We all feel so uncertain that the decision ought to go to a safe pair of hands; if we give this chap the job, it will be like having a grenade with the pin out . . . If the whole executive committee wrote, then that would carry the day. This is the hidden unspoken voice. It's just the sort of lever we need.' But some of the committee were candidates.

The board was to meet on the Monday evening. On Tuesday morning I went down to Wimbledon with Alan Yentob to announce a new five-year contract for the television and radio coverage. Alan was still restless about the appointment process, convinced that he had not had a proper chance to do himself justice in the one interview and angry that he'd heard nothing for sometime afterwards. He cheered up when we gave the press conference at the All England Club, after which he and I larked about on centre court for photographers.

The intelligence on our return was that it was Greg. He was coming in to see the board again on Wednesday but it was more or less a done deal, to be announced on Friday. It had been very close between him, Mark and, I later learned, a second outside candidate. John was low. His plans and his strenuous efforts to influence events had failed. I wondered if there was anything else I could have done.

On Thursday I was in the car on my way to the governors' meeting at Television Centre when the phone rang. It was a consultant who did some work for me. 'Will, I understand that it's Greg and they're going to announce it tomorrow.' I had to admire his spy network. I arrived a little early at the meeting room in the windowless basement. When the governors entered, the thunderous look on the face of Sir Kenneth Bloomfield, the long serving Northern Ireland governor, told all, even if John hadn't whisked over to me to mutter, 'It's Greg.' He'd clearly been hoping up to the last fence.

I doodled through the meeting playing with many versions of 'The British Blaircasting Corporation', 'British Broadcasting Cronies', and so on. Nothing was mentioned about the appointment but everyone in the room knew. When the meeting was over, I went upstairs to see the television channel controllers for a chat.

I returned to where lunch for the executive and the board was to be served, to find that the governors were still in private session below and there were only Tony Hall, Mark Byford and a couple of others in the room. The mood was slightly hysterical, hiding disappointment. They were telling stories. How Chris Cramer, a famously tough news editor, had rung Mark at home in Lincoln on Christmas Day. Mark's father, a former chief constable and chairman of Yorkshire cricket club, answered the phone. Cramer, 'Is Mark there?' Byford senior, 'Yes, he is.' Cramer, 'Put him on.' Byford senior, 'Certainly, and may I take this opportunity, Mr Cramer, to offer you and your family my heartiest good wishes for a very happy Christmas?' Cramer, 'No, you fucking well can't. Put him on.'

Noisy laughter, and on to another. A famous home news editor in London received a letter, signed in a slightly odd hand. It read: 'Just to let you know, sir, that Jesus will be coming again at 12 o'clock next Wednesday in Brixton in South London. I thought that I should tell you so that you can cover it for the BBC news.' A couple of days later there was a telephone call to the news editor. 'Sir, I only wanted to follow up my letter to make sure you were aware and got my message that Jesus is arriving in Brixton on Wednesday at 12 o'clock.' The newsroom phone was slammed down. Wednesday morning arrived. The editor starts going over the letter and phone call in his mind. It was rubbish, of course. But what if? What would people say afterwards? He'd had a tip off and did nothing. At 11.00 a.m., in as casual a manner as he could muster, he called in a reporter and said, in an off-hand sort of way, 'Take a crew down to Brixton will you?' The reporter looked puzzled. 'What for?' he asked. 'Do it,' said the news editor. 'Just got a feeling in my bones. Might be worth looking out for something. Sort of tip off. You never know.' Nothing made the lunchtime bulletin.

I wandered off, as I knew that John wanted a word. We met in a spare office. He unburdened himself for half an hour. It would be presented as a unanimous decision. It may not have been as close as we had hoped. Then he was positive. Now our job was to do everything we could to make things work for Greg, teach him about the BBC, help him understand it.

From when I took over as managing director of television in 1991, I had given a midsummer party for the writers who worked for the BBC. It was an enjoyable, occasionally drunken, beano. The hope was that good company, good wine and good welcome could make good relations. I would make a short speech, telling the guests some positive things about what we were doing and – the high tariff dive – try to make them laugh. This year's was held that evening in the Imagination Gallery, off Tottenham Court Road. It was crowded and hot. Shortly before I was due to speak, I was summoned out to be told, 'It's all over London. Everyone knows. It's been leaked from William Hague's office, after the chairman had called him. You might as well tell them when you speak.'

There was no real need. As I went back in I was caught by Laurence Marks and Maurice Gran, the writers of *Birds of a Feather* and *Goodnight Sweetheart*, whose company had been bought by Greg at Pearsons. 'So, it is Greg, then, Will. What do you think?'

'Well, Laurence . . .'

Chapter two
MEET THE ANCESTORS

The BBC began with one as it meant to continue. 'You agree to devote whole of your time and attention to the service of the Corporation to attend for duty at such hours . . . and at such places . . . as shall from t to time be decided by the Corporation.' The contract arrived at the enc my six months' probation, enclosed with a letter from R. Short, 'E&AAN(that was Establishment and Administrative Assistant, News (Sound), off ing me an 'engagement on the unestablished staff as a Sub-Edit Newsroom, News Division'.

Backing me against the wall, the contract warned that if I invented (came across anything useful to broadcasting, I should 'forthwith commun cate the same to the Corporation and if so required by and at the cost of th Corporation (as to out of pocket expenses reasonably incurred) supply . . all necessary information, drawings and models'. Models? I could barel} manage a paper dart. Bending a little, it offered that, if a patent were tc follow, 'the Corporation will pay you the sum of £10 (such sum to be divided between the inventors if more than one in such shares as the Corporation shall decide)'. The Corporation was going to decide pretty well everything.

A booklet of BBC regulations came too. It informed me that holiday entitlement ('annual leave') was three weeks, 'four weeks if the individual's salary is above a certain figure', that gratuities and Christmas boxes should not be offered or accepted, and that women staff were eligible for maternity leave and grants 'under certain conditions'. Recognizing that a carrot might be needed to encourage a young fellow, the Corporation reached out to offer one: 'members of staff are eligible for admission to the Caxton Convalescent Home, Limpsfield at moderate charges'.

I had first applied to the BBC in the spring of 1965 for a post as a radio studio manager. Many graduates entered by this route. I was invited for interview at 5 Portland Place, home of the appointments department, across the street from the curved west side of Broadcasting House, the BBC's ocean liner-like headquarters, moored a few hundred yards north of Oxford Circus. I did little or no preparation, convinced that my general

ll at 100 paces. At the second interview I was
bout working a tape recorder, a central part of
inspired. I sank like a stone.

Mr Moriarty, when he wrote to me with the
d not been selected, suggested that I consider
id some journalistic experience (six months as a
orning Telegraph), why didn't I try news? As it
itly advertising for sub-editors in radio news and
ad and an application form.

nmoned for a half day of interviews and tests.
question paper on current events, a pile of news
boiled down to a story, against the clock, and a
bledegook which had to be turned into something
terviews were exploratory rather than inquisitional.
ed editor offered, as so many do when interviewing,
rily dressed as questions. 'The *Sun* [then a brand new
you think of it, it's a paper aimed at a young reader-
te middle-aged, wouldn't you say?' On the whole, one

C news training scheme in those days but, feeling their
tey took on people two at time, one a horny-handed pro,
hopeful. I was let in as the greenhorn. It paid £1,570 per
ly twice the salary of a trainee studio manager. I couldn't
uld spend all the money. The blessed Moriarty went on to
nusic and arts television producer and Labour mayor of

tat time appeared a commanding presence in the land. It had
the dominant cultural force in my young life. First, as both
isic hall in the corner of the living room: *Variety Bandbox*,
*time, Family Favourites, Big Bill Campbell, The Billy Cotton
Henry Hall's Guest Night, Dick Barton*. Also, as the ministry of
*Take It From Here, Ray's A Laugh, Ignorance Is Bliss, Much
te Marsh, The Charlie Chester Show, Hancock's Half Hour, The
.* It had been, too, a world of 'Nelly the Elephant', 'Three Little
te Laughing Policeman', 'The Lost Chord' and 'The Stargazers
heair'.

t awareness of television had been in 1949. We'd driven to visit my
Iewbury in our army surplus Austin 7 pickup truck. No sooner had
I up outside his house and moved to clamber out, than my uncle
he front door to greet us. How had he known that we had arrived?
is within to marvel at his new console model television and explained
tenever a car drew up outside, it caused a snowstorm of crackly inter-
t to the picture. I was impressed, aged seven, to have discovered a
he that not only gave reliable early warning of relations approaching,
thich offered football, Mr Pastry and the fetchingly posh announc-
t Jennifer Gay.

The BBC was television for me. My parents had been what would now be dubbed early adopters. In 1951 they had bought a single channel K.B. television set, which had never gone wrong. So, although ITV had been around for ten years by the time I joined the newsroom (and for part of that time taken 75 per cent of the BBC's audience), I had hardly ever seen it. Thus, it was not *Sunday Night at the London Palladium* that had provided my entertainment, but Max Wall, Benny Hill, Fred Emney, Tony Hancock, *Great Scott It's Maynard*, *Ask Pickles*, *Saturday Night Out* and latterly, the thrilling *That Was The Week*. It was cricket with the cheery Brian Johnston and the grumpy E.W. Swanton; rugby league with Eddie 'this lad's looking for an early bath' Waring; rugby union with Peter 'that's an impressive pair of thighs' West.

Above all, there had been *Panorama*, in which Richard Dimbleby, Robin Day, John Morgan, Jim Mossman and Ludovic Kennedy had told me about the world; *Monitor*, where Huw Wheldon introduced me to Robert Graves, Henry Moore, Peter Brook and a hundred other artists, and *Tonight*, where Cliff Michelmore, Kenneth Allsop, Derek Hart, Alan Whicker and Fyfe Robertson practised a witty and confident journalism that I took to be just as smart and as modern as could be.

If, to me, the BBC was a pantheon of these gods, to others, both friends and enemies, it was the subject of criticism. In what has become a refrain over the years, many felt that it was behaving too competitively and was too timid in its peak time programming. 'Much of the BBC's competition is merely head to head; a film is put against a film on ITV, a series against a series. It assumes that a mass audience cannot be held by anything unfamiliar, and its effort is mainly towards making the familiar better than the opposition's.' That was one of the great television critics, Peter Black.

The Clean-Up Television Campaign had just issued its manifesto: 'We men and women of Britain believe in the Christian way of life . . . we deplore the present day attempts to belittle or destroy it, and in particular we object to the propaganda of disbelief, doubt and dirt that the BBC pours into millions of homes through the television screen . . . suggestive and erotic plays which present promiscuity, infidelity and drinking as normal and inevitable.'

Little enough of all this disturbed the tranquillity of the radio newsroom, which I joined in August 1965. It was a large room, divided by several pillars, in the extension at the stern of Broadcasting House. Its role was to prepare the news bulletins and summaries for the BBC's domestic radio services: the Light Programme, 'a friendly and companionable service for those who are in the mood for entertainment and relaxation'; the Home Service, 'serves the broad middle section of the community'; and the Third Network, a classical music service during the day, in the evening it became the Third Programme, of which the BBC was anxious that you should not feel afraid. With a reassuring chuckle, it informed everyone that 'the broad appeal of the plays of Shakespeare and the music of Beethoven is just as characteristic of the Third Programme as the challenges of its more adventurous broadcasting'.

The atmosphere was peaceful, studious even. Occasionally, there were raised voices as a brief surge of current animated one or two figures when time for the bulletin approached. There would be the odd flurry as a late story was completed and rushed down the corridor to the studio. Otherwise, the only kerfuffle was when the tea trolley and its noisy and ample guardian appeared in the passage outside.

We sat at wide tables down the centre of which, at intervals, were jacks into which we could plug earphones. These were for listening to recorded reports, 'voice pieces', from reporters and correspondents. 'Erik de Mauny coming up on line three' or 'it's Conrad voss Bark from Westminster', someone would announce importantly, and the bulletin editors and whichever sub was writing the story would plug in and listen with expressions of visible concentration. You could also listen to the cricket this way.

On a board near the door were pinned notices from the pronunciation department. These related not just to unusual and foreign names currently in the news, advice that continues to this day, but also to everyday English words. There was a confident view on how the language should be spoken. 'Eckonomics' not 'eeconomics', 'finnance' not 'fiynance', 'r'search' not 'research'. Lost causes all.

This and the Mufax machine, a cylindrical contraption that sent or received the occasional page of information very slowly to or from another BBC building, was all the technology. The television news was frowned upon as flashy and insubstantial, and Alexandra Palace, from which it emanated, was where the bad boys were sent. A few members of the radio newsroom had visited colleagues at Ally Pally, but mention of the place would produce a shudder.

There was a senior duty editor, whose office was partitioned off at the top corner of the newsroom. Everyone else sat in the main room, a duty editor, with chief sub on one side and copytaster on the other, senior subs and then subs in descending order of seniority down the table.

Copytasting was a job usually given to a junior. The source of all stories was tape from the various news agencies. It arrived next door in a room of machines that rang a bell as each new transmission began. Armfuls of the tape were brought into the newsroom by uniformed attendants, and the copytaster's task was to sift this, spotting anything new or significant and stuffing it into one of the upturned pigeon holes in front of the editor, while discarding, 'spiking', the dross. The PA, Press Association, came on rolls of plain white paper and was to be relied upon for home stories. Reuter came with a green border and was the one to be trusted for foreign stories. AP was brown. It was American and, therefore, suspect from anywhere but North and South America. UPI, yellow, was also American, and only useful in the last resort for confirmation. Agence France Presse, mauve, was not to be taken notice of at all, save from China and francophone Africa.

Finally, there was the dark blue edged tape from the BBC Monitoring Service at Caversham. This, transcribed from foreign radio stations, was valuable but came in daunting quantities. Yards of presidential speeches, party decrees and conference communiqués were hard to digest, and over the shoulder of all copytasters hovered the spectre of 'The Man Who Spiked The Nationalization of the Suez Canal'. Local folklore recorded that Egypt's decision had been announced deep in the entrails of an interminable speech by President Nasser, the transcription of which had been rolled up and spiked by the copytaster on duty. This had gone down in the annals alongside 'The Night They Lost The Shipping Forecast'.

For the first few weeks I preened myself on the importance of my role as the first journalist in the BBC to see and alert the great Corporation to major news stories. In truth, it was a largely clerk-like job. The agencies themselves screamed 'Flash' if anything was of consequence, and quite often when it wasn't. They duplicated their own and each other's stories, so it was hard to miss something big. To be safe, I erred on the side of more rather than less when passing over copy, but handing on too much caused irritation.

'What on earth am I looking at all this crap for? There's nothing new here,' one editor would rasp.

'Well, um, I thought you might like the UPI stuff,' I would lamely reply. 'They're, um, saying the explosion was at 6.46 rather than AP's 6.48. Could be important.'

If not copytasting, I was down the desk contributing stories to the bulletin. One would be summoned to the chief sub's side, given a piece or pieces of agency material and told, 'Give me fifteen seconds on this please, Will. I should go on the number of new schools.' This last to tell me where to begin. In time the stories got longer, thirty seconds and, exceptionally, a minute, which would be lead or second story.

The chief subs and editors were mostly kindly fellows and in their briefing tried to give you some room to shape the story. There was one, though, an implacable Yorkshireman who, before calling you, would write over the tape in heavy pencil exactly how he wanted the story written. 'I think it goes like this,' he would say, before reading out the combination of his handwriting and print, moving his pencil along the words as he did so. 'Have you got that?' It was my job to go away, turn that into fair copy and bring it back. If I changed so much as a word, he would signal me again. 'No, Will, I think that it's better this way,' and he would adjust the new copy to match his own, always remembered, original.

He would read and re-read the stories given in by the more experienced subs, searching for the mistake or the unfavoured usage he always managed to find. This was a man who would have sent back the miracle of the loaves and fishes for the absence of salt and vinegar. After his first reading of a story, he would lean back on his chair and, without taking his eyes off the paper in front of him, reach into one pocket for tobacco, into another for cigarette papers, into a draw for his rolling machine and then roll himself an encouraging fag. Drawing greedily on the cigarette, he completed his diagnosis; then, picking up his freshly sharpened pencil, he would make the first incision. In a minor operation, 'started' would be changed to 'began', or 'began' to 'started'; 'two fewer' would become 'a drop of two'. In major surgery the steady, determined strokes of his 6B would strike out whole lines, even whole paragraphs, and rewrite them in a crabbed but irritatingly regular hand. No departure from orthodox journalese was tolerated as he shortcut his way through the niceties of reported speech and sprinkled the copy with 'clashes', 'plans', 'schemes' and 'disputes'.

Occasionally, I had to write an intro to a recorded piece from a correspondent, even editing it, though this simply meant cutting it short somewhere. It was around this time that Frederick Forsyth, the BBC's correspondent covering the Biafran War, was deemed to have gone jungly. His dispatches took on a distinctly partisan tone. I seem to recall reading one that concluded, 'I could not bring myself to support a British government that . . .'. Suddenly he was not our correspondent any more. He continued to cover the war, putting Biafra's case and writing a book about it.

One of the best things about the newsroom was that you did get close to the actual broadcasting. The junior sub would deliver the Light Programme summaries down to the studio and often take the full ten-minute bulletin to the Home Service newsreaders. These were distinguished looking gents with Adam's apples that looked like a swallowed walnut. It was, for a while anyway, a thrill to sit alongside them in the brown windowless studios, passing the foolscap pages one by one as the news went direct to all corners of the country. With a long bulletin most of it was in a sacrosanct order, but you always had three or four shorter stories for the end. These you juggled to get in as many as possible while running as close as you could to nine minutes and fifty-five seconds without the newsreader having to speed up. There were jesters, of course. The reader had a mute button he could press if he wished to cough or clear his throat. One used to try to make new subs laugh by pressing, turning with a grin to say, 'I'll now adjust my balls for greater resonance', before releasing it and continuing in the measured BBC tones the nation expected.

Next to each sub sat a typist – all of them women. When you had constructed the story, you dictated it aloud and the typist bashed it out on her sit-up-and-beg machine. We had no typewriters ourselves, the theory being that by having to read out our copy as would the newsreader, we would hear any infelicities, accidental rhymes or alliterations. It was not an infallible system and, famously, someone let through a story about a steel strike in South Wales that began, 'There were scenes of delight in Port Talbot last night, as the news of the settlement spread.' (Say it aloud.)

Some of the old hands would dictate loudly and grandly, especially if it were a lead story for the bulletin. Some would stand and lean over the typist's shoulder; others stood and declaimed to the room. Voices tended to rise as time for the bulletin drew near. In the early days I usually tried to twist myself away from others and offer my piece in a near whisper, embarrassed at how little I had had to do and, if the Yorkshire pedant was at the helm, to hide the fact that I was merely dictating what he had already written.

The typists, who were nearly all helpful and friendly, spent most of their day reading, chatting or knitting. They would type two or three stories for each of the day's three main bulletins and that was it. Times being what they were, they fetched lots of tea and coffee. The sub-editors, too, spent only a minority of their time actually working. If someone was doing a big story, a minute or more, say, on something developing or requiring material from several sources, he would probably do only that and a short item per bulletin. Others would do one, two or three stories of perhaps half a minute each. This was not a full morning or afternoon's work, so there wasn't much one missed in the newspapers.

We worked a twelve-hour shift starting at either 9.00 or 10.00 in the morning, three days on and three days off. When I started, one in four shifts was a night shift, but there were times when this became alternate shifts, a routine I hated. After the midnight bulletin and the shipping forecast, there were just the Light Programme summaries till 2.00 a.m. Broadcasting didn't start again till the Light Programme opened up at 5.30 a.m., so there was often a dead period when it was possible to achieve a kind of sleep, slumped forward, head down on the desk. I always woke up after an hour or so feeling terrible, yet rarely resisted the opportunity.

The newsroom was occupied twenty-four hours a day the year round, and was not the sweetest of environments. It was at night that you noticed this most. The pale yellow light gave the inhabitants a cadaverous look. The body odour, a background effect during the day, now asserted itself as the sickly sweet, piquant smell of sweat. As morning drew near, the air thickened with the stench of old sandwiches, spilled drinks and the stale, coffee-laden fumes of bad breath.

One or two people chose to work only night shifts, among them a grumpy, mostly silent duty editor who kept a bottle of whisky in the drawer. He spent his days writing historical novels set in Roman times. They were rumoured to be very raunchy but no one admitted to having read any. One perk for him and for all the overnight editors was writing the daily review of the papers, a rare chance to stretch the literary muscles.

One typist, to me then a woman of great age, worked permanent nights. As a consequence her face was the colour of yellow parchment, interrupted by deep, grey lines. One night, as I was dictating a story to her in the corner of the room, she stopped typing and hissed out of the side of her mouth, 'I know more ways of sexual intercourse than anyone else in this building.' Now, I was a young, newly married 24 and was taken aback. Was she boasting? Settling an argument? Auditioning? I sought to combine both surprise and congratulations in my response, wrapped in a defensive jocularity.

'Well, I'm blowed,' I said. I could have put it better.

There were few women journalists. The most senior was Mary Edmonds, the cheery editor of the Third Network bulletins. She was middle-aged, unmarried but said by all to be 'close' to one of the newsroom bosses. They waltzed off to lunch and supper together, anyway. She was a jolly presence who would announce interesting snippets of news to all around, as if discovering new triumphs by the clever girls of the lower fourth: 'I say, everyone, listen to this . . .'. She specialized in expressions of jovial horror at the running orders of the television news.

With a work pattern that gave you plenty of time at home or elsewhere, there was a sense that, for some, what happened in Broadcasting House was an interruption of their real lives. One chap, a friendly source of interesting and arcane information on architecture, literature and history, was a cardiganed, schoolmasterly fellow whose main interest, one felt, was the study of Victorian churchmen he was writing, not that he was anything other than conscientious in his work. One duty editor, who rarely seemed to speak, lived for his sailing. In summer, two horns of white hair either side of his bronzed pate, he would wear polo shirt and long khaki shorts and sleep in his office, as if that were below deck. A fellow junior sub, an old Etonian with spectacles and a little turned up nose, was a photographer in 'real life', specializing in portraits and action shots of young girls and their ponies. He was still on the deb circuit and would often nip home at supper time, after the six o'clock news, and swan in for the evening session in dinner jacket, ready to go on to a party or ball. It paid off. He married the daughter of a duke.

The boss was the splendidly named Palmer Ritzema, 'Ritz', a rather glamorous figure, with an upright stance and swept back grey hair, who was said to have once been a dance band singer. I could believe it. It was he who brought down and interpreted comments and messages from above, that is, from the head of radio news and from the distant, and only to be imagined, seniority of ENCA, the editor of news and current affairs himself.

Beneath Ritz all was not well. One senior news editor was on the bottle, to the extent that subs working under him would occasionally concoct telephone calls, fake messages, invent errands even, to prevent him from drunkenly disrupting the bulletins he was in charge of. Once, when the clerk who arranged the rotas suddenly left, this editor took on the job himself. The arrangement was short lived. When the first of his rotas were pinned to the noticeboard, people clustered round, breaking first into argument, then into laughter and finally scornful hysterics, for journalists were down to do two jobs simultaneously, scheduled to work consecutive twelve-hour shifts and placed in authority over their seniors.

Another boozy editor, a Scot, once arrived three days late for work. He had a dreadful temper and had memorably chased an Irish colleague around the newsroom, holding him personally responsible for leaving the lights on in Dublin during the war in order to guide German bombers.

My fellows and I beneath the salt were joined after a year or so by a softly spoken Cambridge graduate, John Simpson. He was a somewhat grand and scholarly party, who showed little interest in doing more than was strictly required. He spent much time reading intently the antiquarian books that I took to be part of his studies. I assumed that he was engaged in a further degree of some kind, the newsroom appearing to be beneath his talents, as indeed it was, but providing an income and a warm place to read.

Simpson was a Christian Scientist and thus didn't join the group that sloped off to the Windsor Castle pub in Devonshire Mews to talk football, pensions, mortgages and the embarrassment of sitting opposite girls with short skirts in the train, for this was the time of the mini pelmet. I could hold my own with the first of these, had a view about the last but it was not embarrassment; the rest I was not ready for.

· Then there was the gossip – the analysis of who said what to whom, who appeared in favour and who did not, the inferences to be drawn from glimpsed memos, half heard remarks and the expression on a face up the corridor. This, for some, was the material that held the key to the universe.

One of these was a creepy senior sub – he kept his money in a purse – who would pounce on anyone he had spotted speaking to a superior, hungry for droppings from the conversation. These he would carry back to his hoard of hints and reports, there to plan. With whom should he drink at lunchtime? To whom should he speak about likely jobs? Most of all, he relished the occasional huddle with a duty editor or two. Then he would smile knowingly to himself, with a child's wonder at his own achievements. Yet when he heard that a fellow sub went to football matches at weekends with the kindly duty editor, Edwin Harrison, he displayed hurt and shock. 'Oh, I'd never mix with senior men off duty. They'd only think that I was after promotion.' He had worked out seniority levels with a slide rule. 'I think that should be my seat,' he said at the start of one shift, pointing to the chair next to the duty editor.

'Does it matter?' asked the colleague about to sit in it.

'Well, I am the senior of us. It should be mine.'

'We're both senior subs. In fact, we were promoted on the same day. So I can't see that.'

'Yes, that's all very well,' said the creep, 'but I joined the BBC a couple of months before you did, so I do have seniority.'

This was not a place to stay. There were good people. It was a job that needed doing. But the newsroom was an island away from the world, not in it. My first indication of this had come a week or two after I had joined. A bronzed, smiling man in a grey shiny suit breezed in full of bounce and good cheer. 'Who's that?' I asked the sub I was talking to.

'Ah,' said my colleague, looking across the room with a mixture of awe and envy, 'that's Elphick, he's a correspondent.' He gazed for a moment at the sight of Elphick chatting away, radiating bonhomie.

'You can tell he doesn't work here, can't you?'

I encountered for the first time resistance to change, by no means unique to the BBC, but which ran deep in many corners of the Corporation. Encountering is too neutral a term: I signed up to it.

Within a few months of joining the newsroom, the current affairs unit started *The World at One*. The former Fleet Street editor Bill Hardcastle was brought in to present this new lunchtime programme, into which the one o'clock news, until then a proudly free-standing edifice, was inserted. Hardcastle wrote and delivered his own headlines – a revolutionary development, this – before handing over to the newsreader. Those who shuddered at television's news values rolled their eyes and shook their heads at Hardcastle's urgent, tabloid style and breathless delivery. His bustle and vitality, his pointed journalism and lack of deference changed radio news and current affairs for good.

The World at One was a success, and with the wind behind it, the current affairs unit's ambitions grew. The six o'clock news was to be reduced to five minutes and become part of Radio Newsreel. In the newsroom we were outraged. We went through the full behavioural cycle that I was to see repeated many times over the years. First, hatred and loathing for those at the very top. Always important to start there. Then came hatred for the victorious rival unit, together with envy of its leadership. This was followed immediately by scorn for our own bosses, who had been outmanoeuvred and then had capitulated. Next came letters to the top, calls for delegations and a rush to the press.

I wrote a piece that no one in his right mind would have published, but which captures the mood:

> The way the decisions had been taken has shattered the already declining morale of the news staff at Broadcasting House and revealed once again the bungling incompetence of BBC executives . . . The Director General's [Sir Hugh Greene] reply to the staff's letter – condescending in tone and insulting in content – was indicative of the BBC's unsurpassable flair for arrogance . . . A typical snub was that he could not see the union delegation for a fortnight as he would be busy entertaining his Russian opposite number. It would seem, though, that there is little Sir Hugh has to learn about the authoritarian aspects of broadcasting.

Some of it is even more embarrassing. Apart from the bit about Russia, it could have been about any of the great BBC squabbles over the following thirty years. Many of the phrases came to have a sing-along familiarity. It was a classic example of the old BBC rubric, 'once the decision has been taken then the debate can begin'. Naturally, there was little enough in what we were steamed up about that concerned what might be best for the listeners. The argument was about 'us' versus 'them', about the way things had always been done, albeit dressed up as anger at the way decisions had been made.

Swept up in all this, John Reynolds, a fellow sub, and I thought that *Private Eye* was the place to bust this story wide open. Frankly, we could not have bust a toy balloon. Knowing that the Coach and Horses in Soho was the *Eye*'s pub, we gauchely door-stepped the *Eye* grandees at lunch. Our garbled account of the likely immolation of radio news made Ingrams' eyes glaze over and, as only toffs can, they let us know that we should leave.

Ineffective as we were as whistleblowers, Reynolds and I were already planning our escape to someplace where responsibility would not be doled out by the teaspoonful. John Simpson, anxious to spread his wings, had already disappeared up the corridor to enlist in the flourishing current affairs unit. Reynolds, a knowing looking figure, amusing and amused by everything, had impressed me greatly when I first joined. He flicked ash off his cigarette in the dismissive way of a battle-hardened journalist, which, as an ex-lobby correspondent for the Scottish *Sunday Post*, to me he was. He won an attachment to television current affairs in Lime Grove, the elite corps of the BBC, and was soon a producer on *Panorama*.

I passed up the chance to apply for promotion in news because the level I was on was the one at which most opportunities came up elsewhere. I, too, fancied television current affairs. I was, after all, exactly the sort of person who should be in the eye of the storm. I was interviewed for an attachment by a senior current affairs executive, Stanley Hyland. Again with the confidence that comes from arrogance and naivety, I did little preparation.

'What do you think about party political broadcasts?' Hyland asked me. There had been a bit of a run of them, the Prime Minister Harold Wilson rather pleased with his fireside manner. I launched into what I took to be an entertaining dismissal of their usefulness and demolition of their execution. The atmosphere cooled. My interviewer pursed his lips with irritation. Only afterwards did I discover that Hyland, a fellow Yorkshireman, was the producer of all Wilson's television appearances.

As the interview came to an end, I mentioned something about 'when I was canvassing'. Hyland leapt on this.

'Are you active in politics?'

'Um, I have been. A bit.'

'Why didn't you mention this before?'

'I don't know. I didn't think.'

'Might it not have been relevant in an interview for a place in the BBC television department that handles all its political programmes and where an understanding of politics and the political process is an essential requirement?'

'Um, yes.'

So, current affairs was out. If I were to move to television, I would have to look elsewhere. Jane had just given birth to our elder daughter, Hannah. I wanted to be getting a move on. On the noticeboard by the lifts I spotted that there were attachments going to the presentation department in television. This unit was new to me. Its main task was to run the networks, ensuring that the right programmes were put on in the right order, to make the trails for forthcoming programmes, to keep the whole show to time and to make what changes were necessary in emergencies. It also had a modest programme arm that made *Late Night Line Up*, a nightly programme on BBC2, *Points of View*, a viewer's letters column, and programmes about films. This is what I was attracted to.

I applied. The competition was much softer than that for current affairs and I sailed through. After the six-month attachment, I had to return to the newsroom for a while, as no job was available. However, one soon came up, I was successful and I left Broadcasting House for a new life four miles west at Television Centre.

Shortly before I went, I was summoned to the office of the new E&AAN(R), who greeted me with some formality. She ushered in a secretary and a clerk to attend upon our little ceremony, then, as 'an agent for and on behalf of the BBC', signed a pale blue document which lay on her desk. On the front, illuminated letters announced an agreement that I had joined the monthly permanent staff. I signed, the witnesses signed, the agent of the BBC solemnly shook my hand, offered congratulations and informed me that I was now 'established'. Surprisingly, no uniform was produced.

Chapter three
TESTAMENT OF YOUTH

Presentation was the Cinderella department of the television service. Its job was to take the channel schedule, as decided by the channel controllers and their planners, and turn this into an operational reality by assembling all the pre-recorded and filmed programmes, checking timings, liasing with live programmes, making and placing the promotions and supervising the transmission. It was the final port of call for BBC programmes before they were handed over to the public, and it was fiercely proud of its role as the controllers' agent. It could be rather hoity-toity about this, as those who serve at the right arm of the powerful often are.

This transmission operation was not where I wanted to work but I had to do a stint as part of my training. I viewed programmes to check that their openings and closings complied in picture, sound and length with the transmission forms. There were no cassettes, so you viewed film on a Steenbeck editing machine or, more luxuriously, in a small viewing theatre. Videotape was two inches wide and was played on the mighty Ampex recording machine: two grey spools on a slab of electronics as tall as a man. These were clustered in a basement area, where the scarce time on them had to be booked. This was an exciting place, the background hum intensified by the whirr of speeding reels, broken by loud stabs of music, laughter or dialogue from the programmes being recorded or edited. Cocky sports producers dashed back and forth between machines, shouting timings and instructions to the operators. Next door drama directors in toggled neckerchiefs would sit frowning as they watched the playback of a new production while the operator yawned. Perky girls with clipboards flirted with the manager in charge in the hope of wangling some extra editing time.

I spent time in the network control suites learning the ropes as the network directors called up the different sources of programmes by telephone and intercom. These suites, at the back of Television Centre between the fourth and fifth floors, were like small air traffic control centres at night: dark, calm, with panels of switches and flashing lights, and smelling of warm electronic machinery and coffee. There was a glow from the array of television screens. These command capsules felt snug, insulated and important.

Quite quickly trainees were given a turn at being in charge, and the day came when I was network director for BBC2 in the evening for the first time. I settled into the gallery and did plenty of confident-sounding 'VT 25, are you standing by?' and 'News, we should be with you on time tonight.' I was flying solo, high over West London. A crash landing followed. In mid-evening, nearly fifteen minutes into a gardening programme, the telephone rang. The assistant who answered it listened for a moment or two. I saw a shadow cross her face. 'You'd better take it,' she said. 'It's the producer.' He was agitated. Somewhat more than agitated to be honest.

'You've got the wrong bloody take. The WRONG bloody take,' he screamed.

'It all seems to fit with what the form says,' I replied.

'So far. So far,' he shouted. 'Any moment now it stops and that's it. We did it again.'

Hardly had I put the phone down when the programme stopped in mid-sentence and went to black. Music and a breakdown caption occupied the screen for nearly ten minutes. By the time I arrived at work the next morning I had begun working on several new career strategies. But no one said a word.

I was still excited by everything to do with television. BBC2, the United Kingdom's third channel, was only three years old and had just begun transmitting programmes in colour. There was something magical about the brightness and clarity of the pictures shining in the dark on the studio monitors. Even the still photographs of flowers or microphones used in the junctions between programmes seemed to assert that this was a new age. The very word 'colour', used by announcers introducing a programme or under a programme title in the *Radio Times*, was one to savour, like 'cash' for a business or 'shpin' for Richie Benaud.

Television Centre in Shepherds Bush, the concrete doughnut, was still new. The plan, for a circular building with an extending wing, like a question mark, was not yet complete, nor was it to be for thirty years. Before I had ever worked there, I had driven past it, marvelling at the glamour and excitement it radiated. John Reynolds had taken me in for a drink in the bar. The place was populated by pretty girls and expansive men. The eight main studios were arranged round the outside of the circular office building, enabling access from a perimeter road. In the central courtyard was a statue of Helios, the sun god, above a fountain that never played, because, it was said, the echoing sound of water made people want to pee. Inside, at first-floor level, there were observation galleries, from which you could see and hear what was going on in the studio below: *Dad's Army*, *The Generation Game*, *Blue Peter*, *Softly Softly* or *Top of the Pops*. In those days there was activity in every studio: building or striking a set, rehearsing, recording or live transmission. The drama, both series and the many single plays, was all studio based and produced in the Centre, along with the children's programmes, entertainment and comedy.

It was a fun factory. Trailers of scenery would clog the perimeter road:

interiors of humble cottages and grand houses, trees, bushes, boulders, garden gates, temple columns, cut-away cars, the Tardis. At lunchtime in the canteen there would be Romans, cybermen, policemen, citizens of Dickensian London, ancient Britons. The BBC Club bar on the fourth floor would fill up at lunchtime and, again, at 6.00 p.m., for the hour between rehearsal and recording in the studio. There was a small bar to the left as you went in, which was where both presentation and light entertainment staff and stars gathered. In the large main room groups of sceneshifters sat with all the pint glasses in West London spread on tables in front of them. There were BBC colleagues having a beer or glass of wine before going home, and actors, extras and production staff waiting to return to the studio.

Television Centre was a place where only first names were used, where everybody affected to know everyone else, and all walked, or minced, a little taller for being a baggage carrier in the showbiz army. I loved it. Mind you, it took a while to become confident about whether to strike off clock-wise or anti-clockwise when stepping out of a lift, especially in the basement. I once heard a man, showing a group of baffled visitors round the building, doing his best to make a virtue of the layout: 'And now, you see: we come once again to . . . the noticeboard.'

Why the presentation department made any programmes was a mystery to most people in the BBC. The reason was a mixture of opportunity and expediency. When Television Centre had been designed, it had been assumed that the channels would continue to use in vision announcers. Two small presentation studios were built for them. Policy changed and announcers were henceforth heard but not seen. What to do with the studios? Weather forecasts were broadcast from one, and both were used for such trailer-making activity as warranted studio space, but mostly they were empty. There was often a need for short programmes, fillers, to bring a BBC1 junc-tion up to the hour or achieve a common junction with BBC2. Here was a place to make them. Thus began *Points of View*, a five-minute letters column of the air. When BBC2 opened a ten-minute preview programme, *Line Up*, it kicked off the evening's viewing. It quickly became more convenient to place this at the end of the evening and, instead of previewing programmes, *Late Night Line Up* reviewed them.

I moved to the programme side to work with Iain Johnstone, an ex-ITN newscaster and scriptwriter, who had just arrived to produce *Points of View* and its children's equivalent, *Junior Points of View*. It was as if the bell had rung for playtime. For the next three years Iain and I made these pro-grammes, dreamed up others and tried our hand at whatever took our fancy. Or so it felt. We were aware that somebody somewhere was saying yes or no, probably the spoken-of-in-hushed-tones, but never glimpsed, controller of BBC1, Paul Fox. But the world, or at least the little Studio A, was our oyster. We had so much fun that we often told each other that, if we worked else-where, we would be happy to come in of an evening to do what we were doing for nothing.

A great part of that fun was Robert Robinson, who presented both the letters programmes. He was funny, clever, older and famous and welcomed us as buddies, encouraging us in japes and mischief. Iain and I shared an office with an experienced PA, who had worked on far more illustrious programmes in the music and arts department, the senior common room of the television service, but who enjoyed our company and the jokes, particularly when Bob Robinson was around. Several mornings a week the widow of a television music director was employed to open the viewers' letters, have coffee and chat.

From the letters that arrived, Iain or I would write a draft script, using quotes from viewers and choosing an illustrative clip. If there was a deluge of letters on one programme, we would reflect that, otherwise humour and controversy were our aims. We sent the draft round by taxi to Robinson, who would re-write the whole thing, though usually keeping our train of thought and, occasionally, a joke. Once we had the final script, we could organize the graphics. The letters were too small to use on screen themselves and having them blown up was expensive. Not that I knew what things actually cost, it was simply that you learned what sorts of things were feasible. We stuck photographs to caption cards and rewrote the relevant extracts from letters in suitably characteristic hand, forthright, spindly, backward leaning, in capitals and underlined, either to imitate the original or to emphasize the tone. This allowed us to improve upon the originals to bring out a joke, and we did.

We made what we thought were funny little films, the ideas for which sprang out of the letters. The arts programme *Omnibus* had just begun, and I shot a vox pop outside Harrods asking people what they thought a programme with that title would be about. No one knew. (Thirty years later, when we were agonizing about the lack of impact of BBC arts programmes, we commissioned some research into *Omnibus*. People still had no idea what it was about.) Another viewer asked what the factory in *The Brothers* made. I decided it was hobnail boots and shot an ad for them. And so on. Of course, we had ideas for jokes for which there was no inspiring letter. This was easily remedied.

In the studio we had three cameras. One was on Robinson, who sat on a stool so that he could work the primitive teleprompt with a foot pedal. The others pointed at two music stands, on which were stacked the black caption cards bearing letters and photographs. Alongside each caption stand stood a studio operative, whose job it was to whip the used captions away as soon as they had been screened. As director, I had to rehearse our letter readers (who included good actors like Miriam Margoyles and Frank Duncan), organize the whole sequence of shots and do the button pushing to change cameras

From our position outside the big battalions of the BBC, we took a schoolboy pleasure in throwing darts at the rest of the output, especially drama, entertainment and the mighty empire of sport. The ammunition was mostly supplied by the letter-writing viewers, but we sharpened what they gave us with a superior glee. Other departments were not happy, the children's department especially.

This came to a head when, for *Junior Points of View*, we did a little spoof of *Blue Peter*. Graeme Garden rewrote my script to make it funny and played John Noakes, Jo Kendall played Valerie Singleton and, mindful of the cost of employing a third actor, we used a life-size photograph for Peter Purves, which at one point was tapped to see if he was paying attention. Biddy Baxter, the brilliant and formidable creator of *Blue Peter*, took this to be a cruel and heartless satire at Purves' expense. We compounded the heresy by placing the Purves figure facing outward in our office window, which, as it happened, looked across to the east tower of Television Centre, home of the children's department. First, an agitated security man burst into our office telling us to take Purves down, as people opposite had been given a nasty shock, thinking a suicide attempt was being made. Secondly, we were summoned to see Monica Sims, head of children's, who gave us a bit of a wigging.

For me it was learning through play. I failed to put at ease the seventeen-year-old George Best, already a pin-up for little girls, when filming an interview with him, trembling with nerves, for *Junior Points of View*. I discovered how not to treat actresses when I filmed the Watling sisters, Dilys and Deborah, who were both starring in series the children liked. I interviewed them together, found that it was all too long, so simply cut one of them out. A tearful phone call followed. It was less ham-fisted production than bad manners.

Iain and I wanted to branch out and made pilots for other programmes with Bob Robinson in a similar vein: a late Saturday night review of the Sunday papers and a review of what overseas newspapers were saying about Britain. Neither became series. We proposed that BBC1 fill its, then, void in the middle of the day with a lunchtime magazine programme, hosted by Iain and me. BBC1 thought otherwise. Then we came up with an idea that was commissioned as a series: a weekly account of what had happened month by month in the 1950s. Bob kicked off by recalling what he'd been doing in 1950, acting at Oxford, playing the lead in *Perkin Warbeck*, 'a work which had not been performed for 300 years and on the opening night, we discovered why'.

The Fifties was a television essay by Robinson, a cross between *What the Papers Say* and *All Our Yesterdays*, using quotes from newspapers and magazines, still photographs, newsreels of the time and occasional short contributions from others. The result was an entertaining, if selective, social history, relying much on the pleasingly wrong notes struck by the old material. Over the Pathé coverage of a football match between England and a skilful Italian side, the voice of Bob Danvers-Walker boomed about 'the acrobats from spaaaghetti land'.

Bill Hardcastle contributed a short piece on Adlai Stevenson, Rene Cutforth on the Korean War and Huw Wheldon on the Festival of Britain, for which he had been the press officer. I wrote to Wheldon, then managing director of BBC television, explaining where the piece would sit in the programme, what I hoped it would cover and that it should be exactly three minutes in duration. I arranged an appointment to run through it with him. Come the day, I arrived in his office with stopwatch and notebook. Wheldon, though polite, enacted an elaborate pantomime of not being sure who I was or what I wanted. I explained. 'Ah, yes the Festival of Britain,' he mused. 'Let me think a moment . . . how much do you want? . . . Three minutes, you say? . . . I see that you have a stopwatch . . . Sit down. Let's try this . . .'. He leant forward across the desk and unleashed a well-turned piece, not a word out of place and ending with a flourish. He paused for effect then asked, 'How was that for time?'

I looked at the watch. 'Two minutes, fifty-eight seconds.'

'Splendid,' he said. 'I'll try to do the same on the day.' As he ushered me out, he fixed me with a smile and added, 'I'm sorry that I didn't see your note and so had to do it off the cuff, so to speak.' The smile continued, challenging me to contradict him.

Iain Johnstone's passion was films, which were hardly covered at all on BBC 1, and he won the go-ahead to make a thirty-minute documentary about Dustin Hoffman, who had just triumphed in *The Graduate* and *Midnight Cowboy*. He was in Cornwall, making a film directed by Sam Peckinpah, *Straw Dogs*. We went down for three days' filming, I sniffing, with a tourist's excitement, the heady air of a movie location and trying to pretend that I had been doing this sort of thing all my life. One of my tasks on our shoestring production was to take the photographs we would use for publicity. We went straight to where they were shooting an exterior. Iain was directing our film camera; Peckinpah was directing Hoffman and Susan George in what I took to be a rehearsal. It was not a rehearsal but a take, I had missed his grunted, 'Turn over.' In the midst of some quiet dialogue I took a photograph, the shutter sounding like an aircraft hangar door slamming. Peckinpah, a man with a well-publicized reputation for drinking, fighting and temper tantrums, shouted, 'Cut,' paused, and added, 'We are shooting SOUND for Chrissake!'

We were not thrown off the set, but when we filmed our agreed interview with him the following morning, Peckinpah chose to conduct it while he repeatedly threw a large knife into a wooden door, punctuating his replies with the sound of the blade hitting the wood and being wrenched out. Each of the mornings we were there began with reports of how much drinking, brawling and wrecking had taken place the previous evening. For someone from a sheltered existence, it was an uninhibited atmosphere. At dinner in a restaurant Hoffman cried, 'Ever see an Eskimo pee?' He leaped to his feet, poured the contents of an ice bucket down his trousers and unzipped his flies.

The movie publicist, who enabled and monitored our filming, invited us to dinner with his wife who was making a rare visit to see him on location. As drink was consumed, a little cabaret began. 'We haven't had sex for twelve years,' proclaimed the wife. There was an embarrassed laugh from her husband.

'Yes we have,' he countered bravely, 'what about last night?'

'Call that sex?' came the reply. We were to film the sunrise next morning, so this was the moment to offer our thanks and retire.

The documentary went down well and Iain went off to do a similar project with John Wayne filming in Mexico. He got on well with Wayne, although when he and I sent treatments for a Wayne movie to the great man, he thanked us, said he would send them to his 'special reader, Mr Art Kane', and, strangely, we heard no more.

I now got a job as a producer on *Late Night Line Up*, which had blossomed over the years into a wide ranging arts and discussion programme, increasingly ambitious in its production. It ran at thirty minutes to an hour, or until overtime rates kicked in for the technical crew, seven days a week the year round. Because nothing followed, it was allowed to be, dread phrase, 'open ended'. For five nights it was a studio-based magazine programme, once a week it was about films, *Film Night*, and once a week a pop music show. This had begun as *Colour Me Pop*, became *Disco2* and, later, *The Old Grey Whistle Test*. The second change was spurred when, to the amazement of all who knew him, the rather naïve, blazer-wearing producer was sacked for accepting sexual favours in a house in Notting Hill as a reward for featuring bands on the show.

Jane and I now had a second daughter, Rozzy, and as I worked very late and was released from rush hour, Jane and I moved to near Thame in Oxfordshire. My job was to run a small team, an assistant producer, a researcher, a PA and myself, producing two live magazine programmes a week. It was expected that we look first for material to the evening's television, the *raison d'être* for *Line Up*'s existence. There might be a review of a play or series, a discussion about a genre of programmes, an interview with a writer or a performer, or a general thrash around the subject of a documentary. But there was nothing to prevent us scouting more widely, to cover books, theatre, architecture and the press. The one essential was that we ask male contributors not to wear white shirts, which strobed on the new colour cameras. The programme had earned a reputation for radical chic, a cosy home for liberals to converse with lefties. The archetypal *Line Up* item would have been a black, homosexual, Marxist coalminer interviewed by Joan Bakewell, her head cocked, so her hair could fall as a curtain as she asked, 'Tell me about having to bathe in front of the fire?'

I can remember no debates about the overall stance or balance of the programme. We sought to find conflicting views when casting discussions, but our main protagonists tended to be contributors to the newspapers and magazines we read, the *Guardian*, *Observer*, *New Statesman*, and authors of books we agreed with. I remember colleagues pulling faces when, in one of my first programmes, I invited Dr Rhodes Boyson, traditionalist headmaster and later Tory minister, to argue the case for education vouchers. In retrospect, we had a pretty blinkered view of the world while believing the exact opposite.

When a friend saw a *Line Up* researcher pick up a five pound note from the floor and pocket it, he asked why he was not going to try to find out who had dropped it. He was told solemnly that, 'All property is theft', something

the researcher demonstrated over the following months by slowly disman-
tling and spiriting away a Steenbeck editing machine.

No one in authority would have condoned that, but the programme had
been born in the 1960s and remained a child of that time. Michael Dean, an
excellent interviewer who always worked without notes, had made his first
appearance on the programme interviewing Leonard Cohen. Beforehand, he
had suggested to Cohen that he should read a poem on air, which he did. It
was a poem about fellatio, which Cohen claimed to have written for a girl
with whom he was having difficulties. As soon as the show was over, the
telephone rang in the gallery. It was the channel controller, David
Attenborough, demanding to speak to Dean, to whom he complained
angrily. Immediately, the telephone rang again. This time it was the director-
general. There was fear and trembling: was a career to end after just one
interview? Not at all.

'Wonderful,' said Sir Hugh Greene, 'can you get me a copy of that poem?'

The founder and editor of *Line Up* was Rowan Ayers, a dashing figure, a
ladies man, who looked somewhat like Rex Harrison. He was an ex-naval
officer, quite formal in manner, but easily enthused by people and ideas. He
encouraged the free wheeling nature of *Line Up*; he relished rows with the
rest of the BBC and, indeed, seemed to define himself by engaging in these
conflicts to protect his producers. He was more a publisher than an editor.
He never stayed around or came in for the programme, but would nearly
always ring as we came off the air with some, usually, encouraging words.

'Hello, Will?'

'Yes, Rowan.'

'Yeees. Pretty good, I thought. I liked the discussion. Pity the old chap had
nothing to say. Did you know the other one was going to be drunk?'

Drink was a problem. We were often not on air till well after 11.00 p.m.
Participants had had dinner and spent some time in our green room before
going into the studio. I remember two great comedians, Arthur Askey and
Jimmy Wheeler, both arriving very early for a discussion about music hall.
Wheeler was already plastered, so, trooper that he was, Askey said, 'Leave
him to me,' and took him off to the canteen to pour coffee in a (successful)
attempt to save the show.

Rowan liked to be surrounded by young people, best of all by the offspring of famous parents. Thus the staff included Dan Topolski, son of artist
Felix; Catherine Jay, half of the twins and daughter of cabinet minister
Douglas; Sally Dimbleby, daughter of Richard; and Cherry Britton, daughter of actor Tony. He collected mavericks, too. The senior producer was
Mike Fentiman, an East Londoner, who would argue about anything and
everything, always with a cigarette in hand, usually gasping laughter at a
funny story he had heard or an idea which had just come to him. Fentiman
was the programme's conscience, and played this role more widely in BBC
television in years to come, asking, with genial good humour, the pertinent
and awkward questions that those around him had not brought themselves
to face up to.

Jim Smith was the programme's plenipotentiary from the working classes. I am not sure how working class he was, but he came on a bit rougher than the rest of us. He was a wild and, occasionally, inspired producer, who once, when faced with an empty show because items had fallen through, sent three taxis down to Piccadilly Circus to collect any hippies or similar and bring them back to fill the studio floor for a live discussion about whatever came up. On another occasion the participants invited for a discussion about television comedy, a *Line Up* hardy perennial, all arrived early and went to the bar. There Marty Feldman, Johnny Speight, John Chapman, Dick Clement and Ian le Frenais began the discussion and were well away by the time they went on air at 11.15pm. Another comedy writer, John Antrobus, who had been part of the bar debate but was not a guest on the show, watched from the gallery until he could restrain himself no more and burst into the studio to join in. Jim Smith, who was producing, spotted a drama and instructed the director, 'Go to a wide shot,' then went in himself, to be seen dragging out the loudly complaining Antrobus from in front of the cameras. Jim, who was having a tempestuous affair with Joan Bakewell at this time, was a volatile fellow, who resigned regularly and then reconsidered. Eventually, he pushed a letter of resignation under Rowan Ayer's door so far that he was unable to retrieve it. Rowan, who had had enough, accepted it. Jim claimed that he was resigning only from the programme, not from the BBC, but was told that there was no mechanism for that, so from the BBC he went. He did work as a freelance elsewhere in the Corporation, but came to a sad end.

Tom Corcoran was a merry fellow with a wild streak and did much to brighten our lives. He was a very talented studio director who brought adventure to everything. His favourite trick was to cause the producer's blood to run cold by leaving the gallery for a pee three minutes before you were due on air with a live show, not to return until the PA was counting down from fifteen seconds. He would sweep in, sit and roll his chair to the desk in one movement, picking up with, 'OK. After titles we come to a wide shot on three, then Mike on one . . .'. Tom liked a drink – 'refreshed' was his term. It was impossible not to warm to him. Once when he returned happy after lunch in the bar, Tom spotted an upright piano parked on a landing. He pushed it into one of the lifts and went up and down for much of the afternoon, playing it to the surprise and pleasure of the passengers. He specialized in forged memos, issued in the head of department's name: 'This year Christmas Day will be on December 25th and Boxing day on December 26th. If there is any change in these arrangements, I will inform you. Rex Moorfoot.' Another, at a time of economies, ran, 'In the light of the shortage of stationary, verbal communication will now be permitted.' His authorship was never traced. Moorfoot changed his signature.

The *Line Up* offices were on the second floor of the spur of Television Centre. Rowan's office, where he would hold the daily programme meeting, was at one end of a run of three rooms joined by ever open doors. At the other end was a glazed office for the presenters, in which interviews would be prepared over games of darts. This space was known as the bankruptcy and adultery line, it being the only spot for a private phone call. Along with Joan Bakewell and Michael Dean, Tony Bilbow and Sheridan Morley made up the presenting team. Joan, attractive, flirtatious and intelligent, was the star. She was good with writers and intellectuals, and at charming contributions from men, diffident or otherwise. She was the most frustrating to brief, as she liked to plan for herself. Tony, a jolly figure, was most at home with show business, comedy and films. Sheridan was first choice for theatre and good with political books. Mike Dean could handle anything. He had an intimate and near stammering style, but established a good rapport with guests and held the line of questioning in his head. All of them were at home with television subjects, our bread and butter.

Because of holidays and filming requirements, we sometimes needed others. As a newcomer, I wanted to introduce my own protégés. I looked to the radio and hired the young Jonathan Dimbleby for his first television appearance. I also rang David Jessell, a rising star on *The World at One*. 'Would you be interested in chairing a discussion on BBC2?' I asked.

'Do you know what I look like?' he replied. Oh, my God, I thought, how crass. He must be hideously scarred or deformed. I should have known.

'Um. No,' I said. 'Perhaps we should meet before we go any further?'

'It's just that when someone else asked me to do television, he backed out because I looked so young.'

'Ah, you just look young?' I said, relieved.

'"Babyface" was the term he used,' said Jessell. He was, and was nicknamed 'Dorian Gray' by Michael Hill, an old chum of Rowan's from his Navy days, who had arrived to act as a sort of deputy without portfolio. Jessell did two or three items for me, but the *Line Up* team had limited room, so I was unable to import either him or Jonathan.

Dealing with television on television was to walk across fields mined with the ambitions, the self-regard and the insecurities of producers, writers, performers and, not least, BBC executives. Originally, *Line Up* had covered only BBC programmes. To escape from this restriction, a 'special' edition reviewing three ITV programmes was proposed. When news of this dangerous innovation reached the Moorfoot ears, a fierce debate ensued. The outcome was Rex rehearsing a justification worthy of the medieval Vatican: 'The programme will not be reviewing commercial broadcasting as such, but that which comes within the experience of BBC viewers.'

There were problems enough with BBC issues. I discovered that the tape of a programme from which I hoped to find a clip had been wiped. I probed further and found that many, to me, interesting plays, comedies and studio interviews had all gone. The two-inch tapes were issued by the engineering division of the BBC. They were expensive and were to be wiped and reused wherever possible. The criteria for deciding which to keep were unsophisticated. Important political programmes, state occasions and live outside broadcasts of sport and other big events were, quite rightly, retained. The archival and social historical value of the remainder of the output was recognized dimly or not at all. Alan Bennett's comedy series *On the Margin*, and Peter Cooke and Dudley Moore's *Not Only But Also* were mostly destroyed. I began to set up an item, gathering stills of lost treasures and finding contributors, who would proclaim the error of the BBC's ways. I needed some one to answer for the BBC, so I put in a request for Huw Wheldon to take part. Within the hour, a Monty Python-like foot descended on my item and me. Wheldon would not take part, nor would any other BBC executive; what's more, this was a discussion that would not take place. Rowan, for all his in-scrapping abilities, could not win this one.

The attitude of the heads of the big television departments to on-air criticism was epitomized by Aubrey Singer, the competitive impresario who ran the features group. He refused us clips of features programmes: 'We are not fattening frogs to feed to snakes.' The loose brief of *Line Up* did spawn a diverse cast list: I filmed an author who wrote pot-boilers to order, giving him the subject for a book, which he immediately began typing, delivered to the studio the following week and which was in the shops the week after; interviews with B.F. Skinner, the behavioural psychologist; Jimmy Reid, working-class hero from the Upper Clyde shipbuilders; Rex Reed, camp Hollywood film critic; a whole programme in which Sir Oswald Mosley and Richard Crossman debated the 1930s; George Melly, another favourite, on Luis Bunuel.

Melly was famous among the programme team for his antics in the hospitality room, B055, a basement hideout, the carpet of which, if it could speak, could have been charged under the obscene publications act. On the night in question Melly had been on with Dominic Behan and afterwards both were drinking with the production team and studio crew. At mention of 'the man, the woman and the bulldog', Melly piped up. 'Of course. I think it's time. I need someone to come outside with me.' Mike Fentiman obliged. In the corridor Melly stripped naked, handed his clothes to Fentiman and re-entered the room to stand with his legs apart, arms raised and biceps flexed. 'The man,' he announced. He went out and came back in, with his penis pushed back between his legs. 'The woman.' He went out again to the corridor and made his third entry, this time backwards, on all fours, his testicles pushed back between his legs. He shouted over his shoulder. 'The bulldog.'

Dominic Behan, plastered by this time, volunteered, 'I'll do it now.'

'Oh no, you won't,' said his wife.

On Sundays we began an anarchic show intended to be humorous and topical. John Wells, John Fortune and John Bird would write and perform a sketch or two, Vivian Stanshall or Neil Innes a song, and James Cameron would contribute a comment piece. There was no host; the links were snatches of silent movie and a Santana record. Ian Keill and I produced alternate editions, my main contribution being to bring in Clive James, whose television criticism I read in the *Listener* and who, then, had done almost no television. Clive would bustle in of a Sunday morning, in the manner of one with barely five minutes to spare, and sit down to write his piece, always with a freshly opened pack of twenty cigarettes alongside the typewriter, and underneath that pack, an unopened twenty as a comfort blanket.

He liked to dress up. In those days BBC costume and make-up were on call to provide for whatever he required. One week he would imitate Henry Kissinger, the next Arthur Brown singing 'Fire', complete with flaming head-dress. He was not a great mimic, but he wrote funny scripts and threw himself into the performance with the gusto of an English master in the school panto. John Fortune has it that he once suggested to Clive that he should deliver his planned parody of *Morte d'Arthur* in a full suite of armour, complete with visor, then persuaded the director to rehearse this item at the beginning of the rehearsal time and record it at the end of the recording session, thus com-pelling Clive to spend hot, uncomfortable hours encased in heavy metal. Clive walked fast, talked fast, thought fast; he was writing literary criticism, television criticism, poems and, with Pete Atkin, excellent songs. He was in a hurry to be famous and was cast down when Frank Sinatra announced one of his retirements. 'I've written songs for that guy to sing,' he complained. 'He'll never sing my stuff now.' The exposure on *Up Sunday* helped Clive on his journey. He was spotted by Granada and went off to present *Cinema*, the pro-gramme that first brought him to general notice.

In the autumn of 1972 *Late Night Line Up* was moving towards the midnight of its own history, but not before I had come up with another wheeze I was pleased with. I would produce the first television phone-in pro-grammes. The technicalities were not easy then. Tom Corcoran sorted them out. I booked Germaine Greer and Esther Vilar, author of *The Manipulated Man*, to argue answers to the viewers' calls about feminism. 'Pioneering' and 'could be an important development' was the BBC's verdict, so I set up two more, Tony Benn and William Rees-Mogg on protest or anarchy, and Malcolm Muggeridge and Bernard Levin on porn, it being the time of Lord Longford's crusade against rudery. They worked well enough and I had blazed a trail. Unfortunately, it was into a cul-de-sac.

Robin Scott, the controller of BBC2, announced that *Line Up* would close at the end of the year. We were to come up with ideas for new pro-grammes. I proposed a regular programme about the press and, while people were making their minds up, went to look for a job at ITN. They offered me one but my proposal, *Edition*, was accepted as part of the new pattern, so I stayed at the BBC to begin planning for it and to see out the final weeks of *Line Up*.

There had been 3000 programmes in eight and a half years. *Line Up* had been the first regular programme in colour in Europe. While it may have been easy to caricature, it had provided a civilized and welcoming outlet for ideas and argument, and had brought to the screen unnumbered writers, artists and performers, as well as a menagerie of eccentrics. The final edition was an interview with David Attenborough, who had turned in his executive job as director of programmes, and the near certainty of becoming director-general, in order to return to writing and presenting programmes. The approach for the interview, as I recall, was that here was as near to a broadcasting saint as we were likely to get. An approach that would still hold good today.

I was asked to use Kenneth Allsop as presenter for *Edition*, which I dubbed as about 'the world of information, comment and persuasion'. I was happy to agree. He was evidently coming off the nightly current affairs programme *Twenty Four Hours*. I did not know Allsop but he had been a hero of mine when one of the original *Tonight* team. I had admired his easy command of literature, American history, politics and popular culture. I had read (well, purchased and glanced at) his book on prohibition in America. I had liked his mod haircut and snappy dressing, especially the neat, tab collared shirts. He was also, though this wasn't my territory, a naturalist and an early and passionate environmentalist, and had written a prize-winning book about the peregrine falcon. We met, got on well and he agreed to do the programme. I suspect, now, that he had been pushed out of current affairs against his will.

Beside from myself, the programme team consisted of the clever and entertaining assistant producer Peter Foges, a researcher and a PA. Each programme had three or four items, including a ten-minute film story. The series seemed to go well enough, that is, *we* thought it was good. There was little enough response from above. Mike Fentiman, the executive producer, was helpful and around. Such comment as filtered down from the channel controller I blithely ignored. I was the producer, not he. Such was the mind-set of the time. Audiences were small, but they had been for *Late Night Line Up*, so that was not of much concern.

I had picked up whispers of doubt that Ken Allsop was right for the programme. In May, a few weeks before the end of the run, Mike Fentiman told me that 'it had been agreed', under pressure from above, that if the programme was to come back in the autumn, as we hoped and expected, there should be another presenter. I remonstrated. We liked working with Allsop and thought he was fine, a bit grouchy at times, but we knew that he was often in pain from his artificial leg. The message was clear, however: there had to be a change. Fentiman said he would see him and tell him.

When Ken Allsop came in for the programme the following Wednesday, he, Peter Foges and I had lunch, as we usually did, in the waitress service restaurant at Television Centre. We would go over the programme items, then talk generally. Ken had chided me previously about going out with a gun to shoot rabbit and poach pheasant from my home in Oxfordshire: 'Don't take a gun, why not take binoculars if you want to give purpose to a walk?' Now he wanted to hear about the goldfinches attracted by the dandelions on our grass. He asked about the campaign to prevent a motorway being built across Otmoor, a low-lying area of unusual plants and birds near Oxford. He said he hoped that the army would hand over their range at Tyneham, near to where he lived in Dorset, so that it could be preserved unspoiled, but thought there was little chance. He expounded on the virtues of cabbage, 'a terrific vegetable'. His one comment on his meeting with Fentiman was, 'Don't let me be an embarrassment to you.'

After the programme, which included gossip columnists Paul Callan, Peter Mackay and Nigel Dempster, Ken stayed for a drink, which he often did not. Learning that neither Foges nor I had ever been to Muriel's drinking club in Soho, he insisted that we go with him as soon as we could arrange it. He reminded us, too, that a documentary he had made with the natural history unit, on the wild life of New York City, was to go out next Sunday, 20 May.

On the day of the next *Edition*, Wednesday, 23 May, the driver of the car we sent to pick Ken up from Waterloo Station rang to say that he was not on the usual train. I told him to wait for the next one and rang Ken's home in Dorset, but there was no answer. It was unlike him not to ring if there was a change of plan, but it could be that he had driven up in his Jag and been held up. When he had not arrived by 2.30 p.m. I was becoming alarmed. I checked for train delays and road accidents, and made more calls to his house. I sent a telegram to Mrs Allsop, asking her to ring urgently, explaining that Ken had not arrived. Eventually, I called the police and asked them to go round to the house.

In the meantime, I rang Chris Dunkley and asked him to come in to be ready to present the programme if Ken did not turn up. When I rang the police again, they reported that all was quiet at Milton Mill. I told them that I was now convinced that something was seriously wrong and urged them to break in. We went ahead with rehearsals. Then, in the early evening, the police told me that they had broken into the house and found Ken dead in bed. It transpired that he had taken an overdose of painkillers and was found with a copy of Dorothy Parker's works open, a passage about the pain being underlined. Mrs Allsop and her daughter had left early that morning to join the Women' Institute's annual trip to the Chelsea Flower Show and could not be reached. So we made the programme with Dunkley and with no reference to Ken's absence.

The funeral was at Powerstock the following week. I drove down to a Dorset at the high tide of spring, hedgerows full of bluebells, cow parsley, buttercups and cranesbill. Outside Powerstock church the lanes were full of parked cars, a clutch of black BBC limos that had brought the bosses down huddled protectively together.

Inside the church was full. The Bishop of Salisbury, who was officiating, began: 'We have all gathered here today to say farewell to . . . Julian.' An intake of breath. The Bishop recovered. 'Er . . . to Kenneth. We begin with some music played by Julian Bream on the guitar.' Ken's daughter read Thomas Hardy's poem 'Afterwards' – 'He was a man who used to notice such things.' At the internment she was grief-stricken. I avoided the bosses and drove home, going over the events of the past few weeks.

Ken Allsop was a man who could become despondent. He set high standards for himself and all around. He was often brought low by pain from his leg. But was his broadcasting work drying up? Had some in the BBC decided that his better days were behind him? I discovered subsequently that his work on *Edition* had been criticized from the first. 'They've bought a pup,' was the comment of Derrick Amoore, the head of current affairs. Was the sacking from *Edition* the final straw? If so, how far should the guilt be shared? There was no note. The coroner recorded an open verdict.

In the summer I went to the United States to film some stories for the next run. In those days, you had to fill in a foreign travel form in order to go overseas. The head of department and the controller of the channel both needed to endorse it before it was passed to the foreign travel department who, only then, would make the booking. I went alone and did my own reporting, interviewing, among others, James Reston, who avowed that he accepted no invitations from the White House or government departments; Gloria Steinem and her team at *M/S* magazine; and made a half-hour programme about the *Readers' Digest* at its home in Pleasantville, New York. It was then selling 29 million copies in thirteen languages. Its editor in chief told me, 'On every page of the magazine you will find something which will help you be a better person.'

These were good stories for the programme, but for years BBC producers were overly excited by the attractions of America. There were strong reasons, political and cultural, for covering the USA, the most likely place to spot early warning signals of what might happen here. But it was the glamour and excitement of the place that stimulated the disproportionate interest of British television. And it was an easy place to work. Thus for the next few years I managed to dream up reasons to go filming there, most of them plausible.

In the fiefdom which had been *Line Up*, and from which *Edition* and a clutch of other programmes now came, there was trouble afoot. Rowan Ayers, our laissez-faire protector, was leaving. He had sniffed some radical new air and had become infected. In the final year of *Line Up* there had been political debate about access to the airwaves. Tony Benn had made a speech in which he had proclaimed, 'broadcasting is too important to be left to the broadcasters'. Rowan was interested. He arranged a meeting with Benn. Half a dozen of us took the tube with him two stops down the Central line for a lunchtime discussion at Benn's house. There was a conspiratorial air to the proceedings. On the table, alongside the cold buffet, was the famous tape recorder, which Benn switched on before addressing us. His remarks can best be encapsulated by his question, 'Why shouldn't the lift man have a say in what you put out?' Rowan was inspired. As we walked back to the tube, there was much 'Yeah, why shouldn't he, and the canteen staff?' in his and some of my colleagues' reactions.

Around this time *Line Up* filmed some Guinness workers in their canteen discussing the television schedules with Tony Bilbow. They were sceptical about the whole process. 'You'll take this back and cut it about and make us say what you want us to say.' Bilbow soon found himself apologizing for interrupting them and for introducing topics. The rushes were, unusually, shown to Rowan, who was much excited. 'Run it all, unedited. Make it the whole programme.' He was aware that he was onto something new.

Rowan was determined that *Line Up* should strike out in this direction.

Soon after, he lectured the production team on the need for new sorts of people to play a part in the programme. What was more, he had met a woman who had some fascinating ideas about television and where it should be going. Her greatest virtue was that she came to it fresh, had never worked in it, had never visited a studio and watched it hardly at all. He was going to hand over an entire show to her to do what she wanted. This was the way to give the medium a shot in the arm. She had something important to offer. The team listened patiently to all this. When Rowan finished there was a momentary silence, then Tom Corcoran piped up: 'Rowan, this woman, has she got big tits?' And when she arrived, sure enough, she had.

Rowan Ayers went off to set up the new community programmes unit, offering members of the public unmediated access to the screen. The resulting vacancy precipitated an outbreak of 1960s' style syndicalism. It was quite clear to us what should happen and the staff were of one mind. Mike Fentiman was the obvious successor. He was an excellent editor, he knew the programmes, we all liked him and he would let us carry on as before. The thought that someone up there might like things not to carry on as before never crossed our solipsistic minds. The job went to Malcolm Walker, a leading light from the other side of presentation. There was outrage of the kind only the naïve can muster. There would be massed letter writing, a withdrawal of labour, a march of allies upon Television Centre (we envisaged Upper Clyde Shipbuilders, Harold Pinter and Richard Hoggart at the head).

We held a meeting to decide what to do first. Some hotspurs began to get carried away and proposed a round robin threatening much of the above. I volunteered to write it, thereby deciding what it should say. Everyone could sign but I intended that it be cool and specific. We signed in alphabetical order and sent the letter to Alasdair Milne, the newly appointed director of programmes, whom we identified as a programme maker's friend. He met a whole gang of us and was friendly but firm. Of course, for all our chest puffing, we got nowhere. How could it be otherwise?

Malcolm Walker wanted to reorganize and have three executive producers to run the output. One of these would naturally be Mike Fentiman. Another would be dear old Mike Hill, who didn't trouble himself with too much work but was the much-loved source of gossip and jokes and already the senior man. The third would be up for grabs but was most likely to go to Janet Hoenig, a close colleague of Walker's. I applied and was successful, as were Hill and Hoenig. Fentiman was again rejected, this time for the job he was already doing. More trouble in the ranks, this time with me as one of the villains. It calmed down, as things do.

Chapter four
THE ASCENT OF MAN

'A word, Will. Don't put your prick in the payroll.' I was now an executive producer, so our genial head, Rex Moorfoot, was giving me my first piece of management training. I am sure that Rex followed his own advice, though young women in the department did claim that when they saw him for their annual interviews he liked to pat their knees to emphasize a point – lots of points. Rex had once been the editor of *Panorama* and will exist for ever in some early film of what purported to be a *Panorama* meeting with Rex mentioning a story to Richard Dimbleby, who replied in the third person pompous, 'Yes, it's in the Dimbleby diary.'

Rex had then become head of the new presentation department, but we all understood that his career had been fatally blighted and that he would go no further. The reason for this went back to the evening of 22 November 1963, the day of the assassination of President Kennedy. The news came through in the early evening when all the television top brass were at a black tie knees up at the Dorchester hotel. At Television Centre, the presenting editor rightly interrupted programmes to make the announcement but had then reverted to the advertised schedule. So the BBC went from announcing the death of the president to the Harry Worth show. It was a crass error. The emergencies file specified that for the death of a foreign leader, this was the agreed procedure. But the written instructions paid no regard to the manner of Kennedy's death, nor to the affection in which he was held. Rex, so we were led to believe, had taken the rap.

You would not know it to see him. He was short, stout, fair-haired, with a hopeful, smiling expression and a will o' the wisp manner. He was bouncy, full of ideas, many of them daft, and would come up to you in the corridor, tender some off the wall thought, then tap you on the arm and add in hush hush tone, 'Think about it', before waltzing off. Occasionally, he would advance on you with a frown, pat your back and mutter, 'Don't worry. The future is assured.' Nothing was more calculated to cause apprehension.

Rex was meticulous about the protocol of meetings, though most of the decisions had 'already been resolved in my office'. He would try to get a discussion going, but if it became critical or too spontaneous, his round face would fall and he would bring matters to a close with, 'I think that we should leave this for further discussion outside the meeting.' He was actually a kindly man and one you ended up feeling protective about. He was planning his retirement from the moment I first went to television. Indeed, the first thing I can remember him saying to me on my arrival was that I should know that, under the new pension scheme, it was now possible to retire from the BBC at 50. It was not what I was looking for at that precise moment.

I now had a new immediate boss, Malcolm Walker. He never breathed a word of recrimination about the campaign to resist his appointment. He was efficient, outwardly confident, ambitious and backed my ideas with the channel controllers. I think that he was a bit in awe of programme makers and relished the excitement they generated. I respected Malcolm and sought to support him, especially as he came bravely through a serious illness soon after taking over

For the remainder of the 1970s, as executive producer and then as the programme head, I had a busy and happy time in our little corner of television. We had space and I was good at getting things going. The channel controllers used us as a release valve to mount discussions and programmes about editorial or broadcasting issues, as their praetorian infantry to take on projects that did not fit the ambitions of the proud independent regiments of music and arts, features and documentaries and as a source of new ideas slipped into the interstices of the big departments.

The first new project was a regular programme about books, *The Book Programme*, which Robert Robinson, with some enthusiasm, agreed to present. It went out late but there was a repeat, and with a following wind from the press, the programme ran for several years. I produced the first series, then handed over to Philip Speight, a fellow *Line Up* alumnus, and became executive producer. The opening programme included Lord George-Brown reviewing biographies of Aneurin Bevan and Herbert Morrison, Kingsley Amis reading (we were keen on readings) an extract from *Girl 20*, and an interview with Laurence Durrell that Robinson and I had filmed at the author's home in Provence, where we had got the giggles as we both thought that Durrell, a very short man, was walking on tippy toes as he moved round his house and garden. The programme began with a couple of notables, to whom we had given £5 each to spend on new books, explaining their choices. In those days you could buy a decent pile of hardbacks and paperbacks with a fiver and still have change for a Double Diamond and a first class stamp. Angus Wilson, author of *The Old Men at the Zoo*, and Margaret Powell, author of *Below Stairs*, were our first big spenders, their exchanges memorable for Margaret Powell holding forth persuasively on 'Pwoust. When I first opened it, there were all those pages and pages of lovely pwint.'

Robinson used to complain that all the people I chose for this spot were 'nabobs', and I have to plead guilty to wheeling on all the usual suspects: Malcolm Muggeridge, Germaine Greer, Tom Stoppard, A.J. Ayer, Anthony Burgess, Jonathan Miller and so on. The only near disaster was when one

Rosie Swale, who had written a book about sailing round the world and was a bit of current newspaper pin-up, was invited on with John Arlott, the great cricket writer. As we were having a cup of tea beforehand, she announced that she would only talk about her own book. I pointed out that this was not what we had invited her on for. She was adamant. 'In that case,' I said, 'I don't think you should take part. The idea is that you talk about other people's books.' She moved to the corner of the room, examining her tea. At this moment, Arlott, eyes agleam at the possibility of a solo performance, came over to me and grasped my elbow.

'Don't worry. I can fill,' he whispered. And so he did.

The most valuable thing that the programme did over the years was to capture writers for the screen and for the archive, including Alexander Solzhenitzin, Alberto Moravia, Heinrich Boll, Jorge Luis Borges and Vladimir Nabokov. When Jan Morris wrote *Conundrum*, the account of how she had changed from James, I filmed a programme with her. To arrange this I went by train to Bath, where she was living in a flat in Royal Crescent. She met me at the front door of the house, dressed in a tweed skirt, jumper and pearls. She led me up the stone staircase and at the first landing twirled theatrically, brought her hands together under her chin, which she thrust out and asked, 'Not too shocking, is it?'

'Um. Good Lord, no,' I said, embarrassed lest my face had indicated otherwise. In truth, it was not. But the lipstick, perm and clothes could not hide the man she had been. I was touched later by the way her son greeted her with the most natural of warm filial embraces.

Everyone enjoys being feted, and most of the writers we filmed basked in being the object of pilgrimage, none more so than Richard Adams, author of *Watership Down*. We filmed him on the Isle of Man where he was living, having retired from the civil service on the strength of the earnings from his hugely successful first novel and subsequent book deals. He greeted Robinson, the film crew and me with a glass of sherry, then stood in front of the fireplace in his large sitting room and offered his thoughts on what we might film, breaking off now and then to issue instructions to his wife in a lordly tone. 'I would like you to see this,' he said, raising his voice and indicating with his eyes. 'It's in a drawer in the other room. Would you bring it in?' No name or 'please' accompanied this. He reminded me of a certain kind of old fashioned Oxbridge intelligentsia who tolerate and are amused by the little people.

The film went out and Adams was in touch to say how he had liked it. The review in *The Times* commented on the final image. 'There was the writer seated in glory at his table, his papers in front of him, when up walked a mute and nameless female who humbly handed him his tea and then stood back in indulgent veneration. Rightly or wrongly, just or unjust, a heavy point was made.'

Meanwhile, I devised opportunities for Robinson and me to harvest American authors. In Boston we netted John Updike, whose prominent and curved nose fascinated and prompted speculation about what part it might play in the sexual antics about which its owner wrote so well. In Chicago we were allowed into the presence of Saul Bellow, whose prickly demeanour implied that the genuflections we were making did not sweep close enough to the ground. Back in England, did the transcriber of the tape know this and tease when, typing Bellow's reasons for getting no closer than Poland to his family's Russian origins, she typed that he had decided to end his journey 'at Walsall'? John Cheever behaved better than I would have done when a member of the crew broke a glass door. He provided a lengthy, often intense interview that nodded towards even darker aspects of his life than he chose to talk of. There was a frisson when he said during a pause in the filming that he had been very close to his brother, for a time, too close. Even before the revelations of Cheever's active homosexual life, Robinson and I wondered what it was that he was almost telling us.

One happy, sunny day Bob and I drove for a couple of hours up Long Island from New York City to Remsenburg, where we were to interview P.G. Wodehouse. He was 93 and his latest novel, *Aunts Aren't Gentleman*, was about to be published. We set up chairs and camera in leafy shade, close to the garden door of his house, a large single-storey dwelling, insulated from the world by several acres of grass and trees. We had been told that he would be with us just after 3.30 p.m., when the soap opera he watched every day had ended. He emerged promptly, accompanied by his wife, Ethel, and immediately embarrassed his interviewer by congratulating Bob on the detective story he had written nearly twenty years earlier, coming back to the subject during the interview. Whether he had remembered it or mugged it up for the occasion, it was a splendid touch of old-fashioned gent's politeness. He talked about Jeeves, named after a Warwickshire cricketer, about Psmith, 'the only character I've not actually invented', and about his early days in a bank. The filming was followed by tea and book signings, before he bid us goodbye.

Over the years I developed a theory of the television deliberate mistake, a theory well illustrated in my own work. Many programmes contain a mistake that is not merely a misjudgement, casual omission or error of fact, but a carefully considered production decision that is wholly wrong. In drama it may be the casting of an actor or director, in documentary the choice of presenter or avoidance of commentary, in a discussion programme the number of participants (too many) or the set. One of my best contributions to the theory was in a programme I made about the American humorous poet Ogden Nash. It was an uneasy combination of filmed interviews about the man and actors reading some of his poems in front of an audience in the studio. The subject was a good one; the presenter, Robert Robinson, well suited to the task; the actors, Prunella Scales, Dinsdale Landen and Clive Swift, excellent. The problem was the audience. I had decided that they would be on banks of seating on the studio floor, worse still, 'in the round'. They were, therefore, visible in all their peculiarity and, most distractingly, behind the performers – not just occasionally, but in every shot. Watching the tape back in the edit, one only had eyes for them. Who were they? Where had we found them? Why were they dressed like that?

The best offspring of *The Book Programme* was *Writers and Places*, in which some good young filmmakers took authors to locations important to their life or work. Anthony Burgess went to Malaysia and Frederick Raphael returned entertainingly to Cambridge and, while casting an amused eye on his vanities as an undergraduate, managed to reveal his then current ones plainly enough. Credit for the series goes to Antony Rouse, a clever, charming man who came from current affairs to work with us. He was a chain-smoking, old Etonian, always dressed in a thin, black polo neck jumper ('It's not the same one as last week'), who attracted talented young people to work with us, Nicholas Shakespeare and Dominic Lawson among them, because he was a delight to be with. He was taken to Thames Television by Nigel Ryan, an old friend of his who was also tall, slim, attractive and top public school. When Ryan departed after two years, Antony stayed on until rumbled. 'I don't think that they realized that there were two of us. It was a bit of a surprise for them to see so similar a creature still turning up for work.'

When not away filming or on a studio day, life was not overly pressured. Office hours were nominally 10.00 a.m. until 6.00 p.m. Indeed, it was not unusual to see people rolling in at 10.30 or after. Then, if not out to lunch with a contact, contributor or chum, we liked to lunch in the waitress serv ice restaurant, sharing a bottle of wine between two, or two bottles between three, occasionally with a glass of port to follow. This was, after all, the golden age of television. I will not say that work was never done over lunch, but I do not remember it as the chief purpose of the exercise. The waitresses in our corner, Sally, Eileen and Margaret, would keep tables for us and warn us off dishes they did not like the look of. Iain Johnstone and I let them down badly when Telly Savalas, with whom Iain was making a programme, asked to eat with us in the 'studio commissariat' and the PA booked a table away from our usual spot, so they were not able to serve him.

We put our expenses in every two or three weeks and, as long as they were reasonable, few were queried. I know of no great scams, but the regime was laxer than it should have been. Taxi journeys were plentiful and receipts were not required, first class train travel was allowed and names of lunch recipients rarely interrogated. None of this was unusual by the standards of the time, but every now and then there would be a dark secret. When Peter Foges wanted to do something with Sam White of the *Evening Standard*, doyen of Paris correspondents, he rang to arrange a meeting. White took matters into his own hands: 'Wednesday. One o'clock. The Crillon.' When Peter arrived, White was well into the first bottle of vintage champagne and lunch continued in this style. The bill, which it was made clear was for Peter to pick up, was in the hundreds. Peter returned shaken and anxious. Each department's money and administration person was called the 'organizer', and Peter went straight to the organizer's office, explained and asked for mercy. Soundings were taken at higher levels. The expense would be met as long as news of it went no further.

Peter fell in love a lot. He would arrive in the office, tall, elegant and bleary eyed, balancing newspapers, a book, coffee and toast from the canteen, and a cigarette and describe the happiness or otherwise of the previous evening. He would talk until the toast was cold and he no longer fancied it, whereupon he would throw it out of the window into the car park below. The less his affections were returned, the more besotted he became. At one time he yearned for a beautiful, but married, researcher, who laughed and joked about his attentions. Peter was determined to demonstrate the depths of his feelings and told her that if she would not respond to him, he would 'do a toast'. More laughter. Peter walked to the open window, put his legs out and let himself down until he was hanging by his fingers from the window ledge. There he hung, to the alarm of the commissionaires who spotted him, until the subject of his affections promised that she would laugh at him no more. Which was not quite true.

When it came to dealing with the talent, I was not yet a grown up. We did a series about television, called *In Vision*, presented jointly by Chris Dunkley and Paul Barnes. Before it was over, I decided that we needed to make a change. They did the job perfectly well, but the producer was unable to attract enough of the leading writers, producers and executives, and I thought that a heavyweight presenter would help. I approached Bill Hardcastle, who agreed to take on the next run. At the end of the series I did the unforgivable: I sacked Dunkley and Barnes by letter. I could try to comfort myself that I needed to move quickly, as Hardcastle was a journalist and news of his booking would leak, that I wanted to tell both at the same time. The fact is that I funked it.

Dunkley was a sportsman about it and we remained on good terms. Twenty-five years later the radio programme *Feedback* sacked him from the presenter's job he had done for many years. It was badly handled and he was bruised. I had overall responsibility for radio and, although this was not a decision that did or should come to me, I felt that he was owed an apology and invited him for a drink.

'I'm sorry about the way this was done, Chris,' I opened. 'It may or may not be a good idea to have a new presenter for *Feedback*, but it looks as though you were treated clumsily, for which, apologies. I'm doubly embarrassed because I did the same or worse to you when pushing you out of the presenter's chair of *In Vision* all that time ago. I told you in writing, if you recall?'

He looked at me blankly. 'I don't remember anything about that'

'You must have been upset? I was told that Paul Barnes carried the letter around in his pocket so he could show people proof of what a shit I was.'

With saintly generosity, Chris repeated, 'I've completely forgotten.'

I was right about Bill Hardcastle. He did attract bigger names onto the show. He was terrific fun to work with and had a great sense of devilment. I was told the story of how, when editor of the *Daily Mail*, he was briefed on the phone by his New York correspondent at the time of the Cuban missile crisis. Many people were convinced that there could be nuclear war at any time. Bill put the phone down and rubbed his hands with excitement 'Oh boy,' he said, 'This could be the big bang.' He came at every programme with enthusiasm, and there was no question that breathless Bill could not or would not ask, however eminent the interviewee. He told me that he could have asked Harold Wilson the question about his finances which, when put by the young David Dimbleby, caused the former Prime Minister to stomp out of the studio. 'It's just that I'm too old and fat for anyone to take offence.' He was fat but he was not old when he died at the age of only 57.

Through all this period the work still felt like an extended playtime and I was now able to make a first fifty-minute documentary. I had developed the outline for a series in which Robert Robinson would retrace famous journeys, and lobbied the controller of BBC1 when I first met him at a Christmas drinks. Convinced of something but not convinced enough to commission a series, he funded a single film in which we followed the journey of the Mormon pioneers from Keokuk, Iowa to the valley of the Great Salt Lake. Our aim was to tell the story of that heroic trek, using it as a frame from which to hang our own observations and discoveries along the same route 130 years later. I even dipped into the book of Mormon, which I found to be an impenetrable pastiche of the Old Testament.

I wanted a suitably arresting opening sequence, and we shot one on a pontoon on the Mississippi, but in Wyoming, Bob had a better idea. He would deliver the opening piece to camera from horseback.

'But can you ride, Bob?' I asked. 'I've never heard you talk about it.'

'Oh yes, I've done a fair bit.'

'Whereabouts?'

'Oh, in Richmond Park,' he replied airily.

'OK.' I drove off that evening to find a horse, asking at several establishments before a friendly rancher agreed to let us have one. It was a flashy, Palomino-like creature. I returned to our motel to give Bob the good news and warn him of an early start.

'Good. I've written the piece. I'll give it to you,' he replied.

'One thing. You'll have to ride long. Western style.'

'That's all right. Does the animal have a name?' he asked.

It was when I replied that I sensed that Bob was not as sanguine about all this as he let on.

'Yes,' I said. 'He's called Bullet.' Bob's eyes widened. There was an awkward pause.

'Aah!' he said thoughtfully. In the event, Bullet was a docile fellow who might well have been strolling through Richmond Park as we filmed our opening.

The best sequence in the film was one that posed some questions about what is or is not proper in a documentary, a subject that was to be much debated in my next job. As we drove between locations we tried to save as much time as we could, ignoring the measly 55 mile per hour speed limit. I had told the crew that if the police stopped Bob and me in the lead car, they should pull over and film it. There was a point to be made about the speed at which we could travel and the laborious progress the pioneers had made. In Nebraska, Bob was at the wheel when we were stopped and ticketed by the Highway Patrol. As luck would have it, several big lorries came past us as we were pulled over, shielding us from the camera car, which steamed by, oblivious to what was happening. We were doubly irritated. We had been fined and we had failed to film it. So, that evening I rang the Nebraska Highway Patrol. I explained what had happened, laid on the visitors-from-England charm with a trowel, told them how courteous the officer had been (true) and asked if they could possibly do it all over again the following morning for our camera.

'Sure.' This was not England. 'What time?'

'Say eight o'clock?'

'Sure thing.'

'And can we have the same officer?'

'You betcha.'

The patrolman and we did exactly as before: stopping, getting the ticket, following him to a post box where he witnessed Bob posting the fine, this time with the camera in tow. In so much as anyone ever remembers the programme, this is the bit they recall, especially Bob's hair flying in the wind as if released from long imprisonment. At the time I wondered briefly whether re-enacting an event like this broke some cardinal rule of documentary-making, but once we were in the cutting room nothing could have made me cut it out. No bones were broken. No deep lies told.

Changes were underway at the top of the BBC. There was a new director-general, Ian Trethowan, and, in his place, a new managing director of television, Alasdair Milne. Before any of the subsequent ripples agitated the waters around me, I had a call from the channel controller that sent me on a memorable jaunt. The BBC had bought the American mini-series *Roots*, which had been a sensational hit in the USA. The programmes were a dramatization of Alex Haley's book of the same title, in which he told the story of his family, tracing them back via family lore and his own twelve-year search to the very village in the Gambia from which his ancestor had been taken as a slave. The story ended with a satisfying click as he heard from the mouth of an African elder the very name his family stories had carried through generations, Kunta Kinte. My job was to make an introductory programme in which Michael Parkinson would interview Haley.

I read the book and flew to Los Angeles where Haley lived, a couple of days ahead of Parkinson in order to set up the filming. There were the usual problems with people you had spoken to a few days earlier expressing enormous surprise at your requests, listing the reasons why nothing would be possible, then asking for money. Once I was able to speak to Haley, all was well. I met Parkinson off the plane. He was zonked. 'I hate flying. The only way to deal with it is have a drink,' he told me as I took him back to the Beverly Hilton to crash out. I went to my room to prepare the line of questioning, looking forward to a hamburger and a quiet night. A couple of hours later the phone rang. It was Mike.

'Will. Get ready we're going out.'

'I thought you were exhausted?'

'So did I, but we're going to a party. Dress up.'

This was a difficult request to comply with. This was a three or four day filming trip and I had no suit. The best I could do was a lightweight pale blue jacket and a tie. When we met in the lobby, Mike was in a midnight blue velvet jacket. He appeared to ignore my outfit.

'We're going to Kirk Douglas' son's wedding party,' he announced.

'Who is Kirk Douglas' son?'

'He's called Michael. He's in *The Streets of San Francisco*.'

'If you say so. Who invited us? I doubt if it was Kirk.'

'Well, no one invited us as such, but my friends Sammy Cahn, the song writer, and his wife Tita are going, and they cleared it for us to tag along too.'

The Cahns picked us up and took us to the Beverly Wilshire Hotel and into the sort of Hollywood party impressionists used to base their act on. I met Kirk and Gregory Peck and Billy Wilder and Karl Malden and many more. Everyone was very polite. They were surprised that Michael was marrying this young nurse, as I think she was. They hoped it would work out because 'Michael, you know. He's been AROUND.'

All this would have been fun if only every other man in the room had not been wearing a beautifully cut dark suit. I looked like the ice cream man. They all knew it. Afterwards Sammy took us to dinner. 'We always have what we call the "in spot". That's where we're going.' The 'in spot' was an unpretentious little place. It was definitely 'in' and I was introduced to Angie Dickinson. However, I sensed that ice cream men were not her type.

When we filmed the interview with Haley, he welcomed us graciously and told his stories with well-practised skill. He was, he said, a conduit. We were pleased with our programme and the mini-series was a success here too. *Roots* was instrumental in raising the sense of pride and understanding of their history among the black people of America. We have learned since his death in 1992 that Haley lifted plot, character and whole passages from a novel by a white author, that most of his genealogical claims were false and that the final satisfying click of his story was more of a clunk, in that the African villagers knew what they were expected to say and were pushed into doing so. The legend lives on.

Chapter five

'CONTINUING TO PROSPER . . . SHOULD BUILD'

In the spring of 1977 the Annan committee reported on the future of broadcasting, advocating the introduction of a fourth channel, to be run by a new authority on a publishing model. The report endorsed both the licence fee mechanism for funding the BBC and the Corporation's independence from government, but gave the place a pasting for 'loss of nerve', 'organizational fog' and for the 'palsy' in its current affairs programming. It also proposed an independent broadcasting complaints unit. All this stirred the BBC up a bit. My own attention remained firmly on the programme road ahead, but in October I was put in charge of presentation programmes and began to take more notice of the passing scenery and the broadcasting weather conditions.

I now became a regular attendee, every Wednesday at 10.00 a.m., at the television weekly programme review board, or 'programme review', a gathering of mythological significance in the BBC. When Bill Cotton retired as managing director of television in 1988, he said, 'I have been coming to this meeting for thirty years. It's the heart of the place.' It is worth dwelling on for a moment.

The myths surrounding programme review were often contradictory: that it was the forum where producers' careers were damned and that it was a mutual admiration society for the production departments; that it was nothing but an internal public relations exercise and that it was where you heard what people 'really thought' about a programme. The purpose of the meeting was to review the previous week's output, the programmes, of course, but also how difficulties or emergencies had been handled and any major events responded to. It took place in B209, a large basement, and thus windowless, conference room in Television Centre, and was chaired by the managing director of television or the director of programmes. He sat at one end of an open oblong of tables, flanked by the channel controllers. Around the oblong sat the heads of the London programme departments, a couple of visiting programme heads from the regions, two or three of the schedule and resource planners, one or two heads of the resource units (outside broadcasts, studios, film editing, film shooting, scenic servicing) in rotation, an

executive producer or two, according to which new or important programmes were under discussion, and the head of press and publicity –
thirty-five to forty people in all.

The big beasts would sit in the same place each week. Desmond Wilcox,
reporter and presenter as well as head of general features, was at the far end
facing the managing director, from where it was easy to intervene, which he
did often. Shaun Sutton, whose longevity and experience as head of the big
spending drama group gave his views weight and influence, sat at the same
end. Cliff Morgan, head of sports and outside broadcasts, himself a broadcaster and rugby legend, was halfway down on the left, just past Monica
Sims, head of children's, who had lots to say because she appeared to have
watched everything.

Nearby was music and arts, represented by Humphrey Burton, who liked
to lean back out of eye line and work through his in-tray until roused, or by
the imposing John Drummond, until he went off to run the Edinburgh
Festival. Drummond would boomingly argue the cause of high culture. He
was a master at damning with faint praise. He once met a fellow arts producer in the corridor remarking, 'I enjoyed your programme last night. Yes,
I've been defending it around the BBC all morning.' Another undercut was,
'Mmn. An interesting programme. So glad you're back on form.' The light
entertainment heads, expecting the most criticism, sat immediately on the
right, nestling close to the top table for comfort.

As well as its editorial function, the meeting was an opportunity for
senior management to report occasionally on high policy, such as licence fee
and charter negotiations, government committees of inquiry and so on, and
to communicate about financial matters and industrial relations. It was also
an important social occasion, enabling the editorial leadership of BBC television to meet weekly face to face, a chance to know each other better,
transact bits of business, gossip and jokes.

Depending on the chair, the meeting could last as little as an hour or go on
for two, even two and a half hours. Alasdair Milne would belt through the
whole thing, betting himself or others that he could be out in less than 60
minutes. The discussion was brisk, at times peremptory. Bill Cotton, on the
other hand, relished the exchange of views, enjoyed the company and was
often in confessional mode from the chair, explaining the history of a programme or decision, tossing in anecdotes of his own and encouraging them
from others. Brian Wenham, when director of programmes, ran a sharp
meeting in which he would rifle waspish comments at programmes or individuals whose work he held to have fallen below the required standard.

My first appearance as a regular was on 19 October 1977, along with the
new head of variety, Terry Hughes, a tall, good-looking and permanently
tanned entertainment producer, who looked as if he was on his way to
Hollywood, as indeed he was, to win an Emmy for directing *The Golden
Girls*. When there were management issues to report on, the meeting would
begin with them. Terry and I heard that there was to be a meeting about pay,
a problem that was coming to a head.

Throughout the late 1970s and early 1980s there were regular industrial disputes, resulting in disrupted and cancelled programmes. That autumn the Labour government condemned the BBC to a hand to mouth existence by granting a licence fee increase, £25 for colour, for one year only. There was pressure on pay through a national pay policy and high inflation. For many weeks programme review kicked off with bad news. A shortage of make-up artists and prop buyers was threatening production. 'The BBC is facing disintegration,' was Bill Cotton's apocalyptic view. Someone claimed that many staff were drawing social security. Unable to move on pay, the BBC reduced canteen prices and offered interest free loans for season tickets. In one week in November *The Generation Game* was interrupted fifteen minutes from the end and editions of both *The Two Ronnies* and *The Duchess of Duke Street* were lost.

In the main, Television Centre was a throbbing production factory with most of the drama, comedy and entertainment made in its eight main studios. Each week there was a report on the late starts and studio overruns that incurred costs. This was a naming and shaming: 'Late arrival of artist on stage', 'complicated show technically', '41 retakes', 'meal breaks overran because of many costume changes'. After management issues, came 'Programme comments from the Board of Governors.' In those days, the governors met every two weeks and had an agenda item on programmes, in which they reported on what they had seen and heard. Their opinions were passed on down, often perfectly sensible but resented by us as merely the views of a random group of the great and good. Mostly they 'commended' and 'praised', and this was reported back to producers. It was when they 'questioned' and 'criticized' that we scorned and kept it to ourselves. One week the programme review minutes contained four and a half pages of governors' comments. We would then hear the headlines from the telephone log and correspondence: 'the total of criticisms of *Play for Today* is now 180; *Key to the Universe*, four appreciations, two criticisms and two comments; eighteen more appreciations of Johnny Mathis', and the like.

The big surprise for the first time visitor was the amount of time spent in going through the latest audience figures. It was not that one was unaware or uninterested in audience figures, but the discussion in the office, bar and canteen was about whether a programme had worked, was it any good. In my fairly rarefied quarter of the schedule, protected from competitive responsibilities, the size of the audience was an incidental. Not here. First the overall figures, in October 1977 BBC1 all hours 44 per cent, ITV 50 per cent, BBC2 7 per cent. Then each channel controller would go through the week's figures (ten days out of date) highlighting, or lowlighting, individual programmes, only rarely commenting on ITV, though their figures were in front of us too.

The controllers and senior pros used a lexicon of comments about the figures, which to the newcomer sounded wise, knowing and all in all terribly grown up. 'Continuing to prosper', 'should build', 'decent figure for a concert', 'Act of Rape, two and a half million, nothing like a title to lift a programme', 'gratifying', 'encouraging', 'losing out badly', 'steady', 'rock steady', 'holding up', 'highest ever figure' and, with a shaft of the blindingly obvious, 'would have liked another million'. For a few shows that had big audiences but did not display all the qualities we aspired to, there was 'distressingly popular'. When the audience stayed away, we could fall back on the RI, reaction index, later AI, appreciation index, a scale of how much the audience enjoyed a programme. It was a proper measure for the BBC to seek and could be a valuable indicator of a show that would blossom in time. It gave a figure out of 100. David Attenborough carried a personal AI of 88, which he bestowed upon any programme he appeared in. Many one-off plays in the 1970s would record figures in the forties, 'apparently, an acquired taste,' the drama head would mutter.

The guts of the meeting was the critique of the week's programmes. We went through the *Radio Times* day-by-day and channel-by-channel, rubbing the itch of our opinion. Anxious producers always hungered to know 'what they said about it at programme review', but the meeting erred on the side of generosity and was often less than honest about failure. There was a tendency for the top table to wish to end things, as Edward VII did after visiting a naval dockyard, with 'treacle pudding all round'. After all, it was their triumph too. Still, the meeting was, in part, a market place where reputations were, if not ruined, priced and discounted, and where one could identify the producers to buy futures in.

It was also political. Heads sought to jump in first when programmes from their department came up in order to fly the flag for them, or at least put upon them the best construction possible. Or they might keep mum, in the hope that no one had seen a dud show and the discussion would move on. My own contribution to this economy of self-congratulation was strong advocacy on behalf of the programmes for which I was now responsible. A colleague offered me a backhanded compliment: 'If I'm ever in court, I want you on my side.' I was an eager beaver, keen to bring the virtues, as I saw them, of our programmes to the attention of all.

The exchanges were generally good humoured. There was much joshing and when sport was the subject, especially rugby, blokeish banter. Yet the debates could be serious and searching. When one of your programmes was at the centre of a public row or had gone badly off the rails, you went along on Wednesday morning with your case prepared, arguments marshalled, wits sharpened and not without some anxiety. This was the forum of your peers and superiors, and you carried not only your own reputation but also that of your producers. I have seen experienced executives shake with nerves.

The quality of criticism was much aided by new voices from outside the BBC, particularly heads of plays who came on two- or three-year contracts. People like Christopher Morahan, Bill Bryden and Richard Eyre were unconstrained by the BBC's institutional interests and always more likely to spot imperial new clothes.

Bushfires could break out around you, ignited by a spark struck off a strong opinion. Others would then unleash their hitherto withheld views and, suddenly, the bonhomie was gone and the club became a cockpit. Sometimes this would be a clash of professional rivals, as when the head of sport, where they felt they knew a thing or two about going live with breaking stories, would make a two-footed tackle on news. Sometimes it would be mischievous. Desmond Wilcox specialized in the *faux naïf* question, 'Was that a broadcasting first last night in *Film 78*? I'm referring to the full frontal male nude we saw for a moment, which I'm sure the controller was informed about.' All part of the rough and tumble. Most often, the impassioned debates would be about ethical and moral aspects of programmes, whether the participant in a documentary had been properly handled, whether it was right to show, say, children in distress, whether the BBC should be transmitting certain films or kinds of programmes. After the first two or three weeks of *Blankety Blank*, Alasdair Milne asked for a show of hands round the table on whether or not it was a suitable programme for the BBC. About half the hands, including mine, voted against, blind, as I soon realized, to the wit and dexterity with which Terry Wogan subverted the conventions of such programmes.

The meeting in October 1977 was not untypical. There was hearty pleasure at a Sunday evening that offered *Treasure Island*, *Poldark* and *Anna Karenina* across the two channels. The run of *Gardeners' World* had ended and several people hoped that BBC2 would bring it back (it's still there). The BBC1 arts strand *Omnibus* had opened its new season with a programme on early medieval Japanese court music (it is true). This had bemused Bill Cotton, the channel controller, who said, 'You know, it reminded me of peculiar dreams I sometimes have.' The new series of *Multi Coloured Swap Shop* had begun on Saturday mornings and a drama head reported that he had recently spoken at a Mothers' Union in Somerset at which this programme had been accused of left-wing bias. BBC2 had transmitted *Fidelio* and John Drummond complained that he had been misquoted about it by James Thomas in the *Daily Express*. He was advised that Thomas was best spoken to about programmes in the mornings. The longest discussion was, as often the case, about the *Play for Today*, *Stronger Than The Sun* by Stephen Poliakoff, directed by Mike Apted, another who was on his way to Hollywood. One present said, 'I found it very hard to get involved for the first three-quarters of an hour . . . but then it became very powerful,' testimony both to the conscientiousness of our viewing habits and to the fact that there were but two other channels. The *Play for Today* often needed spinning by the drama folk. I recall one protesting, 'The whole was not nearly as bad as the first ten minutes.'

The minutes of the programme review board were widely believed to be both a sanitized account of the bloody encounters that had actually taken place and the official record of praise and blame. They were written for years by one of the best-loved figures in the Corporation, Roger Cary, or rather Sir Roger Cary Bt, as he was, but did not seek to be known as. He had been a guards officer and leader writer on *The Times* before joining the BBC as a talks producer in radio.

'When I was in external services, I remember Miss Owen of music copyright ringing me up one day and asking if I realized that the act of recording was a sin,' he told me. He had made a series of programmes about prime ministers, interviewing those who had known them. 'Word was going round the London clubs, "See Cary and die." When I took the recording car down to Lord Mersey's home in Kent, I was met by the doctor with a stethoscope round his neck. "He's still alive," he said. I had written, you see, on December the sixteenth and booked to come on January the seventh. The excitement of having been asked to talk about Lord Salisbury had caused a heart attack. But the idea of doing the broadcast brought about an almost complete recovery.'

Roger was famous for the way that he dressed BBC rooms at party conferences with the appropriate books from his personal library. For the Tories he would bring shelves of Disraeli, Burke, Adam Smith, Churchill and Blake; for Labour, Tawney, E.H. Carr, the Webbs and G.D.H. Cole. There was a small room in Broadcasting House that was lined with Cary books, overflowing from his house and ready to be deployed in the interests of the Corporation. Roger was rarely glimpsed without at least a couple of plastic bags filled with papers and books in each hand, whether waiting at a bus stop or walking distractedly in and out of the building. He cut, and still cuts, a memorable figure in grey suit and old Mac, tie off-centre and his face sprouting whiskers in unusual places missed by his razor.

Roger is a scholar, particularly strong on politics, military history and the Italian renaissance. I once mentioned that my wife and I were going to Rome and the following day he sent me five pages of hand-written notes in sloping capitals on what to see and where to go: 'If the villa is closed, go down the alley to the right and ring the second bell. The caretaker is an old friend and will let you in by the rear gates.' Any reference to military matters at programme review would produce a long minute explaining the origins of that particular regimental uniform or the tactics employed in the battle or the subsequent fate of the commanding officer.

For Roger the BBC was both an idea and a community of brothers and sisters. He sought to celebrate that. I kept his closing minutes of programme review on 8 October 1980:

> MR. ROBIN SCOTT
>
> M.D.Tel. said this had been Robin Scott's last meeting as Deputy Managing Director, Television, now – alas – due to retire on grounds of age. M.D.Tel. said he had been a marvellous deputy, who had presided over the meeting so often and would now be universally missed in the Service and throughout the BBC. There was a burst of spontaneous applause.
>
> A HALF CENTURY
>
> C.BBC-1 drew attention to the fact that M.D.Tel. himself had that day joined the ranks of BBC staff who were halfway to their centuries. A fresh burst of applause was interrupted by the approaching sound of pipe music . . .

Our little department was something of a speciality act on the playbill of the television service, and I set out to raise its profile, and mine, by increasing both the number and the scale of its programmes. The channel controllers used us as, in effect, an in-house independent producer (not that there were real independents then): a unit that was hungry, flexible and responsive. I began to have regular meetings with the controllers to chew over routine business, float new ideas and deal with running problems. At one of the first, Bill Cotton intimated that he might end *Film 77* with Barry Norman and leave coverage of films to the music and arts department. The film programme was a central province of my little empire and its loss would have been a severe blow. Quite out of character, I launched into an increasingly angry tirade. 'You must be out of your mind. It does a good job, gets you a decent audience and the idle prats in music and arts haven't got a clue about making popular programmes or dealing with anything except the precious, longwinded stuff you get on *Omnibus* . . .'. I surprised myself and, to judge by his wide-eyed, anxiously smiling face, Bill as well.

'Well, I'll think about it,' he said, and we heard no more. I wish I could say that this had been a ploy to let him know who he was dealing with, but I do not think that I was wily.

Around this time came the day when I was first asked to go out and speak for the BBC. The public libraries group of the Library Association had invited the director-general to speak at their annual conference. He had other things to do, as had all the other people in the BBC across whose desks the invitation passed. Eventually it came to me, possibly due to my connection with programmes about books. Bright-eyed and bushy-tailed, I accepted. I beavered away and produced a thirty-page speech on the requested theme of resolving the pressures to give the public what it wants with the desire to give it what you think it should have. I touched on how programmes came about and how we used audience research, appropriating arguments and quoting from the likes of Huw Wheldon. It does not read too badly now, a bit holy, mind you. I finished it in note form on the Sunday that it was to be delivered and drove swiftly up to Warwick University where I was to speak after lunch. I felt reasonably confident until the chairman introduced me.

'Welcome back everyone for the final session of our weekend. This is the session that we all look forward to.' I began to worry. 'It's when we let our hair down and enjoy our last hour together. You will all remember last year's marvellous address. We were laughing for days afterwards.' I was now seriously alarmed. I looked down at my sheaf of papers. This is what I had and this is what they were going to get. 'That was a splendid occasion. This year we all hope that today's speaker will emulate it . . .'. By now I sensed that the audience realized the chairman was digging a pit for me to fall into and I grimaced, I hoped winningly, at the friendliest faces I could spot. This did seem to win some sympathy, and the few humorous remarks that I had included raised a smile or two. The response to the remaining forty minutes of my earnest address is, happily, lost to me. It was a while before I offered myself again.

The search was on for savings. Everyone had been invited to come up with ways to save money and I had put up two. To save money on taxis, which were often used to take letters and packages around London that people did not wish to entrust to the post, we should have a motorbike picking up and delivering twice a day. The second, more radical, was that there was no reason why the BBC should be any good at catering and we should contract it all out via competitive tender. In the late 1970s this was not thought to be serious.

I was more successful with programmes. I had the idea for a film about what people were doing when President Kennedy had died, which Peter Foges turned into an excellent documentary for BBC1, *Kennedy's Been Shot*. This established a credibility that led to biographies of Richard Dimbleby and the American broadcasting hero Ed Murrow, both written and narrated by Frank Gillard, former war correspondent and director of radio at the BBC; and to *Scars of Autumn*, in which three correspondents who had covered the outbreak of World War II, Clare Hollingsworth, Patrick Maitland and Sir Hugh Greene, returned to Poland to retell the story for the 40th anniversary. Both Gillard and Greene enjoyed spending time with junior BBC folk like Foges and me. Frank was more formal. He was slim, straight-backed and brisk at the age of 70, and remained so for the next twenty years. He was punctilious in his manners, a cheery host in Somerset or at the Farmer's Club, a lively and gratifying guest in one's home or a restaurant. We enjoyed hearing his stories of BBC bosses, into which he would drop the odd, carefully considered indiscretion. 'Of course, when Hugh Greene was director-general I often used to travel with him as a sort of minder. Not that I could prevent him from doing what he wanted, but I could, at least, watch out for him. That included waiting in the hall of the brothels in various cities round the world while Hugh was enjoying himself inside.'

Frank and Hugh put pen to paper for their scripts, which cannot be said for all presenters over the years. Often it was the producer who wrote the scripts for documentaries and, more often than should have been the case, the presenter changed nothing. There were plenty of other series when the presenter put in little time on location either because of other commitments or because the budget would not run to it. One such was an expensive series of six fifty-minute films all shot overseas. The writer-narrator (he did write) was only available for filming for two days of the fifteen-week shoot. These had to be dedicated to statements to camera, all shot within a mile or two of each other. One was the opening of the series. The next, shot a few minutes later, was the closing statement from the last film, which went, 'And so, at the end of the journey that we have made in these programmes, I return to where I began my story . . .'.

The film programme with Barry Norman was a mainstay of our portfolio and, in order to capitalize upon it, I suggested to Barry Brown, the producer, that he work up a proposal for a series of biographies of the big stars. Choose only the dead, I said, so that contributors can be less gushing than they would be with the living. Barry and Barry and their team made a big success of what became *The Hollywood Greats*. It gave rise to a favourite among the location stories, brought back by production teams after filming. Many of these are to do with the shenanigans of who got off with whom, the all night activity of the assistant cameraman heard unavoidably through the paper-thin motel walls, the jealousy of the producer who, having at last made it with the long fancied PA, sees her swept off her feet by the new cameraman and so on.

This one did take place in a motel. *The Hollywood Greats* team always stayed in a low cost place on Sunset Strip. One night the sound recordist thought he heard someone in his room. They were in a dangerous area, so he held his breath and listened, his heart racing. There was definitely someone there and the intruder was beginning to go through the possessions scattered on the table. The sound recordist knew he had to do something and spoke. 'I don't know who you are. I haven't seen your face and I'm keeping my face to the wall so I don't see it now. Please take whatever you want and go. I won't look. OK?' The intruder was still for a moment. The recordist tensed his muscles and prepared to fight for his life.

The intruder said, 'Hey man, if you just knew what my life was like, you wouldn't think bad of me.' To the recordist's horror, he felt the man sit down at the end of the bed. 'You can't imagine. My life is shit, man. All I get is trouble. I ain't gonna hurt no one . . .'. The man continued in like vein, spilling out an autobiography of misery and bad luck, until he felt he had made his point and left.

The Old Grey Whistle Test, as part of the legacy of *Late Night Line Up*, was a star in our output. The name, by the way, was provided by a researcher who had a boyfriend in the music business. It was the practise, she said, to bring in people off the street, the 'old greys', to listen to a new record. If they could whistle it after a single hearing, it would be a hit. Mike Appleton, a genial, ever-optimistic teddy bear of a man, who had a passion for old gramophones and cricket, produced the series with entrepreneurial flair. It was never a surprise, said one colleague, that Mike was only able to interview Mick Jagger in the West Indies while the Test was on. For many years Mike kept rock music on television almost single-handedly, spotting the rising talents and bringing them into the tiny Studio B to record or play live. Dave Bowie, The Police, Bob Marley, the Eurythmics, the Ramones, Talking Heads, Alice Cooper and John Lennon were among those who appeared and whose performances have proved invaluable in the BBC archive.

One series of rock concerts went out live late on a Friday evening and was repeated the following day in the early evening. One Friday I saw a good show with Bob Geldof and The Boomtown Rats but one of the songs was about suicide and Geldof more than once mimed the slitting of wrists. I went to bed worrying about this. It was too simple to assume that people imitated what they saw on television, but I could not get it out of my head that there might be a child watching at 6.00 p.m. on Saturday who was playing with the thought of suicide. A graphic, almost celebratory, demonstration of how it might be accomplished just could be the trigger. I did not sleep well, got up early and went for a walk to argue it out with myself. When I came back I rang Tom Corcoran and asked him if he would go into Television Centre to edit it, which he did.

On another Saturday the newly famous Ian Dury and the Blockheads gave the concert featuring their hit 'Sex and Drugs and Rock and Roll'. The song and Dury, who cut a subversive figure, were not meant for grown-ups to bump into. On Monday morning the telephone rang in my office. It was Aubrey Singer, the channel controller, shouting, 'What the hell were you playing at? That programme was a fucking disgrace.' He had seen some complaints in the telephone log and viewed the end of the programme. 'You've got to keep tabs on these people or someone's for the high jump. I won't have that sort of thing on my channel.'

That was Aubrey. The next time I spoke to him it would be as if it had never happened. He stormed regularly but was full of pep and brain waves, always with a new enthusiasm, always looking for big splash. As controller of BBC2, he introduced the idea of seasons. Opera month was, I think, the first, but there were also, reflecting his relish for travel, China week and Russian week. Life with Aubrey could be a pain but an interesting and lively pain. He would ring up from distant continents with brainwaves, instructions and requests. In the office he would shout to his assistant, 'Get me Time Life on the transatlantic phone,' as if this required a wholly different piece of equipment from the usual telephone. He introduced a poem at close down. His interest in philosophy led him to ask us to make *Men of Ideas*, in which Bryan Magee, a philosopher himself as well as a professional broadcaster, conducted prepared and structured conversations with philosophers from around the world.

Aubrey Singer was a keen photographer and, when travelling, would be festooned with cameras and camera equipment. He had an endearing enthusiasm for the latest gear. Sitting next to him on a plane once, I admired his smart leather bag. Aubrey glowed like a schoolboy with a new Dinky toy, 'Do you? Yes, I'm a bit of a luggage freak, like David Webster [the BBC's man in the United States].' I said that I had seen Webster with a new portable word processor, with which he could type on the plane. Aubrey cut me short, animatedly, 'I've got one. I'm a bit of a gadget freak, too.' He was a portly figure who lived well. One afternoon I looked in to the sixth-floor suite at Television Centre, the place for big meetings, lunches and dinners, to see Aubrey helping himself to a handful of cigars from the cabinet. It was one of those sights that you wish to be protected from, like the kitchen of your favourite Indian restaurant. Likewise, I have an image of him leaving the big room at the Grosvenor House Hotel, at the end of a BAFTA awards dinner, carrying the hardly touched bottles of brandy and whisky from his table. When he caught my eye, he laughed disarmingly, 'Well, there's no point in wasting them is there?' When he became managing director of television, he turned the annexe to the big suite into a dining room. 'It's not my personal dining room, you understand. I don't want that appearing in *Private Eye*.' A laugh. 'Mind you, anyone else will have a hard time booking it.' It was impossible to be mad with him for long.

I wanted to do something about photography and approached Lord Snowdon through his agent Peter Lyster-Todd. We met for lunch at Langans and threw around ideas until 5.00 p.m., a record for me at the time. It was a bonding lunch. I was getting better with presenters and had discovered that long, bonding lunches did wonders. My annual contract discussion with Barry Norman took place over a mountain of crustacea and two bottles of Muscadet at Le Suquet. Snowdon agreed to make the two programmes and I asked Iain Johnstone to produce. I roped in Harry Evans to help, and one of the best documentary cameramen, Ian Stone, was recruited. Through Snowdon's good offices, Iain was able to film Terence Donovan, Karsh of Ottowa and the legendary and rarely seen Ansel Adams. There were tensions, and worse, on the way. Iain constructed his films out of good moments and, within a broad outline, shot his material in a freewheeling way. Snowdon, as you might expect, was a perfectionist about the lighting and framing of individual shots, but without, according to Iain, who would unload himself on me, much idea of how it would be used and linked.

I watched Tony Snowdon directing one sequence in Hyde Park as a fashion photographer exhorted a model to 'shimmer' and 'sparkle', assisted by two young men in pegged trousers. I was surprised by how nervous Snowdon was. His hands shook so much that he dropped his cigarette while trying to light it. He eventually managed to get it going and told me how pleased he was with the team. The previous evening they had filmed Peter Sellers, who had provided a turn, imitating an Irish, handicapped (the word used then) photographer before the introduction of the zoom lens. Iain Johnstone had told me how funny it had been. I asked Snowdon about it.

'Yes, we filmed Peter. I'm afraid it didn't work at all. It was my fault, I arranged for him to do something. But it was very black. We can't use it I'm afraid.' Then, cheering up, gave me a funny imitation of an advertising photographer who had spent his whole life photographing ice cream and sherry. He affected a deep, artificial voice, 'You must only have two bubbles in a glass of sherry. Three are hopeless. Where would they go? Up and down or in a straight line?'

The completed films, *Snowdon On Camera*, were nominated for the BAFTA award, thanks to Iain's skill and wit and to Snowdon's down to earth views about photographs. He pooh poohed talk of art and was slyly funny in his disapproval of galleries that hung and sold photos. In the afterglow of successful transmission, Peter Lyster-Todd and Snowdon took me to lunch to talk of other possible projects. When we left the restaurant, Snowdon slipped into the back of Lyster-Todd's Rolls-Royce with me, so that Peter looked like a chauffeur, and giggled at his trick as we went back to his house. Snowdon liked to poke fun at grand cars, pomposity and airs and graces, but he did so not as one who had renounced grandeur for ever, rather as one who could have access to it any time he pleased but, right now, chose not to.

There was a new controller of BBC2, Brian Wenham. He was a clever, cultured and funny man who became a close friend. He was ambitious and retained a reputation for scheming and plotting. It was true that he speculated often to himself and others about which moves might lead to which appointments in the BBC, but I was never aware that he did much, or anything, to make these come about. He did want to try his hand at some senior jobs and was impatient. His father and his father's brother had both died of heart attacks in their early thirties, and Brian had suffered a serious heart attack at the age of thirty-two, soon after he had joined the BBC from ITN. When he returned to work he sought to create more relaxation in his life, but from then on would always preface thoughts about the future, be they career hopes or holiday plans, with the proviso, 'If spared.'

He had been head of current affairs, an area of programming that had been criticized by Annan, and had become moody. One member of his staff said, 'You could always tell when Brian was feeling depressed. He didn't take his raincoat off and lay on his desk all day.' He was a shy man. In private or in small groups he displayed his intelligence, wit, insight and sense of fun. He invented nicknames for colleagues. Alan Yentob, then editor of the arts programme *Arena* became 'Nala Botney'; Ian Trethowan was 'the defector general'; a BBC executive, who left suddenly after allegations of an active interest in flagellation, was 'Dick Bondage' or 'The Chief Whip'. But he hated formality and large groups. After announcing a big change around in current affairs, he walked into a staff meeting in his raincoat, said, 'Well, it's all going to be different', and would have left it at that if not deluged by questions. He was thrilled to become channel controller. 'I think it began to swing my way when they realized that Humphrey Burton [his chief rival for the job] meant it when he said it would be a good idea for the channel controller to introduce each evening's output in person.'

Brian wanted a new programme for late on Fridays. I persuaded him that I could provide and chewed it over with Iain Johnstone, who came up with the bold, possibly foolhardy, conceit that there should be a different presenter in the chair every two weeks. We would be able to try hosts who would not otherwise have the time for or be risked on a whole run, and this would also broaden the range of guests. *Friday Night, Saturday Morning*, as it was called, began well. The first host was Ned Sherrin, who kicked off with a funny, highly scripted news quiz, and then Iain followed with Simon Hoggart, Willie Rushton and Tim Rice, all of whom acquitted themselves well, as did the Cambridge Footlights team of Martin Bergman, Emma Thompson, Stephen Fry and Hugh Laurie.

Then came a daring throw. Iain had met Harold Wilson when producing the *Frost Programme*, and suggested we invite the recent prime minister to do a couple of the shows. It was an eye-catching move and I urged him to go ahead. Afterwards, colleagues were loyal and supportive. Wilson was a public man, said one, he had chaired conferences, committees and the Cabinet. You would imagine that he could chair a television show. Well, perhaps not if we had thought a little harder. The guests included Pat Phoenix, from *Coronation Street*, Dicky Bird, the cricket umpire, Freddie Trueman, the fast bowler, and Harry Secombe. Wilson began with a lot of saloon bar nudging and chuckling about Lancashire versus Yorkshire and continued in this vein. Watching from the gallery, I realized after five minutes that this was the first time that I had seen terror in the eyes of interviewees, not because they feared a merciless grilling, but because they might not be asked any questions at all. Harry Secombe began whistling to himself, as if to say, 'Don't forget about us.'

The sickness in the stomach was intensified by knowing that Wilson would be back the following week. Somehow, the programme was completed and in the one-hour delay before transmission Iain achieved a brutal edit and a show went out. Much of the BBC's top brass was due to come down to the Greenwood Theatre where we recorded for the second programme and to have supper with the former prime minister afterwards. Oddly enough, they chose not to.

There was an extraordinarily likeable and talented man called Ian Keill in the department. He habitually wore an owl-like expression of beatific surprise and came up with inventive, occasionally whimsical and utterly original ideas. He had produced *Up Sunday* and *One Man's Week*, in which intelligent celebs were filmed for a sort of diary of the week. I helped Ian get off the ground a delightful series with the singer-songwriter Neil Innes, once of the Bonzo Dog Doo-Dah Band, which featured charming films cut to Neil's songs. Like much of Ian Keill's work, it pleased an enthusiastic cult audience but did not break through more widely.

One of Ian's collaborators in his programmes lived in a mill in Dorset and with his wife ran a mail order business selling mackintoshes, Ian hinting that their interest in rubber went well beyond useful rainwear. A few years later I ran into the journalist and author Simon Winchester. 'I've just come back from a family holiday,' he told me, 'we went to the West Country and rented a nice old mill.'

'Successful?' I asked.

'Yes, we had a terrific time. Though something pretty amazing happened. The people who owned the place had put most of their stuff away, but one day we opened a cupboard that was full of the most extraordinary rubber gear. There were rubber clothes and a rubber mask from which protruded . . .'. He described the oddly placed rubber organ attached to the mask.

'Ah!' I said brightly, 'I know about that house.'

Winchester looked at me oddly. I tried to explain, but I'm not sure that I convinced.

With Ian's productions we were into drama, and I came up with a proposal that led to the dubious honour of two drama firsts. It would be the 20th anniversary of the trial of Penguin Books for obscenity for publishing

Lady Chatterley's Lover in 1980. What better way to mark this than a dramatization of the court proceedings. I read an account of the trial and was sure this could make a good programme. The language of the book was one of the central issues of the case and it would be impossible to do justice to the material without using some of the court exchanges in which the four-letter words were used. I knew that the channel controller would have to clear the programme with Alasdair Milne, the managing director, and decided to recce the path myself.

Alasdair was a strong-minded Scot, thought not to be sympathetic to bad language on the screen. He had been, however, the editor of the great *Tonight* programme and, more to the point, the person under whose auspices *That Was The Week That Was* had been conceived and produced. Sympathetic or not, he was the person who would make the decision. I went to see him and explained my proposal.

'Good idea, boy.' Prolix, Alasdair was not.

'If Brian wants to commission this, and I'm sure that he will,' I said, 'the script will have to contain the words "fuck" and "cunt".'

'I can see that.'

'There is absolutely no point in our going further, if, at some later stage, you or any one else has second thoughts or wants to reconsider. Whatever the climate about language at the time, we will have to broadcast these words.'

'You'd better see if Brian wants it,' said Alasdair. 'Tell him it's all right by me.'

'Thanks, Alasdair. This is worth doing. The governors? Do they need to know?'

'You leave them to me, boy.'

I asked Phil Speight to produce and he did a terrific job, casting Edward Woodward as Mervyn Griffith-Jones, the prosecuting counsel who asked the famous question, 'Is this a book you would wish your wife or servants to read?' Thus occurred the first scripted use of the word 'fuck' and the first ever use of the word 'cunt', a word I hate, on British television. This did not open the floodgate. 'Fuck' was not permitted in scripted work for many years after. It was more difficult to keep it out of documentary films that captured people at play or under pressure. Judging by the falling number of complaints, the audience understood that. Today, for much of the younger audience 'fuck' carries little charge. 'Cunt', I am happy to say, remains exceptionally rare on television.

By now I was living within a couple of miles of Television Centre and was to do so for the next eighteen years. We had moved to a hamlet just outside Thame in Oxfordshire with our young daughters while I was on *Late Night Line Up*. I worked odd shifts then, with days off in the week and never needed to travel at the rush hour. Our garden was the scene of a memorable *Line Up* summer lunch party, at which people appeared and disappeared all day and at the end of which, when we locked up at night after the final guests had gone, we found a pair of yellow knickers on our doorstep. No one ever claimed them. As a baby executive, I now worked a more usual pattern with some evenings thrown in. The travelling had become a pain and I was staying one night a week in London, presuming on the hospitality of different friends. This was going to become two nights and that did not seem a good idea, so we gave away the pony (a day of tears for daughters and guilt for father) and moved to Shepherds Bush. Well, at least it sounded rural.

In a burst of what came to be called 'accountability', the BBC began a pattern of public meetings around the country, at which some BBC big, or biggish, wigs would answer questions from whoever turned up. A governor would welcome people and assert how open we were to criticism and how keen we were to explain ourselves. In the front row there would always be someone from the BBC's local radio station and an engineer who could answer the inevitable complaints about poor reception. Members of the public regularly told us that the FM radio signal was not receivable in many of the places that BBC engineers insisted it was. The panel would comprise a couple of people from television, someone from radio and the head of the BBC's regional services for that part of the country. A prominent presenter, such as Esther Rantzen, Sue Lawley or Nick Ross, would be in the chair and declare, 'I'm freelance. The BBC doesn't own me.'

These meetings continued until the 1990s. The mayor, in chain of office, would sit in the front row. The audience was, by and large, made up of just the sort of person who would bother to leave the warmth of their fireside to travel to an echoing hall for what was, however you looked at it, a BBC supporters' event. They were predominantly radio listeners, kindly, older, genteel folk, who wanted to make a strongly felt point or just be in the same room as Sue Lawley. In time, a wider representation of the public was induced to come and special interest groups twigged that this was a place to air their case. Mostly, the evenings were good humoured and sometimes the panel had to liven it up for themselves. Once, Bill Cotton, then managing director of television, was on the panel with Jim Moir, the head of light entertainment. There was a long aggressive question about entertainment, during which Bill scribbled a note to Sue Lawley and Jim, 'Come to me not Jim on this, I'll deal with it.' Jim relaxed and let his mind wander. The question ended and Sue turned and said, 'Bill Cotton?' To which he replied, 'This is tricky. It's one for Jim Moir.'

On television, I thought we should mount intelligent criticism of our programmes. The first stab was called *Armchair Critics* but it was not quite right. I felt we needed to anchor it with someone whose company the audience would look forward to of a Sunday evening. I invited Ludovic Kennedy to take it on and he did. The title was *Did You See?*, and Kennedy made the programme his own, opening with his view of the week's television, in which he offered his enthusiasms and brickbats, along with occasional mischief. From the first transmission it was one of those programmes that you cannot believe has not been there forever. Not that this prevented some BBC executives being upset, 'I can't understand why we kick ourselves in public like this.'

One of the reasons that the BBC was putting itself about a bit was that the world was becoming more threatening. So much so that in May 1980 Alasdair Milne summoned forty people from London and the regions to a seminar at Avisford Park Hotel, near Arundel. This was a first for most of us. Two people remembered something like it fifteen years before, but away days, let alone away weekends like this, were not part of the BBC conduct of business at the time. Hence the frisson of self-importance that ran through the group as we assembled on the Friday evening. We all knew that the Corporation was in a tough position financially. The rampant inflation of the 1970s had made broadcasting costs rocket and, combined with a squeeze on public sector pay, had opened a chasm between BBC and ITV pay rates. £100 million had just been cut from the annual budget.

The opening discussion at Arundel was about money. When Alasdair asked for a show of hands on whether the BBC should take some advertising, I was amazed to see a majority raise arms in favour. To some colleagues it looked like a financial quick fix. The argument against it then, as now, is that once embarked upon, advertising would inevitably spread throughout the BBC's services, for governments would always prefer this to raising the licence fee. Thus the BBC would become another commercial broadcaster, reducing the range, choice and upward pressure on quality in British broadcasting and, of course, destroy the business plans of existing commercial broadcasters. A little advertising would have been the beginning of the end.

Most of the weekend was concerned with how the BBC's channels and programmes should develop in the face of competition from both ITV and the impending fourth channel. It was the first time that I heard the word 'punter' for viewers and 'product' for programmes. I did not like it then and still do not. We expected ITV to launch breakfast television and, if it did, we were adamant that we had to do so as well. We could not allow them a free run to colonize a new audience that would make them the place to turn to when big things were happening in the world.

We discussed and rejected a repositioning of the channels, making BBC2 more obviously popular, say, or making BBC1 an entertainment only channel, with all factual and minority appeal programmes on BBC2. Strong factual programmes were seen as crucial on both channels, 'to reveal the flaws in society', as the minute put it, jutting our jaws as Mrs Thatcher was getting stuck in.

We were much exercised by the effect on viewers of the videocassette recorder and the videodisc that many thought would quickly replace it. More live programming was one way to persuade people to watch in real time, we thought. This was one of the ideas in a paper I wrote with help from two heads closer to the front line, Graeme McDonald, drama series, and John Howard Davies, comedy. It was becoming increasingly difficult, we said, to draw attention to good programmes. Once, a 50-minute documentary, say, was a serious piece of work, the standard hardback edition of television. Now they were routine. We admired ITV's success at creating a splash with an evening dominated by one long programme and urged then, as the cry has been ever since, that every night should be 'an event'. We were both perceptive about the planned fourth channel – in warning that if it encouraged independents, much of the talent in drama would wish to work that way, and complacent – in a certainty that 'there will not suddenly be a plethora of wonderful and revolutionary programme ideas that no one had ever thought of before'.

A theme of the weekend was that we were stuck with people who had done perfectly good work but had now run out of ideas or energy, or were unable to move with changing styles or tastes. 'Orbiting debris' was the memorably unkind phrase that one head came up with. I proposed army-style contracts for fifteen or twenty years, with arrangements for a lump sum and pension at the end of that time. No one coming in to television with their dander up at the age of 25 would be put off by the thought that they might not make the cut at 40. The odd thing was that I considered this 'a hard hearted proposal' and began backing off.

I was feeling even more pleased with myself than usual at Arundel, for that very week there had been excellent reviews for my newly published book, *The Man Who Was B. Traven*. This was based on the last programme that I produced myself and the one I was proudest of. The seed for it had been planted the evening after Bob Robinson and I had filmed P.G. Wodehouse. We wondered into a New York bookshop after dinner and Bob waved in front of me a book of short stories by B. Traven. I knew nothing about him. 'You must do,' said Bob. 'He's a mystery man. Supposed to be the President of Mexico, I think. Anyhow, he lives in South America, in the jungle or somewhere, and no one has ever found out who he is. Now there's a story we should do sometime.'

Some months later, I came across a short piece in *Time* magazine about Traven. There was a still from John Huston's Oscar winning film *The Treasure of the Sierra Madre*, based on the best known of Traven's novels, a study of greed and betrayal among gold miners. The article said it was more or less certain that he was one T. Torsvan who had died in Mexico City in 1969. But who was he? No one knew. Bob Robinson and I set off to make a documentary about the mystery. Traven had claimed to be an American but his books had been published first in Germany. Neither publisher nor agent had ever met him. The only way to get in touch with him had been via a post office box number in Mexico City. He typed all his letters and never signed them.

By the time that we got on the trail, much was already known. The old man in Mexico must have been Traven. His cover had been blown by a Mexican journalist who intercepted his mail. Torsvan had used the name of Hal Croves and passed himself off as Traven's representative when he turned up on the set of *The Treasure of the Sierra Madre*. He had earlier called himself Ret Marut when a revolutionary pamphleteer in Munich during the socialist uprising there in 1919. Marut had been wanted for treason but escaped. No one knew whether that was his real name, where he had come from or whether there was anything in his background that might have prompted his strange behaviour.

Robinson and I interviewed people who had written about the author. We interviewed John Huston and travelled to Mexico City to see the writer's widow, who was generous with her time and hospitality but offered contradictory snippets about her husband's origins: he had been born in San Francisco, not in Chicago, not in Norway. When Robinson asked, 'Why did he make such a mystery of his identity?' Señora Lujan replied, 'He didn't.'

We had fun chasing up blind alleys. Then I discovered that all the names we had come across were indeed of the same man and that he been imprisoned as an alien without papers in London in 1924. At the Home Office there were mug shots. Through the Freedom of Information Act I found FBI and state department papers that revealed intriguing parallels between the man and the books.

He had given the Americans a new name and birthplace. We checked this and after many months learned that of the twenty-five names Traven used, here at last was one, Otto Feige, that fitted a recorded birth. Robinson and I went to Poland to see the original documents and discovered that there were further parallels with the writer's life. Also, he had siblings. Could any be alive? We found a brother and sister in Germany and filmed them. What they told us fitted with a pleasing click into the known facts of Marut/Traven's life. What was more, there were photographs of the child and young man that matched those of the middle-aged man in Mexico.

Bob Robinson came up with a new title for our programme: *B. Traven – A Mystery Solved*. It went out, I was asked to write a book by Tom Maschler at Cape, did some more research, including a further visit to Germany, and began. I wrote every word in my own time, evenings, weekends and holidays. I made enough money from the advance to buy a car, which I had to sell two years later to pay the tax, fortunately, just as the BBC decided to provide me with one. The reviews were good. Two stick in the memory: the one snide one, of course (I have his name), and that of Paul Theroux, who picked it as his 'thriller of the year' in *Time* magazine.

The evidence and the argument convinced nearly all who watched the programme or read the book, which earned me a parenthesis in the *Oxford Companion to English Literature*. I say 'nearly all', as a few Traven scholars clung to a romantic notion that there were two men. A few years later I had the clincher. I found a medical expert on the human face, gave him two photographs of the man that no one now doubts was Marut/Traven and two photographs of the young man from Poland and asked him if they were of one man or two. He took measurements and made calculations. His verdict was that it was several hundred million to one that they were photos of the same man or a brother. No one has yet suggested another lost brother, but knowing the obsessive intensity of the Traven buff, it may only be a matter of time.

Chapter six
'NO SUBJECT WILL BE SACROSANCT'

There was a spectacular bust up at the BBC in the summer of 1980. Desmond Wilcox, the noisy, talented and high profile head of the general features department, was forced to resign. All ten of his senior producers had protested to senior management about the way the department was run now that Wilcox was married to the department's leading star, Esther Rantzen, presenter of the hit consumer programme *That's Life*. Wilcox had also given her production responsibilities and many of the staff thought things were getting out of hand, especially as Wilcox himself still produced and appeared on screen. Producers seeking to launch new projects felt that they were competing with the head of department and his wife. There was a BBC rule that husbands and wives should not work together. The complainants' aim had been to have *That's Life* and its presenter moved to another department and to keep Wilcox in the office more; the unintended upshot was that Wilcox, who felt betrayed but seemed unable to grasp the seriousness of the rift, had to go.

Soon afterwards, the head of the documentaries department, Christopher Ralling, said he wished to return to producing. The television service seized the opportunity to merge the two departments under the name of documentary features. The job was advertised. I had no career plan, although I did fancy the idea of controlling BBC2. I had also been asked if I would be interested in running music and arts, but the new job was a big one, so I put in and was successful. In January 1981 I moved into Wilcox' former office in Kensington House, a long, thin four-storey office building that snaked alongside the railway line behind Shepherds Bush. Outside the window was a shapely, red flowering hawthorn tree, which dazzled for three weeks each year. Ken House was also home to music and arts, science, sport and religious programmes, which was now to swap offices with documentaries in the east tower of Television Centre.

I knew relatively few people in the general features department, and on the evening of my appointment went to have drinks with the producers, after which, Tim Slessor, then editor of *Man Alive* and whom I made my number two, told his wife, 'I think he's going to be all right. He wears black lace-ups.' When I left eight years later he presented me with a pair of child's size six black lace-ups to confirm that it had worked out. I tried to ignore the rivalries and resentments of the Wilcox fracas. To have done otherwise would have meant finding out who had allied with whom and perpetuating the divisions. I was an outsider and clean of either party.

It was, however, impossible to prevent people telling me something of what they called 'Desmond: The Final Days' – how people entering his office found him slumped dramatically, head on desk. Peter Bazalgette, who had been an assistant producer on *That's Life*, described how Wilcox had called in members of the programme team one by one to tell them that he was taking the programme to London Weekend Television and asking if they would come too, at LWT pay rates. Some had agreed. I said that I did not want the names. For others, seeking to take a BBC programme to ITV was the final straw. *That's Life* did move, but only to Lime Grove, home of the BBC's current affairs department. The heat subsided. Wilcox' talent and self-confidence enabled him to bounce back swiftly as a successful freelance and independent documentary producer. When I came to clear away the books he had left in the office, I discovered among the titles *The Male Menopause*, *Sex in Later Life*, *Divorce and After*, *Managers and Their Wives*, *How To Survive As A Working Mother* and *Relations in Public*.

My first task was to make the merger of the two departments work. There were 200 staff altogether, fifty of them producers, not an easy bunch. Documentaries, moving reluctantly, was something of a gentlemen's club. There was only one woman producer. It had most of its regular output on BBC2 but made a clutch of Tuesday Documentaries for BBC1 and had just had popular successes with *Sailor*, a ten-part portrait of HMS *Ark Royal*; *Strangeways*, a series shot in that prison; and *Public School*, a series about Radley College. These documentary serials that featured returning characters were forerunners of the docusoap. Lighter, more portable 16mm film cameras, new lenses and new kinds of film stock that reduced the need for lights had made possible a new way of capturing life as it happened. The documentaries department had embraced this, though there were some older producers whose better days were behind them and whose film-making style was stiff and old-fashioned.

This film-led culture was now joined with the journalist-led culture of the much larger general features. Apart from *That's Life*, the other chief spine of the output was *Man Alive*, a film and studio series that ran with a wide public affairs brief for twenty-six weeks a year. Like all other studio or documentary programmes from the department, it was always fronted by one of a team of reporters. These were able enough, but not stars, and some were leisurely in the way they went about things. My ex-*Line Up* team-mate Michael Dean was the best writer and most productive; the former *That's Life* reporter John Pitman was the most original and most artful. The department had far more women producers and directors than docs and a wider span of talent in general. There were bright young sparks who had learned popular television journalism under Esther Rantzen, the adventure and anthropology producers for *World About Us*, the programme teams of *Holiday* and *The Sky at Night*, as well as some talented film-makers. I inherited as my manager the financial and administrative officer for the department, Brian Elliott. He was a rock for staff during the Wilcox saga and a rock for me, a calm and wily administrator and a wise and kindly handler of people.

A good way to get people to work together is to start something afresh. I discussed this with Brian Wenham and we agreed to end *Man Alive* to create space for something new. Tim Slessor was disappointed but he had had a good run as editor. I asked him to oversee the journalistic output of the department as my deputy. Tim had been one of the producers on Alistair Cooke's *America* and had experience of most kinds of programme. He was tough-minded, straightforward and a man in whose hands you would place the life of your child. He looked a toughie, with a broken nose and wiry frame, appropriate for an ex-commando who once shared a bivouac with Maj-Gen. Sir Jeremy Moore, and his eyes would gleam at the thought of a scrap, but was kind and thoughtful about his friends and staff.

In place of *Man Alive* we were to launch a new six-month long series of documentaries. I told Brian Wenham that too many of the fifty-minute documentaries I saw were overstretched and that thirty minutes would be too constricting, so I would like the programmes to be forty minutes in duration. Could he cope with that in his schedule? He could. He suggested that I ask Roger Mills, the de facto leader of the docs people, to be the editor. Mills had hoped for my job. He was one of the best documentary makers in the country but was in prickly mood, put out by the merger and by a perceived threat to the BBC tradition of documentary. I told him about my plan. He liked the idea of forty minutes and my proposal that this be the title, thereby avoiding debates with producers who, as most producers did then, wished to overrun. He wanted the series to be defined by the range of styles and film-making techniques rather than by subject matter. 'Whatever night the new run is placed should be an event, something not to be missed,' he wrote to me. 'No one will ever quite know what to expect. There will be sociology but there will also be biography, history, religion, sport, art. Some will be off-beat; some conventional. There will no doubt be huge successes and huge failures. No subject will be sacrosanct.'

Roger was a brilliant editor. He was a former classics teacher who had a clear sense of structure and enjoyed bringing the best out of his producers. These skills were allied to the nose for a story, even a streak of yellow journalism, and a competitiveness. He wrote beautifully, whether it be an annual report on a producer or a *Radio Times* billing, a printed collection of which I gave him at the end of his spell as editor. He was, and is, the best commentary writer I have come across in television and no mean deliverer of it. He liked to provoke and test his bosses, would argue fiercely his own case or on behalf of his producers, but once a decision was taken, whether or not it went his way, he was dutiful to the BBC and the most loyal of colleagues.

Most of the producers in both the original departments were on the long-term staff, and these had to provide the backbone of the *Forty Minutes* team. Roger embraced the former *Man Alive* people as his own, urging them to be free of reporters and to take on authorship of their films; the reporters were given the same opportunity. He was able to hire one or two freelances and to offer some film cameramen and editors their chance to direct. I should explain that producer and director were for the most part interchangeable terms for the maker of a documentary film. In theory, it is the director who selects what scenes to film, directs the shooting of them and supervises the editing; the producer assembles the required people and resources, is responsible for the budget and probably chooses the subject. On nearly all documentaries one person carries out these tasks. On a series there may be a producer and several directors, or a series or executive producer and several episode producers.

The first *Forty Minutes* was transmitted in October 1981. It was called 'Rough Justice', about a Welsh working man's club, and produced by Karl Francis, who had both documentary and drama credits to his name. I saw it ahead of transmission and was so relieved that there was such a strong and enjoyable film to kick off the new series that I missed at first the signs that, good as this film was, life caught on the wing it was not. Some of the action had been either re-enacted or, at the least, nudged along. When it was transmitted, the journalistic arm of the department was outraged. Here was the clash of cultures. I summoned a packed departmental meeting to debate the issues and took the chair. Nick Ross and Tim Slessor led for the journalists. Roger and Karl Francis argued that most of the film was not set up and that, in any case, they held by definition of documentary film given by John Grierson, father of the documentary movement, as 'the creative treatment of actuality'. The documentaries of the 1930s and 1940s had featured ordinary people acting out their lives for the camera in staged scenes. There had been no other way then, given the cumbersome equipment and lighting needs. Just because you no longer had to film that way, argued Roger, did not disqualify it as a documentary technique.

The issue, as with the Robinson arrest or any other incident of re-enactment, is whether or not the audience is deceived and, if there is sleight of hand, whether the audience would feel cheated if they knew about it. It is always wrong to offer any material of this kind as evidence, in an investigation, say, without labelling it as re-enactment. It cannot be evidence, only illustration. There is an argument for allowing it as illustrative material as part of an impressionistic portrait, when the weight attached to any sequence may be much less. You have to judge case by case. If in a film portrait of a busy place, perhaps an airport or a station, there is a touching shot of a crying child, apparently lost, does it matter if it is the director's own child, left while the parent disappeared to cause the distress? It happened. Or, if in a series about an institution, one of the characters the director wants to follow had just come out of hospital when filming began, so the director took him back to film a scene in the hospital bed, bandages and all? I felt cheated when I learned about this one after the event, though I am not sure now that any great untruth was told.

The first *Forty Minutes* did much to achieve what Roger Mills must have hoped for. It provoked a passionate discussion about the purposes, methodology and techniques of documentary making and sent a signal that this series was different. There followed a film about a nun running a school on the Falls Road, children's parties, a high security borstal, Gary Glitter, dyslexia and hunt saboteurs. A film about the heart transplant unit at Harefield Hospital was extended to a series of seven and concluded the first run in triumph. I remember being moved and uplifted in the cutting room by the first of these I saw, as a heart is delivered by helicopter and carried in a cardboard box to be sewn into the waiting, already opened, chest. The Broadcasting Press Guild gave *Forty Minutes* its best documentary series award and it was nominated for this category at BAFTA for the next seven years, winning three times.

Roger was an inspirational figure. He let producers make the film they wanted to make, but saw all the rushes and early cuts and was not slow to intervene if necessary. His passion for cricket revealed itself in a *Forty Minutes* biography of Geoffrey Boycott and one on the 'bodyline tour' in Australia. Roger's populist touch brought 'Package Tour', 'Mistresses', 'Gigolos' and 'Rent Boys'. His search for new talent brought in the Polish director Witold Starecki and gave Lucinda Lambton her first programme. He experimented. One film was Earth as seen by an alien, shot entirely in slow motion, thought by many to be the worst documentary ever made. His eye for a story led to a film about a little known British army mutiny at Salerno. This was followed up on *Newsnight* with a confrontation between a sergeant, who had been condemned to death and reprieved, and the chairman of his court martial: 'So you think that Mr Binns here should have been shot in 1943?' 'Yes.'

After four seasons I felt it right for Roger to move on to other things and for a new editor to take over to keep *Forty Minutes* fresh. I chose Eddie Mirzoeff, the cultivated producer of many of the most delightful documentaries of the past decade, among them John Betjeman's best known programme, 'Metro-land', the influential 'The Front Garden' and a BAFTA-winning portrait of the Ritz. Eddie also had an eye for audiences and, like his predecessor, was a great documentary craftsman. He maintained the series' upward trajectory, both in audiences and prestige, for Eddie had a genius for publicity. He cruised past the BBC press office's attempts to control him, summoning previewers, hustling reporters and, when they became available, sending cassettes (it was against BBC policy for journalists to watch cassettes at home or anywhere outside BBC premises). No opportunity to promote was too small for Eddie to seize. Alastair Campbell could have taken his correspondence course.

He brought in a marvellous new film-maker, Jonathan Gili, who made films full of both wit and human warmth, and forged a partnership with Lucinda Lambton. Her programmes surprised, amused and informed, drawing fan letters from the great houses of England and urgent invitations to dinner. Eddie recruited Gerald Scarfe to make several films, including a celebration of Max Miller. There were programmes on leek growers, on love at first sight, on the Englishwoman's wardrobe (they secured an interview with Mrs Thatcher, whom I insisted they ask where she bought her underwear: 'Marks and Spencer. Doesn't everybody?'), on page three girls, on the return of a kidnapped child, on Holloway prison and on Hollywood wives. The series averaged just under 4 million viewers. Two programmes attracted over 8 million, one under each editor, 'Star Paws', on the blush-making subject of animals in films and advertisements, and 'Stop The Wedding', about late cancelled nuptials. The Mirzoeff mantra for the good documentary was 'narrative, tears and laughter'.

One of the best of the series followed a visit I made to the National Film and Television School, not always an encouraging experience, for I found many of the documentaries made there too long, boring and self-indulgent. After my talk I had a cup of tea with some students and, as I left, a young woman ran after me and asked if I would look at her film if she sent me a cassette. When it came I was bowled over. *Home From the Hill* followed an old colonial, Colonel Hilary Hook, as he sold up his house in Kenya and sought to come to terms with life in an England where he felt like a beached whale. It was utterly original, warm, funny and kindly to its subject. I rang the producer, Molly Dineen, and told her we would like to run it, probably in *Forty Minutes*. Eddie loved the film too, and took on the delicate and fraught task of helping Molly reduce it from an hour to the required length, which did improve it. Hilary Hook, a delightful man, received several offers of marriage by post and an offer to clear up his house from a senior BBC woman executive. Molly became a star director, making films in Kenya again and in an underground station, before a famous series that chronicled the agonies of change at London Zoo.

Eddie could be a bit of a tartar. He was a perfectionist with an impressive quiver of techniques for getting what he wanted, from fulsome praise to a flounce, from the most winning flattery to the full freeze-out treatment. But people liked to please him because they respected his standards and admired his talent. He was, too, a most encouraging and helpful mentor for young film-makers and he built a strong team spirit. The producers, researchers and film editors clustered in offices, canteen and bar. They even passed each other stories. There were end of season awards, voted for by the producers, Eddie and myself. Categories included the most entertaining programme, best writer/reporter, highest audience and most economical.

This was the heyday of the powerful strand editor. Roger or Eddie would see the channel controller once a year and go through the long list of possible stories; otherwise, everything was managed within the department. I would have regular meetings with them to monitor progress, discuss the programmes, hear about staff and budgets, help sort problems, advise and, very occasionally, warn or intervene. By and large, the editor got on with it. The series was his.

The programmes were all shot on film. If shooting in Britain, every day the crew would send the cans of exposed film back for processing; if abroad, every few days. The following morning the film manager and series editor viewed the processed rushes: the film manager to check on technical quality, so he could alert the camera crew if there was a problem with the camera or the stock; the series editor to see what material was being shot, check the quality of coverage and whether the director was capturing the story. The strand editor could be on top of every film as it was being made, able to con-gratulate and encourage or step in to call for a change of approach, even to pull a film that was going nowhere.

When directors returned from location, they would view all the synched up rushes, that is, with the sound married to the picture, with the film editor. Together they would assess the strength of different sequences and the direc-tor's job was then to give the editor a cutting order. When the editor had roughly assembled each sequence and put them in the scripted order, editor and director viewed again, most likely deciding to change the order around. Now began the task of cutting each sequence in a near final form. The film editor's skill was to use the shots available, bemoaning where director or camera crew had missed a crucial image or angle, to make the best sense of the story, to structure and pace the scenes and to help shape the whole film.

Each coupling of director and film editor worked together in its own way. The film editor's contribution to a film was often the most significant creatively. They cracked structural problems, disguised the absence of mate-rial that should have been shot but was not and made sense of miles of film shot enthusiastically, but without much sense of how it might fit together, by young and not so young directors. Alan Lygo, Andy Willsmore, Jim Latham and Tony Heaven were four film editors at the heart of *Forty Minutes*' success.

The strand editor could look in at any stage in this process and always at the rough-cut stage. Great editors like Roger and Eddie were skilled at spot-ting how films could be improved by re-ordering the material. They would often insist on going back to the trims, the discarded rushes, to find shots or whole sequences that brought a film to life or helped it make sense. Even so, there was the odd disaster that no artifice could conceal.

In my eight years as head of documentary features, only one *Forty Minutes* and one other completed documentary were not transmitted. The former was about a family of criminals and was never run because it was always *sub judice*, such was the frequency of the family's offending. The other was a film for BBC1 that I inherited. It featured the producer, Hugh Burnett, and John Allegro, who had written about the Dead Sea Scrolls, striding around the Middle East, always in shot together, talking about the 'myth of Jesus', as if Jesus' non-existence was an established fact. Allegro had a case to make but he was not even gently challenged at any point. Short of sending them back on location, I could not see how it could be made trans-mittable and told the controller of BBC1 that we should forget it.

I wanted to build on *Strangeways* and *Radley*, documenting other aspects of life in the United Kingdom. I suggested to Richard Denton, the bouncy, floppy haired, ferociously determined producer of *Radley*, that he follow it up with a comprehensive school. Because people would make judgements about the comprehensive system from such a series, we should find one that was neither a showcase, full of middle-class children, nor a big city problem school. He found Kingswood School in Corby, Northamptonshire, and made a riveting series. I went up to meet the head, Brian Tyler, a likeable and confident leader of the school, who was happy to take the risk of the series and enjoy the limelight. Denton had many showdowns with Tyler in the course of filming, as the producer pushed for access to film or did it anyway, and the head tried to control matters and to protect his staff. Both were doing their job and became firm friends.

In the great majority of cases, producers left on good terms with their subjects (every so often, intimate terms) and remained so, sometimes for years, after the programmes were transmitted. This was important personally and professionally. One of the ways to persuade people to let you film them was to show them the films you had made about others and refer them to previous subjects for a reference. You cannot do that if you betray people. I can think of at least one producer to whom this course would be fraught with danger.

We wanted to crack an Oxbridge college. I went with one producer to make our bid at New College, Oxford, where, as it happened, I knew the Warden, A.H. Cooke, the father of an old school friend. 'Look, Will,' he said when we arrived for lunch with the fellows. 'There are two kinds of college head: grandees and people like me, working dons. Neither would be able to help you with this unless you win over the governing body. I'll do what I can.' The producer and I addressed a college meeting and were quizzed for forty-five minutes by the gowned fellows. As we left, someone threw a final question, 'Do you have a second string to fall back on?' We had not, but playing on Oxford snobbery, New College being pretty grand, I answered, 'Yes. Oriel.' It raised a laugh but next day New College telephoned to say it did not want us.

The following year I received a message that Queens' College, Cambridge might be interested. It was essential that we keep this quiet and deal only with the senior tutor, Dr John Green. One February evening Roger Mills and I drove to Cambridge, had a sandwich in a pub and made our way to the rear entrance to Queens' to meet Green in his rooms, along with the college president and two senior fellows. All present enjoyed the clandestine nature of the gathering. We had sent them cassettes of *Radley* and *Kingswood* and they had been impressed, but were anxious lest we choose a producer 'who was ideologically opposed to Oxbridge'. We chose Michael Waldman, a young producer of great charm who could talk his way into anywhere. He once arrived at the Cannes Film festival on his own and ended up dining that evening in a small private party of stars and moguls. Queens' did agree, but only after Waldman had been scrutinized separately by fellows, graduate students and undergraduates, and the fellows had invited Brian Tyler and Denis Silk of Radley to dinner to be debriefed. The deal was that Waldman filmed anything he could but that people could have second thoughts if they registered them within twenty-four hours. The series provoked a surge in applications to Queens', in spite of (or because of) the programmes reflecting aspects of college life that the fellows were unhappy about and that excited some of the newspapers.

One or two documentary series were underway about the armed forces and I urged our producers to look elsewhere. I approached the Foreign Office and had several friendly meetings with senior people, but they shied away from a series. In those days the BBC gave television training to senior diplomats, and when I discovered that Sir Anthony Acland, about to be our ambassador in Washington, was coming in, I arranged to give him lunch. He listened politely to my requests but no more. I do remember that he told, evidently believing it to be true, the well known urban myth about the British family on holiday in Spain who brought grandma's body back to England, wrapped in a carpet, on the roof rack of the family car. He even offered provenance from his time as ambassador in Spain. Either this *was* the origin of the tale or I feared we were sending an ambassador who might be a bit of a pushover for enemy disinformation. We tried the FCO again later when David Mellor was a junior minister. 'You should definitely film a ministerial visit,' he said, adding, when he spotted a knowing expression on our faces, 'Of course, it needn't be me.'

The magic ingredient in eventually getting onto the FCO was a remarkable researcher/assistant producer called Roger Courtiour. He had been half of the team responsible for the book, based on interviews with Harold Wilson, that alleged a conspiracy against Wilson by right-wing forces from South Africa, the CIA and from within MI5. Courtier was a self-effacing fellow, slightly built and very softly spoken, his thin face framed by a severe black beard. He could have been a Spanish spy at the court of Elizabeth I. Unusually for a television researcher, he always wore a three-piece suit. Roger was enormously hard working, persistent, assiduous in his dealings with people and was responsible for securing entree for a number of scoopy series, including *The Duty Men*, Paul Hamann's brilliant ten-part series about Customs and Excise.

This series, like Roger Graef's on the Police, like the schools and Cambridge series, like many other individual programmes and less controversial series, such as *Life of an Orchestra*, and *Animal Squad*, about an RSPCA inspector, all formed part of the verité or fly-on-the-wall debate. The filming was fluid, following people and events, often with minimal or no commentary. Were the results a true picture of these people's lives? Could the camera ever be forgotten by them? Was there something spurious about the authenticity of a technique that dispensed with the overt tools of interview and narration, and thus appeared to be without artifice, but which employed all the other, less evident, tools of construction? Did the producer not shape and point the film just as much by deciding what and whom and when to film, and by the choices of inclusion and exclusion made in editing?

The answer to this last question is, of course, yes. You are in the hands of the producer whatever his or her editorial apparatus. I could see nothing dishonest in the absence of commentary or interview. Viewers may not be familiar with all the conventions of film-making but bring their own responses to what they see, dividing the material by their own experiences. They are quite capable of wondering what was not filmed or whether some-one is trying to pull the wool over their eyes. As to spurious authenticity, that is a charge that can be brought as easily, if you choose, against ex cathedra pronouncements from presenters. Again, you are reliant on the honesty and fairness of the people involved, producer and presenter. The audience makes its own judgement.

But does the camera influence what goes on in front of it? By definition, a film cannot show you what goes on in a particular police station or class-room when a camera is not present. When the camera is there, much depends on how used people are to its presence and how engaged they are with whatever they are doing. When people are busy, occupied with prob-lems, mentally or emotionally involved with something testing and if they are accustomed to a small film crew being around, then it is possible to record at least the surface of what is going on. There will be times when people play up to the camera to emphasize their own charm, toughness or what have you, even arrange meetings and encounters that they believe will show them to advantage. Producers know this. Sometimes it can be revealing in itself, as when the board of the Royal Opera House acted up like mad as a bunch of hard types in The House. At others, producers simply exclude it from the programme.

There is less angst about these issues today. Producers are less ideological about styles of film-making and work with a full palate of techniques; the audience is ever more sophisticated about how television works. Also, the development of the returning docusoap has blurred the line between docu-mentary and entertainment. There were always entertaining documentaries; there were films with subjects outgoing enough to make asides to the camera; there were characters in films whose face to the world was a sort of performance of themselves; there were central subjects of series who were picked up by the press and invited onto talk shows, like Sid Jenkins, the RSPCA inspector from *Animal Squad*. But now, with the likes of Maureen from *Driving School* and Jeremy Spake from *Airport*, we have documentary subjects who have become celebrities, are encouraged into show business and who give their turns when the camera rolls. It is a picture of life in inverted commas.

One of the institutions that said no to being filmed was the BBC. I argued the case with Bill Cotton when he became managing director of television. 'You couldn't do it,' he said. 'All the interesting stuff, the stuff the public would really want to see, is about the talent. The agents would never have it. They're not going to be filmed with me telling them what I think their artists are worth. And how could you film the head of light entertainment and the channel controller arguing about where to place a show or whether to cancel it? You'd destroy people in public. They don't deserve that and I'm not going to let it happen.' I tried to tell him that entertainment was not the only thing the public was interested in, but to Bill, who had spent his career in entertainment, this was not a winning tactic.

Why then, you might ask, when I was in charge did I twice turn down requests to film BBC television? In part, because I had learned that there was a lot of truth in what Bill had said. So many of the crucial discussions were about people, not just on-screen entertainment talent, but about writers, producers and executives. Then there was the nuisance factor of having a producer trying to wangle a film crew into every meeting, while I and others struggled to find out what material the crew was netting and seeking to exert some kind of control. This was a feasible task in a school; impossible in a place with 8000 staff making hundreds of programmes in dozens of different places every day.

When we filmed a college or an orchestra, the producer would have certain preconceptions but would, essentially, come to it fresh. What he or she would not have that a television producer would in the BBC are dozens of contacts and previous connections, let alone a history of working in the place, with friends and enemies old and new. These were the arguments that I deployed. I sound a bit defensive, do I not? I probably was. I should say that on both occasions I sounded out colleagues who would also be in the camera frame and they were of like mind.

By the 1980s most agreements to film included the promise of a viewing for the subjects before transmission. At one time this would have been anathema, and for investigations and similar hard-nosed current affairs programmes it would remain so. But whereas film-makers had once asked for interviews and illustrative or linking shots, now they were saying, in effect, can we come and film everything we are interested in and edit this into a programme? The level of risk and exposure for the subject was far greater. It became practical, and it was only fair, to offer an opportunity to comment. The BBC could never concede any editorial control but did promise to correct factual inaccuracies and to listen and take note of comments. There were arguments about whether something was or was not inaccurate and debates about the comments. Most producers would not have left something in if they felt it unfair, so would fight their corner. The strand editor or head of department could be brought in as a court of appeal by either producer or subject.

These viewings were nerve-wracking occasions. It was the moment that the court painter turned the canvas round to show the monarch. The *mise-en-scène* was arranged with care. Some producers provided a glass of wine and sought to create an atmosphere of bonhomie. The viewing would be a jolly present for the guests. Others would imply terrible pressure of deadlines, hinting that they were up against it if they were to complete mysterious technical processes in time for transmission. Sometimes, they would deliberately leave in a small horror to give the subject an easy trophy when they agreed to take it out, thereby acquiring some leverage in any disputes that might follow. Many times, the viewing would be a perfectly straightforward encounter.

There was a significant difference between showing to the actual subjects of a film and to people viewing on their behalf, especially when the latter came as a group from an organization. Then, they could not be uncritical, for all had to justify their presence. They would top each other's criticisms. Producers usually knew when they had got something wrong. When Jenny Barraclough showed a film she had made to mark the 30th anniversary of the coronation to several staff from Buckingham Palace led by Sir Phillip Moore, the Queen's private secretary, it still contained a critical interview that did not fit. Sir Phillip went rigid when it came up and was implacable afterwards. I began to argue the case for retaining the interview to create some room for manoeuvre, when Jenny said, 'All right. I've never liked it. I'm happy to take it out.' On another occasion she felt differently. The Somali ambassador came to a viewing of her film on the BBC World Service, for which she had filmed in his country. Part way through, Jenny cunningly struck up conversation to cover disparaging remarks on the sound track about Somalia.

On most occasions the subjects of documentaries felt that they had been fairly treated and were happy with what they saw. There is a duty of care on producers who have persuaded people, especially vulnerable people, to take part in a programme, and most take this seriously. Many will have excluded shots or sequences that might be harmful to the subject even though the person concerned may be content with them. At the same time, when grown-up people give permission to film and for the programme to go out, it is fair to assume that they mean what they say.

The Fishing Party was a film about four rich, loud young city men. One of their number had rung *Grandstand*, the Saturday afternoon sports pro-gramme, saying that they were going sea fishing and would someone like to film them. 'We don't do docs here,' was the reply. 'Try Eddie Mirzoeff.' They did. Eddie smelled a story and it was filmed that week. The programme revealed these men in all their glory: at play, enormously pleased with them-selves, shouting, drinking and, among other things, shooting a passing seagull. A viewing had been promised. They came in to Kensington House one evening. The producer lured their wives away on the more or less true grounds that there was not much room in the cutting room. The men loved the film, laughing as they relived their riotous weekend trip. When it was transmitted, all hell broke loose. The demise of the seagull, to my mind no great loss given their numbers, was what caused most upset. The men's own view of their behaviour was not shared by the rest of the world and they were savaged in the press. The lesson being that vanity smears your spectacles.

The question for the producer was also when to show. In the days of film it was usually best to offer the film when near its fine cut, with the com-mentary written but not recorded, so changes could be made. In short, when it was possible to assess the near final version and to tweak it but not to make huge alterations. The absolute critical moment was when the neg-ative of all the included bits of film was cut to match the edited copy, the neg. cut. Thereafter, changes were made only in emergencies. Today most documentaries are made on video and edited electronically. Anything is possible up to the last moment.

At the end of 1981 Ian Trethowan retired from the BBC and was replaced as director-general by Alasdair Milne. The governors had advertised the post but Milne was the obvious candidate and had been groomed for the job. Like most programme makers, I admired Alasdair Milne. He was notably Scottish, black haired, always dressed in a grey suit, white shirt and single coloured tie. I did not know him well but he had been decisive and helpful over *Lady Chatterley* and he had behaved like a gent when I had had to tell him that a lecture by his mentor Grace Wyndham Goldie, which we had recorded at his request, was untransmittable. He had been a dashing programme editor in the pioneering days of the 1950s and 1960s. He was tough, a BBC person through and through and a fierce defender of the Corporation's independence. For all that, I felt that he was not right for the top job. He had an almost caricature brusqueness, addressing males of any age as 'Boy' and, in the face of any challenge, thrusting his face combatively forward and squaring his shoulders. He would, I thought, and still do think, have made a terrific colonel on the battlefield, a brave leader, protective of and loyal to his men. I just did not see him as commander in chief devising the strategy, planning the war and forging alliances.

The sound of doors opening and closing echoed through the organization as subsequent vacancies were filled. Aubrey Singer became managing director of television after four years running the radio. Brian Wenham, who had been a conspicuous success as controller of BBC2, was disappointed. He stubbornly refused to take the role of assistant director-general, in charge of all the journalism, in spite of being pressed by George Howard, the chairman. Brian had been duffed up by the Annan report over current affairs and could spot a bed of pain when he was shown one. He was low: 'There's always the Arts Council or the IBA. The BBC is stitched up for some time.' As it turned out, it was not. Bill Cotton, who had been doubling unconvincingly as director of development and director of programmes for television, moved full time into the development role, and Brian became director of programmes. The most delectable job in the whole Corporation, controller BBC2, became vacant. I was one of the candidates seen by Howard, another governor, Stuart Young, Milne and Singer. I looked at my watch as I left the chairman's office. The interview had lasted only twenty-eight and a half minutes. It was not going to be me. Graeme McDonald, head of drama series, was selected.

Brian was famous for his notes, Wennograms, hand-written or typed on his old typewriter. 'Last night's 40. Bit rum?' was one. Another, in reply to a note from a reporter asking 'Can we have lunch to discuss my future?' read 'No lunch. No future.' He sent me one the day after the interview. 'So, they went for the older man. They tend to do that . . . However, these things have a way of righting themselves in the end . . . You have every chance of finishing at the top of this heap sometime around the end of the decade. And a decade in television is a short time.' In truth, I was not fussed. I had not expected to win, was enjoying my job and learning how the place ran.

I did not like everything I saw. That summer the BBC had celebrated its 60th birthday with a service, in the presence of the Queen and the Duke of Edinburgh, in St Paul's Cathedral. As soon as I entered the cathedral, I sensed that the whole pompous exercise was a huge mistake, dreamed up by the chairman, George Howard, who owned Castle Howard in Yorkshire. He was a big, overweight man prone to wearing kaftans. From the middle ranks I always felt that he rather made use of the BBC to travel and so on, but I did not know him well. No kaftan for him this day. He was up and down the aisle two or three times before the royal arrivals. The congregation rose to its feet and sat down again; rose again and sat once more. It was getting silly. The Queen and the Duke looked lost as they processed up the nave to the sound of 'All people that on earth do dwell'. They scanned the rows of gawpers for a friendly, even a recognizable, face. Two of the hymns no one knew. This was also the 50th anniversary of the external services, so there were Hindu, Buddhist, Sikh, Muslim and Jewish prayers. Archbishop Runcie gave a good address and there was a splendid new anthem, full of mystery, by Michael Berkeley. But even those who are suckers for such occasions were left cold. It was the BBC as the establishment rather than BBC the broadcaster.

Much more fun was a visit to the BBC's written archives, kept in a single-storey building at Caversham in the suburbs of Reading. The librarian invited several programme heads to come and see what they held and asked each to specify something he would like to have brought out. I wanted Lord Reith's diary for the day that the television service started, 2 November 1936. The published diary omitted this. I noted the entry: 'To Alexandra palace for the television opening. I had declined to be televised or to take any part. It was a ridiculous affair and I was infuriated by the nigger stuff they put out. Left early.' A bonus was a note from the Broadcasting House librarian that was produced for us. It was dated 20 September 1951 and said that the previous Saturday, Mr G. Burgess had come in to return library books that he had had out so long, for years, that they had been given up as lost. The writer passed on this information, as 'I am aware that the Foreign office is looking for Mr Burgess.' It must have been one of his last acts before fleeing to the Soviet Union.

Chapter seven
TOP GEAR

'Yes please.' 'No, thank you.' 'Subject to a pilot.' 'No, overtaken by other ideas.' 'Has gone away.' 'Develop please.' 'Send me a tape of the presenter.' 'Let me see a treatment.' 'Not with him.' These were typical comments on programme proposals, as recorded in the minutes of the annual editorials meetings between the channel controller and each production department. The minute takers enjoyed a joke: 'Four x thirty minutes. *Adultery* – Let's do it.' Editorials, which took place in the late spring, were when departments put up ideas for new programmes for the financial year that would begin the following April. It was not the only time to talk new ideas, but it was the opportunity for the controller to survey everything that was on offer from the twenty or more production units around the BBC. The minutes were the draft order book for the department.

I would spend a lot of time preparing. Throughout the year, I encouraged producers to come with their ideas, tell them where I knew that BBC1 or BBC2 had a need, push thoughts at them, held brainstorming sandwich lunches in my office, mixing staff from different parts of the department. Over Easter I read and sifted all the submissions, followed up with further discussions with producers and then wrote the department's editorials document as tightly and as persuasively as I was able. My strategy was to limit the number of proposals that I went with, so there were not more than three or four contenders for each chunk of the money and airtime we were likely to get. This entailed a ruthless cull. Some proposals were limp in themselves, some clashed and I made a choice, some were interesting but I doubted the originator's ability to deliver. In time, channel controllers wanted longer and longer lists of ideas and more and more background material and lengthy treatments. Even so, it often came down to the controller saying, 'I like all three but can only take one. Which should I go with?' The face-to-face meeting was the opportunity for the controller to question and probe and for the head to sing loud and seductively.

Each channel was planned on an April-to-April year, the money apportioned season by season: spring and summer, autumn, Christmas and winter. The draft schedule identified where big sporting events would go, where fixed output such as news and religion would sit, where long running shows were likely to be placed and where the controller wanted new drama, comedy, entertainment and factual, if he could afford it. In those days the channels worked to a baseline of money for each department, on top of which the controller kept back what he could scrounge in order to create some flexibility. It was a system in which the controller was king but not an absolute monarch.

After the editorials, there were far more ideas in play than possibly could be afforded. When every department had submitted their proposals and been seen, they provided budgets for the accepted programmes. Then came the crucial moment of the year when the controller and his team of planners went away for two or three days to cut the plan. This was the time when the money and the ambitions were fitted roughly together, the possibles were junked, the probables weeded and some definites reneged on, as the controller faced hard reality and had second thoughts. The final stage of the process was the round of autumn offers meetings. By then the departments would have received intelligence of the cut plan, some projects would look even more enticing than in the spring, other projects would have struck icebergs or costs would have been revised. Offers were the business meetings. The channel team pinned down delivery dates and interrogated the budgets, both cash and bids for film, studio time and editing.

Large-scale series were made over more than a single year, and it could be three or more from the first agreed proposal to transmission. Some ran into trouble. I inherited a project about France for which the old documentaries department had approached the historian and philosopher Theodore Zeldin to present. I asked Eddie Mirzoeff, who had worked with many academics and intellectuals, to produce. He came to me worried that Zeldin would not be convincing on camera and that, brilliant intellect that he was, he did not have things to say that would drive a television series. I said they should make a fifteen-minute segment that would enable us to decide. This they did, encountering a nasty little hiccup, nothing to do with the presenter, that I only heard about much later. On the evening before filming at his house, the Duc de Rohan dined the full film crew in some style. The following morning the Duc entered the room where the camera was set up and addressed all present. 'Gentleman, when last night's dinner was cleared away, it was discovered that one of our silver forks was missing. I am now going to leave the room for half an hour. When I return, I shall hope to see that fork. If I do, we shall proceed as if nothing had happened. If I do not, I shall ring the police.' When he left the room, one of the crew evidently produced the fork. The filming was finished as intended, but Zeldin was very diffident on camera and I felt it too big a risk to go ahead. I saw him and, in an uncomfortable interview, explained the position. He went ahead and wrote his book *The French*.

We made a series called *Year of the French*. This comprised twelve portraits of twelve different French people in different parts of France, each shot in a separate month. This elegant conceit was rigorously adhered to and the series was a joyous celebration of the country and its people. We followed up with *The Italians*, again a string of charming portraits. Both series were subject to debate within the BBC, some criticizing them for their lack of analysis. What they had were detail, texture and strong characters. The next target was the Soviet Union. Could we get good film-makers in with a free enough hand to make similarly interesting and detailed profiles?

I went to Moscow with our executive producer, Peter Pagnamenta, to open negotiations. We were put up at the art nouveau National Hotel on Red Square, and had the frisson of walking past room 107, in which Lenin stayed on his return to Moscow, on the way to our rooms. These were high and dingy with a fridge that did not work. I half hoped and half feared that my door would open in the middle of the night and one of the pretty young women that sat by the stairs would burst in dressed only in a fur coat and followed by a photographer. Our experience was far more prosaic. At Gostelradio, the Soviet broadcasting organization, we explained what we wanted. At first the response was boot-faced: 'Get in touch with the London office of *Soviet Weekly*. They will know what the British people would like to find out about the Soviet Union.' Then, more sophisticated people took over and we began to get somewhere. Further meetings over coffee, with delicious cakes that were baked on the premises and of a kind we did not see in shops, began to make the project seem possible. It would clearly be a struggle. The Soviets were attracted by the idea of a series like *Year of the French*, with no reporter galumphing about, but they were nervous about what a film crew might pick up in the two weeks we demanded with each subject. For our team there would be a continuous fight to resist or get round the inevitable attempts to manipulate, with the risk of being conned or a terminal showdown.

The producer for the Soviet series was Richard Denton. He had two Russian speaking assistant producers but learned the language and threw himself into this hugely exciting and exhausting project to such an extent that he married a beautiful Russian actress. Denton fought the Soviets to a standstill to get what he needed. He rejected eight collective farms for film-ing until he arrived at one where the puzzled farmers asked, 'Why have you come here? We have no Soviet Heroes.' He would send me postcards at the BBC with 'secret message under stamp', scrawled down the side. We took a chance with the final film, which was about a jazz/rock musician and shot clandestinely by a young director, Olivia Lichtenstein. It was only in the middle of a thank you lunch I gave for the Russian minder and our contact at the Russian embassy that I was passed a note to say that she had returned safely with the tapes.

Denton and his team filmed near Vladivostok and in Estonia, in Uzbekistan and Siberia, in Azerbaijan and Samarkand. They provided a unique picture of life in the Soviet empire, something recognized by the reviewers. It was reported to me that at the board of governors the vice-chairman, William Rees-Mogg, launched into an attack on the series for presenting too rosy a view of Soviet life, the implication being that the team had been duped. Not so, said a newly appointed governor, Sir Curtis Keeble: this was exactly how it was in the USSR. His views carried weight and the day, for he had recently been our ambassador in Moscow.

In the spring of 1983 Mrs Thatcher was re-elected with a thumping majority. This was to bode ill for the BBC. Its coverage of the Falklands War had upset many Tories; there were plenty in and around government who believed that the place was run by lefties, and, it later transpired, there was a growing sense that the Corporation needed to be sorted out. The election was a bonus for me, as I was chairman of the year's Edinburgh Television festival. This opened with a lecture on August bank holiday Monday and closed with a panel of industry heavyweights at lunchtime the following Friday. With my committee I had to fill the days with sessions, and I knew that for the festival to be considered a success, I needed one noisy event to excite the newspapers. A debate on the election coverage provided it. This erupted when Robin Day lost his temper with Tam Dalyell and blurted out, 'Michael Foot did not think that the sinking of the *Belgrano* was an election issue and told me that the Prime Minister had no alternative but to sink it.' Whereupon Roy Hattersley, looking thunderstruck, wheeled upon Day, 'I shall have no more private conversations with you.' There was more of this. The papers went to town on it; the delegates had something to chatter about.

For the opening McTaggart Lecture I had hooked Jonathan Miller. He had announced that he was having nothing more to do with television, so I went to see him to invite him to offer a valedictory address. He said yes, gave me three good ideas for documentary series and wanted a gossip about the BBC. 'It is like the Navy,' he said, 'full of able people who were clearly not in it for the money, doing their best work. Lots of super efficient WRENS to help the drama directors.' A week before the lecture, Jonathan was in a panic and asked if he could do the whole thing as a question and answer session. I said no. On the day he held reporters spellbound in a press conference in The George Hotel and then delivered a tour de force on the impossibility of doing Shakespeare or classic serials on television and on the awfulness of the medium, 'Insatiable at one end, incontinent at the other.' Our job then was to shovel endlessly the material that would satisfy the loose sphincter of the mighty tube.

Afterwards, Stuart Young, the new BBC chairman, confided, 'Wasn't he good? I knew Jonathan from the Jewish Youth Club. I've just asked him if he would like to be a BBC governor.' (He would not.) Jonathan, ordeal over, was flying. A group of attractive women latched onto him and joined us for dinner, where he recalled an obsession with stocking tops acquired in days of jiving at the Jewish Youth Club. He imitated the gum-chewing, eye-avoiding way the Teddy girls jived, in studied denial that their partners existed at all. We then had Jonathan on old Etonians at King's College, Cambridge, 'peeing carelessly as if they were hosing the place down', and his dread of staying in faculty members' houses when on a lecture tour of the USA. 'Listening to hear if the bathroom is empty, the awful damp reminder of the presence of others, the fantasy that the whole family is listening to one's evacuation, "Oh dear, honey. We listened to his lecture but just listen to that."' This was, of course, only Jonathan Miller's first farewell to television. A few years later I was able to help to the screen his series *Museums of the Mind* about mental illness. In more recent times he made some riveting programmes about directing opera.

In 1982 and 1983 we had a number of debates at the programme review meeting about the BBC's television programme strategy, a mirror, no doubt, of even more intense discussion among the senior bosses. The central conundrum was no more or no less than that which the BBC had faced for twenty-five years and was to go on facing to this day. In order to justify the licence fee method of funding, the BBC must provide programming that people choose to see, and yet, because it is protected from commercial competition for revenue, it must provide services and programmes that would not be provided if there were no BBC, both provide them itself and create a climate in which others need to as well. As Huw Wheldon famously put it, the BBC exists to make 'the good popular and the popular good'. The demands of popularity and what is now always referred to as 'quality' can and must be balanced.

The long arm of its former monopoly influenced what many defined as quality for the BBC: concerts, highbrow discussions, church services, academics telling us things, adaptations of classic novels, all of which BBC television should offer, all of which can be done well or badly. If the latter, is it still 'quality'? Entertainment and other kinds of popular programmes are part of what the BBC is funded to do but have to work much harder to win acceptance with the chattering classes. The most difficult moments are usually when new kinds of entertainment emerge, new tones of voice are heard and enjoyed, or someone demonstrates that taste has moved on. The question for the BBC is do we lead or do we follow? At what distance? And with our nose in the air? Hence the debate about *Blankety Blank*. Hence the agonizing over the need to produce a soap. The first semi-soap was *Angels*, about a group of nurses, which ran twice weekly in thirteen-week seasons. *Triangle*, set on board a North Sea ferry, had the same pattern but was less successful. Channel 4 had now arrived with *Brookside*. The consensus was that we needed a twice a week, year-round show. 'Put enough money in to make it *Coronation Street* not *Crossroads*,' was the plea to drama from round the table. By the autumn of 1983 Alan Hart, who had three tough years as controller of BBC1, had already commissioned *EastEnders*.

Within two years of ITV's launch in 1955, the BBC's share of the television audience had fallen from 100 per cent to a little over 20 per cent. The shock of this had left a permanent scar on BBC television's psyche. It had been a long hard road back to respectability. By the mid-1970s, with the aid of the second BBC channel, the share was ITV 53 per cent, BBC1 and 2 together 47 per cent. By 1982, the launch of Channel 4, it was ITV 49 per cent, BBC1 40 per cent and BBC2 11 per cent. Some readers may be rolling their eyes to the heavens, spotting, they believe, the beginning of 'this obsession with ratings'. They may even be muttering, irritatedly, 'They are not the only thing.' No, they are not. Not even the most important. But they are *an* important measure of how the BBC is doing, and the most obvious. Others will make much of them; they are not going to go away, and, if the BBC slips too far, there is a perception of failure that can corrode every other aspect of performance. In any case, I have never met a producer who did not want more rather than fewer people to see his or her programme. A producer who had expected half a million and got three-quarters would come running along the corridor to my office as swiftly as one whose programme was watched by 10 million when the previous week it was 8 million.

The fear was that we were losing touch with the public who paid for the BBC. A big debate at programme review threw up the concerns: the BBC shied away from the popular; it had too many people on the staff who were talented but could not make programmes with wide appeal; there were too many factual programmes not doing very much; there was only enough money for ten months of new programmes. We had launched breakfast television, but while ITV provided new programmes for people at home in the daytime, we were running pages from Ceefax.

This all came to a head in January 1984, when BBC1 ran an American mini-series, *The Thorn Birds*. There was nothing wrong with the series as such. It was popular fiction turned into television and had its place. The trouble was that the channel did more than simply drop it into the schedule. To accommodate the long episodes on a Monday evening, it moved the news and dropped *Panorama* for the weeks in question. Compounding the felony, the BBC promoted *The Thorn Birds* by taking its first ever poster advertisements. So far, so dodgy. But there was worse, for in the very same weeks, ITV ran its triumphant production *The Jewel In The Crown*, an adaptation of Paul Scott's novels, The Raj Quartet. The press poured scorn and worse on the BBC from a great height. Within, there was a bitter debate. Why were *we* transmitting 'unmitigated rubbish' while *they* were 'producing exactly the thing that we should be making'? What was the BBC's programming philosophy?

Unknown to us, at the turn of the year, returning from a day's shooting together, Alasdair Milne had told Aubrey Singer that he had to go. It was announced in February that he was retiring early to set up as an independent producer. That evening I was buying a programme at the Royal Opera House when there was a tap on my shoulder and I turned to see it was Aubrey, looking shell-shocked. 'Has it been a bloody time?' I asked.

'It's been dreadful,' he replied. 'Why do we always cock up things like this?'

He had been managing director of television for less than two years and had been seen at his best when he could charge head down at a clear target, as with the swift and dramatic launch of the BBC's breakfast news.

Aubrey was full of enthusiasms and grand schemes but volatile. His head of press, William Carrocher, wore a permanent expression of worry. 'He's a walking time bomb,' he muttered to me as he trailed after Aubrey at the Prix

Italia festival, 'I can't let him out of my sight.' Aubrey was never happier than when making announcements. These could be sudden. At Edinburgh one year he, the chairman George Howard and Brian Wenham were to give a press conference. I thought that I ought to go along to hear what they said. It was a fine morning, so I strolled in a leisurely way through the New Town, arriving a quarter of an hour after the start time, only to find our press people looking strained. They swept me straight in and on to an empty chair alongside the chairman. 'Ah! Now he is here we can begin,' said Aubrey.

'Yes,' said the chairman. 'Today we are announcing that the BBC is to make a large scale series charting the history of television for the 50th anniversary in 1986. Over to you, Will.' Lucky I turned up.

There were times when Aubrey had to put Carrocher right. Bill was a delightful man who had come via the Foreign Office and Buckingham Palace ('I was warned never to get in the lift alone with Mountbatten') and was permanently bemused by the antics at the BBC. He christened me 'Major Wyatt' because everything that emanated from documentary features was claimed as a 'major' series. At home with politics and international affairs, popular entertainment was not Carrocher's strong suit. Thus when he took a call from the head of entertainment to say that Bob Monkhouse was returning to the BBC and that we needed to announce it forthwith, he was thrown by detail. He went immediately up to Aubrey Singer's office and burst in. 'Aubrey,' he cried, a little breathless, 'we need to call a press conference. I've just heard, from light entertainment. Tony Hancock is coming back to the BBC.' Aubrey, who was typing a note, swung round on his chair.

'What? If it's Tony Hancock who's coming back, it's not a press conference that we need, it's a fucking séance.'

Aubrey had been the chief architect of the BBC's unique science department, and would get rattled by programmes on animal rights protestors or complementary medicine, ones that challenged the orthodoxy. He was leery of rows with overseas governments, of which there were several following programmes we made about South Africa, Nicaragua and the Philippines, but was fair in his warnings. 'Producers don't always treat people abroad as they do at home. They change tack on a story and don't tell people who have helped them fix things, the British embassy, say. That's what brings governments onto the offensive.'

On his many travels Aubrey had brought much co-production money to the BBC. One country that we almost never worked with was France and, as managing director, he decided to do something about this. He took the channel controllers, several programme heads, including me, and Michael Checkland, then in charge of finance and resources for television, on a mission to Paris. We had a dinner on the Friday evening with the French television bosses and programme chiefs, and spent most of Saturday in discussions with our opposite numbers in the hope of identifying projects that we could work on together.

We were getting nowhere, so in my meetings with the documentary heads of their three channels, I punted what I thought to be a witty proposal. I said, 'Look. It's clear that you do what you do in your way and that you are not much interested in what we do, which is rather different. And, to be frank, we have our way of doing things, which works for us and I don't see how we can sensibly work jointly alongside you on a big series or anything. But we could take advantage of our differences. What if you made a film on what the French don't like about the British: our rotten food, football hooligans, the weather and so on? We could make a film on what the British don't like about the French: killing and eating songbirds, smelly lavatories, dog shit all over Paris and so on. We could put the two together and at the end the two reporters could shake hands and go their separate ways, perhaps row off in different directions in the channel. How about it?' The documentary head for channel one looked at me as if I was crazy. It was impossible, he said. His equivalent at channel two seemed to think that there would be a diplomatic incident, followed by a political row, followed by his dismissal. The chap from the more radical channel three grinned. He got the idea and we agreed to try it.

When I returned, I put a talented young French-speaking director, John Paul Davidson, onto the project. He went to see channel three in France and began work. A few weeks later he showed me his rough-cut. He had worked with Auberon Waugh and produced an entertaining half-hour. The most memorable sequence began with the close up of the gnarled face of a French countryman evidently concentrating on some manual task and talking at speed about how this craft had been practised by his family for generations, how proud he was to continue it, how much he enjoyed it and valued the participation of his dear, gentle wife. All the while, the camera was pulling back slowly, eventually to reveal that the couple were cutting the legs off live frogs and throwing the severed limbs into one wooden half barrel and the remainder of the frog onto a huge mound of twitching amputees in another half barrel. The wide shot of this scene was held for some time for the audience to digest the wonder of it while the French couple continued to chatter away. I told John Paul that he should send the film to Paris with a letter asking for their comments and for news of how their part of the film was progressing. He did so. We never heard from channel three again.

At Aubrey's farewell dinner he made a very funny speech and let everyone know that he was not going of his own accord. 'It's been a rum old year so far. On January the 1st I was awarded the CBE, on the 7th I was asked if I wanted early retirement, on the 23rd I was asked to act as director-general for two weeks, and in February I pick up a newspaper to read what my plans are.' Afterwards there was, as so often at such dos, much boozy approval, 'honest . . . brave . . . just right . . . respect . . .'. But I knew that Aubrey was playing hardball to get a gold-plated production deal. In a neat stroke he registered the name White City Films, the name he knew the BBC had intended to use for its own planned film company. A co-production fund of £500,000 was established for him to draw down for agreed projects. Eventually he delivered two good documentaries about China and Vietnam, but in the first two and a half years he spent £250,000, some from IBM, on setting up his company, on development and on a showreel for an ambitious helicopter-borne history series that was too expensive to be commissioned.

The new managing director was Bill Cotton, the BBC's Mr Entertainment, who for two years had been in charge of the abortive plans for a BBC satellite service. He was the son of the famous bandleader, a former entertainment producer and long-time head of light entertainment before becoming a successful controller of BBC1, and was now welcomed back warmly. He believed passionately in the BBC's role as entertainer to the nation. Bill could be as ruthless as they come but he inspired affection. He reached out to people and would unburden himself about life, jobs and his health over a drink or, better still, a Chinese meal. He was never good with names and over the years relied more and more on his own shorthand for those that did not come to mind. A woman he respected would be 'Madam', one he considered a nuisance 'Old Mrs Clutterbritches'. Any man who worked for you might be 'your man of affairs', a nuisance was 'Old Bugalugs', and someone he did not much like but had to take note of, 'Jolly Jack the Sailor'. In the most innocent and old-fashioned way he would throw his arm round women and call them 'darling' or 'love'. I once gave a talk to a BBC women in management course, at which the participants complained about this practice. It demeaned them, they felt. 'How do you think I feel?' I replied, 'I am a bloke and he calls me "petal".'

On taking over, Bill addressed a meeting of senior staff and said firmly, 'There is too much gossip and too much drinking at television centre.' Certainly white wine flowed plentifully on the sixth floor, site of the senior management offices, and any meeting that began after 11.00 a.m. was opened with a corkscrew. I took these remarks to be Bill's way of saying, 'I'm in charge and I will keep Brian Wenham in check.' Brian stared straight ahead. Bill Cotton had an absolute certainty that the public paid their licence fee for good television programmes. To him, all the rest was so much parsley round the plate. He was not much interested in radio and moaned regularly about 'the Oxford Street branch', by which he meant the governors, the DG and all who served at their tables.

This focus on the strength of the television networks made him suspicious of the BBC's regions, which were then always looking for extra money and for times to opt out of the main BBC1 service, supported by heavily lobbied governors. 'You've got to keep them in check. For, I tell you, if there's a conflict between us and the regions, with this lot of governors, the regions will win.' Bill could not hide his centralist and metropolitan instincts, even when he wished to. He once journeyed up to Scotland on the sleeper with Jim Moir, then the head of light entertainment. Over dinner Bill tried hard to persuade Moir to apply for the job of controller, Scotland. He was fulsome on the importance of the post to the whole of the BBC, explained what a significant step it would provide in Moir's career and waxed eloquently on how enjoyable a job it would be. He told Moir to sleep on it. In the morning they alighted from the train together on a cold, wet Glasgow morning. 'You know, Jim,' said Bill, looking around at the puddles and litter, 'if God ever wanted to give Britain an enema, this is where he would apply it.' Jim Moir stayed in London.

Bill Cotton had a plan to restructure the television service. He wished to abolish the jobs of channel controllers and have a director of programmes – who would schedule the two channels – and four output controllers – drama, entertainment, factual and sport – who would have money and airtime and supply the programmes. 'Neither channel controller is up to it and the job's not really a job anymore,' he grumbled. 'The output heads are marginalized, controllers take the praise for successful programmes and apportion blame for the unsuccessful. In any case, the place is too laid-back and the sixth floor is travelling too much. I wouldn't want to work for the current regime here. We need more discussion of failure, more balling out.'

Much of this was aimed at Brian Wenham, the director of programmes. Brian was consciously laid-back in manner and drank more than he should – both in response to his early heart attacks – but he was tightly wound within. He was shy and hated performing in public, and because of this could appear brusque and discourteous. He was disarmingly aware of his failings. I once bumped into him as I was coming in through the rear gate of television centre and he leaving. 'Where are you off to, Brian?' I asked.

'I'm just going down to Lime Grove,' he replied, 'to lower morale.' On another occasion, I upbraided him for bullying my departmental manager about our staffing levels while I had been away. Brian looked forlorn. 'I stand rebuked,' he said, and then, as if to make friends again, 'I've got four tickets for *Andrea Chenier*. Would you and Jane like to come with us?'

At the same time he had been a brilliant channel controller, was the rock upon which Graeme MacDonald, the current controller of BBC2, leant and was a thinker about the television industry. He was quickly bored and refused to waste time when, to him, a decision was clear. As channel controller, when he had dispatched the day's business, he would slope off to the cricket or the cinema. He judged programmes according to their MEGO factor – 'My Eyes Glaze Over'. He was an avid reader – one year while director of programmes he read ninety novels as a Booker Prize judge – and an opera buff, who almost made a BBC2 hit of *The Ring* cycle by scheduling it one act at a time on Sunday evenings. He was not much interested in money and once wrote that his epitaph should be 'He Never Shopped.' His office and his home were places of merriment and gossip. He was also, for many of us, a wonderfully encouraging patron and mentor, the person, above all, whose good opinion one sought and continued to seek well after he had left the BBC ('What do you do now, Brian?' 'I'm a media waif') and well after he was in any position to affect our careers.

Bill Cotton failed to implement his new structure. After a year he announced, 'The programmes are going well and "if it ain't broke, don't fix it",' he said. We all knew that the director-general and the governors had overruled him. He had another scheme, to integrate radio and television staff, but that had little life. Bill had been having a difficult time. His marriage had ended and he had been pursued by the *Daily Mail*, as always sniffing for carrion at the BBC. Bill Carrocher had been beside himself with worry about his boss, who would suddenly disappear and who was between marriages and between homes. 'A night with his daughter, a couple at his club, his clothes in a dressing room at television centre. It's no way for a 57-year-old man to live.' Carrocher knew what the problem was: 'It's romantic love.' He said, 'The worst thing mankind ever invented.' Not, as it turned out, for Bill, who happily married his new love, Kate.

After *The Thorn Birds*, Alan Hart's days as controller of BBC1 were numbered. Bill Cotton knew who he wanted in the job, the former programme controller of London Weekend Television, Michael Grade, now having a not entirely happy time producing for American television in Hollywood. It was Brian Wenham who first put forward Grade's name, and Bill, who knew him well, was convinced that Grade had the flair the BBC needed. Alasdair Milne and the governors agreed, and Michael Grade arrived at television centre in September 1984.

He was popular from the outset. I thought that his greatest virtue was that he was very un-BBC. He was steeped in entertainment, had great showmanship, was a sunny and optimistic presence and a funny, punchy and persuasive performer on the air or with the press, who loved him. He had been a show business agent and you rarely left Michael's office unhappy, whatever might happen later. Once I had a quite acrimonious argument with him about when a series was to be scheduled and finished my routine meeting with him to step next door to Graeme MacDonald. Ten minutes later Michael burst in with a big grin, clutching the audience figures. 'Good news in week 2,' he proclaimed, pointing to the improved figures for one of our documentary series.

He watched the programmes and was swift to respond to producer or department head with a telephone call or one of the many notes he wrote from his office first thing in the morning in his slightly girlish hand. Best of all was his enthusiasm for discussing programmes, the ideas for them or the mechanics and style of their production. In all the jobs I had, from assistant producer to chief executive, brainstorming, analyzing and arguing about programmes was the most enjoyable part, and swapping thoughts with Michael on a pilot, say, or a series idea was always a pleasure, even when we were at odds.

We did not get off to a great start. Michael had a feel for programmes across the board, but his first need was to brighten up the audience appeal of BBC1 and his attention was straightway on entertainment. My department had a history of providing entertaining factual programmes, which have always been a strength of the BBC's. We had on air a particularly bold, not to say foolhardy, show called *Hotline*, presented by Chris Tarrant. It was a glorified grown-up swap shop, transmitted live and dependent on audiences bringing to the studio things they did not want in order to exchange them for things they did. To compound the difficulty, the programme was transmitted from a different regional studio each week, putting a huge strain on the production team. The producer was brave but the show was not working. We tried to fix it but the new controller had had enough. 'You'll never get it right,' said Michael, 'it's too ambitious and the presenter is charmless. I'm going to bring it off before the end of the run.' He did and, at my request, came down to Kensington House to talk to the production team, for which he won high marks.

We had a studio show that was a hit in *The Time of Your Life*, a nostalgia and celebrity format, which Noel Edmunds, who presented it, Henry Murray, the producer, and I had worked up. It was the top rating BBC programme for several weeks and ran for three series. Noel demonstrated his quick-witted ability to drive and sustain a live, or as live, show. Critics, not the audience, came to deride him because he was an entertainer who did not sing, dance or tell jokes. He had other television talents. Noel was always involved in creating his shows. He understood where the surprises, the laughs and the drama could be created, prepared himself carefully and had the energy and speed of mind to propel a programme forward and maintain its buoyancy. To watch him in later years present *House Party* for fifty minutes, live and without a written script, was to appreciate that this sort of high wire act was a lot more difficult than much singing or dancing.

I got on well with Graeme MacDonald, controller of BBC2. He was a lovely, warm man, personally and professionally generous and, uniquely in the annals of television, one who was content to take less than his due. He had been producer of *The Wednesday Play* and *Play for Today* in some of their great days, and had presided over a shining era of BBC popular drama. He doted on his dog, loved all animals and it was his battling determination that had brought *All Creatures Great and Small* to the BBC.

As controller, he was in awe of Brian Wenham, a great friend. Graeme maintained an urbane demeanour but often shook with nerves if we were dealing with a controversial programme and, if he or Brian wanted any cuts, his voice would quaver on the phone. His rule with his PA was that she must never give him any kind of urgent message of a morning until he had passed through the outer office and was seated at his desk and prepared for what the day might bring. Before his first press briefing he was in such a state that he told Bill Carrocher he would have to give it. 'I think it would be better if you did it,' said Bill. 'Would you consider having a dram?'

'No,' said Graeme.

'Well,' said Bill, 'I'll see if Dr Newman has any suggestions.' The doctor came to the office and, as Bill put it, 'I don't know what he gave Graeme, but when the press arrived half an hour later he was all smiles.' Graeme was a great traveller but hotels rarely came up to the mark. Rooms were changed, hotels were changed, even cities were changed. He loved his annual visit to the Prix Italia, especially when it was in Capri. It was there that the Italian chairman introduced him as 'Il Ditorre di Canale Due'. This caused much mirth in the auditorium, for the two entrances to the funicular railway that everyone had to use on the island were designated Canale Uno and Canale Due. Forever afterwards, Graeme rejoiced in the title of Canale Due.

Graeme had a great liking, as did most of us and the public, for the work of John Pitman, one of Esther's first young men on *That's Life*, by now an off-screen reporter and director. Pitman had the best nose of anyone for a popular subject and a gentle, sly way in telling a story. A list of his *Just Another Day* series is to list the documentary serials and factual hits of the following decades: Heathrow, Selfridges, Waterloo Station, the AA, Soho, Battersea Dogs Home, Sotheby's, Driving School. Pitters got to most of them first.

I wanted to resurrect the idea of a programme reporting what the foreign press said about the United Kingdom, with the same title I had used for our failed pilot in presentation, *Do They Mean Us?* My number two, Tim Slessor, had the inspired notion of asking Derek Jameson to present it. Jameson had just sued the BBC and lost, leaving him owing the Corporation £75,000. In his and Tim's hands what might have been an interesting, rather esoteric, series became a hit for BBC2. Jameson, the broadest of cockneys, was a sharp ex-Fleet Street editor with a flair for the demotic. He created a catchphrase out of the title 'Do They Mean Us? They surely do', and beamed with pleasure when people shouted it at him in the street.

When Derek married in 1988 he invited those of us connected with *Do They Mean Us?*, as he felt we had thrown him a lifeline. It was a spectacular affair. Arundel Cathedral was stuffed with pink and white flowers and at the entrance Derek greeted guests as if they were popping in for a drink. Anne Robinson, not yet a television star, was matron of honour. The reception was at the same Arundel hotel to which Alasdair Milne had taken us for his conference. Derek's speech began, 'I shall be including the names of various sponsors, as you have to make a bob somehow in this cruel world . . .'. And then, as with the credits at the end of a programme, named all those, who had or were employing him or contributing to the nuptials – an extensive list.

Prompted by my own predilections and spotting similar in others, I thought we should create a programme reflecting the growing interest in better eating and drinking. We made a pilot that did not work. I changed the team and persuaded Graeme MacDonald to commission a first series of what I imaginatively titled *Food and Drink*. Henry Kelly presented. He was an appealing fellow whom I liked all the more when one week he came in looking low to confess, 'Will, the bank has just refused to honour three of my cheques, one to my wife, one to my mistress and one to my bookmaker,' before bouncing on to the set to do his cheery professional best.

The programmes failed to engage with the subject but I convinced Graeme that we could get it right and asked a young producer, Peter Bazalgette, to take it over. Baz was a pink-cheeked ex-president of the Cambridge Union. He had been a researcher on *That's Life*, where he had learned a lot but was one of those outraged by Desmond Wilcox' plan to take it off to London Weekend and had fallen out irretrievably, or so it seemed at the time, with Esther. When I arrived at Kensington House, he was a reporter. I saw him deliver a piece to camera with his jacket slung over his shoulder in a camp and affected manner, suspended on his crooked finger. I told him the next day. 'Peter, for God's sake, you looked like something that strolled in from *Brideshead Revisited*. If you want to be a reporter, do it properly.' He stopped reporting, showed himself to be an energetic and talented producer, but soon after left to set up a video company.

He returned and made *Food and Drink* a success by creating a pleasing cocktail of presenters – Chris Kelly, Michael Barry and Gilly Goolden – by being serious and consumerist about the subject matter and by being fecund in production ideas. He used some of the department's best film directors to make inventive, short films: in one the preparations for a Women's Institute lunch was shot as a British war film, with the ladies moving models on a plotting table. He challenged well known chefs to cook school lunches and hospital dinners and, in a charming series of short items, took Anton Mossiman to Sheffield to cook Sunday lunch for a council worker and his family for £10 and followed by taking the Sheffielder to learn some dishes in France with Raymond Blanc.

Baz was the first producer I knew who took audience research seriously. He commissioned research into which items the viewers liked and disliked, what they wanted more of and what they thought of the presenters, and developed the series accordingly. All this would be routine now. In the early 1980s many producers hated the very idea of it. They should follow their instincts, they felt, offering their work in hope and expectancy. There is no programme of any kind that does not require the producer's intuition. Baz's insight was to realize that if you are producing a long-running programme that aims to provide a service as well as to interest and entertain, then you are more likely to succeed if you understand what the audience is looking for and tune your instincts accordingly.

I invited two of the BBC's audience research department to give a presentation to our producers. It came as a shock. A team in Oxford had fitted video cameras to television sets in people's homes and recorded what happened in front of them when they were on. The footage was later used in a Channel 4 series. It revealed, to the horror of some producers, that viewers did not sit in rapt attention from the beginning of the programme to the end, but came in halfway through, wandered in and out of the room, read the newspaper, looking up from time to time, chatted, snoozed and snogged. This should have come as a surprise to no one, for at home, outside of diligent professional viewing, we were no different.

The inference that I wanted producers to take away was that you should not be afraid of giving a bit more information rather than a bit less, of reminding people of what had already been shown, of going out of your way to attract and retain attention. For this was a time when producers liked to dispense with commentary if they could and were prone to the elliptical in constructing programmes. Some subjects leant themselves to such approaches; some producers were far more skilled in achieving this than others. Too often at viewings I would say, 'I don't understand who this man is?' to be told, 'There was that remark in the conversation at the bar which you could hear that mentioned him,' or 'Didn't you see? He came out of the next door house in that shot at the beginning.' I had not heard because I was straining to hear what someone else was saying or I had not noticed because I was taking in other implications of the relevant shot. Producers and film editors lived with their material over several weeks and were well acquainted with every nuance of sound and picture. First-time viewers will miss much of this and need help if you want them to pick it up.

When I first went to viewings in Kensington House, producers booked the viewing theatre, a mini cinema with several rows of seats and the film projected on a large screen. We would take our places, the lights would dim and in a near religious atmosphere we would watch the programme. It created a sense of occasion, it allowed you to see every detail on the celluloid, but it was not television. I stopped this and insisted on viewing at a Steenbeck editing machine where the screen was no larger than that of a domestic television.

Baz went on to be one of the country's top independent producers and a leading voice in the industry. After 1982, when Channel 4 began as a publisher–broadcaster, commissioning all its programmes from independent producers, British television would never be the same again. In 1986 the Home Secretary Douglas Hurd announced that ITV and the BBC would have to have 25 per cent of their transmitted programmes made by independents within four years. The measurement was by hours but had to apply fairly evenly across the output. Given the lead times for commissioning and producing, four years was not long. Unless I was to take all new programme propositions from the independents, thereby stifling the in-house producers, I had to shift one or two current series to be produced independently. I thought of *Food and Drink*. In the six months of the year that Peter Bazalgette was not producing it, he ran his video company, so he had a basic infrastructure in place. He was entrepreneurial in spirit and I trusted him to maintain the quality of the programme. He jumped at the chance. Neither of us could see it then, but it was the beginning of a lucrative business. Others had similar opportunities and were far less successful.

I loved the job of head of documentary features. I was surrounded by interesting and talented colleagues who cared passionately about their work. They were difficult, as creative people often are, but that did not make encouraging them, leading them, supporting them, managing them any less rewarding. There was an unending flow of programme ideas to be argued over, programmes to be cast with presenters and producers, judgements to be made, budgets to be sorted. Programme review board on Wednesday morning was the fulcrum of the week, which began with a Monday morning prayer with Tim Slessor and Brian Elliot, the departmental manager, a shy, wise and utterly supportive man who checked my wilder flights, warned when danger loomed, persuaded people that the bad news I was about to give them was in their interest and cheered me up when times were rotten. At the other end of the week I held a meeting with them and the team of five executive producers. This was often followed by lunch with a guest, a politician or a BBC senior executive or a governor. I would have an individual meeting with each executive producer every couple of weeks and see Brian Elliot every day to chew over staffing needs, people problems, budgets and intelligence from the rest of the BBC or beyond. There were lots of sessions with individual producers, assistant producers and researchers about their ideas, their work or their futures and then the annual rounds of interviews for promotions, new recruits or trainees. Every now and then we had a union liaison meeting, Nick Ross fronting for the National Union of Journalists.

At intervals I received deputations from the South African and Sri Lankan High Commissions, from the Chinese and the Soviet Embassies, all complaining. In part they were going through the motions so they could report their vigorous activity to the chief back home. I visited locations and occasionally viewed morning rushes with an executive producer. I tried to turn up to as many studio productions as possible, and living, as I did, only a mile or so from Television Centre, could nip in on a Sunday afternoon for the live transmission of *Holiday* or return after dinner at home for *Crimewatch*. I would drop in informally to the big production teams and wander round the corridors at least once a week. There was no better way to pick up what was on people's minds. Without thinking, this slipped into a regular Friday afternoon wander and the suspicion grew that I was checking to see who had skived off early. I was not, but, when in scratchy mood, I could never decide which irritated me more: that offices were empty, so where on earth were people? Or that they were full, so why the hell were they not out making programmes?

I lunched busily. There were writers and presenters I wished to court, schmooze or assuage and those who wanted to pitch ideas. There were agents proposing work for their clients and those whose clients I wanted to hire. I would see journalists, contacts in other companies and visitors from overseas. And there were lunches with producers or executive producers and with friends, bosses, colleagues and talent from elsewhere in the BBC. My favourite place to take non-BBC guests was Sally Clarke's restaurant in Kensington Church Street, where the food was inventive and never heavy. For the home team I would stroll down to the Klefitiko, a friendly Greek Cypriot restaurant opposite the Kensington Hilton, the birthplace of many programmes and the last resting place of many duff ideas. Best of all was lunch ad hoc in the Ken House canteen, where there was always a debate underway.

Then there was watching the programmes. Most I was content to see when completed in cutting rooms, increasingly on cassette or on transmission. Some I wished, or was asked, to view at rough-cut or even earlier, so I could ask for changes or give a steer on construction or taste. I watched everything we made. I was responsible for it, wanted to monitor quality, spot talent and I owed it to the staff to know their work. I also kept my eye on documentaries and feature programmes at ITV, Channel 4 or from other parts of the BBC. Saturday mornings were the time to sit down with a pile of cassettes to catch up on what I had missed, for there were many evenings out for work and for play. I made sure that I had time for the opera and theatre with my wife and in 1986 was even a judge for the Olivier drama awards.

I travelled a bit, too. I went as part of a British Council jaunt to Delhi and Bombay to show some programmes and give some talks as part of the festival of India. Aubrey Singer sent me, and I took Jane, to a two-week seminar at the Aspen Institute of Humanistic Studies in Colorado, where we made good friends. I was not a great festivalgoer but I did attend the Prix Italia, held in a different Italian city each year in September. An organized excursion to a cultural site was followed by an heroic five pasta course lunch at which it was crucial to avoid the Norwegian producer expounding his 'documentary concepts'. There would be a polite dinner or two at which arch little speeches were received with nodding, teethless smiles. 'Ze BBC ees ze essential olive in ze Martini zat ees ze Prix Italia.'

I viewed enough of the programmes to keep my conscience clear and sometimes bought one, but the chief pleasure was Italy at that time of year and the chance to get to know documentary heads from around the world and ITV moguls and programme heads. For a time there was a harassed BBC man from the foreign relations unit who went out early in the year to recce the billets, book a suitable place and take care of arrangements when we all arrived at different times. It all came to an end the year the festival was in Venice. While ITV were staying in the Danieli and the Gritti Palace, and the BBC chairman George Howard in the Cipriani, the rest of the BBC were in a hotel without a proper message service, fifteen minutes walk – carrying our own luggage – from the quay. Aubrey, cut off from the office and puffing from the hike, went wild. The recces and the man who conducted them were no more.

All first-time visitors to the Prix heard how Alasdair Milne had arrived to give a reception at the festival in Lecce, in the far south of Italy. Alasdair, in casual gear, arrived on time but his luggage did not. The town was scoured for a gent's outfitters and a new suit purchased. News of this spread through all the delegations. As Alasdair greeted his guests that evening, many of them eyed his suit up and down, smirked and remarked that, all things considered, the suit just about did. BBC folk made remarks like: 'Well, I suppose it's better than what you were wearing.' Alasdair was not best pleased. Unknown to his guests, his luggage had arrived after all. The suit was his own.

Chapter eight
'WE MUST ALWAYS FOLLOW THE EDITORIAL IMPERATIVE'

When I arrived in Kensington House in 1981, one of my ambitions was to generate a regular flow of good history programmes. I had studied history at Cambridge and when I went up with a history scholarship I was under the illusion that I wanted to be a historian. I soon realized that there were plenty of people cleverer than I labouring in that vineyard, and while I enjoyed working alone in a library some of the time, I did not fancy it all the time. I believed that history programmes were an important part of the BBC's remit but thought that performance was fitful.

Almost the first thing I did was to suggest to Malcolm Brown that he make a programme about the Christmas Truce of 1914 for transmission the coming Christmas. Was it a myth? If not, what happened? Brown, one of the senior producers of the old documentaries department, had made a memorable programme about the battle of the Somme and written a book about soldiers in World War I. He not only made the definitive programme about the truce, but he and his researcher also went on to write the authoritative book on the subject. Old soldiers never die, at least not until interviewed by Malcolm Brown. When he retired a year or so later, he went on to become a leading historian of World War I and an authority on T.E. Lawrence. Malcolm's letter of application to the BBC in 1954, dug out when he left, gives a flavour of the man and the time: 'I am looking for a career of scope and interest in which such gifts as I have will find congenial and useful employment . . . I admire style and the taking of pains and feel that the BBC admires these qualities, too.' Happily, it did.

Another early decision was to accept Rex Bloomstein's proposal for a film on Auschwitz and the Allies: what and when the Allies knew of Hitler's Final Solution and what they did about it, based on Martin Gilbert's book. I persuaded ABC News in America to put some money in and Rex produced a powerful ninety-minute epic.

The breakthrough for a big series came when I received a telephone call from Peter Pagnamenta. He was a former star of BBC current affairs who had left to run factual programmes at Thames Television. He expected to be pushed out following a change of boss and had an idea. We met for him to explain. Peter is a tall, shy man, so quietly spoken as to be almost inaudible, with two main expressions. One is an impish grin as he retells a story or the nonsense meter in his brain registers a new idiocy. The other is a worried frown, furrowing high up his bald dome. I received the latter as he outlined his idea for a documentary series telling the story of British industries through the twentieth century. 'The story will be told industry by industry,' said Peter. 'There will be no pundits in the films. I will write an outline for each programme and then the producers will interview managers and workers to bring the subjects to life. They will tell their stories within the framework of the overall story. There's a mass of good archive film, much of it never seen on television.'

He would use historians to help shape the series and to ensure the authority of each film. There had been a number of series of *Yesterday's Witness*, an enjoyable and interesting oral history programme, but it was essentially anecdote driven and, I felt, lacked a presiding historical intelligence. We had run a good series, *The Thirties*, but what Peter was proposing was something new. In many ways he was to do for history programmes what John Birt had been doing at London Weekend Television, and would do later at the BBC, for current affairs programmes: impose a firm analytical framework by conducting thorough research in order to understand and map the story, then film people who would contribute the essential detail and arguments that told the story. Peter's project would be expensive and would not attract co-production money, but I was determined to make it happen.

Two years later, when I watched a cassette of the first near complete programme, about shipbuilding, I was thrilled. In it and through all twelve films Peter delivered exactly what he had promised. The individual episode producers made their contributions but the consistency and intelligence of approach was down to him. In the programme on the aircraft industry there was a magical moment when we saw ancient archive film of young women assembling an early aeroplane, heard a woman's voice describing the work and identifying individuals and then cut to the woman in shot, to realize that the programme team had found one of the very women in the film. It was the first time this technique had been used, bringing history to life before one's eyes. *All Our Working Lives*, as the series was called, deservedly received critical praise, won awards and set new standards for history programmes. I encouraged more and a rich stream of such output flowed. One of the *Working Lives* producers, Angela Holdsworth, made *Now The War is Over*, a social history of Britain from 1945 to 1951, in similar vein, and then *Out Of The Doll's House*, the story of women's lives in the twentieth century.

The other big series I set underway early on was *Soldiers*, a thirteen-part history of men in battle, made over three years for BBC1. John Gau, a former head of current affairs, now an independent, brought the idea to me. The programmes were written by two leading military historians, John Keegan and Richard Holmes, and traced the history of warfare from earliest times to the present day. The production values were high, with re-enactments and much travel. Some of the programmes, 'Infantry', 'Fighting Spirit' and 'Casualties' among them, were magnificent. Yet the series took a while to catch on. It was scheduled on BBC1's historically weak night, Wednesday, but by the end audiences were rising as more people discovered it. Even so, it never received the success it deserved. With the BBC's main channel in mind, John Gau had suggested Frederick Forsyth to present and I enthusiastically agreed. He was a former war reporter, a writer himself and a convincing presence on screen. He did us proud but I felt there was a disjunction because, outstanding as the scripts were, they were not his scripts. An example, perhaps, of a deliberate mistake.

Another way with history was to use the historian to write and present. However diligent or skilful producers may be in their own study and research, they have, one way or another, only mugged it up. A good journalist or producer could compose a passable biography of Winston Churchill. I wanted Martin Gilbert, who had spent half a lifetime studying Churchill, writing the final six of the eight-volume biography. I had to wait because Martin was busy – he has written two dozen other books as well as the Churchill magnum opus. While waiting, Martin arranged 'a Churchill London day' for me. He provided a running commentary as he took me to several of the houses in which Churchill had lived. At 12.45 p.m. we were in St James's.

'It's time for lunch,' Martin announced. 'We are going to go where Churchill would have gone if he were with us today and we are going to eat what he would have eaten.' He led me round the corner to the Ritz, where a table was reserved. Martin ordered. We had a clear beef soup followed by lamb cutlets. 'Now, pudding,' said Martin. 'Churchill liked to have what he called "an important pudding".' The waiter was summoned. 'What would you say was your most important pudding?' Martin asked. The French waiter was baffled and consulted a fellow. After further negotiations we were served an excellent queen of the puddings. Martin wisely drew the line at brandy and cigars.

Martin Gilbert did write and present a four-hour television biography for us, but not until he had finished the final volume of the written biography. In the meantime the eventual Churchill producer, Jeremy Bennett, worked with another biographer, Nigel Hamilton, on his subject, Montgomery.

I was a great admirer of Max Hasting's books, so when he told me that he was writing a history of the Korean War and would like to do a television series alongside it, I leapt at the idea. Could we film and access film libraries not just in the United Kingdom, the USA and South Korea, but in North Korea as well? Britain had no diplomatic relations with North Korea, so getting there to find out would not be easy. To my surprise, I discovered that a BBC colleague, Philip Lewis, had already penetrated this veiled land to negotiate coverage of the famous North Korean State Circus. He was confident that he could get himself back in and me with him. We had to pick up our visas in Beijing and fly North Korean Airlines to Pyongyang, the capital. Thus began one of the longest and strangest of weeks.

We were met by two minders and driven into the city in a large and ancient black Russian Zil. The buildings were all new. We were told, not for the last time, that the whole city had been destroyed by the fighting and American bombing in the war, and rebuilt under the guidance of the The Great Leader, Kim Il Sung. Rebuilt, it appeared, with concrete Lego.

Where were the people? It was late afternoon but we passed just one other car, another official Zil, and one empty lorry. There were no bicycles and just a few pedestrians. 'Bicycles are not permitted in Pyongyang,' said young Mr Kim, one of our minders. 'They would make the city untidy.'

Down the centre of the wide empty streets were two yellow lines, marking a central lane. This was, we were solemnly informed, so the President's car could travel unimpeded – unimpeded, presumably, by the non-existent traffic. The exception was a modest fleet of tricycles, each of which had a large basket attached behind, all of which were pedalled by women. Their purpose was to carry the luggage of rail passengers who reached home on foot, the underground or buses, for there were no taxis for people. Smartly uniformed traffic police stood at all the main street crossings, swinging lighted batons to control the imaginary traffic, halting and waving it on with stern formality. On a later occasion Phil and I absented ourselves from young Mr Kim and his colleague and went for a walk. There being no wheeled vehicle in sight, we strolled across the road only to be sharply whistled at by a traffic policewoman who indicated that we use the underpass or there would be trouble.

Make-believe cloaked everything we saw. Spotting a few neon lights in the main street of the capital, we explored, only to discover that the one or two restaurants and shops beneath them showed no sign of ever being open. Just as a big city had to have traffic controls even if there was no traffic, so it had to have neon lights even if there were no shops or cafés.

The public face was the only one we were to see. Our minders were pleasant enough but anxious. They, and everyone else who spoke to us throughout the week, began always with the mantra, 'The Great Leader, Kim Il Sung, and the Dear Leader, Kim Jong Il . . .'. There was no teasing them.

'Isn't it odd,' I asked, 'that it was already decided that Kim Jong Il would take over from his father? This is like a western royal family.'

'No,' was the reply. 'This is the unanimous will and desire of the people in response to the Dear Leader's outstanding ideological and theoretical activities and great revolutionary practices.'

Everyone wore lapel badges with a portrait of Kim Il Sung. 'People have to wear these?' we asked.

'No, no. All people wish to show love and respect for The Great Leader.' There was never a flicker of the eye or twitch of a muscle to indicate that they knew all this was ritual. In my limited experience of Eastern Europe, translators or guides had a hundred ways of signalling their individuality through the communist liturgy and alone, over a drink, would damn their masters and the regime. Not here. One shuddered to guess what sanctions ensured such uniformity. We did manage to get our minders up to my hotel room, where we plied them with Scotch. But even in the drink, one watching the other and both aware of those who might be listening, no chink opened. Surely, there must be some things which they did not like about their country, everyone feels that, however patriotic they are? 'If I have a problem, I can go to the People's Committee. I am a party member. I can say something not very good happened to me. We find a solution that way.'

It is hard to have a discussion about politics in a place where all the books in the hotel bookshop are written by the President save for one, which was about him and probably not wholly unadmiring. There was an English language newspaper, upon which Peter Simple could not have improved. The front page headlines in our week were: 'President Kim Il Sung receives Yugoslav People's Army delegation', 'President Kim Il Sung to visit USSR' and 'President Kim Il Sung nominated as SPA candidate'. At the last, 'thunderous cheers "long live The Great Leader" burst out at the meeting from workers, farmers and working intellectuals'.

The meetings about filming were postponed and we were kept busy with a round of visits. Everywhere we went the first thing we saw on entering was a large painting of Kim Il Sung surrounded by beaming farmers, engineers, children or soldiers. The first thing we were told was how many times The Great Leader had visited to give 'on the spot guidance', the dates listed beneath the painting. He had visited the farm we saw eighty-two times, his son twenty-three times. 'We are so proud even though this is a normal village.' What's more, the President had invented a new method of collective farming. A room full of photographs recorded him giving guidance. A diorama depicted the bad days 'before liberation', complete with wicked landlords. 'The farmers here believe they have a happy life now thanks to Kim Il Sung . . .'.

We were shown a newly completed barrage across a sea inlet, this too, evidently, Kim's idea. He had brought his extraordinary engineering knowledge to bear, coming many times to give his 'on the spot guidance'. At the Children and Students Palace the President had said that every child should learn to play a musical instrument. We saw classes for guitar and accordion. The effect was like synchronized swimming, the children not without charm, but drilled, mechanical heads swaying in unison, mouths rictus-like. Italia Conti goes mad in the orient. They did, however, amaze with a spectacularly accurate mirror dance.

The most extraordinary place we saw was the film studios. Here, in the centre of a vast, grassy square, was a twice life-size statue of Kim Il Sung dispensing the usual to the artists making *The Flower Girl*, a film that Kim had written in 1930 whilst fighting the Japanese. No mention of him inventing the computer and a cure for cancer in the evenings. He had made eighteen visits to the studios, his son more than 300. There was a huge back lot with permanent sets: two villages, two Japanese streets, a Chinese street, a group of ancient buildings in a square, a grand house to show the lives of the rich (with its own cleaner and caretaker), other European houses, an enormous office building, a university building, a church, the studio's own railway station and huge water tanks. The unspoken question was why Kim Il Sung (often referred to as 'Ultimate Genius of All Mankind') had not explained that there was no need to build all this in bricks and mortar to have film sets. The spoken question was why was there no one shooting a film, preparing a film or, indeed, any sign of life at all? 'Ah! All the camera teams are out in the countryside capturing footage of the beautiful autumn colours.'

We did manage to get some business done. We outlined our plans and viewed some of the archive film. Our most useful visit was to the Fatherland Liberation Museum, room after room dedicated to the war. It had Kim's microphone, telex, binoculars, uniform, the car in which he had visited the front and the machine gun he had personally stripped and reassembled, along with a reconstruction of his H.Q. Oddly there were no photographs of him with his troops, only paintings. Elsewhere in the museum were captured American and British weapons. Several spectacular dioramas depicted important battles and the climax was a vast panorama of Taeson, where the visitor is placed in a revolving central seat and moves 360 degrees round more than 130 metres of painted battle.

Eventually we were promised our meeting with the man who could make the decisions we required. First, though, came a trip to the border with South Korea at Panmunjom. Our Zil swept us out of the city and into the countryside, where we saw groups of women and children working at the roadside with buckets and birch brooms. They appeared to be doing no more than tidying up. The way our driver sped past them and the ox carts bringing grain from the fields revealed that those who travelled in official cars felt little concern for the comfort or safety of the remainder of the population. We sent a cart crashing backwards into a ditch as we startled both ox and driver. Bicycles were evidently permitted outside of Pyongyang, for in one town we passed through a crowd of them, clipping one, knocking it and its rider to the ground. Our driver stopped grudgingly, exchanged some angry words with the fallen and bleeding cyclist and returned, laughing, to the car with the comment, 'Drunk.'

At the border our guide took us to an observation post, from which we could look out across the demilitarized zone to the line of South Korean defences, as he told us more tales of American sins. Panmunjom, a name that echoed from my first reading of newspapers, was the site of the talks that led to the armistice in 1953 and had continued for many years after the war. In a long building overlooking the cluster of huts that straddle the border, we were addressed by a North Korean colonel, an impressive figure, who spoke excellent English and exuded sophistication and controlled menace. When he had explained the history of the talks and the scale of the American presence on the South Korean side, we went out onto the steps. Directly opposite, 50 or so yards away, was an American observation tower where an American soldier had his binoculars trained on us. We looked down to the buildings in between and, from the far side of the central hut, another American soldier leaned into view and began photographing us. A moment of alarm. My photo would go into the file of Commie troublemakers. I envisaged the scene at US Immigration the next time I went to America, when the officer

Above: WW reads instructions on how to be a director while filming for *Late Night Line Up*.

Left: In producer's uniform at first recording of *Edition 1973*.

Above left: Brian Wenham.

Above right: WW as baby executive.

Right: Robert Robinson and WW meet B. Traven's brother in Germany 1977.

Roger Laughton
Head of Daytime Programming

Anthony Geffen
Assistant producer, South and East region

Hugh Purcell
Editor, *Day to Day*

Peter Bazelgette
Editor, *The Food and Drink Programme*

Chris Terrill
Director, *Crimewatch*

Tim Lambert
Researcher, *Rock School*

Will Wyatt
Head of Documentary Features

Mike Casey
Independent film director

Andrew Hornig
City financier

Harvey Woolfe
Assistant producer, *Newsnight*

Above: Tatler features the BBC Mis-Hits as an ambitious cabal in 1985. Far left, Roger Mills begs to disagree.

Left: The first two editors of *Forty Minutes* and two of the BBC's finest, Eddie Mirzoeff (left) and Roger Mills.

Right: WW auditions as imperialist lackey at Pyongyang film studios.

Below: The Pope realizes a lifelong ambition.

Left: Alan Yentob (BBC Photo Library).

Below: Prix Italia in Capri, 1988. *From left:* Jane Wyatt, Alan Yentob, Ron Davies partner of 'Canale Due', Graeme MacDonald, WW.

Above: January 1993, the new director-general's board of management assembles at Amberley Castle as 'Martin Gibbons Associates'.
From left: Ron Neil, Bill Dennay, Michael Stevenson, Bob Phillis, Margaret Salmon, Tony Hall, Pamela Taylor, James Arnold-Baker, Liz Forgan, John Birt, Patricia Hodgson, David Hatch, WW.

Right: Marmaduke Hussey (BBC Photo Library).

Above: Executive committee 1999. Back from left: Mark Byford, John Smith, Tony Hall, Rupert Gavin, Matthew Bannister, Colin Browne. Front: Margaret Salmon, John Birt, Rod Lynch (leaving as chief exec resources to run Olympic Airways), WW, Patricia Hodgson.

Right: Leaving party for Paul Fox 1991. From left: Anne Tyerman, Michael Bunce, WW, Paul Fox, Bill Ansbro, Jim Moir.

Five managing directors of BBC TV at the hanging of a portrait of a sixth, Huw Wheldon. Back row: Paul Fox, WW, Bill Cotton. Front: Alasdair Milne and Aubrey Singer.

in the booth would leaf through that hefty volume they have to hand, and instead of stamping the passport and waving me through, would have me bustled away and put on the next plane home. The photographer slipped silently out of sight and we walked down to inspect the hut where the United Nations–North Korean talks had taken place.

We had one more night before we were due to leave and, by this time, getting out safely was at the front of our minds. We were to meet the main man at last. I took with me a large bottle of Johnnie Walker Black Label, a drink much prized in the East, I had been told, and kept for this moment. We were ushered in to meet the smooth senior party man, who was expensively dressed in a silk shirt and shiny well-cut suit. There was nothing for it but to hand over the present, which he received and passed to an aide, much as Her Majesty might a bag of doughnuts from a guest arriving for a dine and sleep. He heard us out, asked about money and what our view of the war was. After three-quarters of an hour he rose to leave and said that we would hear the decision when we were back in London. The good news in this was that we were, indeed, going back to London. We had begun to fantasize about becoming Missing In Action.

A month or so later we did receive our answer. We could not film in North Korea and could not use their archive. A rival project had offered more money and, according to the North Koreans, would be more sympathetic to them. We went ahead and Max Hastings and his team delivered a series to be proud of. My heart did pound the next time I entered the United States, but the immigration officer was no more interested in me than usual. What happened to those photographs?

It was not just for history programmes that the right presenter on the right subject remained one of the best documentary formulas. I courted David Attenborough to write and present the history of television that I had been jump-started into announcing at Edinburgh in 1983. He had other series in mind, and when I discovered that Granada were underway with a big series on the subject, we had a rethink and instead produced a series of essays on different aspects of television. They worked well in the overall TV50 season, marking the anniversary of the world's first television service that the BBC had opened in 1936.

Among the films was Robert Robinson's delightful rumination on being on the box, *The Magic Rectangle*. Part of his thesis was that being on the television was a trick that more or less anyone can pull off, the essential requirement being a desire to show off in public. Bob exaggerated, but the explosion of programming to feed today's plethora of hungry channels has revealed hundreds of, mainly young, people who can more or less do it. Or do enough. And there are school bus loads of others queuing up to follow. Some have charm; some have wit; when it comes to brass neck, Jeffrey Archer could have been their tutor. But they are mostly the audience writ slightly larger and in 'Omygod' mode. Their appeal is their attractive ordinariness. To that extent, Robinson was right. What Robinson did not point out is that many of those who have sustained long careers have been abler than much of their work strictly demanded. I think of, among others, Robin Day, who would bemoan that he should have used his talents for something other, Ludovic Kennedy, Robinson himself, James Cameron, David and Jonathan Dimbleby, Clive James and Esther Rantzen, who, if she had been in politics, would surely have reached the front bench, there to give hell to some government minister. The audience watching them do not think, as do the audience of the young manics, 'I could do that', but rather, 'I wish I could do that.'

From a broadcaster's point of view, such people brought qualities and abilities that raised television's game. They helped make television in the United Kingdom a trade to which able people, even outstanding people, were pleased to devote themselves. The Canadian born Robert MacNeil, one time BBC current affairs presenter, was asked whether his mother expected him to have a career in broadcasting. 'Oh, no,' MacNeil replied. 'I think that she had hoped for something better than that.' Long may television attract the overqualified.

The relationship between producers and presenters is a struggle as old as television itself. It needs to be a partnership, and is often a happy one, but it is a partnership coloured by mutual insecurities, fears and resentments. In the producer's mind grow the questions: 'Why is she getting all the glory when I am doing all the work? Why is he getting all that money when I am doing all the work? Why don't they even read the research I've given them?' and 'Why doesn't he just do what I ask him to?' Meanwhile, in the presenter's mind lurk other questions: 'Are this lot capable of delivering what they promise? Will the interviewees for once say what the researcher says they will say? Why am I in the hands of people who can't get us a decent transmission slot?' and 'Don't they realize that it's me who will get rubbished?' It is a struggle for glory. Many producers have not only devised, researched and directed films, but written the presenter's script too. It can then be galling to hear the programme referred to only by the possessive of the presenter's name.

At the same time there are presenters who feel they could make things a damn sight better if they were in charge of camera and editing. I once saw a letter from Alan Whicker to Roger Mills when they were making a series about Australia. 'I had long feared your notorious inflexibility,' wrote Whicker. 'After thirty years, I am too old to be given orders . . . I *won't* be put into your mould. This is a series I suggested and I know what we should get out of it . . . Let me repeat: I would like the first two episodes rearranged as per my cutting notes, and if you feel incapable, perhaps you should retire gracefully.' They made up. The show went on.

I had learned how not to give bad news to presenters. That did not make the right way comfortable. In one of the more disconcerting interviews, I told one presenter that we were changing a programme and her role on it was over. She spent half our subsequent time together staring soulfully at me and the other half performing a version of the Hollywood guide to negotiation. 'I want to know what your other offer is and I want to know yesterday.' The whole point was that there was no other offer. I had sympathy then, as now. The people who do these jobs are all volunteers and know the risks, but they are at what you hope is not merely the whim of producers, executives and channel controllers.

No wonder presenters sought to protect themselves. A producer was talking to Freddie Raphael about an idea for a series on memory. The producer told him candidly that we had also discussed it with Michael Ignatieff. Raphael rang me. 'I'm not going head to head with anyone.' He went on to tell me several stories, with added references to the transience of all executives, especially television executives, just to let me know that he had seen my kind and better come and go. And what's more, that once we were gone, we were soon forgotten. All true, of course.

Raphael was the real thing. Not all were. One arch bullshitter was in the cutting room one day, boasting of the visit of a famous author to his house the previous week. 'What an evening. He told wonderful stories all night. We all drank too much, of course. He left at 2.00 a.m. after signing a copy of his new book for me and my wife – "To you both, with thanks for an evening I'll never forget".'

The film editor, who had come to loathe this man, looked up. 'Did you say last Tuesday he came?'

'Yes, last Tuesday.'

'But he's dead. He died three months ago,' the film editor said.

'What am I saying? I mean last July.' Our hero sought to recover. 'Funnily, my wife said he wasn't looking too well then.'

Sometimes the presenter was almost the sole author of a series, as was Bryan Magee with *The Great Philosophers*, for which he chose the participants, shaped the discussions and conducted them on air. On one occasion a presenter who had devised a series about people and their houses, Robert Robinson, came to me with a unique suggestion. 'Will, I think that the producer is excellent and the programmes will be good. However, I don't think that they need me.' He stood himself down. This was the reverse of the usual situation when people known for other talents wanted to 'make some documentaries', possibly to establish a different credibility, possibly because they thought it was easy. Sometimes a channel controller would throw a short series at someone to keep him around, fill out a contract or flatter.

Paul Daniels walked into my office one day in search of such a series; Jimmy Young's agent volunteered the ageless wizard of the mike. The young Emma Freud came to see me with a programme idea. She would interview some big names in circumstances that would encourage relaxed self-revelation: on a desert island. Not such a daft idea and this was a decade before the fad for desert island programmes. There would be an additional attraction. She would conduct the whole affair in a bikini, 'And, Will,' she held my eyes, 'I look pretty good in a bikini.'

In 1986 Robert Kilroy-Silk, then an MP, rang me and asked for a chat. I met him at a cafe in St Martin's Lane, where he told me that he had written

a book that would lead to his de-selection. In any case, he wanted to leave
the House of Commons and wished to make his living from television.
Needless to say, he had an idea for a series of documentaries. I heard him
out, then told him: 'Look Robert. If you want to make this series I will consider it. But if you want to make a living from television, you won't do it this
way. It will be at least two years before the programmes would be finished.
The fees would be spread over that time, and even with a book, you won't
make what you are looking for. To make a good living from this business,
you have you be on the air a lot, earning each time. As it happens, I know
that they are piloting a morning discussion programme from current affairs.
Why don't you try that? I'll ring them, if you like.' I did. He hosted one of
the pilots and was chosen. The following year I went to see John Harvey-
Jones at ICI at the behest of his agent. Harvey-Jones was stepping down as
chairman and he, too, fancied a broadcasting career. He had four ideas:
three were for big series, the fourth was something I both liked and thought
we could get into production quickly. His idea for 'a business masterclass'
became *Troubleshooter*.

Celebrating some of the great figures, we made Ludovic Kennedy's television autobiography, a retrospective series with James Cameron, and one
with John Betjeman. The last is remembered by many for the end sequence
of the final film, when the producer, Jonathan Stedall, questioned Betjeman
in his wheelchair in Cornwall.

'John, is there anything you regret in life?' he asked.

'Not enough sex,' was the reply. We gave a launch for the series at the
British Academy of Film and Television Arts, which Betjeman much enjoyed.
'I am surrounded by lots of friends. It's like being in heaven,' he said as one
who shortly expected to be visiting the real thing. I noted the pleasing incon-
gruity of him sitting in the seat dedicated to John Wayne. I had only met him
once before, when he came in for *The Book Programme* and I vacated my
office so he would have a place to rest. When I returned to it, Bob Robinson
introduced me.

'John, this is Will Wyatt who let us have his office to sit in.'

'How do you do? I say, it is awfully kind. Thank you so much,' said
Betjeman, adding in the loudest of stage whispers, 'Gosh! I am an old
humbug, aren't I?'

In 1987 Clive James was in touch with Michael Grade and me about
coming with his producer, Richard Drewett, another *Late Night Line Up*
alumnus, on contract to the BBC. The four of us had dinner to open discussions. Michael was in his element on these occasions, telling stories to create
a relaxed atmosphere: how Lew Grade slipped a five pound note to a
snooker club owner asked to adjudicate on a free ball; how Marilyn Monroe
reacted when at her third Passover meal with Arthur Miller, 'Are these
Matza balls again? . . . Don't they cook any other part of the Matza?' We
planned some high profile documentaries for BBC1 and some late night talk
shows for BBC2. Negotiations dragged on; Richard and Clive always came
to negotiate as a pair, both wound up, one nervous and one very nervous.

Finally, after an emergency meeting in Michael's house, we agreed terms. Then a late tackle on me from Drewett: 'Clive will need a car to bring him to and from work every day.' No.

An almost separate unit, at least when I went to Kensington House, was *The World About Us* team, under Tony Isaacs. That series was half natural history, from the BBC in Bristol, and half anthropology, exploration and adventure, from documentary features. Tony had been a current affairs producer in ITV, had an eye for strong stories and would talk of 'knocking off a "doco"'. In the 1970s and early 1980s Tony exploited gaps in the BBC's current affairs output to make some dramatic films about famines, earthquakes and the disaster at the Bhopal chemical factory in India. I inherited from him a run of drama documentaries about political prisoners, among them Bukovsky and Nelson Mandela. *The World About Us* was runner-up for the Prix Italia with an episode about Vietnam veterans, and did stories on the opium harvest, corruption in Nigeria and the Amazon gold mines, as well as lighter subjects such as the Indian film industry and Hawaiian boat racing. The channels had the money and the appetite for regular and extensive foreign filming.

Tony, who had a bald head and a beard, had looked exactly the same for thirty years. His wardrobe was a symphony of safari suits made in Hong Kong. He had enormous drive and energy, but trying to pin him down to arrangements or a delivery date was a nightmare. He was a pirate, an operator of the old school, and his dealings with the (mostly) reasonable requests of the rest of the BBC sounded a consistent note of exasperation, the bold explorer replying to interfering sponsor. 'I have just returned from a ten-week location in Africa . . .', 'I have only a few hours to catch a plane . . .', 'I am just back from a month in Ethiopia . . .', 'I go on location in India tomorrow morning for some weeks.' No wonder I never knew whether he was at home or in Honolulu. He could be utterly disarming about it all. When I bawled him out for wasting time in India at the end of a shoot, he faffed and blustered before blushing into a grin. He would come into my office with a ruse – he usually had a new ruse – that he would try to persuade me to back, and the more sceptical I became, the faster he would speak, until I was drenched by an unstoppable waterfall of words.

Tony's constant travel brought some exotic claims. 'Trousers ruined. Slipped while descending from a Beaver aircraft at Masawa airstrip, the door being blocked by a can of insecticide.' The last detail, a brilliant touch. 'I recognize that the tropical clothing allowance should normally be sufficient to cover a year's requirements. However, the conditions I shall be facing at Lake Chad will be such . . .'. Tony was a passionate fisherman, went nowhere without his tackle and was somehow often caught between planes where there was a trout stream, a salmon river, a lake or good sea fishing. I treasured one of his many telexes from distant parts: 'Cannot repeat cannot make meeting on Monday. Have been held up and robbed by Dacoits in India.' It was true. He could be maddening but it was hard to remain angry with a man who had offered himself to the BBC as, 'Fit, usually of sound mind and have my own mosquito boots.' When he left, I gave him a book, *Far Eastern Jaunts*.

Brian Elliott, the departmental manager and, in effect, my chief financial and administrative officer, had worked with Tony for some years and handled his unit's claims and costs with an amused firmness. Overall, the factual departments were not extravagant and operated with an awareness that it was licence payers' money they were spending. We looked with resentment, mingled with envy, at the two departments that appeared to operate with an open chequebook: drama and current affairs. Television had grown as a combination of show business and journalism, administered, in the BBC, by the civil service. The practises and style of the first two, stoked by the rank prodigality of ITV, wrestled with the last. People knew what they could get away with, which was more than they should. Some pushed the allowances to extremes; others took less than their due. There was a system of payment for work on off-duty days, WOODS. Popping in for an hour or so could prompt a substantial payment, as could simply claiming to have popped in. It was very difficult to police. The hardest working producer in the department, who I knew was in for one or two days most weekends, never claimed.

The macro financial framework had its problems, too. Production was not linked closely to transmission. Thus when Bill Cotton became controller of BBC1, he discovered a documentary mountain, programmes commissioned but not scheduled by his predecessor, Bryan Cowgill. Michael Grade discovered much the same when he took over that job seven years later. Working capital was managed at director of finance level. It was not a major constraint upon the channels and of little concern at departmental level. At the Year End we would sweep as many problems as we could into 'work in progress', where some would lie until the next year end and beyond.

The budgeting of television programmes had been modelled on radio and split into 'programme allowance', essentially cash, which was what producers were held to account for, and 'resources', studio time, filming, editing, design and so on, which producers had to estimate but which were policed and controlled by the planning departments. A McKinsey's study into the BBC at the end of the 1960s recommended a total costing system, treating budgets as a single monetary sum that producers could spend on whatever they believed their programmes required. The BBC could not face such a radical step, which would have thrown into high relief the huge fixed costs of staff, equipment and buildings, and questioned their viability. Consequently, the 'total costing' introduced was hedged around with limitations and caveats.

Given that there was much tighter control of cash than of resource usage, producers sought to stuff a budget with the maximum resource load they could get away with, fully intending to 'convert' out of this, by under using the studio or filming allocation, say, in order to spend more cash. The financial arm responded by imposing additional rules. This led to regular arguments about the amount of work achieved in a day in the studio or by a film crew and about the slow returns of information on what had been charged for. Each programme had an identifying number against which charges were allocated. This was open to abuse. Producers could be careless in specifying which programme incurred a particular cost, some even getting hold of another programme's number to exploit. (The General Election's number was thought to be the ultimate golden goose, a large budget that, it was believed, was only added up every four or five years.) The resource departments could balance their books by allocating charges to a programme knowing that it would be some weeks, even months, before the programme department would be able to challenge it. All this was against a background of industrial disputes that were so much part of British life in the early 1980s. In 1982 a dubbing mixers' strike was 'one of nine disputes in the BBC nearing a critical stage', we were told.

In fact, the BBC prided itself on its financial performance and kept within the targets set for it. Overseas broadcasters came regularly to learn about the BBC's systems of planning and financial controls. In 1984 the chairman Stuart Young, a top flight accountant himself, said: 'I thought I might find the BBC careless with the licence payers' cash but soon learned otherwise . . . three major efficiency audits by external consultants have given us a pretty clean bill of health . . . we are up with the leaders in efficiency.' By the standards of the time, I am sure it was. The tensions arose because the financial management sought to give the maximum amount of creative space to producers, an entirely laudable aim, but with a system that still relied on a high degree of central allocation.

Most years there was some sort of crisis. Brian Elliott controlled our spending on the programme strands well, but occasional big projects went off the rails. The worst was a four-part drama documentary about the Antarctic explorer Shackleton, shot on location in Greenland, around London and at the BBC's Ealing studios. The producer, an experienced drama production manager, was unable to say 'no' to the director. *Shackleton* went a disastrous, and I seem to remember record-breaking, 50 per cent over budget. I told the producer he was finished with us and should return to drama and I abandoned all plans for further drama docs.

I was shaken by this but it did not prevent me from taking advantage of the BBC system by generating as much new work as I could and putting it into production as soon after the controller had commissioned it as possible. The bow wave of costs and resource needs was for the planners to deal with. My job, as I saw it, was to get as much work as possible for my producers and provide as many good programmes as I was able. There was much game playing. An offers meeting with Brian Wenham, when he was running BBC2, revealed a muddle over the financial year in which a big series should be costed. In a stage managed gavotte Brian and his planner pretended they did not know we were in production, I pretended not to know that some projects were not yet loaded in the financial plans, and Brian Elliot pretended to know only what was written down.

The following year Brian Elliot and I paraded before Aubrey Singer at the managing director's finance meeting for a severe wigging. A six-part series had grown to a highly acclaimed ten parts, backed enthusiastically by the channel controller, who nonetheless refused more funds. A triumph sat in our books as a big overspend. I took the offensive. 'This was a terrific series we were all proud to have. It would have been crazy not to make the extra programmes. Anyone in this room would have done the same.' I knew it was going to be all right when Aubrey Singer rose to my fly.

'Yes, of course. We must always follow the editorial imperative.' Michael Checkland, the director of resources, kicked him hard under the table.

'We must, though, be aware of our financial imperatives, too,' Aubrey added lamely. But I had to cut back our plans for the coming year and returned to the department to bollock overspending producers.

Every year there were cuts. In 1984 Bill Cotton announced that the television service was forecasting an overspend, the BBC was in the third year of a licence fee settlement and there was said to be no reserve. All departments must trim. The next year the new licence fee was much less than hoped for and a senior group, 'Black Spot', conducted a blitz on spending. In 1986 we had to make 10 per cent cuts in secretarial and clerical staff or surrender the cash equivalent. There was another round of programme cuts and we were ordered to slow down the production timetable to lessen the pressure. Bill summoned a meeting of all programme heads, at which we were handed a document headed 'Creepage and Wastage – A study in the decline of productivity in BBC television.' It charted the long-term fall in the amount of edited footage achieved for each filming or studio day. I asked how long it would be before this document was in the newspapers, and the copies were hurriedly collected as we left the room. What we lacked was a mechanism to make us decide what we deemed a necessity and what was just nice to have.

The shortfall in the licence fee brought more than an annual swing of the scythe at programme budgets. The BBC began to think about sponsorship as a source of extra revenue. In 1986 Mike Checkland, director of resources and deputy director-general, came down to programme review to talk on a paper proposing relaxed rules for this. As a group, we did not like them. Mike and Bill Cotton became testy about us being 'negative', but here we were, ten minutes after arm wrestling with the Peacock Committee about maintaining the non-commercial funding of the BBC, making a 180-degree turn. The paper remained a paper. Anna Ford came to see me with an idea for a series about the English landscape to be sponsored by Shell. We could not do it.

We were, however, increasingly seeking and using co-production monies. This had begun back in Huw Wheldon's day with big series like *America* and *Civilisation*. Time Life was the co-producer then and the BBC's attitude was, 'You give us the money, we make the programme as we choose.' For most big projects, the channel controllers began looking to the programme department to come up with some co-production funds to bridge the gap between the usual level of production spend and the full, *bombe-glâce*, travel-anywhere level of spend. In 1987–8 I had overseas money in fifteen programmes or series in documentary features. I went to the USA, the chief source of such funds, most years to see the people who might or did invest in our programmes: the public television stations in Boston, New York, Washington and Los Angeles, RKO/Lionheart, the Arts and Entertainment Network, CBC in Canada and Turner Broadcasting.

They travelled to London regularly and by the mid-1980s each department made a presentation at Television Centre to our main co-producer, A&E. Many of the visiting co-producers seemed to have London shopping high on their agenda and two men from Westinghouse appeared out of the blue on a trip that appeared chiefly geared to buying a London flat. The American public television people were kindred spirits in many ways but were niche broadcasters with rules more like an educational body, which, in effect, they were. They had to pass big series through committees of experts and advisors and would recite the mantra of the day: 'It must have impact, be of the highest quality. It must be popular but serious. It must be beautifully shot.'

Turners were different. They did not fund many projects but they had swagger. The man I dealt with was Bob Wussler, a suave, expensively dressed and dined executive, who oozed confidence and authority. He arranged for me to meet his boss at the headquarters in Atlanta so I could pitch some ideas in person. When I arrived I was met by a different Bob Wussler, who was edgy and moving around nervously. He explained that Ted Turner had arrived back in the country that day after three weeks away. He would see me though. I was led into Turner's vast office, furnished with sofas and easy chairs and bedecked with trophies and photographs. Turner was direct, enthusiastic, quick and impatient. 'What else? What else?' he kept asking before I had finished. He made some jokes, fell back on his sofa laughing, then leaped up to show me two paintings he had commissioned from an English painter, one of the Battle of Trafalgar, the other of an eighteenth-century American sea battle. He pointed out a bust of Nelson and photographs of himself with Gorbachev and with Castro. We talked about television. He had strong views about violence and would not let his stations run *Miami Vice* or *Cagney and Lacey*. 'I want to show people some of the good things going on in the world.' He engaged and gave me an hour. I was impressed.

'We were lucky. We caught him in a good mood,' said a relieved Wussler, who had, I felt, feared a bawling out for wasting his boss's time with a nobody from England. And Turners came through with money for the series I had pitched about the Caribbean.

Staff for this series, as for others, were a mixture of 'permanent' and 'contract'. All job vacancies were advertised and open to competition. This brought an annual round of interviews to decide upon promotions at different levels. I always gave people in the department the results in person, a pleasure with the successful candidates, not so with the others, who responded with resignation, bitterness or tears. I headhunted for some editorial posts but the BBC has never been *dirigiste* in moving people, as are many companies. In the 1980s I was asked if I would like to be controller of Radio 4, the secretary to the board of governors and, extraordinarily, controller BBC Scotland. No one said, 'You will do this.' Always the BBC way was, 'Would you be interested in? . . . Oh, well.'

At one time of organizational head scratching, Brian Wenham asked if I would be interested in a new post of controller, news and current affairs. This was easy.

'Brian,' I replied, 'I have thought about what has happened to heads of current affairs. There was John Grist, who took the rap for *Yesterday's Men* and was sent to the English Regions. You took a public rubbishing from the Annan Report. John Gau was tarred with the Carrickmore incident, punished by being denied the controllership of BBC1 and then parachuted out. Chris Capron [the current head whom I had just seen leaving Brian's office, spluttering for a drink of water] is exhausted and wants out. Then there is the news. Derrick Amoore cracked under the pressure, hit the bottle, was sacked and is now exiled to Radio London. Alan Protheroe has been resurrected, but was previously sacked from news. And Peter Woon has taken endless flack about the superiority of ITN and cannot be long for this world. Your kind offer invites me to be responsible for both areas. No thanks. Anyway, it would put me out of the running for BBC2.'

Programme editors and executive producers were intensely competitive in seeking the best producers, assistant producers and researchers for their teams. The staff economy worked partly on a market system – A wants to work on B's programme and B wants A – and partly by soviet planning, I allocated people. I knew my priorities and had a better idea than anyone else, or so I believed, of the strengths, weaknesses and need for experience of all the staff. Because there was limited movement in and out, there were a few duffers who had to work somewhere. This was not a big problem for me, but Brian Wenham, when he was head of current affairs, had operated his 'every home' policy. When programme editors complained about being sent drunks or incompetents, they would be informed that such liabilities were being spread evenly around on the basis that 'every home should have one'.

Productivity varied. Some producers would turn out three or more films a year. Others gave birth slowly and painfully to one a year. Some would wax and wane then happily surprise. At an annual interview with Clem Vallence, an experienced *World About Us* producer, I was halfway through warning him that his strike rate was problematically low when he passed me the idea for a programme following Phileas Fogg's footsteps going round the world in eighty days by surface transport. We immediately began discussing how best to make it. An early thought was to do it live with the traveller linking by satellite, daily, but this would be expensive and difficult to schedule effectively. A series of documentaries was a better bet. With whom? Alan Whicker needed a new project. We talked to him but this would be an uncomfortable and tiring shoot. He was not keen. Clem wrote a list of possible presenters and showed it to me. Near the top was Michael Palin, who had made a railway journey documentary we had both seen. I said that I knew him and would sound him out. I rang Palin.

'Michael, can I come to see you?'

'What's it about?'

'I'm not going to tell you until I see you.'

'Why not?'

'Because I may not get to the end of what I want to tell you about before you decide that it is all too much trouble and say no. I have a much better chance if I see you face to face. Can I come?'

The series would take nearly three consecutive months on location, away from family, friends and any other work. Whoever did it would have to clear their diary and be prepared to rough it. Michael was intrigued enough to see me, and over tea at his house he heard me out and became excited. Some months later I went to Victoria Station one Sunday morning to see him, Clem Vallence and Roger Mills, who was to make three of the programmes, off on their journey. They made the best ever television travel series and to this day I receive postcards from Michael or Roger Mills as they chronicle subsequent adventurous journeys.

The BBC had been very much a boys' club. Saying farewell to a retiring picture researcher who had joined the BBC in 1945, I discovered two stains on her record. As a young secretary she had been reprimanded because she 'joined in the general conversation in the office,' and was later seen formally by her personnel officer for having 'addressed radio correspondents by their Christian names'. Thanks in large part to the inheritance from Desmond Wilcox, my department had a cadre of excellent women producers, among them Jenny Barraclough, Angela Holdsworth, Patricia Houlihan, Ruth Jackson, Louise Panton and Ann Paul. The male bias in the make-up of BBC staff was rapidly changing in the face of talented women applicants, and among those I took on were Sue Bourne, Sarah Caplin, Nikki Cheetham, Elizabeth Clough, Molly Dineen, Sally Doganis, Belinda Giles, Olivia Lichtenstein, Anne Morrison and Jane Treays, all of whom have distinguished television careers.

The cry then and later was that there were few women in senior posts. This was true, but I was aware of the quality of women at other levels and knew that they would take their chances when their time came. In the 1980s they were producers, in the early 1990s editors, in the late 1990s heads of department and, as I write, BBC television is run by a triumvirate of women, with others in leading roles in commissioning and production, among them head of entertainment Jane Lush, once my PA. It should have happened sooner, but it is a battle won. Already, by the end of the 1980s, the entrants were overwhelmingly female. Of twenty-eight researchers in documentary features in 1988, an interesting bunch with diplomat, stuntwoman and ballet dancer among their former occupations, only four were male.

Nevertheless, I caused consternation when I started a cricket team, the BBC Mis-Hits (motto: 'Semper Dignus in Adversis'). It was soon reported to me that this was now believed to be the sole route for advancement. Women were excluded, naturally. Even when I ended the contract of our best fast bowler, suspicion of a blokeish conspiracy lingered.

Only twice did I come across the famous 'Christmas trees' in a BBC personnel file. These markings, a double arrow pointing upwards from a horizontal, indicated that the person concerned was deemed a security risk and should not be appointed without reference to the top. A shadowy figure in Broadcasting House acted as a link between the BBC and the Ministry of Defence, liasing over the Corporation's role in emergencies or war-time broadcasting and providing a channel for security clearances. The aim was to prevent the BBC being infiltrated. Until Alasdair Milne reduced the number of posts subject to this procedure, the vetting had reached far beyond senior posts and news and current affairs staff.

The first time I bumped into this was in the 1970s, when interviewing for attachees to presentation programmes. The personnel officer chairing the board announced that we could not appoint the next candidate, a video tape operator, whatever we thought of him. I asked why not and received a blurry reply. As it happened, he was quite unsuitable, but I pursued the matter afterwards. A more senior personnel officer told me: 'He has a "Christmas tree" because he is a member of the Communist party.' I laughed.

'But that's like being in a train-spotting club. If he'd been in some shady Trot splinter group, I could just about understand. Anyway, he could do plenty of harm where he is if anyone is serious about this.'

The next occasion was in the 1980s when I wanted to rehire someone who had left the BBC and was working in Fleet Street. I was sent his file with a note explaining the problem and there was the double upward arrow. I ignored the note and offered him a contract. He proved crucial to many of our most successful projects and is still working in the Corporation.

For several years in the 1980s I chaired the BBC's graduate television production training scheme. This took a dozen or more people each year, offered them a two-year contract, provided some basic technical training and gave them spells in three or four different departments, though it was up to them to apply for and get a job or contract. We tried to steer each of them towards a department in which they had a reasonable chance of success. Each year one or two fell away and one or two found only tenuous employment, but the great majority made it and some of the BBC's brightest talents were recruited on this scheme, among them Mark Thompson and Tim Gardam, as I write chief executive and director of programmes at Channel 4; Peter Salmon, controller of BBC1 and now controller of sport; Catherine Everett, head of interactive at the BBC; Anne Morrison, Alan Bookbinder, Peter Maniura and Laurence Rees, four of the BBC's creative leaders in television.

Over 2000 graduates applied each year, of which 200 would be interviewed. Before I chaired, I helped with the preliminary interviews. This was not altruism. It gave me a look at the incoming trainees and an edge in trying to lure one or two to the unfashionable presentation programmes when I was still there.

Some applicants tried too hard. 'I was snapped up by the university newspaper' was a hopeful boast. We noticed after several years that an awful lot of people were claiming to have been editor of *Varsity* at Cambridge or *Cherwell* at Oxford. On inquiry we discovered that, in the interests of the students' CVs, both papers now had three joint rather than a single editor each term, thereby tripling the number of those who could legitimately claim to have been 'editor'. 'At Oxford,' another hopeful began, 'I have steered clear of the traditional attention-grabbing ploys of union membership and university sport.' So, having rejected presidency of the union and a double blue, what was the private, self-effacing activity he chose instead? Acting. Was the young woman volunteering for the casting couch when she wrote: 'I hope to persuade you to give me a personal interview so that I can show that I have those aptitudes which cannot be listed or labelled.' Or did she just put it badly? We never knew.

We were offered more than enough about 'the challenge of the media' and 'the potency of the visual image'. Other applicants were way out of their depth. 'My zest for documentary programmes is breathtaking,' began one innocent. They listed their holidays, told us that 'Jimmy Greaves, Tony Hancock and the Beatles are my favourite people; kindness, humour and irreverence my favourite qualities,' or announced proudly, 'I am fire monitor for my end of the corridor' or lapsed into a stream of consciousness: 'I toyed with the idea of taking a pottery course but eventually (for practical rather than academic reasons) decided against.'

The interviews were run by a warm and friendly appointments officer called Barbara Todd. She always provided home-made flapjacks or short-bread that would be opened to 'oohs' and 'aahs' at coffee and tea times. At 12.45 p.m., after six interviews, she would announce, 'I think we have earned our lunch.' It was a tiring but pleasurable task to see so many bright, personable young men and women. They mostly sparkled. I warmed to the young chap who, having displayed limited knowledge of current pro-grammes, came clean. 'Look. The television is a mile and a half away in college. I have to tell you, it's not quite such a compulsive medium when it's a mile and a half away.' They all had to offer a programme idea, about which we gently questioned them. 'Who would be your presenter?' I asked one. 'The person I have in mind would be sort of halfway between David Attenborough and Desmond Morris,' he replied, adding mysteriously, 'Like, maybe, Jonathan Miller.'

Were we recruiting people like ourselves? We were aware of this danger and sought to aim off but I am not sure we succeeded at that time. Successful candidates were by no means all Oxbridge but, apart from a good balance between the sexes, we did not achieve diversity as we would define it today. Things improved later. We started a scheme specifically targeted at ethnic minorities and then, after a few years, rolled all into one.

Chapter nine
'TRANSMIT OR BE DAMNED'

Saturday, 27 July 1985 was a breezy day of sunshine and cloud, and Jane and I walked from Kew to Twickenham and back along the Thames. We saw off some American friends who had been staying. I watched Petoski pip Oh So Sharp to win the King George VI and Queen Elizabeth Stakes on television. Then the telephone rang. It was Keith Samuel from the press office: 'The *Sunday Times* is winding up the Northern Ireland story. They'll make a big play with it. It will probably lead the paper.'

The programme in question was a documentary in the *Real Lives* strand, called *At The Edge Of The Union*. It contrasted two hard line politicians in Londonderry: Martin McGuinness of Provisional Sinn Fein and Gregory Campbell of the Democratic Unionists, both elected members of the Northern Ireland Assembly. The original title for the programme had been *Elected Representatives*. The producer was the talented and ambitious Paul Hamann, who had made many programmes in the province about the army, about IRA bomb victims and other sensitive subjects. I had been told the previous day that the *Sunday Times* were after us. Mrs Thatcher was in the USA and, after the Arab hijack of a TWA plane in Beirut, had made a speech insisting that terrorists must be starved 'of the oxygen of publicity on which they depend'. A *Sunday Times* reporter lit the blue touch paper by asking her at a press conference what her reaction would be if a British television company were planning to interview a leading member of the IRA? She gave a vigorous response to this hypothetical question and the *Sunday Times* had its lead. Thus began a row that nearly brought the Corporation to its knees. I am pretty certain with hindsight that the newspaper was tipped off by a member of the production team, intent on stirring up some eye-catching controversy.

Paul Hamann had shown me the film in the cutting room a month before. It was a bleak reflection of the bitter struggle going on in councils throughout Northern Ireland between extreme loyalists and extreme republicans. I told Hamann that it was OK for transmission.

'But did you like it?' he asked eagerly.

'Like is not a word I would use about two bastards like that. I found it depressing. It's a good piece of work, though. Has Jimmy Hawthorne seen it yet?'

'Yes. Both he and Cecil Taylor have okayed it.'

Hawthorne was the BBC controller Northern Ireland and Taylor his deputy, who had been standing in while his boss was off sick. The BBC had strict rules about covering the province, at the heart of which was the need to keep the controller in Belfast informed from the outset and, for sensitive projects such as this, to secure his approval both to begin production and of the finished programme. The controller, the person on the ground, living with the daily pressures and intelligence, was the crucial figure for the BBC.

The sinisterly named News and Current Affairs Index, the BBC's editorial guidelines, also specified that 'Interviews with individuals who are deemed by ADG [the assistant director-general, responsible to the director-general for news and current affairs issues] to be closely associated with a terrorist organisation may not be sought or transmitted – two separate stages – without the prior permission of DG.' Back in March, Cecil Taylor advised Eddie Mirzoeff, the strand editor of *Real Lives*, that there was no need to refer the programme further. Later I had specifically asked if Campbell and McGuinness fell into the category that needed to be referred to the director-general. Advice from Northern Ireland said not. When a newspaper article alleged that McGuinness was chief of staff of the IRA, a claim also made in the film by Campbell, I checked again that Alan Protheroe, the assistant director-general, known as 'The Colonel', was aware of the programme. Yes, Cecil Taylor had informed him. For several months the film had been included, with names of the participants, in the list of programmes in production, the 'target' list.

I labour this because of the way events unfolded. The weekend that the story broke, Alasdair Milne, the director-general, was away on holiday in Scandinavia, knowing nothing of the programme. Had he been told about it earlier, I am sure that it would have been transmitted, unaltered and as planned, but he might have alerted the chairman and the BBC might have avoided the damaging impression the programme had sneaked up on it. This could have averted the constitutional crisis that developed. At the time and in the immediate aftermath I was racked with self-recrimination. Why did I not alert Protheroe myself? I had referred another possible Northern Ireland story to him in this period. How could I have omitted to mention the Derry film? I believed that it was all under control, no big deal and that he was already aware of it. Why did BBC Northern Ireland advise as it did? Possibly because it wanted to demonstrate that men such as Campbell and McGuinness were a regular part of output in the province, and if the people of Northern Ireland were used to this, the people on the mainland ought to get a face full of it too. Possibly chests were puffing out to emphasize that this was their patch and they were quite capable, thank you very much. There was also the ambiguity over McGuinness' position. He might well be IRA, but he and Campbell were both eligible for a salary from the British taxpayer as elected representatives. It was in this capacity that he was included in the programme and in this capacity that he was featured in local programmes. The BBC rule had been introduced to cover interviews with avowed terrorists, men in balaclavas and so on, not local politicians. For whatever reason, the programme was not pushed at Protheroe. Even if it had been, it is quite likely that he would have taken the same relaxed attitude to it that almost everyone else who was to see it did.

That Saturday, Michael Grade, controller of BBC1 to whom I had given a cassette, rang in the early evening to say that he thought the programme was fine. We would wait to see how the *Sunday Times* looked the following morning. It looked lousy. We devised a plan to show the film to the press in Broadcasting House that afternoon. Paul Hamann and I would go in to introduce it and answer questions. The previewers, who had seen tapes a couple of weeks early, had written quietly about the programme. If we let more journalists see it, so we reasoned, they would describe how uninflammatory the film was and we might quieten things down. Not a chance. The tabloids went to town.

When Bill Cotton rang me in the office on that Monday morning and simply read out the passage quoted above from the News and Current Affairs Index, I felt that a lorry load of ordure was heading my way. Hints from the press office indicated that I was standing in the middle of the road. Then things moved swiftly. I spent much of the morning establishing a clear, agreed narrative of what had happened and when. The board of management met, saw the programme and planned to advise the governors at a special meeting, called for the morrow, that the film should go out with a following discussion. By the time I attended a reception at television centre for Chief Buthelezi, the talk was all of the hand grenade lobbed by the Home Secretary, Leon Brittan. Seeking to please his boss, as it seemed at the time, or simply acting precipitously, governing without due care and attention, he asked Stuart Young, chairman of the BBC, not to let the programme go out. Brittan followed his telephone call with a letter. Reading it now, it is shameful in its hectoring tone and the simple-minded assumptions about the affect that a programme he had not seen would have on the public. Brittan asserted that the very existence of a programme about McGuinness would 'boost the morale of the terrorists' and 'give succour to terrorist organizations'. 'Even if the programme and any surrounding material were, as a whole, to present terrorist organizations in a wholly unfavourable light, I would still ask you not to permit it to be broadcast.' The most generous verdict one can offer is that the tensions of being responsible for both security and broadcasting got the better of Brittan.

On the morning of the specially convened governors' meeting *The Times*, *Telegraph* and the *Guardian* all called on them to take no notice of Brittan, who, in effect, should either ban Sinn Fein or pipe down. It was a long day. In the late afternoon I was summoned over to Television Centre, where I waited with the two channel controllers, Michael Grade and Graeme MacDonald, for Bill Cotton and Brian Wenham to return from seeing the governors in Broadcasting House. The governors had two decisions to make:

whether or not to see the film, and whether or not it should be transmitted. They got them both wrong. At 6.30 p.m. Queenie, Bill's PA, came in. 'They're on their way back. The decision has gone against us.' Bill returned to give us a blow-by-blow account. 'Stuart was confident the meeting would go easily; the newspapers would help . . . The trouble is, with Rees-Mogg in the lead, they've been dying to see a programme ahead of transmission, looking for a chance, and here it was . . . two said "Don't", but were pretty well on their own . . . When they saw it, they hated it . . . They watched it together. There were little intakes of breath and head shakes and glances . . . Only a couple were for showing it.' Stuart Young, who was ill, had let the meeting get away from him, said Bill. The three of us watched the Channel 4 news coverage, then Bill applied his preferred balm for any wound: a Chinese meal at his current favourite haunt in Holland Road. 'Whatever anyone had done beforehand, once the *Sunday Times* trapped Mrs Thatcher into her comments, we would have been in exactly the same position,' said Bill as we returned to his office to watch *Newsnight*.

Something momentous had happened. The board of governors had over-ruled the board of management on an editorial matter at the prompting of the government. The line between this and overt government censorship was a fine one. Programme makers throughout the BBC and beyond were rightly angry. The programme review meeting on Wednesday morning was tense. Bill handled it marvellously, his warmth and common sense holding the place together. I made the point that Paul Hamann had conducted himself with discretion and some dignity in difficult circumstances. I knew he was feeling low and sent him and his wife a bottle of champagne. I was due to go on holiday for two weeks, fortunately, in England. I discussed it with Brian and Bill, who said to go. Alasdair would not be back until the weekend. They would regroup then.

I left on the Thursday evening, calling Tim Slessor twice a day over the weekend as we monitored the press and developments. As it happened, we had to take our little dog to a vet in Exeter. We found a Mr Shattock, the Mr Shattock whose wife had been killed by terrorists in the Brighton bombing.

I returned to London on the Monday. There was a cheerful augury. This was the week the BBC was finally transmitting *The War Game*, a drama documentary on what might happen after a nuclear attack on Britain, banned since it had been made exactly twenty years before. Hopes were rising. The governors were to meet again on Tuesday, 6 August. Alasdair was back, had seen the programme, thought it was a good one and wondered what the fuss was about. The serious papers had pronounced on it in similar vein. In the *Sunday Telegraph* Sebastian Faulks wrote: 'Its technique was to allow the subjects to express themselves at length without the insistent questioning which would be the norm in a news or current affairs programme. In this sense it did give a "platform" to terrorists, though it was a platform with rope and trap-door.' The *Daily Telegraph* called it 'carefully made, well balanced and well-crafted . . . succeeds in conveying the frightening depth of emotional commitment to the opposing causes.' David Watt in *The Times*:

'you have to take a totally contemptuous view of the public's intelligence and decency to believe that it would do serious damage to the national interest. The "publicity" which it gives to the IRA, for example, and to which the Home Secretary takes exception, is wholly bad. To anyone who is not already a supporter, Martin McGuinness is clearly identified in the programme as a thuggish fanatic.' *The Economist* described the programme as 'averagely well-made, unremarkable . . .'.

A compromise looked likely: one or two additions to the film and a discussion after. 'The upshot of today,' said Brian Wenham on the phone first thing, 'could be that Rees-Mogg resigns, which is an outcome devoutly to be wished.' This optimism drained as the day wore on. We expected a decision by lunchtime. It was not till 4.30 p.m. that the chairman issued a statement that affirmed 'the Board considered the programme flawed in its present state and, even if amended, unsuitable for viewing in the prevailing atmosphere'. It made great play of 'the failure to observe the detailed guidelines at the highest level'. In the strained circumstances of the day I was convinced this was aimed at me. Bill Cotton rang. I said, 'Bill, I have to go now one way or another.'

'Don't think of it.'

'They'll want a head to roll.'

'They didn't seem to want that. In any case, my friend, they would be looking for a more highly paid one than yours.' A moment or two later Alan Protheroe called.

'Sit tight.' Bill Cotton's voice was hushed and tense. 'It's not Armageddon yet. Don't do anything. There are great issues at stake.' His melodramatic tone made me laugh as I regaled what he had said to those with me, Paul Hamann, Brian Elliott and the ever supportive Tim Slessor, whose dander was now well and truly up about the whole business. I rang Jane at home with the news and then took the typed statement into the crowded *Crimewatch* office where the department had gathered. As I went in, they were passing a motion of support for me, which also called on me not to resign.

I read out the statement in full, and then urged them to be calm while we waited for a board of management response. 'I don't have to tell you that this is a black day for the BBC. Our enemies would love us to make some wild gesture. They would relish the chance to point gleefully at a rabble, so they could say, "Look. This is the gang who made this programme. They can't be trusted. They're out of control." Don't give them that chance. Thanks for your support. It's terrific and I'm very grateful. By the way, though, I'm the one who is supposed to raise the issue of resignation, not you.' Much laughter. I went back to my office and rang Aubrey Singer, who had extracted a famously good deal out of the Corporation when he was tipped overboard.

'Aubrey, I might need the assistance of a tough lawyer. Could you give me the name of the one you used?'

'The governors are mad, quite mad.'

'The lawyer's name?'

'I warn you, he is very, very expensive.' I took down the name and number.

A strike had been called for the next day, 7 August, the day that *At The Edge Of The Union* should have been transmitted. When we met at Television Centre to decide what management should do, there was a feeling that the television service was at one. Bill was positive and encouraging, but he was fond of Stuart Young and moaned again about Rees-Mogg. 'He doesn't behave like a vice-chairman, he's more like the leader of the opposition.' I walked back to Kensington House with Alan Yentob, the head of music and arts, to find that Heather and Tracey in my office had stayed on 'to see if we still have a boss'. Tim Slessor, in a typical gesture, insisted on taking me out to dinner.

On the day of the strike I walked to Television Centre and chatted with the staff demonstrating outside, before going in for the programme review, which Alasdair came to brief. He was firm, practical and in his best 'no fuss' mode. We let him know that we wanted the board of management to emphasize its distance from the governors' decision. As we broke up, many colleagues came to commiserate and wish me well. They were a touch over solicitous for my taste. 'I hope that you are not saying goodbye,' I said.

Nothing could change before the governors met next on 5 September. I returned to the West Country and kept in touch by phone. The staff held further meetings but things slowly quietened down. My biggest worry was during the following weekend. Chris Serle was skippering a boat in the Fastnet Race for *In At The Deep End*. A gale blew up, several boats were wrecked and crewmembers drowned. I feared for his safety and had a bad night before I learned that Serle had put into Dartmouth and, like many other competitors, retired from the race.

When I returned to London, the question was how quickly could we get the film out. Alasdair seemed to promise soon; the governors had intimated not before the end of the year. The formal position was still that the board of management believed there should be some changes to the film 'for greater clarity'. Alasdair indicated to me that he expected only minimal changes. We added thirteen seconds of archive film of the aftermath of an IRA bomb and changed two of the captions. I rang the assistant director-general to check them with him. 'Oh, no,' said Protheroe. 'There is no need to do that. You just change them.'

'I don't want to have to go back to the film for another nibble,' I replied. 'I want to check the wording with you before we touch the print.'

'I don't want to back away from this or anything.'

'Then let me read them to you.' He did, and approved the changes.

Alasdair agreed to see a group of programme heads. We wanted him to know the strength of feeling against the governors' actions. We debated beforehand how best we could bring pressure to change the decision. One or two were strong for giving the director-general our written resignations. If he went in with these and the resignations of board of management in his pocket, he would have a powerful weapon – only if the governors were aware of this, for he would not want to detonate it.

Michael Grade and I favoured an outside broker who would carry influence. To this end I made contact with Sir Michael Swann, former chairman of the BBC, who promised he would ring some governors, and possibly Stuart Young, to urge them to reverse their decision. I rang Huw Wheldon, whose first response was 'I want to stay out of this', but then said he would try to help.

Alasdair saw us in the antiseptic office kept as a pied-à-terre for him at Television Centre. We sat in an arc facing his empty desk. He was in bouncy mood, made a joke or two and, it being 4.30 in the afternoon, made sure we all had a glass of white wine. Yes, he knew how people felt. 'Do you give me no intelligence at all?' We told him that the staff had collected money for an advertisement headed TRANSMIT OR BE DAMNED, which they intended to place in *The Times*. We did not think this would help and might be able to delay it if there was a likelihood of a change of mind on 5 September. He thought that was possible but could not promise it. The next day Michael Grade, Alan Yentob and I saw the committee behind the ad, which included Jeremy Paxman and was chaired by Ritchie Cogan, a thoughtful and incredibly hard working executive producer in my department. We put our case and, while they went off to take stock, chewed over the situation the BBC was in. 'Of course, Alasdair will have to go,' said Michael, 'but not till after the Peacock Report.' Who should replace him? What about Jeremy Isaacs? 'No fear,' said Michael of the man he was to replace at Channel 4, 'he would be a disaster. He's got no administrative ability and is full of crazy ideas.' Ritchie Cogan, who was impressive throughout the *Real Lives* saga, came back to agree a delay.

By the week of the board meeting the BBC had received 614 letters against showing the programme, 473 in favour and 560 in appreciation of the music that had replaced programmes on the strike day. The day before the meeting Paul Hamann and I went to Alasdair's office to show him the changes so he could say that he had seen them. We were with him for five minutes. On the day itself I was at the launch of our big series *Soldiers* at the Army Museum. I had introduced the viewing and we were three minutes into the first programme when I was called to the telephone. It was Bill Cotton: 'The *Real Lives* thing is resolved. Can you get back as soon as possible?' I dashed out and found a taxi. The statement was better than expected. There was, in passing, an elbow in the management's eye with mention of the 'full system of reference' not working, but the rest read like a climb down. The 'amendments originally required by the board of management' had been made and 'the general climate is such that an early showing of the programme is acceptable'. It would go out in October. The madness was over.

I rang Paul, Eddie and Ritchie to read each the statement. 'Just say, "I'm delighted that the film is going out" when the press call you. The two boards have agreed to give no interviews.' Unknown to me, Ritchie Cogan had just been on BBC radio. So, Bill Cotton rang me later, only slightly irritated.

'I've got the Chairman bugging me about why he is not allowed on the air but our friend Ritchie Cogan is. Remind me, which one is Cogan? Doesn't he do any work?'

'Whatever you could accuse Ritchie of, it is not idleness,' I said. 'He produced *Drugwatch*.' Bill chuckled. 'And he was the originating producer of *Crimewatch*,' I added.

'Oh,' said Bill, laughing. 'He's good. He's bloody good. Try to calm him down.'

Then Alasdair rang. 'Look, Will, I never told the governors what changes I'd asked for, that they were minimal. So it's a touch embarrassing to have them outlined on the air by a member of staff. No more, please.'

When *At The Edge Of The Union* went out on 16 October it was but a small earthquake. Audience Research reported that 78 per cent of those who saw it were not surprised by any of the revelations in the programme. Both Campbell and McGuinness rang Hamann to say each had come out of it better than the other.

The BBC's editorial procedures were clearly imperfect. They had grown up on the principle of 'reference up'. If you were unsure what to do or operating in certain defined territories, you should consult your boss: the programme editor, head of department, channel controller, managing director or director-general, as the case may be. It was a common law system. Experience, case histories and folk wisdom developed so that, with a largely permanent staff, editorial understanding was 'in the woodwork'. It was only with the News and Current Affairs Index that there arrived an easy to use, written codification of the guidelines, and then not comprehensive. One or two rules existed, such as with Northern Ireland, but the policy was, and remains, that guidelines are more practical and helpful than rules. They offer a way of approaching editorial decisions. This enables producers to confront circumstances or issues new to them by applying principles, whereas rules may remain silent in the face of something outside of previous experience or, even, box you unhelpfully in.

Alongside the 'woodwork' way of thinking I sensed a studied casualness about editorial intervention by executives. The programme editors ruled. They knew what should be done and should be left to get on with it. To intervene could be seen as heavy handed, even censorious. Stretching back to its earliest days, the first *Tonight* programme, there remained in some quarters of the current affairs department cavalier, even arrogant, behaviour towards the people programmes dealt with. Alongside this was an 'OK, try me' attitude towards organizations. Complaints were to be seen off. Libels? They wouldn't dare. There were few worse sins for a boss than to admit that a libel suit might be difficult to defend. The BBC's size and independence enabled it to tackle big issues and powerful interests, and it had an honourable history of doing so. They could also provide a shield to poor practice.

Current affairs, based in the Lime Grove Studios where Alfred Hitchcock had once directed, was a cock of the walk culture. The production teams operated at the sharp end of the BBC: *Panorama, Tonight, Twenty-Four Hours*, the General Election, the American Elections. They attracted some of the brightest and best of their generation; they had money; they travelled the world. They worked with great television journalists, Robin Day, Robert Kee, Ludovic Kennedy, Charles Wheeler, and developed more, David Dimbleby, Tom Mangold, Jeremy Paxman, Julian Pettifer, Peter Snow and Peter Taylor. Some producers, like Tom Bower and Michael Cockerell, became outstanding reporters. Current affairs folk saw themselves as the guards, paratroopers and commandos of the BBC. They looked upon news, an even more important part of the organization, as the poor bloody infantry. When, eventually, the two operations were brought together, the number two in news joined the Lime Grove editors for lunch. 'Don't worry, Tony,' he was told. 'We'll help you with the long words.'

The very number of factual programmes from all round the BBC was a problem in itself. There were clashes and overlaps and it was difficult to keep track of impending fireworks. When he became director of programmes, Brian Wenham introduced the monthly 'target' meeting, at which all factual programme making departments were represented. This scrutinized a list of everything in production in order to avoid duplication and identify likely problems. He would marvel at the vast number of documentaries, features and magazine programmes, affecting to be shocked that the schedules contained so many. However, Brian let the routine slip. When the *Real Lives* bomb exploded, there had not been a target meeting since the beginning of the year.

The 1980s was a time when the BBC was regularly accused of bias by both ends of the political spectrum. For the left, the Glasgow Media Group had established a reputation for bringing a new rigour to scrutiny of television. It claimed to identify implicit as well as explicit messages and saw the BBC as biased towards the status quo. Such was the prevalence of their attacks and the force of their arguments that I used to keep a list of recent programmes that investigated the government view or challenged the accepted wisdom, so that I had ammo to hand for interviews.

The right learned from the Glasgow group and became skilful in their critiques. Were they justified in believing that the BBC was a den of lefties? Not if put like that. There were no conspiracies or co-ordinated campaigns. It was the case that most people in production were of the centre or soft left. When talking to groups of staff, I would often ask what newspaper they took at home in the sure knowledge that, for 90 per cent, the answer would be the *Guardian* or *Independent*. As long as they read the remainder at work, knew whose were the other interesting voices and ideas, this did not matter. As long, too, as there were people around to make sure that in choice of subject and in selection of contributors programme makers aimed off, to compensate for or disguise their own views. In fact, some of the toughest, most questioning of producers and editors I knew were more of the right than the left. What politicians found it difficult to understand was that these jobs attracted not a bias but a temperament, the awkward squad.

At the height of the Tory attacks on the BBC for being biased to the left, the regular surveys of public opinion showed that about a third of the public believed that the BBC was biased. Of them, three-quarters believed it was biased to towards the right, for the BBC was in many people's eyes part of the establishment. Still, one did catch the odd, worrying flash of something dangerous. Dropping into an office one afternoon, I interrupted a debate about who should take part in a programme. They were looking for a strong woman. I mentioned Ann Leslie, who had just written a brilliantly critical piece about the Greenham Common women. 'What, that fascist?' snapped the female researcher. It would have warmed Norman Tebbit's heart to hear his suspicions confirmed. Mostly, such overt partisanship as one encountered was about social issues. Producers would often argue for more personal view programmes that put up a controversial case without any 'on the other hands'. But the cases they wanted to put were always good, liberal causes. Nothing wicked in that, but the BBC was granted money and airwaves in return for offering a rounded and overall impartial picture. I said I would believe in such a series when someone proposed a programme in favour of capital punishment; after all, there was probably a majority of the population in favour of it. I have yet to see that programme.

As editorial decisions went, the *Real Lives* programme was a clear one. Northern Ireland was a stroll in the park compared to dealing with the BBC in its corporate majesty. When I took over documentary features, I was entrusted with one of the BBC's precious things of the shop, the televised Dimbleby Lecture. This was given annually in memory of Richard Dimbleby, the outstanding broadcaster of his generation (father of David and Jonathan) who had died from cancer at the age of 52. It was the chairman who formally issued the invitation on behalf of the board of governors. The producer for the first ten years, Eddie Mirzoeff, was responsible for proposing a suitable lecturer, ensuring that this person, when invited, would accept, and making sure that the lecturer had something interesting and preferably attention catching to say. This was not a simple task. Eddie thought Roy Jenkins' draft too boring and it was only in the rewrite that he requested Jenkins lay out the ideas for the SDP. Arnold Goodman had refused to write a script and lost his way on air.

In my first year Eddie approached Isaiah Berlin, who declined but was happy to discuss other names that might be suitable. It was a matter of later dispute as to whether Berlin came up with the name of E.P. Thompson or merely warmed to it. The left-wing historian Thompson, author of *The Making of the English Working-Class*, was a figure in the land as a leader of the nuclear disarmament movement. Eddie approached him. He would do it, if asked, and volunteered a sketch of his subject, the Cold War. I told Alasdair Milne, managing director of television, who agreed it with the chairman. When Ian Trethowan, the director-general, heard, he blew up. The message came down that this would be 'deeply damaging to NATO' and Thompson was not acceptable. When he heard there was to be no invitation to speak, Thompson and his supporters cried 'censorship' and went public, creating a brief storm.

Eddie and I had to turn over for take two. He proposed Edward Heath and with the utmost caution, inquired: 'Would he, if invited . . .?' He would, his subject the gap between rich and poor nations. Another problem. Trethowan vetoed Heath as well, on the grounds that he was a close friend. Needing no lessons from Thompson, Heath also cried 'censorship', his enmity for Mrs Thatcher cited as the cause. By now you could buy 'I have not been asked to give the Dimbleby Lecture' badges. We struck camp for a while in order to try again in calmer days, when we secured Dr Garrett Fitzgerald, the Irish prime minister, who fitted the brief: a public figure with something to say on a topic of current public interest, but who gabbled his delivery, thereby reducing his impact.

I had learned that this was no ordinary programme. As Eddie Mirzoeff put it in a note, 'everyone in the BBC with initials after their name thinks they have the right to interfere'. The difficulty went back to the origin of the lecture as something in the governors' gift, thereby confusing the normal editorial prerogatives. I instituted a new procedure, by which we put up three names in order of preference. If this was ticked, we could then go about our usual business. It worked for the first year and we went with our first choice, Peter Parker, then running British Rail. The following year the governors suggested we invite George Thomas, the retiring Speaker, ahead of David Sheppard, Bishop of Liverpool. Neither the producer, now Jeremy Bennett, nor I wanted Thomas, a monumental old bore, so I made a song and dance about 'exercising our production judgement' and Sheppard it was.

At least as sensitive were the social arrangements. The production office drew up the guest list, which included the lecturer's guests, but the invitation came from the chairman, so he had to approve and add guests of his own. All this and the director-general, the Dimbleby family and the secretariat had to be kept happy. And then there was the question of who was to sit where, highly sensitive when there were to be shots of the audience. Not a year went by without a tantrum.

When the BBC chain of command operated as it should, documentary features tackled many contentious subjects with only limited hassle: investigations into President Marcos' illegally acquired fortune, the Allies' recruitment of Nazi scientists after the war, whether Marilyn Monroe's death was suicide or murder, the possible existence of living American prisoners in Vietnam and the bombing of Libya. George Carey, a former *Panorama* editor I had brought over from current affairs, was instrumental in developing and seeing through many of these, and we also launched the first *Prisoners of Conscience* season, commissioned Peter Taylor's *Families At War* and kicked off Brian Lapping's extraordinary contemporary histories with *The Second Russian Revolution*.

Crimewatch offered some interesting dilemmas. In 1983 Ritchie Cogan brought me a cassette of a German programme that reconstructed crimes and asked viewers to phone in with information to police officers in the studio. He wondered if we could launch a British version. When I had seen it, I said we could, but we needed to set ourselves some rules for the reconstructions, for the German programme re-enacted a rape as seen from the rapist's point of view. The team worked out some principles, one of which was to use real life witnesses wherever possible, otherwise casting look-alike actors. I suggested a title, *Crimewatch UK,* and found some money for a pilot. The team began lengthy negotiations with the police, who were sceptical that the programme would be of any value. Peter Chafer, the programme editor, and I went to see Peter Imbert, chief constable of the Thames Valley Police, who led support for us among the chief constables. The first live programme narrowly made it to the air (there was industrial trouble) on 7 June 1984.

It was a success with the audience from the start and within a few months was the top-rated BBC programme. I was aware, though, that we could not justify its presence on air unless it led to convictions. It did. Slowly, the Met and other reluctant police forces came on board. Among the reasons that the programme was successful was that it acted as a bulletin board for the police. Officers from one part of the country would recognize faces or trademark techniques from crimes committed in counties far away. Often, too, the programme would trigger information from the underworld.

Crimewatch provoked fierce debate both within the department and within BBC television as a whole. Interestingly, the unit making it was also responsible for *Out of Court,* which was more often than not critical of judicial procedures and the police, and *Rough Justice,* which investigated possible miscarriages of justice. This meant that the programme makers had wrangled out for themselves the arguments about whether the BBC should act as coppers' narks, whether and how it was justified to cross a line from reporter to campaigner and what sort of crimes should be featured. I never had much difficulty with the fact that we helped catch criminals and nor did the public. On one happy occasion a man was actually arrested while watching the end of the programme. His landlady had quietly rung the police.

Life was full of surprises. I was summoned out of the hairdressers to a call from an agitated channel controller. 'Will, MI5 have been on the phone complaining that someone is filming their premises, wherever they may be.'

'Good luck to whoever it is, but it's not us.' Tour operators complained about the *Holiday* programme and so did the town of Scarborough, when a short item was unkind about the weather. The manager of a large hotel wrote to George Howard, then the BBC's chairman, to say that all leaflets and posters for Castle Howard, his house, had been consigned to the dustbin, where they would remain until the Corporation apologized. The town clerk enclosed with his official complaint the town's holiday brochure. The producer briefed the chairman's office with his discovery that the sun-kissed bikini girl who beckoned us to Scarborough on the cover had actually picked up her tan in Spain. The chairman was a bit of an expert on pretty girls. I later learned from one in a position to know that he twice had them provided at the BBC's expense, and when warned about this, his response had been, in effect or verbatim: 'Fuck off. I'm an old man. I'm going to die soon and if the BBC doesn't like it, too bad.'

Many tricky decisions concerned matters of taste. Within days of arriving in Kensington House I was roped in to see the rough-cut of a film about cosmetic surgery. It could have been the London chainsaw massacre. Sequences of bloody slicing followed sequences of gaping flesh. As I watch any operation on television through my fingers, I found this something of a baptism by gore. Some questions were clear-cut. We embarked on a big programme for BBC1, called *Black*, investigating racial prejudice in Britain. A few days after beginning work, the producer, Hugh Purcell, came to see me: 'We need a bit of extra money because we want to carry out some research.'

'Into what?' I asked.

'Nick Ross [who was the presenter] believes that the underlying cause of prejudice against black people is sexual jealousy.'

'So?'

'The reason is that white men fear that blacks have bigger pricks. He thinks we should find out if this has any basis in fact by conducting a survey into comparing the size of white and black men's sexual organs,' said Hugh.

'I don't,' I replied. 'Think again.'

In the early runs of *Forty Minutes*, Roger Mills pushed at the boundaries of subject matter with films on skinheads, rent boys, male strippers (then a novel subject), Hell's Angels and animal rights protestors. The style of filming, 'studied neutrality' according to some, threw up difficult issues. No reporter tidied up the story. How much could you leave to the viewers to form their own judgements? Was it enough to rely on implicit rather than explicit messages? We had torrid debates at programme review, with Colin Morris, head of religious programmes, usually leading for the opposition. 'Voyeuristic', 'brutalizing' and 'pornographic' were among the words on the charge sheet. I argued that if colleagues were depressed or revolted by the lifestyle portrayed, was that not also the likely response of other viewers? There had long been a tendency for documentaries on social problems to conclude on an upbeat note, pointing to some new experiment or a public inquiry that would provide solutions. Mostly, this was not how life was. Bleakness was sometimes as proper an aspect of truthful portrayal.

Issues of taste varied in their intensity. Was it right to include a programme on mistresses in a series which went out on a Sunday evening? This sounds rather quaint now. Female circumcision does not. One Saturday morning in February 1983 Brian Wenham rang me at home. 'I'm just watching the tape you sent me. It's strong stuff. I have a problem with it.' Louise Panton, with an all woman crew, had made a powerful programme which proved, by depicting it, that the practise of female circumcision was an agonizing and horrific operation and that it was going on in the Sudan not just in rural areas among 'backward' people, but in modern hospitals. It was a tough watch but I had seen it and approved. Brian put his thoughts in writing:

> I find it <u>too</u> gruelling . . . I then sense 'prurience' . . . What in terms of <u>essential</u> information do they [shots] give me, that the earlier drawings do not give? . . . I am sufficiently fussed to call in aid both CBBC2 and MD Tel. I think we have a problem in your handling of what Anna Ford rightly called 'a ticklish subject'.

We met to debate the case. Brian and Aubrey Singer wanted the shots of female genitalia cut out. I said that we must not postpone transmission. Louise was passionate that the cruelty of the practice must not be sanitized. She found a way, using freeze frames with the sound of the victims' screams, to leave viewers in no doubt about the horror and yet show no genitalia. The programme retained its capacity to shock and to spur action against the practice.

I agonized more about the effects on participants, especially children, of being in our programmes. One buffer was time. It could be a year or more before material reached the screen. Life had moved on for those involved and they had had time to prepare, to talk through and to forewarn. Even so, I made cuts in the comprehensive school series to protect some of the pupils. A *Forty Minutes* on divorce was a sad, pertinent film that revealed the pain for all concerned. It provided understanding and insight. But there was an unhappy young son who was seen in one sequence breaking down as he told his father that he did not want to see him. Again, there was heartfelt debate when we reviewed the programme. Some were adamant that the scene should not have been shown; some that the moment of transgression was in the very act of filming it. The boy, the mother, the father and the welfare officer had all seen the film separately and were content. The actions filmed had taken place a while ago. I hoped, and from my inquiries about the circumstances and subsequent events, believed that the film had caused no harm. But I do not forget the image of the crying child.

The series I lost more sleep over than anything else in my time at the BBC was called *A Gentle Way With Cancer*. It followed some patients at the Bristol Cancer Help Clinic, which offered dietary (masses of chopped vegetables) and other alternative therapies to cancer sufferers in what it called an 'holistic' approach. The production team was open to the centre's methods and was, naturally, sympathetic to the patients. The series had to avoid promoting an unproven approach, discouraging sufferers from undergoing orthodox treatments and – the long-time risk of programmes on cancer – offering false hope. Although there was little overt scepticism in the films, they tried to skirt these dangers. It was our job to document such experiments, but I was allergic to flaky 'mind, body and spirit' activities, and the doctor who ran the place gave me the creeps.

My difficulties were made worse by Aubrey Singer, the managing director, getting in a bigger flap than I was. His history in the science department had left him highly sensitive to the medical world, especially with programmes about cancer. He rang me repeatedly before and during the run, blustering and threatening, 'I'm telling you that you'd better be right with this one,

Will. This could explode.' I talked the series over with the current head of science who was encouraging. I stayed close to the production team, going through the commentary to prevent it from being too wide-eyed. The Prince of Wales chipped in to help when he gave a speech in support of alternative therapies. The programmes went out to decent, and utterly unhysterical, interest.

It was possible to mount overtly campaigning programmes in one or two carefully chosen fields. In a way the BBC's appeals on behalf of charities were of this order. A committee of external advisers chose the beneficiaries of them, but Children In Need was the BBC's own charity. It had first appeared on radio in 1927, and in the year before I took over at documentary features it had mounted its first television spectacular. The spectacle had been limited. The show was decided upon late in the day, staged at a hotel near Television Centre and had been chaotic. Too many stars had been booked and not all got on the air, to the irritation of them and their agents. All this was spelled out to me by Bill Cotton, controller of BBC1, who said, in effect, 'Sort it.' I spent a lot of time with the producer, Mark Patterson, and we planned how to run the programme, again with Terry Wogan as the chief presenter. The next was a much better show and, with each succeeding year, the quality of the programme improved and more money was raised. I persuaded a wary light entertainment department to help. More stars joined in.

Over the next decade Mark Patterson did more than anyone else to raise the profile of Children in Need and put it on a sound footing. The sums of money raised on the night grew from just over half a million to more than 17 million in 1989. Much more would arrive over the next two or three months and the mechanism for distributing it was increasingly stretched. Children in Need gave its money in many small grants and by the mid-1980s each regional committee was making dozens of decisions every hour at its meetings. The trustees, of whom I was now one, lived in fear of a catastrophic mistake or fraud. We were lucky that, to my knowledge, there never was a serious mistake. We recruited a professional, Julia Kaufman, to run the fundraising and distribution, with Mark Patterson producing the programme. Terry Wogan has been with it throughout. In the 1990s I had to head off a move for someone trendier. The trouble with trendy is that today's new look can become tomorrow's wide lapels, with presenters even tomorrow's named and shamed.

Esther Rantzen returned to Kensington House to make *Drugwatch*, a one-off programme about the dangers of drug taking. There were some frosty looks along the corridor, and Esther blanked both Tim Slessor and Peter Bazalgette, whom she cast respectively as Casca and Metellus Cimber in the historical drama 'The Assassination of Desmond Wilcox'. *Drugwatch*, which originated in a *That's Life* survey, struck a chord. Michael Grade launched it with panache; Jimmy Savile brought Princess Diana to the studio to sign a 'Just Say No' pledge; forty-five sacks of mail arrived in the next week.

We followed up with another subject that Esther had been working on: child abuse. Again, Ritchie Cogan produced. Again, *That's Life* asked viewers for their experiences. Letters poured in. The researchers reading them found it hard, and when Esther showed me some, I could see why. They were from grown-up, in some cases elderly, women, who wrote vividly about things that had happened in their childhood. The pain, guilt and suffering remained with them decades later. The letters were heartbreaking. Over and over they described how the little girl had tried to tell a friend, a neighbour, a teacher about what was being done to them, but how they were not believed or listened to.

As the team worked on the programme over the summer, Esther demonstrated her right to be an early order batsman in the all time first eleven of operators. A programme would raise awareness of this problem, but she was determined to instigate action. She chaired a conference of agencies dealing with children; she corralled Ministers; she persuaded BT to provide free premises and a simple telephone number; and she raised money. The result was that the charity ChildLine, providing a free counselling line for children, was ready to be launched on the day of the television programme, *Childwatch*. The impact was enormous. Until then, few had understood the scale of the problem of child abuse, that it took place in well-off suburban homes as well as in isolated cottages, that it left not a passing embarrassment but a lifelong pain, often rendering the victims incapable of establishing healthy sexual relationships. In time, some simple-minded obsessives caused untold harm by imagining abuse where it did not exist. This was wicked but cannot be laid at *Childwatch*'s door. And it must be weighed against the tens of thousands of children helped by ChildLine and the thousands more protected from such harm by precautions put in place since Esther Rantzen and her team brought this subject into the open.

Such were the waves caused by ChildLine and such were the skills of those who created it that Mrs Thatcher held a reception for it at Downing Street at the end of its first year. The Prime Minister, in her elegant welcome, spoke warmly about ChildLine and thanked anyone and everyone who had made any contribution to its creation, but she could not bring herself to mention, let alone thank, the BBC. You could not help but think less of her for such mean spiritedness. A very nervous Esther then spoke and made good this omission with some generosity. At one point I suddenly found myself facing the back of the Prime Minister's neck, and very soft and inviting it was too. I was in two minds about leaning forward and giving it a peck but good sense prevailed. A few years later Mrs Thatcher visited the ChildLine offices. Valerie Howarth, the director, told her that the only quiet time for calls was between 5.30 and 6.00 p.m., when *Neighbours* was on. 'That's the Australian one, isn't it? Escapism, you see. Now, could you get a message about this into something like that?' I told her about the other things that the BBC had done.

'Could you teach parenting skills in schools?' asked Esther.

'We looked at it when I was at Education. They're just not interested until they have children.' Then she was off into how she was taught domestic science. 'I can put a patch on and all that sort of thing.' She stayed for well over two hours, was genuinely engaged and left a personal cheque for a decent sum.

Female circumcision and *Crimewatch* apart, there were few instances of violence in programmes from documentary features. Yet violence was a subject in which I developed an eye-catching novelty act in the 1980s. Concern about violence on television was not new – the BBC had introduced its first special guidelines at the end of the 1970s – but there was rising anxiety and a consequent increase in noise levels. The genuine worries of parents, politicians, journalists and broadcasters were accompanied by opportunist hoo-ha and scare-mongering. Early in 1983 Aubrey Singer asked me to chair a group to review and revise the existing guidelines.

We aimed for sensible, practical advice for producers and schedulers. The research as to whether television caused violence was inconclusive and looked likely to remain so. Campaigners pointed to '2000 pieces of research' establishing a causal connection, but the advice of serious social scientists was that they did no such thing. I looked at a few myself and they were full of holes even I could spot. But the question for the broadcaster was, even if there were a connection, what do you do? Show no scenes of violence in any programme? Ever? Cut all fights from westerns, all shooting from gangster films, all scuffles from drama, all war footage from news? It would be a nonsense. So, it comes down to the practical questions of how much, of what kind, in what sort of programmes, treated in what manner and transmitted at what time? We sought to lay out the considerations that producers and schedulers should bear in mind, alerting them to particular dangers and audience sensitivities.

In the first review we made few changes. I wrote an introductory essay that struck an uplifting, school prefect tone, offering a parallel with road safety. The way to be certain of preventing all road accidents would be to ban motoring entirely. We choose not to do this because we value the convenience, freedom of movement and economic benefits that the motor vehicle provides. So we regulate rather than ban the motorcar, even though we know the result is a high number of deaths and an even greater number of injuries. With the broadcasting of violent material, the consequences are happily much less extreme. There is not the same direct affect on life and limb. If there is harm, it is only a contributor to the many other causes of violence in the world. Against this, we balance freedom of expression, freedom of communication and the pleasures of films and drama, and regulate accordingly.

The task brought me close to Roger Cary, who serviced the committee with case law, research digests and coherent minutes. He provided his own insights: 'Of course, my family is steeped in all this. My mother rather frightened people. She was a Norman, you see, and was mostly concerned with keeping the Anglo-Saxons under control. She was a Curzon. The badge of shame for the Curzons was that they didn't come over until 1120. They didn't come at the Conquest.'

I examined the issue again in 1986 when the going was tougher. Norman Tebbitt had been sounding off about television violence, and shortly after I had been fingered for this ('Viewers force telly clean up', 'BBC launch big probe in row over TV violence'), the chairman and director-general were summoned to see the Home Secretary who was considering an external monitoring body, later the Broadcasting Standards Council. Winston Churchill MP, in a populist huff and puff move, was seeking to have broadcasting brought within the Obscene Publications Act. This last would have applied tests less stringent than our own and would have had a marginal effect but a high nuisance factor.

We worked hard, examining new research, analyzing complaints, going through letters the director-general had invited on the subject and comparing guidelines of other European broadcasters. We held seminars with staff around the BBC, at which the full range of views, from the laissez-faire to the censorious, were expressed; the drama department explained how it handled violent scenes. News showed how various European news broadcasts had treated airport bombings at Rome and Vienna. All had worked from the same footage. The BBC's coverage was by far the most discreet, to the point where I felt it had sanitized the terrorist's violence. At the other extreme the Italian news had opened with a close-up of a dead victim's face. We looked at how our programme acquisition people rated and edited American films and series. Two episodes of *Starsky and Hutch* had never been shown; several high profile films were rejected for purchase, among them *The Exorcist*, *Friday the 13th* and *Nightmare on Elm Street*. I commissioned Guy Cumberbatch of Aston University to conduct an analysis of how much violence there was in four weeks on all four channels, broken down into detailed categories. My idea was that it would be an objective benchmark against which the results of future studies could be compared.

This time we produced a sharper, redesigned booklet for BBC editorial staff, with rewritten guidelines. I wrote another, slightly less pi, essay. 'The concern about violence is actually a number of quite different concerns . . . What gives a small child nightmares may be the least likely incident to arouse an aggressive teenager to action. What is a shocking scene to an elderly person may be viewed by others as a well-deserved act of retribution. The worries about violence tumble over onto a wider unhappiness about the ways in which human beings behave to each other and how this is represented on screen. The cry that there is too much violence seems often to be a howl of rage that people are not as one would wish them to be, that things are not as they once were and that television not only shows this but, at times, appears to relish it.'

We worried most about the fear that children were, as one correspondent put it, 'growing up accustomed to violence, which they see every day on their screens; it is their norm', and that, similarly, for adults the drip, drip, drip of television violence blunted our sensibilities. In a nutshell, our advice came down to: 'Go careful.' It was prudent to 'work on the assumption that to some extent, for some people, for some of the time, television may well promote violence. But that is not to say that television is a leading cause of violence. It may reflect it; it may exaggerate it. But violence is in people and there is enough violence in human history for us to know that television's role must be tiny.' Sounds a bit defensive now. The trouble is that the broadcaster can only control one end of the exchange: what goes out. It is the indiscriminate nature of the medium that produces the difficulty. More helpful was to remind producers that their programmes went out to 'an audience which may contain one's own and other people's children, one's own and other people's parents, the mentally disturbed and those who have experienced the very acts which are depicted on the screen'. I wrote it that way in order to remind readers that television folk, in spite of many suspicions and their own best efforts to disguise it, are members of the human race, with friends and families too.

In 1986 everything went out to a general audience. That is changing. With the explosion in channels through cable and satellite, viewing has fragmented in households that have these services. Many of these new channels are highly targeted at particular segments of the population, and are hardly visited, save for a passing flicker, by the untargeted. The rules for what is and is not acceptable are different here. The regulators know this, the content announces this and the audience understands this; in fact, it is central to the appeal. This development has affected mainstream channels as well. They are more clearly structured, less surprising if you like, and there are late night canyons where the middle-aged and those of a grown-up disposition rarely tread. Even so, BBC1, ITV, most of BBC2, some of Channel 4 and parts of Channel 5 remain territory where the general audience must be expected to be wandering.

Our group firmly supported the principle of the 9.00 p.m. watershed as the dividing point in the evening, after which schedulers should place the more testing, grown-up fare, whether that be for reasons of violence, sex or language. I support it still. We know that many children watch much later than that, have television sets in their bedrooms and have access to video-recorders which enable them to time shift programmes. But it is for parents to police bedrooms and video-recorders. Unless you argue that because children may be watching at any time, nothing that is unsuitable for children should ever be broadcast, the watershed provides a useful and well understood tool for parents to use and broadcasters to work to.

The real world had a habit of breaking in to remind us that violence was not a theoretical concern. The day after we had published the report in November 1986, I was in my office preparing to do another news interview about violence when the phone rang for the reporter. He put the phone down and said, 'Sorry, chum, this is cancelled. Bigger story. Someone's been killed in a stunt for the *Late, Late Breakfast Show*.' He and his cameraman dashed off to cover the death of Michael Lush, a volunteer from the public. The following year, just a week after we had announced the results of the Cumberbatch survey, generally reassuring for the BBC, Michael Ryan, dressed in combat fatigues, shot and killed sixteen people in Hungerford.

This unleashed a storm of national recrimination and disbelief. How could this happen in our country? Had Ryan been dressed as, and thus imitating, Rambo? Television was quickly hauled into the dock, guilty until proved innocent.

I got to know Mary Whitehouse, warm, friendly and solicitous, but the toughest and most ruthless of campaigners. If you made a good counter or scored a telling blow, she simply ignored it, advancing inexorably with another attack on 'middle-aged trendies, out to make money or a name', dismissing the broadcasters' codes as 'nothing more than a public relations exercise', counting the jokes about condoms in the *News Quiz*. She came in once to see Colin Morris, head of religious programmes, and me. With her was an obedient little chap who only spoke if her eyes gave permission. Ask him a question and Mrs Whitehouse replied. She was past her peak, losing her place in her papers and getting in a muddle here and there, but put on an impressive display, steaming over our questions or defences. She was not interested in argument. She believed.

The violence work began to put my name in the papers, and it was this, I am sure, that brought a letter from the painter John Bratby, a well-known artist. 'Would you like to come to Hastings to let me paint you? Your individuality, what you are, what you have done, and what you are doing, your personal distinction from Humanity's Mass, is the reason.' In search of a nice little earner, Bratby had identified a preening tribe whose vanity and sense of their own importance would respond to such an approach: television people. 'It would take four hours or less. No commercial aspect to it at all,' the letter disingenuously continued. There was a hint that the finished work would appear in an exhibition like the ones he had held at the National Theatre, BAFTA and the Royal Festival Hall. And I would not be slumming it. 'Some of the people I have painted in my studios are the Queen Mother, Sir Alec Guinness and Paul McCartney.'

I drove down to Hastings on a sunny March day. Bratby was a friendly bearded fellow, like a genial garden gnome. We began. He had a disconcerting way of looking at me sideways so that I felt I was not really coming up to scratch. His wife Patti brought coffee and a bacon sandwich, and Bratby several times asked her for 'a bit of green paper'. She would then come in, gaze at the painting, go out again and then return with a little note on green paper. Bratby told me that the photographs I had sent at his request were of the smooth executive but that, in person, I was much more human. So he had noticed? My personality was working its magic on him. He and his wife had established a routine and the day, relaxed and pleasant as it was, felt like a well-rehearsed ritual. The thought occurred that he had actually painted the picture from the photographs beforehand and spent the day dabbing in the sketchy background, an idea not discouraged by his complaint that I was wearing different glasses from those in the photos.

As he worked, he chatted away about the male menopause, in which he believed strongly. 'I left my first wife for an art student. At one time I thought of nothing but young girls.' After four hours, almost to the minute, he asked me to write in his wife's scrapbook and, as I handed it back, he confirmed the sense of a ceremony having taken place by saying quietly, like a priest at the end of a service, 'The picture is finished. You may now look at it.' There was a large close-up head with very blue eyes staring out. A perfectly nice but odd smile played on lips that were nothing like mine. I did rather like the energetic look he had given me. I made appropriate noises. A week or so later, Bratby wrote to say that he was able to offer me the painting, if I wished to purchase it. A week or so after that, Mrs Bratby wrote to Jane, enclosing a Polaroid of the painting, suggesting that she might like to buy it for me or for herself. I wavered. Vanity tugged at my sleeve. I had a soppy feeling that it should be kind to poor old Bratby and his wife, who had only been trying to raise a bit of cash. Jane took one look at the photograph and settled the matter. 'I don't want it. It doesn't look in the least like you.'

Chapter ten
FORTUNES OF WAR

'If it were done when 'tis done, then 'twere well it were done quickly.' It was. Within three months of being appointed chairman of the BBC, Marmaduke Hussey sacked the director-general, Alasdair Milne.

Over the summer of 1986 a new vice-chairman, Joel Barnett, the former Labour cabinet minister, had held the fort since the death of Stuart Young. Hussey was appointed on 1 October. A journalist rang me with the news but I had nothing useful to say. Most people in the BBC had either never heard of Hussey or had a vague memory that he had been chief executive of Times Newspapers when they were kept off the streets for a year by a strike. He now joined an organization which saw 'the ambitious ocean swell and rage and foam' about it. There had just been a noisy row over whether *The Monocled Mutineer*, a drama series about a World War I mutiny, was a 'true story' or not. The BBC now stood accused of not producing a play about the Falklands War it had commissioned from Ian Curteis because it was too sympathetic to Mrs Thatcher. By the time Hussey took up office at the beginning of November, Norman Tebbitt had thundered his attack on Kate Adie and BBC news for its coverage of the bombing of Tripoli. The new chairman had been appointed to calm these waters and, quite likely, chuck one or two people overboard.

He soon made a visit to Television Centre. What with his name, Dukie, his age, 63, his height, his voice and general demeanour, we took him, as did many, for a genuine toff, though as he would readily admit, he was more of 'a threepenny masher'. As he limped round the building (he had lost a leg in action during the war), the first impression was of a bit of an aristocratic buffoon. 'Watch out,' said Bill Cotton, 'he's not as dim as he pretends. He didn't miss much.' Nor did he. There was fear and suspicion in the land. 'You can always tell a dangerous general,' said one colleague after the visit, 'by the way he is affable and friendly to all below the rank of sergeant, while being dismissive of senior officers.'

Even so, Alasdair Milne's departure when it came in January 1987 was a shock. His wife had been seriously ill for many years, so the announcement that he had 'resigned for personal reasons' could be taken at face value at first. The full story of how he had been ambushed in the chairman's office after the board meeting and presented with a letter of resignation was soon round the building. 'I knew something was wrong when we all went in for lunch and there were no place names,' Graeme MacDonald, the controller of BBC2, told me on the phone. 'When the chairman came into lunch late, he tapped his wine glass with his knife and announced that Al had resigned. Then we all went on with lunch in a very English way. There is a special board of management going on this afternoon.'

'What are they doing?' I asked.

'Huddling together for warmth,' Graeme replied.

It was a gloomy television programme review board the following week. Bill Cotton reported on the DG's sacking. We heard that the inquest into the death of the viewer stunt man in the *Late Late Breakfast Show* had recorded death by misadventure. The BBC was at fault. The controller, Scotland, a contradiction in terms if ever there was one, reported on the special branch's raid on BBC premises in Glasgow in search of material from one programme in an investigative series, *Secret Society*.

Too many things had gone wrong too often under Alasdair Milne as director-general. The *Real Lives* episode had been the biggest, but there were many others, and the BBC was struggling to hold the government and much of the press at bay. The previous year *The Times*, owned by Rupert Murdoch, had devoted editorials on three consecutive days to the BBC, why it should not get more money and how it needed sorting out. The executive was at odds with the governors, Alasdair most at odds. 'They're mad,' he said in bemused frustration to me and other guests at his house for dinner of smoked salmon (caught by A. Milne) and pheasant (shot by A. Milne).

'Poor Alasdair must be shattered,' I wrote in my diary the day after his dismissal. 'I admired his toughness and independence. But he should have found a way of getting on with the chairman and governors. Did he know this was coming? Did he know that he was not right in the job?' I do not think he did. While I did not see him often, he appeared to bear the pressure he was under with, mostly, good grace and fortitude. I never saw him the worse for drink, though I had seen him consume quantities of his favourite malt, Glenmorangie. He had seemed genuinely saddened and surprised by harsh things William Rees-Mogg wrote about the BBC when Hussey was appointed. It was a tough way for a 'lifer' to go, a tough way for anyone to go.

Over the years many have commented on the 'cruel', 'barbaric' and 'humiliating' way in which the board dismissed Alasdair. As I have said, I felt for him personally. But I have yet to discover a way of sacking someone that the victim is happy with. However you prepare the ground, however you dress it up, the fact remains that one moment the person has a job and a second later realizes he has not. That is a fall of many thousands of feet that no pile of mattresses can disguise. I have never carried out as clinical an execution as Alasdair's. I have come at it, on those occasions when I have had to, in a more round about manner. The response of one colleague as I sweet talked him towards the news that I wanted him to go was, 'My God, you are a bloody politician.' Evidence, I suggest, that just because the bastard who thumps you has not put a horseshoe in the glove, it does not make you like it any more. Alasdair's thump was the more demeaning because it was so public. The press was never going to relegate the enforced departure of a director-general of the BBC to a diary column.

The search was on for a successor. Ladbroke's got this one wrong. They had Brian Wenham at 2–1. I rang him. 'Do you think that's right,' I asked.

'Those of us not beyond ambition will have to wait and see,' he replied. The word in the press was that Hussey wanted David Dimbleby. Outstanding broadcaster that he was, this did not seem a good idea, as he had no experience of running anything except his small local newspaper business. Some in the BBC feared their spats with him over the years might bode ill for their corporate futures. One or two of those, a couple of other programme heads and I met rather self-consciously and self-importantly to consider the situation. 'This is a meeting which is not taking place,' our chair began pompously, but we had no agreed view on what to do, so we returned to such individual lobbying or gossiping as we chose. Malicious rumours about Dimbleby began to circulate. I heard him asked if he was to become director-general, to which he replied, 'Not if 30,000 people have anything to do with it.'

The *Did You See?* programme conducted a poll of BBC programme heads and executive producers, ITV executives and leading independent producers. They were asked whom they preferred. Jeremy Isaacs, chief executive of Channel 4, had 47 per cent of the votes; Paul Fox, managing director of Yorkshire Television and former controller of BBC1, 35 per cent; Brian Wenham 10 per cent; Mike Checkland, Harry Evans, former editor of *The Times* and *Sunday Times*, and John Tusa, managing director of BBC World Service, 2 per cent each. On the instruction of top management, the poll was not broadcast.

Four weeks to the day after bumping Alasdair Milne, the governors named Mike Checkland as the new DG. It had obviously been close, for the announcement did not come until after 10.00 at night. Mike, in smart pink shirt, made a good fist of his televised press conference the following morning. He promised a slimmer BBC. For most in the Corporation, Mike was an unexpected choice but not an unwelcome one. In the finance and resources cadre of the BBC, in which he had mostly worked, Mike was respected for his quickness of mind and a legendary recall of figures. In the wider Corporation he had the reputation of being the programme makers' friend. He had seen his role as the enabler, who made it possible for the creative and journalistic teams of the BBC to make as many and as well-resourced programmes as possible. In the industry at large he was admired as a string, no-nonsense manager. I had always liked him. A slightly built, unpretentious and approachable man, with traces of the native Birmingham in his voice, he was direct in his dealings and dead straight.

Mike Checkland refused to take David Dimbleby as his deputy. He was determined to bring the news and current affairs arms of the BBC together to strengthen editorial control, minimize the internal competition and sort out its management. It was only a few years since the television news had been in the hands of one whose lunchtime drinks left him largely silent in the afternoon. One day several editors came into his office as usual to view the early evening bulletin. They were waved to seats by the hand not holding a drink. The bulletin began, and throughout it one of the news team kept zapping back and forth between BBC and ITN to compare running orders and story treatments. When it was over the set was switched off and the news boss, who had remained silent the while, spoke. 'Bit of a bumpy programme tonight, wasn't it?' Three weeks after taking over, Mike Checkland brought in John Birt, director of programmes at London Weekend Television, to be deputy director-general in overall charge of the BBC's news and current affairs.

I knew John Birt only slightly through a mutual friend, the producer Jonathan Gili, and from industry gatherings. As head of documentary features, I did not fall under his command, and my first concern in the new order was to protect my troops and own domain from interference. A new word began to appear, 'directorate', as in news and current affairs being the 'new directorate', or as it sounded to many, 'The New Directorate'. John Birt took them all off for a two-day conference. On return, Peter Pagnamenta, head of current affairs, came to see me. 'How did it go?' I asked.

'I think I've talked myself out of a job,' he replied. He had. Peter, the most cerebral of programme executives, who had already put to Mike Checkland the case for bringing the two journalistic departments together, had felt obliged to argue the case for the sort of popular journalism long practised in Lime Grove. He knew this was unlikely to be the style of the new world. John Birt told him that there was no role for him in the new structure.

Peter had an idea for a big series about Japan that he took immediately to Michael Grade, who agreed to commission it. This was both a lifeline and a sensible commission, but when Peter told me of this, I said, 'Get it in writing. Michael won't intend to go back on this, but things happen. Channels get overset and have to cut. Ask Michael to write you a letter formally commissioning the series.' He did. A couple of years later Peter delivered a hugely original and eye-opening series, *Nippon*.

John Birt put the structure for the new directorate in place. He appointed Ron Neil, the editor of television news, a popular and respected figure who had launched *Breakfast Time* and the *Six o'Clock News*, as director of news and current affairs, with separate radio and television arms reporting to him. He set up four new specialist units for politics, economics and business, social affairs and foreign affairs to provide expertise across both radio and television. Each unit was to have a weekly television programme. He introduced new ways of working with more research and scripting before producers began filming current affairs stories. I watched this from the sidelines. I was not alone in feeling that current affairs had had it too good for too long and that the self-confidence necessary for strong independent broadcasting slipped over into arrogance in many places in the BBC, most of all in Lime Grove.

At the same time I was sympathetic to the cries of anguish from colleagues as they railed against the spectres of conformity and castration that they claimed were the intended outcome of the changes. On a personal level I was unhappy about what had happened to Pagnamenta. I shared the insiders' resentment at an outsider digging up the whole garden to replan and replant. I was envious of the extra money the director-general found to fund the new arrangements. I was anxious lest documentary features was on the list of likely acquisitions for the new empire. The line was that the new deputy-director general was in charge of the BBC's journalism, but journalism of various forms was practised in many places outside of news and current affairs.

One innovation did appear to threaten freedom of movement: the new post of controller, editorial policy. There was an Orwellian ring to the title. In the ferment of the time, amidst the fear and loathing begat by the changes and in a climate in which many truly believed that Hussey and Birt were in place to clip the BBC's wings for Mrs Thatcher, this was deeply suspected. I was suspicious myself. In fact, the job was a perfectly sensible attempt to create a source of editorial experience and guidance for the BBC as a whole. The first incumbent was the wise and trusted radio newsman John Wilson, who quickly made the role indispensable. Within eighteen months, you could not imagine how we had got along without it. Wilson and his one or two assistants acted as an editorial special forces unit. They had the time to come to the aid of producers with tricky decisions to make, not just sensitive political matters, but legal issues from the Representation of the People Act to the Children's Act and problems of approach, taste or programme-making ethics. It was a function that helped get programmes on the air rather than, as had been feared, a means of stopping them.

The summer of 1987 was both comical and confusing. Game playing and manoeuvring was rife, as it was not clear how far the writ of the new deputy director-general ran. When Bill Cotton, who was to retire the following spring and hand over to Michael Grade, came to a producers meeting in my department, it was evident that he did not know the answer to the question, 'Who's in charge?' Bill's great fear, and one I began to share to a degree, was that with the extra investment in and huge emphasis on news, the BBC's entertainment role would be diminished. Only a year earlier I had worried in my diary that, 'with Cotton, Grade and MacDonald running television, a cloud of entertainment active dust will settle over the entire output'.

In August I went to a meeting about factual programmes on television with the two channel controllers, their planners, Ron Neil and one or two of his team. We were to hear about the new directorate's output. Michael Grade had an act prepared. 'We have a schedule to fix,' he began, 'We have to know whether programmes will be there.'

'John plans four new programmes,' said Ron Neil. Michael performed surprise.

'What programmes are these? . . . Where will they go? . . . On BBC2?' He turned to his colleague and furrowed his brow in an elaborate display of concern. 'Did you know about this, Graeme?' Ron Neil, who thought this was something already sorted, was thrown. He became tetchy. These questions would be answered when John Birt returned.

When John made his first visit to our department, at my invitation, I heard some of his woes. 'I've never known anywhere as paranoid as the BBC,' he said. The opposition to the changes certainly manifested itself in some pretty unpleasant ways. When Samir Shah, the new television current affairs head brought in from London Weekend Television, came to programme review to defend a programme, an unduly heavy barrage of artillery rained down on him. Samizdat publications circulated. John apparently told someone that he had missed live coverage of the Enniskillen bombing, so the refrain of a seven-stanza W.S. Gilbert pastiche ran: 'Because JB's the DDG who doesn't watch the news.' The BBC is packed with people with good access to the press and many used it.

News and current affairs was to be the BBC's New Model Army. It was to develop its own specialist expertise, pay proper attention to policy issues, not merely report, but analyze and explain. This now sounds like motherhood and apple pie, but at the time the idea of putting the whole news operation on a more coherent footing was taken to be code for control, censorship and sucking up to authority. One or two unhappy editorial decisions, whereby programmes were pulled or postponed late in the day, contributed to this. In the long run, though, the BBC's journalism emerged stronger, better resourced and confident in its ability to originate stories, win scoops and take on the powerful.

The zeal and determination with which this Oliver Cromwell drove through his reforms created its own mythology. It was an article of faith that John Birt never drank and deplored drinking. It was true that he drank more sparingly than BBC folk were used to, but you did not have to be that close to him to know that he liked a beer and, in particular, a strong martini in a proper cocktail glass. Another certainty was that he was straight-laced, interested only in high policy. He was serious about policy and about freedom of the media: he had stood bail for one of the OZ trial defendants. But he had also pulled the stunt of helicoptering Mick Jagger from his prison release to debate drugs with the editor of *The Times*, and, like all journalists, he enjoyed gossip.

'Did you know, Will, that it was evidently a fact that Hitler did only have one ball?' This was John ringing me with a programme idea. He said that Alan Bullock, author of the classic biography of Hitler, was researching the subject again. 'And did you know about his extraordinary sexual practices?'

'No. What were they?'

'I don't think that I can say on the phone. It seems that he didn't sleep

with his women friends but he did do other things. I'll say when I see you.'
He forgot and, some journalist me, I forgot to ask.

In the summer Brian Wenham, after just a year as managing director,
radio, decided to leave. Seven of us gave him (or did we claim it on
expenses?) a dinner at L'Escargot in Soho. As glasses were refilled, the meal
grew increasingly gloomy. Peter Ibbotson, the former *Panorama* editor who
was our convenor, became drunk and dramatic, jotting down notes for his
diary and sinking lower and lower at the table. Brian threw out his pes-
simistic prophecies: departing governors would not be replaced, leading to
an eventual joint board; this, accompanied by a centrally directed news
operation would end in the politicization of the BBC. All wrong, fortunately, but it was a night for black dog.

In the new spirit of communication, the board of management summoned
all us middle ranks to studio six at Television Centre for an address that was
carried on the ring main to all BBC buildings. As was the custom at so
many such BBC events, technical problems, in this case two dud microphones, knocked some of the shine off the occasion. I noted: 'Like an early
party political broadcast. Never have so many Renault 25s gathered in one
place at one time; never have so many men in glasses said so little to other
men in glasses.'

But I had other matters on my mind. Both channel controller jobs were
coming vacant. Michael Grade was to step up to be managing director and
Graeme MacDonald was retiring after five years in charge of the second
channel. He had adored the job and had been a wonderfully encouraging
controller to work with, trusting my judgement, backing my enthusiasms,
always quick to phone with congratulations after a success and with cheering commiserations after a flop or during a rough passage. In his company
a giggle was never far away. His nervousness with the press was, I guessed,
caused by a fear that the tabloids might make a story of his homosexuality.
He was proud of being the first homosexual channel controller but it also
weighed on him. There was no need. He lived a life of domestic stability with
his partner, Ron Davies. Indeed, over dinner at a Prix Italia, a group of us old
marrieds compared how long each couple had been together, and Graeme
and Ron were the winners. They had met in a cinema queue, Ron with his
fiancée, whom he left for Graeme.

This was the first time that both controllers were to be selected on the
same day. The one job that I had always fancied was controller of BBC2.
When I had bobbed for it before, it had been too early. No longer. But I also
bid for BBC1. I had less hunger for it but knew that I could do it, and it
would be both wimpish and high risk not to apply. That same autumn,
Channel 4 were seeking a successor to Jeremy Isaacs, and both friends and
my own ambition impelled me to go for that as well. Thus in the week
beginning Monday, 9 November 1987, ambition did not so much vault as
clatter the hurdles as I competed for three of the best jobs in British broadcasting and was thrice rejected.

On the Monday morning I slipped into the Churchill Hotel to lay out my thoughts to the interview panel for Channel 4, chaired by Dickie Attenborough. With him were George Russell, the deputy chairman, Paul Fox, managing director of Yorkshire Television, Carmen Callil, founder of Virago Press and John Gau, independent producer. I told them that the channel was too glum, it needed cheering up; it should capture a wider range of opinions and assumptions; and the schedule looked like a dysfunctional compromise between competing interests. I would sort it out and improve the share.

Three days later I went to Broadcasting House for the BBC interviews. I was last in at 12.55 p.m. and could almost hear their stomachs rumbling. The interview was in the panelled boardroom on the third floor of Broadcasting House, where green baize topped tables were arranged in a square, and black and white photographs of former chairmen looking suitably important gazed out on all sides. A gang had assembled: the chairman and vice-chairman, the director of personnel, along with Mike Checkland, Bill Cotton, Michael Grade, who as incoming managing director of television should choose the people he wanted to work with, and John Birt, whose presence was perfectly logical but about which, we later learned, there had been a row, Grade not wanting another shadow across his wicket.

The betting in the planners' office at Television Centre had me second favourite for both channels. My thoughts on BBC2 were that Graeme had grown the audience share with a raft of successful magazine programmes but that the channel was clogged with such shows. It needed better arts coverage, to become more intellectually stretching, widen the range of subject matter and create a greater sense of occasion and surprise. BBC1 came down to Saturday nights, more warm bath drama and a stronger early evening. Michael Grade took the lion's share of the questioning, lobbing hypotheticals at speed. I kept thinking, 'This is all about BBC1. Are they only measuring me for that?' Afterwards I went for a walk to clear my head. When I got back to my office there was a message to call Bill Cotton. I did and heard the bad news: Jonathan Powell, head of drama, had BBC1; Alan Yentob, head of music and arts, had BBC2. As I wrote in my diary, 'Balls.' Graeme rang to commiserate. 'I hear you made a big play for BBC1.'

'Did I?'

'So Michael said.' Of course, I knew that the board would have made little difference. Michael, I presumed, had got the people he wanted, which was as it should be. I could, though, have made it more difficult for him. I went off with Jane to hear George Solti conduct an exciting performance of *Die Entfuhrung* at Covent Garden, where we bumped into Mike Checkland. 'The trouble is,' I said to him, 'there is nothing else now I want to do in the BBC.' Kind colleagues rang and sent notes. It was as if there had been a death in the family.

The following day, Friday, there was a message from Channel 4. Would I be ready to see them again the next week? I perked up. The next two or three days were full of fun and games, and what follows is some of how I described it to myself at the time:

Monday, 16th November

Call from Dickie Attenborough: 'Terribly sorry, Will, it didn't work out. There'll be an announcement tonight.'

'Who is it? Can you tell me?'

'I can't say now. It's not someone on the publicised shortlist.'

'Ah, well. I felt I put up a decent show.'

'Yes, you did very well. You were in the last three.' Rang Brian Wenham. He'd been told he had been in the last three, too. 'Only one more to find,' I said, 'and we know it's a kindly fib for some of us, at least.' We speculated. Rang Graeme and he swore me to secrecy: Michael Grade did not meet Peter Ibbotson at the airport for the flight to Los Angeles last Saturday [this was a trip to buy American films and series]. Bill Cotton had tried to find him over the weekend and failed. The housekeeper said the only messages left were from his cousin and Mr Paul Fox. Bill was beside himself. Michael had now fixed to meet him at seven. Graeme took the management meeting, hands shaking. I sat next to him and as I sat down he wrote 'I was right' on his notes and pushed them towards me. Keith Samuel [our head of publicity] said too casually and rather unnecessarily, 'Michael is in Los Angeles buying pro-grammes'. The meeting was over in twenty minutes. As we drifted out, I told Jonathan Martin [head of sport] that neither Brian Wenham nor I had got Channel Four. Did I know who had? I said I thought I did but was sworn to secrecy. 'If it's not Brian, then I needn't rush to renegotiate my snooker contract,' said Jonathan. 'Don't be too sure,' I replied.

Back in the office, more calls. I rang Bill Cotton saying that I'd heard from outside the BBC that there was going to be an announcement that would shake us. 'Oh, yes. What's that then?' asked Bill.

'Channel Four it sounded like.'

'Look, we're all circling round the same thing. We'll just have to see.'

[I went home for dinner with my family] I told them how things stood. 'That's out of order,' exclaimed Rozzy [my younger daughter]. 'That's so wrong.'

Just after ten, a call from Graeme. 'It's definite. He's taken it.' I rang Brian Wenham; we couldn't talk for long as he had a film crew in his house shooting Buster, a film with Julie Walters and Phil Collins. It was 'an act of unmitigated cynicism.' Rang Ron Neil, who didn't know. He was speechless, then: 'It makes a farce of last week. I don't believe what you're telling me.' I told Jonathan Martin, who was equally taken aback. 'As I was driving home I was thinking about what you had said about the snooker. None of the possible candidates fitted. I wondered about Michael, but it just couldn't be. My producers always said that I shouldn't trust him.'

I rang Jonathan Powell who was very low. 'I've stopped being sympathetic to Michael and I'm now angry.' I mentioned the clash with John Birt. 'No, it wasn't just or even mainly that,' said Jonathan.

'You mean that he just couldn't resist it when he saw it?'

'Yes,' said Jonathan. 'It's the exits and the entrances.'

Tuesday 17th November

Rang John Gau. Michael had definitely approached them, said John. The selection board was unable to agree on any one candidate and Dickie Attenborough then revealed that Michael was a runner. They saw him on Saturday morning at Dickie's house in Richmond. Meeting in Bill Cotton's office at 2.30, chiefly for Bill to get across matters that Michael had been dealing with. He looked old and weary and put on a brave face. 'People have to make the career moves that seem right for them.'

I returned a call from Carmen Callil who was exhausted, just going to bed at 7.15. 'I've learned so much about television in the last ten days, I'm really quite hooked on it.' She said I'd done a 'stunning interview' and had been in the last two. Carmen was certain that Dickie had planned the whole thing with Michael. 'It had all been hashed over beforehand . . . too much fitted too easily . . . Dickie told me last Monday that Grade was a candidate . . . I think Dickie has been a lot cleverer than we thought he could be.' There was no doubt, she said, that Michael had approached Channel Four. Watched Michael's interview on Channel Four News played back late – radiantly insincere.

Before I wrote this chapter, I read the relevant pages of Michael Grade's autobiography. He explains why he was determined to leave the BBC when it became evident that John Birt sought influence over television, and that the row over the interview panels for the controller jobs was the defining moment. Fair enough. He continues: 'In the weeks that followed, I just got on with the business of seeing in the newly appointed channel controllers, Jonathan Powell and Alan Yentob, and began mentally withdrawing from the BBC.' No, that is not what happened. Michael must have remembered that there were no 'weeks that followed'. In fact, he left before the new men had even entered their new offices. What is more, he had begun his mental withdrawal, indeed had told Channel 4 that he would take their job if offered, before he had even appointed those controllers. No wonder people were angry and felt betrayed. Jonathan and Alan were shattered. They would both be new to their testing jobs, while the man who had put them there and was to have been their mentor had done a bunk.

All right, all right, I was a disappointed claimant, career forced into the heavy goods lane, if not quite off the road. No wonder I was full of resentment. But I was not alone. Looking back, I think that Jonathan and Alan were the right choices for the two jobs. I have no complaints about that. And the managing director of television must have the people he wants. Lousy behaviour, though, is lousy behaviour. I think Rozzy had it right: 'That's out of order. That's so wrong.' No wonder Michael's book disguises what happened.

Michael was a huge loss to the BBC. Bill Cotton was cast down. Where he had planned an orderly transition, there was a gulf. I concluded that I would have to leave the BBC, as I was now out of the running for the big jobs. Jonathan Powell knuckled down to understanding and running the mighty, all-consuming monster that is BBC1. We got on fine. Alan Yentob was more difficult at first.

I had first met Alan in the early 1980s. He was a brilliant arts producer and editor of *Arena*, already a name and winning prizes. He appeared at the door of my office soon after I had arrived at Kensington House, and my first impression of him, as I recorded, was 'grubby, obsessed, interesting'. He often turned up for a drink and a gossip around 6.00 p.m. Then, when he became a head of department himself, he would wander over to the seat of power on the sixth floor of Television Centre for his sundowner. When Graeme handed over to him, he expressed the hope that Alan would spend as much time on the sixth floor now that he had an office there as he had when just hoping for one. Alan had a way of making friends with some of the people he filmed, famously Mel Brooks and Orson Welles. Myths grew up around him that, say, he had once written to Fidel Castro about a project and had signed off: 'yours in the struggle, Al.' He was often disorganized, late for appointments and could ramble, but he was absolutely obsessed with getting the best, endlessly inventive and utterly committed to the BBC. I loved his impassioned outburst at a briefing about plans for a new BBC building on the White City site: 'We've just been told about "design and build", we've been told about "the constructors",' began his outburst. He continued, turning his gaze on the director-general, whom he addressed as if he had done a pooh on the carpet, 'Why is there no mention of an architect? This is a building for Britain's greatest cultural institution. It should reflect that. This is simply not acceptable . . .'. I offered modest support but should have just cried, 'Bravo.'

Alan was hands on, interested in detail, loath to delegate. On his first day in the job a colleague asked the BBC2 planner if things were all right. 'Alright,' said the planner, with a worried grimace, 'but Alan wants to change tonight's schedule.' Alan's instinct was always to seek out the best talent and if you did not have it then go shopping. He brought the Comic Strip team – which included Dawn French, Jennifer Saunders, Ade Edmundson, Rick Mayall and Alexei Sayle – to the BBC. He wanted a strand of programmes to appeal to young adults and persuaded Bill Cotton that we hire Janet Street-Porter. The intention was that she work to me. We had lunch, after which I noted, 'I can see why she gets through husbands at such a rate; full of ideas and rather sexy' – a view probably not reciprocated. I thought that she would require a lot of attention and I had plenty on my plate, so she worked out of the entertainment department. Janet was impressive. She quickly sussed out how the BBC worked, and few people before or since have come into the place and made things happen so quickly. Her DEF II strand pioneered in the BBC a new style of intelligent, informal journalism in *Reportage*, the *Rough Guides* to places and careers, *Open to Question* and other programmes.

While still running music and arts, Alan had proposed a nightly review, arts and media programme. This now happened, and the young independent producer Michael Jackson was brought in to edit it. I first came across Michael in the early 1980s and was immediately intrigued. He had worked on the Channel 4 campaign, was now setting up as a producer and came to see me with a proposal for a drama documentary. He strode into the building with a nervy, neatly furled manner. I was struck by his serious and business-like demeanour. He had taken an option on a book, which he left me. I read it, liked the idea and said that I would definitely do it but it would have to be the following year. In that case, said the young tyro, he would withdraw the proposal and place it elsewhere. This was unusual. Most young producers were desperate for any sign of interest, let alone a promise of production. I was impressed. As I was again when I saw his Channel 4 series *The Media Show*, not least because he had wisely ignored advice I had given and done something much more interesting. He never did get that book away. *The Late Show*, as the new BBC2 programme was called, was cool, brought new faces to the screen and established a reputation for originality, eclecticism and a post-modernist take on the world. It was famously attacked for refusing to proclaim whether John Keats or Bob Dylan was the better poet, its critics thereby ignoring the altogether closer run decision as to which was the better singer. The show was one of the distinguishers of Alan Yentob's custody of the channel.

Michael Grade's departure was not the end of tensions. For a long while there had been an argument about the placing of *Newsnight*. It came on at a different time each evening, according to the mix and duration of the other programmes in the BBC2 schedule. News wanted a fixed time so that people could make a date with it. Television resisted the considerable constraints this would bring to planning the schedule, procrastinated but promised to have a look. At a press conference at the end of the year Mike Checkland announced out of the blue that he had decided there would be a fixed start time of 10.30 p.m. from the following summer and that Alan Yentob had argued for this at his board for BBC2. This was a facer to Bill Cotton, who was in the audience, knew nothing about it and left the studio in fury. I rang him in his car. 'Checkland's behaviour is despicable . . . he knew I was taking the controllers away to go through the schedule . . . I promised him a paper immediately . . . I've never been treated like this before . . . talk to my lawyers . . . I'm not going straightaway without trying to sort things out for people . . .'. He was convinced that this was the parting of the ways with Mike, who had taken John Birt's side against him. The decision seems small beer now (and perfectly sensible), but at the time I and many other inmates were convinced that news and current affairs would from here on dominate the BBC, that the rest of the output would be downgraded and that a business man would be brought in to manage television to keep it in its place.

The anxiety spread. Alan and Jonathan were still learning their trade and we had inexpert coverage of the Mardi Gras in Rio on both channels. When we had to drop a programme because of a *sub judice* problem and I replaced it with a repeat of the controversial documentary *The Fishing Party*, Alan, reflecting others' concerns, became agitated. 'Why run it at this particular time?' I pointed out that the BBC always used 'this particular time' as a reason for caution. Over the years, Alan was very shrewd about the transmission of difficult programmes. To my knowledge he never ducked out, and by marshalling his arguments and preparing the ground carefully, he was able to bring all kinds of bold programmes to the screen.

When Michael Grade jumped ship, a number of programme heads and others urged me to launch a campaign to become the next managing director. I did not think that I was ready for it and declined. By the end of February and with no replacement for Bill Cotton in sight, I changed my mind. I wrote a manifesto and, even though Dame Rumour whispered that an announcement was nigh, sent it to Mike Checkland:

> Dear Mike, I am told that you already have someone in view for MD Tel. In which case I trust that you have chosen wisely and I wish him good luck. As I had written the attached, I send it anyway on the basis that a/ I may be misinformed. b/ Many a slip. Best, Will.

Five days later Mike announced that Paul Fox was the new managing director of television. When I took back the news to my department, there were smiling faces. Paul was one of the big figures of ITV, yet always ready to speak up for the BBC when political flak was flying. His Yorkshire television chums were quick to point out that this was an opportune moment to leave ITV. The easy days were coming to an end as the companies prepared to slim to bid for their franchise renewals. But before decamping to Yorkshire fifteen years earlier, Paul had been a legendary BBC figure as head of sport, then of current affairs and for six years as controller of BBC1. The chance to return in an hour of need was irresistible. As it happened, he had been party to the creation of that need in his role as board member of Channel 4.

At the press conference Mike spoke: it was to be a three-year term. He had wanted a programme person with experience of scheduling. Paul spoke: he was coming home, ITV was in ferment, the BBC could plan. John Birt spoke: Paul had taken him out to dinner when he got the BBC job and told him that he had to get *Newsnight* fixed at 10.30 p.m. 'No, I said that *Newsnight* should have a fixed time, I thought 10.30 best,' interrupted Paul.

'That's not as I remember it,' said John. At the drinks afterwards I congratulated Mike on a terrific coup. It certainly seemed to restore the balance of power between the different parts of the BBC. Paul was 62, Bill was standing down at the BBC retiring age of 60, and was happy, he said, to be handing over to an older man. The following day he told me, 'Do you know, this is the first morning for two months that I haven't woken up feeling sick? It was just thinking about things not being settled and what might happen.'

I went to see Bill about a programme matter a couple of weeks later. He poured a glass of wine and talked for three-quarters of an hour. Out came his account of the past few months, the climax of which was his description of a managing director's lunch, arranged to clear the air. At this, he said, he had let rip at John Birt. 'I told him he had run a three day a week company and it looked like it . . . There are no programmes worth naming that you are associated with . . . I don't know what your plan is and if I don't know, God knows none of the people working for you can . . . You think you know how to run something? Going round telling everyone how awful your staff are? What you should remember is that those people have wives, husbands, families and you're trying to destroy them . . .'.

He warmed to his tale, the bitterness coming back to him. 'Then Birt started talking about the press leaks. On one leak he said, "There were only three of us there: you, Mike and I. How did that get out?" I said, "I know what you are suggesting. But remember, it could have been me." He didn't laugh. The others did.' There was much more. 'You know all those times you come out of a meeting and you wish you had said this or that?' asked Bill rhetorically. 'Well, this time I said exactly what was in my mind in exactly the order I wanted to say it.' We were eventually interrupted by Jonathan Powell coming in to consult Bill about a blasphemous joke in a programme due to go out that night.

There was huge affection for Bill Cotton. He was the last of the old era, loved the BBC, was sentimental about it and let it show. He had a rare sense of the public mood and was able to communicate this to those around him. He was combative, reassuring and streetwise in times of crisis, and alert to dangers of overconfidence when things were going well – all in all a fund of common sense. His advice was dispensed in the vernacular, as in: 'Tell them it's time to shit or get off the pot.' There was always time for a laugh. I remember a discussion about an outside broadcast that entailed much strenuous rigging in the heat of summer. The producer was worried about the crew.

'They should be OK,' said Bill.

'But what about the ageing riggers?' asked the producer.

Bill thought for a moment. 'Make-up?'

In later years Bill did busk some of the managerial aspects of his job. He once had to hear an appeal against dismissal by someone in studio resources. It was arranged that the personnel officer would provide a briefing on the case and on the man in question. Came the day, and Bill's PA put her head round the door and said, 'He's here.' She showed him in. Bill sat at his desk with the pile of papers in front of him. He pushed his glasses up on his head and looked at the quiet bespectacled man across the desk.

'Well,' said Bill, 'I've been looking through all the paperwork on this. I've got the picture and I'm sorry to say that I'm going to have to let you go.'

'But Bill,' pleaded the man, 'It's not me. I'm Ray Bell. I'm your senior personnel officer.'

Bill was not leaving the broadcasting business. Among other things he was to act as an agent for one or two friends, among them Sue Lawley. He later told me of the first contract meeting he and Sue had with Granada at the Hurlingham Club in West London. Work was going on outside and the noise of the diggers drowned out bits of the conversation about the number and type of programmes and the fees for them. When the meeting had finished and the Granada person left, Bill turned to Sue and said: 'Well, that went well didn't it?'

'I'm not sure,' replied Sue, 'I didn't hear the crucial bits.'

'Bugger me,' said Bill. 'Neither did I.'

On a chilly April evening there was a dinner to see Bill off. Jim Moir produced an emotional occasion. We all waited outside the main entrance to Television Centre for Bill and Kate to arrive. When they had alighted from their car, Mike Checkland ushered Bill onto a small dais and the sound of military drums was heard in the distance. The band of the Royal Marines marched into view playing 'I've Got a Loverly Bunch of Coconuts'. They formed up in front of the building for Bill to take the salute. Trumpeters sounded the 'Last Post' as the BBC flag was slowly lowered. Two marines folded it and marched up to a visibly moved Bill and presented it to him. The bugles sounded 'Come to the Cookhouse Door' and we went in for a candle-lit dinner in the long curved sixth-floor suite, scene of BBC farewells. Bill told some of his stories in his speech and we all chanted the punch line to his much-used, all-time favourite. Eric Maschwitz, the composer of the show *Goodnight Vienna* passed through Lewisham when the show was playing there. He stopped and went in to ask the house manager how *Goodnight Vienna* was going in Lewisham. The manager told him: '*About as well as* Goodnight Lewisham *would go in Vienna.*'

The underlying strains were present even on such an evening. I sat next to Ron Neil, the big, strong and popular director of news, who suddenly turned to me, clasped first my shoulder and then my hand with both of his and said, 'I hate my job. I don't like coming to work and I can't sleep.'

Chapter eleven

THE OFFICE

Towards the end of the 1980s a little fags and mags shop and then a hair-dressers opened up at Television Centre, modest signifiers that the world was changing. The political and economic changes wrought by Mrs Thatcher's government were transforming the climate in which the BBC operated. They, and the new forces they unleashed, demanded both strategic and operational responses from the BBC, and over the next couple of years I was to lead the television contribution to this and tackled a whole range of new things.

First came a little programme matter. *Holiday* was a series that was a joy to have in my department. It was loved by the audience, prized by the channel controller, provided a training ground for young film directors and caused few problems. That is until May 1988 when the *News of the World* ran two spreads on the presenter, Frank Bough, accusing him of drug taking and attending sex parties. Frank was a highly accomplished broadcaster who had been a star sports presenter and the first anchorman of *Breakfast News*. Famous for wearing cardigans on screen, in *Holiday* he provided a cosy, avuncular tone that was right for its early evening placing, and each year made a series of films rambling round France or Italy with his wife Nesta. We had a problem. The producer, Patricia Houlihan, was deluged with phone calls: 'It's like people gathering at the scene of an accident.' Frank admitted some of the accusations and Paul Fox, Jonathan Powell and I agreed that he could not continue to offer family holidays to a public that knew he spent evenings watching people have sex on the carpets of suburban living rooms. He should come off the show for a year and we could then take stock.

I was in touch with Frank through his friend and chosen intermediary, the television reporter Bernard Falk. I had several conversations with Falk, who, in the true spirit of show business, let me know that if by any chance Frank were to be taken off *Holiday* and I was then looking for a new presenter, he, Falk, would be available to take over at short notice. Frank, it appeared, chose his friends as unwisely as he chose the parties he went to. Reporters were besieging Frank's house and hanging around Television Centre, so I arranged to meet him at the Halcyon Hotel in Holland Park, where I booked a suite on the first floor. He arrived in one of his brown patterned V-necked jumpers, a little late and a bit flushed. He looked thinner, strained and red-eyed. I offered him a glass of wine or water. He chose water. 'Let me give you the three-minute John Birt backgrounder on this investigation,' he began. I guessed that he had planned to take the initiative and set the tone. 'A few years ago we had a big problem in our family and that problem was me.' They had sorted it out in the weeks before the story ran. He was not going to sue, as he had admitted some things, but there was a deal: no writ, nothing more in the paper, 'that's if you can believe anything they say'.

I told Frank of our decision. 'You're making a grave mistake,' he said, 'I've had letters from the public asking me to stay on. Tomorrow I'm opening a fête for a vicar. I've just received a letter from royalty asking for my support for a charity. You are the only people turning away from me.' I said that his friendly, chap next-door style made it impossible for him to continue for the moment. 'It will be another big press story just when I am beginning to see some light.'

'We'll do everything we can to mitigate that. You can issue a statement, if you like, and we'll agree with it.' The argument went on for a bit. Frank looked me hard and accusingly in the eye, but I sensed that he was not fighting as vigorously as he could or as I had expected him to. I left him to phone his wife in private while I went to see the *Holiday* team. 'Give them my love,' he called as I moved to the door.

Falk rang me the following morning about the statement, offering his thoughts. 'He's behaved like a child. He's not a journalist, just a television front man and has ruined his whole career.' Then I really did feel sorry for Frank. Desmond Lynam took over on *Holiday*.

That autumn Paul Fox opened a door by asking me to work with him as assistant managing director. It was a new role, one that I would have to create. I was flattered. It meant I did not have to leave and I could see a mass of things that needed doing in the television service, so I accepted and left documentary features after eight years. I had worked with some marvellously talented people, made good friends and learned a lot, not least about my own view of the role of factual television. I had written about this in a trade paper:

> Making television programmes is a valuable occupation but we should be clear about what it is and what it is not. The wish to make a programme about a problem is not to be confused with devoting a lifetime to trying to solve that problem. Our responses should take that into account. I have always mistrusted the kind of reporter (fortunately rare) who addresses himself to one of the great issues of our time or a troubled nation overseas and appears to get angry at what he finds. He makes a programme in which he displays his anger then boards the next aeroplane or hops into a taxi and goes somewhere else where he can become angry all over again . . .

If you are truly angry then you should stay and do something to help. Have less fun, do without expenses, eat less, drink less, have the kind of hard time that is not going to end when the programme ends.

Of course, reporters and producers will be affected emotionally by the stories they cover but their job is to remain clear headed and not allow themselves the easy option of striking a posture. One of the great reporters, possibly *the* great television reporter, James Cameron, has spent much of his life travelling from one human foul-up to another. But you never find Cameron railing in anger. He may find things sad, crazy, extraordinary, cruel, tragic or funny but he leaves the emotion to well up in the hearts of the viewers. And he never takes himself or his role too seriously. He is the passing stranger, detached and on the move. His job is just the telling and trying to understand.

The staff of documentary features gave me a splendid send off and a present I still prize, a portrait of Churchill by David Hiscock that was a moody reworking of a photograph. It was from the title sequence of a series of history lectures we had made. In my last newsletter I grappled with the dilemma of the good and the popular in factual programmes:

It creates a buzz to have programmes in the top ten. It is good for professional self-esteem to know that programmes are reaching a sizeable number of people or doing an important job for controllers in a difficult or exposed slot. After all, we are in *broad* rather than *narrow* casting. It is important, too, that factual programmes remain in the centre of the schedules on both channels, that they are not there on sufferance, that they are seen by viewers and broadcasters alike as belonging to the heart and not the periphery of television. It is not so everywhere.

But the importance of this is not just to show that we have muscles to flex when we choose. It is to be able to put before as many people as possible programmes of the highest quality. A high audience is not an end in itself; good work is. The two can, and often do, go hand in hand. Lest there be any doubt: audience figures can be forgiven; poor quality work cannot.

This sounds, now, as if it emanated from a mouth suitable for the long-term storage of dairy products, but it was a message one had to keep sending and it still holds good for the BBC, or it should.

When Channel 4 had launched in 1982 it was as a broadcaster only, making no programmes itself and commissioning them from a largely new constituency of independent producers. Many of these, mostly small, companies were set up specifically to take advantage of this new market place, often by ex-BBC and ITV staff. Once established, they turned their attention to the BBC and ITV, both of whom commissioned nearly all their programmes from their in-house production base. The independents began to lobby the government, asking that it prise open the locked schedules of the established broadcasters to provide access for them. The Peacock Committee proposed a legal quota. The government liked what it heard from these enterprising young companies. Indie production was an idea whose time had come.

Like most in the Corporation, I was at first unsympathetic. These people had chosen to work this way. If there was not enough work from Channel 4, then that was just too bad. Why should the BBC have to throw them a life belt at the expense of its own programme makers? I came to change my view. Good ideas began arriving in from independents and there were some talented people in these companies. If BBC producers had been at any other industry, their sympathies would have been with David against Goliath. The idea of small, energetic outfits providing some competition to the monolithic BBC was one hard to argue with and the government did not. When in November 1986 Douglas Hurd announced a 25 per cent quota the implications were profound. The BBC would require not just 25 per cent fewer programme makers, but it would also need to make equivalent reductions in production resources and overheads. The quota was to force painful change in both the BBC's financial and editorial processes. The Corporation could never be the same again.

One of Mike Checkland's first acts as director-general was to lay out a plan of how the BBC was going to begin these changes. I now took over our negotiations with the independent producers' association, IPPA. One issue still to be resolved was 25 per cent of what? We were able to exclude from the base all acquired programmes, that is, movies and those shows we purchased as completed programmes from overseas producers, usually in the United States and Australia. Repeats were also not part of the total hours for purposes of the quota. We could also exclude daily news programmes, on the grounds that these emanated from an integrated news machine that it would be uneconomic to fiddle with, though we had vigorous debate about the definitions: *Newsnight*, in or out? Out. Conference coverage? In. We argued the case, and lost, for excluding sport. The 25 per cent was therefore not of all broadcast hours, which would have closed two-thirds of the BBC's programme making capacity, but of all original programming other than news. The government was the arbiter, as the quota would be included in the forthcoming Broadcasting Bill.

Our negotiations with IPPA were protracted and generally good humoured, though Michael Darlow, their chairman, was not slow to write to Mrs Thatcher or even to lead a deputation to her when he felt we were backsliding or obdurate. The BBC was worried about cost. The indies claimed they were cheaper. We employed Ernst and Young to compare costs and their conclusion was that 'there is no evidence that the BBC will save money'. The big problem for us was accurately costing and then reducing our overheads: the cost of buildings, communications, infrastructure and bureaucracy. At the time no attempt was made to allocate such costs to individual programmes. The independents worked on full budgets that included all the elements of a BBC budget plus the costs of running their companies. The BBC was determined to meet the quota, and at the Financial Times Media Conference in 1990 I set out the year by year targets that would get us to the required 1400 hours in 1993/4. They pleased few. The indies quibbled with the numbers; the unions were unhappy with the implied job losses.

Crucial aspects of the negotiations were who owned and who controlled the copyright of BBC commissioned and independent made programmes, and how commercial income from exploiting the programmes (overseas sales, secondary use in this country, licensed products, videos, records and so on) should be shared. These remain bones of contention today. At one extreme some indies wished merely to license the programme to the BBC for one or two transmissions, on the American model. But here, unlike the networks in the United States, the BBC paid 100 per cent of the cost of production, plus a profit fee, plus, sometimes, the cost of developing the programme. Thus, we argued, the BBC, or the licence fee payer, had taken all the financial risk and was entitled to control the exploitation of the programme and a share of the subsequent income. I remember explaining this to a man in a suit, socks and sandals sent by the Office of Fair Trading to investigate our deals. Even his side-kicks, young turks with greased back hair in wide-shouldered suits, the uniformed enforcers of red-blooded capitalism, appeared surprised that after paying the costs and production fee, we always shared the back end income, usually fifty-fifty. I traipsed to Brussels to put the same case to the competition policy people in the department headed by Leon Brittan, who, pleasingly, had not lasted long in government after the *Real Lives* affair and had fetched up in the European Commission.

The growth of independent production was a success story. It shoved a stick firmly in the complacent ribs of the BBC and the ITV companies. It brought talent into television that would otherwise not have wished or been able to work in it. It led to fierce competition in ideas. It inspired innovation. Over time it created a market in which talent, especially on-screen and writing talent in comedy, could extract payment proportionate to its value to broadcasters. Entertainment stars were always the top earners in television. Now many of the new talent chose to work in companies they owned or had a stake in, thereby gaining more control over their work and rewards, not just for writing and performing, but also as executive producers and shareholders. Many stars of what was once alternative comedy, most of whom loathed Mrs Thatcher privately and publicly, made their well-deserved fortunes thanks to her policies. She is the fairy godmother of their children's trusts, the kind fairy who provides winter sunshine, the Lady Bountiful who made possible their country houses and Notting Hill homes.

The impact of satellite broadcasting was not so immediate but in time even greater. British Satellite Broadcasting won the licence to launch a three-channel service via a high-powered satellite to 'squarials' on receiving homes. The company set itself up in some style and spent heavily on Hollywood film deals. In the meantime, Rupert Murdoch announced in June 1988 that he would launch his own subscription service into the United Kingdom, a four-channel operation using the medium-powered, privately owned Astra satellite. This was based in Luxemburg, so bypassing the regulators of British broadcasting. Sky reached the air in February 1989, some months before BSB. This was a formidable achievement. Murdoch turned up at several industry gatherings around this time, intoning with a straight face about how 'we live in a deeply moral society', about 'how the elite in the BBC and ITV have force fed people', with the promise that 'now the standards of ordinary people can be catered for'. By stuffing one's fist into the mouth, it was just possible to avoid gagging or giggling. Sky was heavily puffed in the Murdoch papers, but it and BSB were bleeding cash. There was not room for both, and under the banner of a 'merger', BSkyB, as it became, swallowed its rival in the nick of time as far as Murdoch's bankers were concerned. With the field to itself, it had a chance of success.

I joined the board of the BBC's own subscription television company, BBC Select. This was set up chiefly to ward off the threat of our night time hours being taken away and handed to a commercial operator. This would have been a dangerous precedent and would have cramped our ability to run the schedules late or even overnight for major political or sporting events. Select carried specialist services aimed at the medical profession, lawyers and accountants; very BBC, you might say. I never believed that it would make money, nor did it, but it served its purpose in seeing off the threat to our airtime.

As broadcasting was to be deregulated, there was a need, of course, for more regulators. The government established the Broadcasting Standards Council, an advisory body concerned with taste, decency, violence, sex and the like, under the chairmanship of William Rees-Mogg, former vice-chairman of the BBC and chairman of the firm that published the Kray brothers' memoirs. I went to their first meeting with a small BBC delegation, led by John Birt, to explain our approach to these matters. Rees-Mogg was courteous and punctilious; Richard Baker, a member, tried to be helpful; the Bishop of Peterborough, another member, rambled amiably and autobiographically. They were at that stage all over the place. I had argued against the introduction of the BSC. I thought it unnecessary and potentially dangerous, springing, as it did, from the censorious soil of Victorian values and all that. In the event it was sensibly run for the most part and its approach to complaints provided a heat shield against Whitehousian missiles. The Broadcasting Complaints Commission was a court of appeal for individuals or organizations that felt mistreated by broadcasters, a necessary body, one had to admit. It became too legalistic. Powerful companies used lawyers to amass piles of documents in a cynical attempt to tie up broadcasters in costly proceedings.

Both these bodies were set up to empower the viewers. Although I only dimly perceived it at the time, it was the embryonic satellite services and the cable operations that did most to shift the balance of power away from the broadcasters and towards the public by providing more choice. Murdoch, for all his cant, did see it and had bet the farm on it.

The wind of competition blew in all quarters. Since 1923 the *Radio Times* had been the promotion sheet for the BBC, with a monopoly on listings for its services. The covers were decided in consultation with the channel controllers, programme heads brought pressure to secure features or photographs, producers composed long billings and fought for extended credits. This was to end. The monopoly was broken. To compete against other listings magazines the *Radio Times* would have to carry ITV and Channel 4 schedules, run features on their programmes, reduce the space it gave to BBC billings and, horror of horrors, print fewer credits. I became mixed up in time-consuming negotiations over each of these changes, fighting to retain as much space and priority for our programmes as possible. We won agreement that for drama and comedy the writer's name would always appear and managed, in the face of cries of 'editorial freedom', to extract a promise that the cover would always refer to a BBC programme. The BBC channel schedules had up to then remained confidential until the *Radio Times* appeared on the street; indeed, they were often changed even as the presses were rolling. Now the schedules would have to be released to other magazines and there was understandable paranoia in the BBC1 office about leaks to ITV. A scheme was devised whereby all channels fed their billings to a confidential bank, from which they were released to magazines at an agreed moment. The world was becoming less accommodating and we did not like it.

I joined the Broadcasters' Audience Research Board, BARB, the body owned by the BBC, the commercial broadcasters and the advertising agencies, which produced the audience figures. The interests of the owners clashed and I enjoyed the elegant and patrician style of the chairman, the former broadcasting minister Sir Giles Shaw, as he sought to reconcile them. He was impressively fluent in laying out issues and charmingly old-fashioned in language: 'a matter yet to be determined . . . we agree so to do . . . if colleagues are content . . . it is only just that it be so'. He referred to the meeting as a 'witenagemot', and to chivvy us along after a break he would say, in friendly tone, 'Resume your seat, if you will, sir.' The disagreements of the time were over whether audiences for programmes shown twice within a week, notably *EastEnders*, should be aggregated (we wanted that) and whether there should be a consolidated top ten as well as top tens for each channel. We did not want this because ITV would dominate it, though our argument was that it would mostly feature soaps and thus tell people little about the appetite for different programmes. ITV took unilateral action, so Howell James, the new BBC director of corporate affairs, and I went to see Shaw. Howell revealed to our surprised chairman not only ITV's statement but the already issued BBC response. 'Oh, my goodness!' said Sir Giles. 'How do you spell resign? Oh dear. I thought we were supposed to be gentlemen' He certainly was one.

One of Marmaduke Hussey's aims was to make the BBC less insular, to open it up and establish a wider circle of contacts and friends. He himself appeared to be ceaselessly out and about. Nary a conversation nor a meeting passed without Dukie saying, 'I sat next to X at lunch last week' or 'I sat opposite him at dinner last night' or 'Of course, I've known him a very long time.' Mike Checkland picked up the open doors policy and asked the famously efficient and persuasive Biddy Baxter, originator and long-time editor of Blue Peter, to organize a series of seminars at which senior BBC staff would explain what we were trying to do and hear criticism, comment and questions. These ran for nearly ten years and I and others performed for, listened to, and occasionally took a pasting from, Labour, Tory and Liberal Democrat politicians, government information officers, civil servants, industrialists, academics, educationalists, scientists, artists, arts administrators, officers of various religions, independent producers and on-screen talent. I usually enjoyed them, although at times I was on autopilot, once or twice my mind completely lost in some problem. Biddy was full of praise when one did well, full of encouragement when one did not. On one occasion I must have been looking haggard in the midst of some crisis, for she grabbed me: 'I know what it's like. Think of your lovely daughters, Will. That's what is really important. This is only television.'

The outreach continued with grandees invited to lunch and dinner. Among them was Brian Griffiths, head of Mrs Thatcher's policy units, with a particular interest in broadcasting standards. A sharp, chummy fellow, he almost rolled himself into a ball when he shook hands. Geoffrey and Elspeth Howe were guests at another when John Simpson was telling of his time with Afghan rebels. 'The group I was with objected strongly when they heard that the Iranians wanted to blow up the French embassy.' Geoffrey, who was a little tiddly, looked surprised.

'Oh!' said the pro-Europe deputy prime minister with a giggle, 'I would have thought there would be plenty of volunteers to blow up the French.'

In those days of eating for Britain, Paul Fox had television do its bit with regular lunches for guests. The star charmer of the many Tories was, to our surprise, Cecil Parkinson, dashing in a fancy white shirt with a shiny stripe in it and the monogram CEP. He was full of good stories from the Cabinet that showed him not be Mrs Thatcher's poodle and others that revealed him, quite consciously I was sure, to be a ladies man: 'I was being interviewed for local radio in Umtata in the Transkei and I was chatting away freely to this bird.' Then: 'The Polish women are very striking I find . . .'.

Jeffrey Archer came once and gave a theatrical turn over the likely banning of Sinn Fein from television: 'I want you to know that this is something that I feel very strongly about, very strongly.' Our small lunch became the conference hall: 'You see, some of us happen to believe that saving lives is more important than these people being interviewed on television.' When I took him on, he came down from the platform to become perfectly reasonable.

The public meetings continued; the best for me was one in my hometown Oxford, where I had the chance to show off in front of my Mum and Dad who were in the audience. Having watched me for a bit and confirmed that I had a clean shirt on, they understandably left before the end to make sure that they got a drink before the pubs closed.

One of Mike Checkland's best hirings was Howell James, who came at the age of 33 to be director of corporate affairs. He had been press boss at *TV:AM* and adviser at the DTI. Howell had a will o' the wisp quality, flitting from problem to problem, always beaming, quick with a plan, deft with a line to take. He was a cheering companion, who took neither the BBC nor himself too seriously. When he had complained to me with a 'fancy that' expression that he was not to get an office in the planned new headquarters at White City, I said, 'Ah well, you'll just have to have a tent on the lawn.'

'I suppose a tent could be the answer,' he grinned. 'Do the scouts come with it, do you think?' For all his jesting, Howell had sharp political antennae and was in the first division of his trade. He was a great boost to morale.

Tim Bell, Mrs Thatcher's favourite PR man, was employed to research the BBC's image and advise. The broad message of the research remained the same for many years. People admired and enjoyed the programmes but were iffy about the institution that provided them. One of Bell's ideas was that the BBC should provide a kind of on-air shareholders report. It was called *See For Yourself*, and the first went out at the beginning of January 1988. There was a long film about the BBC with various bits of information about costs and so on, and then the chairman and director-general, in the studio in Manchester, answered telephoned questions. Dukie was not a natural for the television age. His matiness came over rather as the man from the great house looking in at the estate Christmas lunch. To a call from Bristol: 'Hello, John. How is it down in Bristol? I've got a house near Bristol. I hope the weather is better with you than it is here. Ha!' He was, though, firm against the government using the courts to gag broadcasters. Mike was crisp and to the point, an ambassador from the land of real people. Anyone would trust him.

The programme was mocked in the press as the Mike and Dukie show but there was also a continuo of praise for attempting to answer up in this way. So there was another the following year, the upbeat tone not helped by being interrupted for a news flash reporting the British Midland air crash on the M1. The film section scored a massive own goal. In documenting the careful planning and high production values of a new period detective series, *Campion*, it filmed a bus drawing up at a distant location for the design recce. From it alighted, one after another, a multitude of smiling designers and design assistants, for all the world like a works outing. If anyone had ever doubted that the BBC was all too comfortably staffed, here was the beaming evidence.

The next year the programme carried a film about Radio 3, putting on the BBC's most cultural expression. John Drummond, who had left the television arts department to run the Edinburgh Festival, had now returned as controller of this network and was later to run the Proms. Drummond, a clever, cultivated man, disdainful of much around him, was famously hard to please. Opinionated, loud of voice and large of frame, he frightened many people. Ideas, stories, gossip and complaints tumbled from him, the complaints as often as not about other parts of the BBC. 'People say that I dominate meetings too much,' he once said, 'but no one else had anything to say.' Drummond was shown the Radio 3 film and exploded. Unless there were changes, he would resign. Some changes were made; he did not resign. It emerged that the director from the independent production company had got off on the wrong foot with the controller. As the company later wrote to the BBC commissioner, 'I admit that [the director's] arrival in a cassock to interview John Drummond was not, in retrospect, the most sensible or sensitive thing to have done, but in no respect should that be misinterpreted as suggesting a derisory attitude to the project.'

Drummond, surprised and irritated to discover the director in clerical garb, had asked: 'Why on earth are you dressed like that?'

'Well, I'm told you're God,' replied the director, 'so I thought I'd dress accordingly.'

While John could be pompous, he would also tell stories against himself. Years later he had just been to the new Glyndebourne. 'It's wonderful,' he exclaimed, 'although there are 100 seats which have no view *at all* of the stage. It's true. I know because I was in one. I was assessing the production of *Eugene Onegin* which we're having at the Proms and they put me in one of those seats. When I complained at the end they said: "Oh, they're seats we give to people who aren't very . . .!"'

The final *See For Yourself* was in January 1991. Julian Pettifer made a film about the BBC's year and then a panel, on which I was the television representative, answered questions from an audience in the Birmingham City Art Gallery. The format felt better from where I sat and I enjoyed it. I reviewed my performance: 'did passably, once or twice over-defensive, once a bit ingratiating'.

As assistant managing director, I applied myself to every aspect of the television service, learning about areas I knew little of and trying to bring about changes. Under the leadership of Cliff Taylor, the television director of resources, we made a big push to improve our record in equal opportunities. The first step was to raise awareness of what we needed to do, and I chaired seminars on disabilities and on race. For the latter there was a programme of workshops run by a charismatic former American army officer. We hosted an industry-wide seminar on women in broadcasting, at which we listened to, among much good sense, humbug from Janet Street-Porter and others on how 'men lie, women don't; men manipulate, women don't; men play games, women don't'. Really? I did see differences in how the sexes worked, but not those. Women achieved more in a day then men, were better team builders than men and were more supportive of colleagues.

I was the television person on a committee considering sponsorship as a way of boosting the BBC's commercial income. I was never sure as to whether Mike Checkland's enthusiasm for this was genuine, or merely a demonstration of activity to head off external pressures. I was deeply sceptical and had to pinch myself to make sure I was not dreaming when I arrived at one meeting to be shown a specimen title sequence for the BBC Olympics coverage that featured the logos of the games' official sponsors. The trouble with sponsorship for the BBC was that it was the soft drug of commercialism that external pushers would use to lead on to the hard. What the BBC would be selling was worth more to it than any sponsor would pay; even if there were ever fees commensurate with that value, they would be but a drop in the ocean of the BBC's total funding.

I still had overall responsibility for all the factual departments, and this demanded some fire fighting on the *That's Life* front. Shaun Woodward, editor for less than a year, was leaving to help run the Conservative campaign for the next general election. He had worked with Esther on some tough and high profile stories as researcher and producer, and was a loss, though I should have marked him down for politics after he had twice come to my office to tell me what a good job I was doing. We had also walked through fire over a *That's Life* investigation into a private school, Crookham Court, where boys were being sexually abused. The programme team researched this assiduously, brought John Birt and me into the loop early and thus we were able to back the programme makers fully at an ugly court case at which the defence turned on them. The headmaster and two teachers were sent to prison. The BBC lawyers helped enormously, but I had to warn them off when they said that they, rather than the programme team, wished to decide when they should be present in person at recordings. I did not want a regime in which lawyers acted as producers' minders. Esther made enemies. She was brazenly ambitious; she delighted openly in her fame; she engendered a them and us mentality in her teams; she was ruthless in seeking out the seat of power to achieve her ends. But she was bloody, bold and resolute when faced with a wrong she felt she could right.

Under John Birt's leadership the BBC editorial guidelines were pulled together, added to and turned into a single coherent and usable document for the first time. The thoughtful John Wilson carried out this task and the resulting regularly updated booklet has been the producers' bible ever since. It was way overdue but its introduction came in the face of paranoia and suspicion. A song and dance accompanied the launch of the guidelines in March 1989, one eye cocked at the watching political world. Mike Checkland accompanied by John Birt and Patricia Hodgson, the head of policy and planning, came to the television programme review board for the internal launch, to be greeted by a sulky and near silent reception. That there was a BBC rulebook was bad enough for some; that John Birt was the instigator confirmed the suspicions of others; that it carried the imprimatur of the secretive and unloved policy and planning unit, 'the thought police' to producers, was the clincher for nearly all. Sensitive to this and resentful himself at the thought police seeking to interfere in the production process, Paul Fox ordered that the opening page of the booklet, which boasted 'Policy and Planning Unit', be torn out of every copy before they were distributed. I shared a genuine fear of central control. Had we not drawn a line in the sand, the policy unit would have spread its wings and sought to direct. As it was, the advice became invaluable, while editorial responsibility remained where it belonged, with the programme makers and channel controllers. It took a while for them to appreciate that a fund of corporate-wide experience strengthened rather than weakened your hand, and for the centralists to learn that it was dangerously wrong to undercut those at the front, that able people would not take instruction but might value advice.

This all came as free marketeers were arguing the case against the licence fee or against the BBC being its sole beneficiary. The pressures on the Corporation were building up. One government free marketeer developed a strategy of infiltration, though penetration was probably his goal. He was introduced to and then arranged to meet an attractive BBC news producer. 'He's always asking me about the BBC and dropping suggestions on how it should be changed,' she told me. 'People at work kept asking, "Why does he ask you about all this?" Last week I found out why. He fancies me. I went to dinner in his house to meet his wife and he kept rubbing his feet against my legs under the table. I didn't know where to look. This was his house, with his wife there! And he's such a great Christian!'

'Are you sure?' I asked. 'It could have just been an accidental brushing of feet.'

'What?' she exclaimed, laughing. 'And the hand on my thigh in the car?'

While one influential hand clutched a young female thigh, another, Woodrow Wyatt's (no relation), sought to have an impartiality clause inserted into the Broadcasting Act. It would have imposed a statutory requirement on television journalism that every programme argue the case for and against with equal weight. It would have neutered current affairs programming and, in particular, hobble investigations. The BBC has an obligation to be impartial and reflect that impartiality in its overall coverage. That is not the same as every programme being measured for the time it gives to every side. With John Birt and others, I lobbied, spoke and wrote against it. There was strong opposition to it within the Conservative Party and it did not become law.

I could not argue with the director-general Mike Checkland when, at the height of the debate, he asked, 'Do personal view programmes balance out? I doubt it.' The BBC did need more internal vigilance to ensure that it broadcast with the impartiality demanded of it. The day before the Broadcasting Bill received the Royal Assent, Mrs Tebbitt, badly injured in the Brighton bombing of 1984, was at home watching daytime television. She evidently liked the new presenter, who introduced an American comedian. This hopeful, no doubt trying to ingratiate himself with his British peers, opened, 'There's an awful lot of bad news about at the moment. Let's have some good news. Norman Tebbitt is dead.' Not funny; insulting; in appalling taste; a party political jibe.

In the same month, at the height of the Tory attacks, a programme head rang me. 'Two of my producers have had phone calls asking whether or not they agreed with various government policies, how they voted and so on. I thought you should know.' The press office rang next. 'Producers in a number of departments have had similar calls, part of a Gallup poll. We got the research department to ring Gallup to find out what is going on. Gallup said that they could not reveal the name of their client but the results will be available on Friday.' Then Tony Hall rang to say that his news producers were getting the calls. I spoke to the wise television press chief Keith Samuel and to the ever-cheerful Howell James. We were of one mind. This was obviously a stunt dreamed up by an enemy of the BBC, the Freedom Association, say, or the *Daily Mail*, that would be played into the argument against us on the bill. It was a typically cunning manoeuvre. The best tactic in such circumstances is to get in first and knock the shine off the story. I suggested that we drop the story to a sympathetic newspaper, the *Independent*, that someone was conducting a sinister, McCarthyite witch hunt, lists of allegiances would follow and so on. This was done. We felt pleased with ourselves. Quick on our feet, we had stuffed them, whoever they were.

Then came another call. It was David Hatch, director of radio, a warm-hearted colleague but a radio man through and through, always just a wee bit suspicious of the mighty overweening television service. 'Do you know about this poll, Will?'

'Yes, don't worry, David. We're on the case. Made a few moves.'

'Do you know that it's a stunt by one of your programmes?'

'It's what?'

'Yes. It's a bright idea from *The Late Show*.' I could sense the Mexican wave of mirthful pleasure rolling round the rest of the BBC. I rang Roly Keating, the bright young producer of *The Late Show*. Was it true he had commissioned Gallup? Yes.

'You fucking idiot,' I shouted, calmly. 'Call it off straightaway.' Reeling from the terrifying naivety, I rang the press office with the news, then Mike Checkland to make sure that he heard it from me first. There was little in the papers, for that was the evening George Best was incoherent on *Wogan*. I saw Roly formally. By then he realized his mistake and his innocence in the wars of institutional survival. He has deservedly prospered since.

As a result of the troubles over the World War I 'true story' *The Monocled Mutineer* and the Falklands drama *Tumbledown*, Paul Fox had instituted a monthly meeting to consider all forthcoming factually-based drama, and I now took over the chair of this. The idea was to be prepared, to check the research and the provenance of such productions, so we understood their status and could bring them confidently to the screen. My first surprise was how many projects there were on the list. I wondered aloud and to the irri-tation of the drama heads whether writers ever made up stories any longer. The second surprise was how wily the drama folk were. I understood pro-ducers' paranoia. I was accustomed to them dissembling, only letting on half, coming clean late in the day. But these were starred firsts in the tripos of the cunning. One meeting we would be looking at a title and a one-sentence description under the heading, 'script commissioned'. A month later the head of plays would hand over a tape of the completed film. Drama had ever been like this. In 1976 the first that the then channel controller of BBC1 heard about the Dennis Potter play *Brimstone and Treacle*, in which a handicapped girl is raped, was when the senior cameraman from the studio led his crew up to the controller's office to say they hated what they were working on and wanted to halt the production.

I learned more of the strange ways in which the BBC could work. Paying a prisoner for his story was not allowed. However, I discovered how an ex-con man, whose information had provided the basis for a script, was paid with a cheque issued on the precise day promised, the day of his release, while only two days earlier power had been cut off for two hours at the BBC's outside broadcast base because no one had remembered to pay the electricity bill.

The drama heads tended to communicate the explosiveness or otherwise of their projects with nudges and winks. There was a tendency to want it both ways. I said that 'with some factually based drama, we say, "This is true. We've interviewed all the main characters." Then, when challenged, "Ah. But this is the work of a distinguished writer and has its own artistic validity."' Trust was in short supply. I took over soon after a film called *Here Is The News*, produced by Ken Trodd, Denis Potter's producer, a brilliant, difficult and combative man with a string of outstanding dramas to his name. Trodd had a dishevelled appearance, as if he had spent the night in a sleeping bag in his office, which was not surprising, for I was told that this was exactly what he did do for periods at a time. The central character was an investigative newspaper reporter with kinky habits. The question was whether this was a portrait of a reporter called Duncan Campbell. Campbell sued for libel and, on the advice of counsel, the BBC settled. The governors went on the warpath. Had Paul been deliberately misled by the programme makers? Not that anyone could demonstrate. Drama producers were utterly committed to the work in hand. Once bonded with a writer and a director, they would fight anyone and anything.

I became the television port of call for complaining delegations. The chief Girl Guide came in full uniform, upset by an episode of *EastEnders* in which a pack of Brownies had run amok. The Turkish Ambassador was angry about an *Everyman* programme that rehearsed the wrongs done by the Turks to the Armenians. The Romanian Ambassador came about another *Everyman*. This was ritual, in part in order to point out what he claimed were specific errors. I told him the problem was that we were unable to report freely from his country. When the meeting was over, I accompanied him to the lift. As we waited, he said, 'I told you. I not diplomat. In university, I talk with my students. We exchange ideas.' He looked sad.

'This is very different?' I said politely.

'Yes,' he replied as he stepped into the lift and turned to face me, frowning. 'Very different,' he added as the doors closed.

We were at odds, as usual, with the South Africans, and I went with John Birt to dinner at the embassy to argue for more access for journalists and producers. I was going with my wife to Botswana, where her sister lived. We would travel via Johannesburg and I wanted to press our case there. There was doubt over whether I could have a visa, as I was held responsible for *Suffer the Children*, a powerful documentary we had managed to get shot there. I was granted a visa and was able to lobby the Bureau of Information in Pretoria, a waste of time, I sensed. I visited the South African Broadcasting Company in its new twenty-nine-storey building. 'We have what we call a responsible approach,' I was told. 'That is, not criticism for criticism's sake.' They told me, 'TV1, the main channel, is not just for whites; 25 per cent of its audience is black.' Then a moment later when I asked if there were black Africans on the channel, 'No. TV1's audience wouldn't have it.'

I paid a call on the director-general and was shown into his office on the top floor. Its size would have best been computed in acres. 'Come here,' he ordered, and proudly led me across the room to the windows that ran along one side.

'You know,' he said, peering into the haze, 'on a clear day you can see the Voortrekker monument.' For him, this was a religious experience.

'Mmn. Jolly good,' I replied politely.

My other international forays were less exotic. I was the BBC member of the television committee of the European Broadcasting Union, made up of 'mission orientated' broadcasters, that is, those with some or many public service obligations. Initial excitement, prompted by the names of three prominent women in the EBU, Mesdames Luste, Flesch and la Lumiere, was quickly dampened by the bureaucratic meetings, which took place in 'the bunker', a dark brown half basement in Geneva. We were in rows facing a raised dais on which the chairman and other officers sat. Above us to one side were the illuminated translation booths from which speeches and contributions in one of the two official languages, French and English, were rendered into the other and one or two additional languages. The dry air-conditioned atmosphere drew upwards the thin film of cigarette smoke and the cumulo-nimbus from the Spanish delegates' cigars. A large busted Spanish woman of a certain age walked in and out during sessions, self-consciously cooling herself with a fan as her mighty bows swung dangerously before her. A couple of visits to Geneva were not enough to be quite certain of knowing the bureau from the steering committee, a sub group from an ad hoc group, let alone a working group from a working party. And where did a task force fit in?

The crucial activities of the EBU were exchanging news material, winning and servicing contracts for big international sports events and putting the case for public service broadcasters in Brussels and Strasbourg. Views split almost always on racial lines, with the British, Germans, Scandinavians and Dutch lining up against the French, Italians, Spanish and Greeks. There were various programme groups that were mostly talking or networking shops, but which ran the Young Musician of the Year, a children's animation project and, above all, the Eurovision Song Contest, the rules of which were regularly updated: 'A comprehensive drum kit will be provided.'

Europe was awash, at the time, with initiatives on what was called the 'audio-visual landscape'. Initiatives appeared to work in an exactly opposite way from making programmes. With the latter, you decide what to do and then gather the team to do it. With initiatives, you set up a secretariat in Brussels, then decided what its work should be. Still, they kept people busy, including me. I was pleased to note that, flying to a Council of Europe meeting, I travelled with one of our lawyers, while Andrew Neil, then running Sky, was accompanied by two speech writers. In the discussion they kept passing him notes, contributing, perhaps, his most memorable phrase: 'There is no difference between television programmes and refrigerators.' At a big conference in Brussels I was bored for Britain but compensated with a sight of the French culture minister, Jack Lang, in action. He was chairman, and though he condescended to spend most of the day with us, showed little interest. At the point at which the first woman went to the microphone to speak, he picked up a newspaper and disappeared behind it.

Moules and *frites* were only an occasional part of my life. And back home there was a problem: money.

Chapter twelve
'IT'S A BIG JOB'

A series of strikes over pay hit the BBC in the spring and early summer of 1989, taking a number of programmes off the air: two days of Royal Ascot, *Newsnight*, even the news. Mike Checkland, the director-general, had little room for manoeuvre. The years of plenty were coming to an end. As the number of television households had grown from the 1950s on, so the BBC's income had swelled as people took out the television licence. Then came the switch from black and white to the higher colour licence. All in all there had been three decades of inherent growth. Now the licence fee had been pegged to the retail price index. This itself was a first. Until then the BBC had always made the case that broadcasting costs rose faster than the index and had won increases accordingly. Mrs Thatcher had called time. Mike was determined that the BBC would find the money to make a competitive pay offer next time round.

He asked Ian Phillips, the chirpy director of finance, to lead a small team to examine the whole of the BBC's expenditure and identify the necessary savings. I was on it. We questioned activities and expenditure everywhere, toiled long and hard over piles of figures and reports, and consulted widely, including the unions ('get more money from the government'). At that time the BBC had a large store at Ware in Hertfordshire. It stocked stationery, typewriters and catering supplies. Everyday a van would leave Ware to make a round of deliveries to BBC buildings. Stores encourage waste, as did some of the attitudes. At one time you could apply for a free BBC briefcase. I had one for years. Filofaxes had come in, so the Ware stores put them in the glossy stationery order books, with the result that the leather bound version was demanded by the dozen at no cost to the recipients. The store was for the chop.

A Mr H.E. Weston wrote from Worthing to say that he'd read about the search for savings and said that as 'the first professional accountant/administrator to be appointed to Sound Broadcasting's management', he had had to do similar in 1937. 'I noticed that my women staff began to take turns to tidy up half an hour before lunch time, and before leaving in the evening. Once their faces and nails had been made up, they did no more work. I observed that my wife spent about two minutes in washing and five in making up her face. With great difficulty, I obtained permission to view the ladies' loos.' He had altered their design and converted a gents to an extra ladies. 'Saving: an average of half an hour per day for every woman member of staff.'

We, in particular I, were more interested in building plans. I was convinced that we should not build the planned news centre at White City and thereby save £400–500 million. The news executive in charge of the project was a born-again convert to 'the new directorate', and when my line of questioning revealed that scrapping the centre might be on the cards, he was outraged and near to tears. Speculation was rife about what we would come up with, and *The Times* ran a story saying that 7000 jobs would go. This was probably inspired by Joel Barnett, the vice-chairman, who was telling everyone he met that Checkland would not be radical enough. Joel was known as 'the little shit', not because he was wrong in his opinions, but because he was an inveterate leaker and the more management were getting kicked the more he appeared to enjoy life.

When we took Mike Checkand through the draft report that I had largely written, he put his finger immediately on the weak spots but remained scratchy about the news building, which he did not wish to abandon. In January 1990 we presented the report to an all day meeting of the two boards, management and governors, in the council chamber at Broadcasting House. Mike, who had named our report Funding the Future, set the scene. Change was underway and the staff had responded; this was not crisis management but a plan for the future. Joel Barnett said this would have to be presented carefully to the staff, who needed to know that 'there has to be a different kind of BBC or there won't be one at all'. John Birt pointed to good things in the report but said it eradicated symptoms; what was needed was a new management system. He emphasized then, as later, that the television service was under funded. The chairman took the recommendations one by one, and as we debated what seemed at the time to be great issues, we heard the sounds of a mighty storm raging outside, a storm that we later discovered had caused great damage and loss of life.

The climax within came when I led into the discussion on capital spending, questioning the need for the news building and identifying the money that abandoning it would release. Ian Hargreaves, the number two in news, who to Mike Checkland's fury had already refused to offer any savings from news and current affairs operations, now insisted that the building was essential, the whole rationale of the directorate depended upon it, it must be built. His steel spectacles seemed to glint in defiance. Several governors argued against the building and, as they did so, John Birt's knuckles were white as he grasped and twisted the pencil in his hands. He asked if he could speak. He recalled his first meeting with the director-general. He had been asked to come to fix the problem with news and current affairs and from the outset a new building was promised. It was his 'utter and complete conviction' that it should go ahead. Life had moved on, said other governors, we were up against it financially. The chairman said the building must be better justified, they needed to make the case. 'What does make the case mean?' said John. 'You just heard us make it.' No decision was possible then. When the agreed recommendations were totted up at the end of the day, they came, to my surprise, to as much as £75 million per year. After a lager with Ian Phillips, I left to get the tube, only to find that the storm had closed Oxford Circus station and so joined the huge queues for a bus.

Cliff Taylor and I had to find the savings and lead the production efficiencies recommended for television. Cliff was a high-energy Mr Fixit who was quick to diagnose a problem and quick to take action. He was a great chum of Mike Checkland. They were both accountants by training and shared a practical, no-nonsense view of the world. Cliff had the Yorkshireman's eye for saving money and would stop all office stationery orders for scissors and sellotape for the month before Christmas. He hated wasting time and wanted to get a job done and be off to the races, a passion we shared. In one of his earlier jobs, after joining the BBC from the Coal Board, he had been sent with 'the equipment auditor' to the Isle of Wight for two weeks to audit the operation of the transmitter there. They checked into the pub they were to stay at and had a drink. Cliff asked the publican if he would turn the television on and tune to BBC1. The picture appeared true and clear. 'Could you put the radio on now?' asked Cliff. The publican did and out came the sound of music. 'That's all right, then,' said Cliff. 'No one's nicked the transmitter. I'm going home.' The other fellow stayed for two weeks and, apparently, came to the same conclusion. Next month, the West country.

We set targets for savings in programme budgets and talked much of giving responsibility to the producers, but many of the costs lay outside the producers' control. We began plans to contract out scenic servicing, costume making, catering, security, cleaning and building maintenance. We re-examined our annual planning system, which, especially with the growth of independent programme supply, was now something that ran alongside the commissioning and production process rather than the controlling force it had once been. We looked for some specific production efficiencies such as in the handling of props, the smaller items needed for use in a programme or to dress a set. Why was Harrods the shop of choice for prop buyers? When a bottle of champagne was required on set, was it necessary to order a case? And where did props go after use? Some were appropriated by the production team, in the same the way that the *Late Night Line Up* hospitality trolley always went back empty. Each week £10,000 worth of props were disappearing from locations or studios, half a million pounds worth a year. On drama locations producers anxious to maintain their schedule would say that if people would just not remove things in the middle of scenes, thereby ruining continuity, a blind eye would be turned at the end of the day. At Television Centre when one manager was asked for the name of a particular foreman, there was surely a clue in his reply, 'Oh. That's "Take Away Ted".' In great secrecy Cliff Taylor had some surveillance cameras installed and the evidence was gathered. When the man in question appealed against his sacking, Cliff said, 'I have only one thing to ask. If you didn't do any of this, why does everyone call you "Take Away Ted"?' The response was the equivalent of 'It's a fair cop, guv.'

In the light of the reductions made later, it seems amazing now how formidable those savings of 5 per cent appeared to be. The trouble was that we did not then have the tools to reshape budgets.

The BBC exists under a royal charter. This has to be renewed at intervals and the current one was due to expire in 1996. It was already time, in 1990, to be thinking about this. The renewal would need to be enacted in 1995, before which, working backwards, would be a bill, a white paper, a green paper and a public debate. The BBC needed to have its case thought through and its arguments marshalled ready for that debate and in order to try to shape the agenda. It would not be easy. The Corporation was already under political pressure. The broadcasting world was changing fast. For the first time there was competition other than that from the heavily padded gloves of ITV and Channel 4. Cable and satellite broadcasting offered a vastly greater choice of channels and a different economic model. Many believed that the BBC would slowly be marginalized, that the need for its services would be reduced, eventually to disappear, and that licence fee as a method of funding was due to receive the black spot.

I took on the funding arguments in a speech at the 1990 Edinburgh Television Festival in a debate about the future of the BBC. I dismissed advertising as a way of paying for it. If it were intended to replace the licence fee, there was not enough to go round without destabilizing, possibly ruining, the ITV companies; if it were to be a supplement to the fee, governments would always from then on increase the amount of advertising allowed rather than raise the fee, thereby commercializing the BBC. Subscription, I said, would require taking away from the public what they currently received for free and making them pay more (to compensate for those who did not opt in) to have it restored to them. 'This is de-inventing broadcasting.' In any case, subscription had only ever worked for movies and sport, not for channels with a full mix of programmes. As for a grant in aid from the government, it would put BBC services at the mercy of the annual review of public expenditure, threatening its strength and independence. 'Governments should not allow such temptations to be put in their way. It is easier for them to avoid altogether the temptation to behave badly than to resist it.' The licence fee did look odd but 'it has been examined, inquired into, held up to the light, tested in the laboratories of sceptics, thrown against the wall, shaken and stirred, and every time the conclusion is that it is the most cost-effective way of turning money into programmes.'

Then there were those who argued that public funds should only pay for what commercial operators will not or cannot afford to make, labelling such programmes as 'worthy' and 'public service' and putting them into a kind of zoo for endangered species. What was so extraordinary was 'not just the snootiness of this approach but its illogicality. If you believes that certain

things have a particular importance in broadcasting, that these programmes
have great value to people and must continue, then surely they must be
where most people can derive most benefit from them, be where most people
have the opportunity to choose them: on broad mixed channels. It costs as
much to make such programmes for a small audience of committed explor-
ers prepared to track them down in the dark recesses of channel 97, as it
does to place them in the mid-evening of a national channel attracting a wide
general audience.'

Nearing the climax of my *allegro con brio*, I brought in the brass and tim-
pani. 'Let us ask: What is broadcasting for? What is it capable of? How can
we ensure that its capacity to enrich lives can grow? How can we make sure
that all its possibilities are on offer to all the people? Public service broadcasting does not mean whispering worthy thoughts in the corner of the
room . . . Above all, Britain needs a place that is dedicated to providing the
best that broadcasters are capable of and never the least they can get away
with.' It went down pretty well and I quote it at length because it lays out
some of the important arguments of the time, and, mostly, it still holds
good.

The BBC's plan to win a new charter began with thinking through its purposes from first principles. This time we would be asked fundamental
questions such as why we needed more than one television channel, why we
should not be a commissioner only rather than a commissioner and producer
of programmes, why the Corporation should not be split up. We needed to
have bottomed out these issues for ourselves and for the answers to be
widely understood. So Mike Checkland unleashed the 'charter review
process'. He and John Birt took the helm, Howell James and Patricia
Hodgson assembled and directed the crew. The management consultants
McKinsey's were engaged to help design its shape, provide research and
ensure that the interrogation was rigorous. Fifteen task forces were set up
looking at different roles and responsibilities of the organization: the BBC as
information provider, entertainer, educator, standard setter, cultural patron,
employer and so on. The members were some of the most talented people
from all parts of the BBC. The groups were to consult widely both internally
and externally, call for research and grill members of senior management. It
was an energizing and inclusive way of going about things, exciting in its
scope and thoroughness.

The campaign for the next charter was the backdrop to all that happened in the BBC over the next few years, including decisions over the three
big jobs, for the terms of office of chairman, director-general and managing
director of television were all due to end in 1991. Fox would go after his
three years, as he would be 65. I sensed that Hussey would like to continue
and until that was decided no decision was possible about the director-
general. At one time I understood that Checkland intended to go after his
five years, but now the rumour was that he wanted to stay on for at least
two, while everyone assumed that Birt had not come to the BBC to remain
as deputy DG indefinitely. There would be some struggles.

One of the greatest was to be over the work and proposals of the 'television resources study' set up in the autumn of 1990 under the leadership of John Birt, of which I was a member. Funding the Future was delivering savings but, looking ahead, the BBC had to adjust its number of television studios, outside broadcast units, film crews, editors and designers to what would be required when 25 per cent or more programmes were made outside. We had facilities all round the country, the capacity of which had never been measured and set against overall demand. We had an obligation to make programmes around the UK, and if they did not flow in sufficient number, then perhaps one or two programme departments should be relocated out of London.

I got to know John Birt much better on this group. He never showed any resentment at my fierce opposition to his longed-for new news building. In the chair he was always courteous and welcoming to members or visitors. He enjoyed a joke at the outset or conclusion of a meeting, or to break the tension at a sticky moment. An endearing habit then, and in executive meetings in later years, was his response to a joke at the expense of an otherwise sacred cow, the chairman, say. His hands would fall to the table; he would raise his eyebrows and drop his jaw wide in silent, surprised laughter as if to signal, 'I can't believe you said that. I hope the grown-ups can't hear.' John could not disguise his moods. When he faced opposition or when a discussion by the governors was not going as he wished, he would purse his lips, stretch his neck, even go red in the face with frustration or anger. He bore down determinedly on the work in hand. His degree had been in engineering and he worked methodically, beginning with the data he felt he needed and kept demanding that data until he received it all. Then he interrogated it, looking for holes, testing its strength. Only when assured that it was 'robust', a favourite word, could we move on to draw conclusions and formulate plans. It was a rigorous way of approaching problems and new to most of the BBC.

First, we had to measure the total resource capacity, no easy matter, and De Loittes were employed to help. John Birt's analogy was the break up of the USSR and perestroika. The days of central planning were over. 'The BBC should decide the level of its different resources by how much our producers want to use them.' How simple that sounds now, how obvious.

John was the most radical of the group; the regional member the most conservative. I was attracted from the outset by the idea of market mechanisms. My father was a bricklayer who had set up his own small building firm. In my boyhood he had lectured me often on the law of supply and demand. A market system would enable, and compel, producers to take responsibility and force resource managers, who had a monopoly, to become more efficient, reduce charges and put the interests of producers first. It would match capacity with demand. Producers currently argued for and were allocated resources rather than paid for them, and had little incentive to use them economically. Resource managers grew facilities to handle peak demand, creating down time in the troughs. Moreover, there was now a thriving provision of external studios, outside broadcast vehicles, editing and so on. Producers should be able to shop around to use whom and where they wanted for their money. I hoped that the BBC providers would become and stay competitive in quality and price, but they needed sharpening up. The level of overheads they carried was to be their problem.

At the same time, I was still nervous of what the full implications might be. There were arguments about the capacity figures Deloittes had produced, but that there was over capacity was clear. We visited Birmingham where two studios existed when one would do. We went to Manchester to see the new £6.5 million studio of which everyone was so proud but which was used only occasionally. Somehow the dinner of roast beef and treacle pudding our Manchester hosts provided seemed part of the problem in a world of Soho independents doing business in bistros and coffee bars. We heard much talk of how every regional base needed a 'full kit of parts', i.e. a big studio, an outside broadcast base, a dubbing theatre and so on, as a sort of sign that its voice had broken.

This work was going on over the new year of 1991, at which Paul Fox was given a knighthood, an honour that brought pleasure all round and a sure sign that he really was about to go. I thought that I was the person to succeed him. I had driven much of the action in television over the past two years, I had the editorial judgement and I felt that I could run the place with the confidence of the channel controllers, Jonathan Powell and Alan Yentob, and the programme heads. Paul took me to lunch towards the end of January. 'Now it's down to two people, John Birt and you. Ron Neil [who was now running regional broadcasting] has gone away. David Hatch isn't right for television. John Tusa [managing director of the World Service] wants to go back to programmes. Bob Phillis [managing director of Carlton] was a candidate but he's ruled himself out. David Elstein [director of programmes at Thames] and Charles Denton [ex-director of programmes at central, now a leading independent producer] are both very interested but Mike won't have either. The trouble is the chairman can't think about anything but whether he'll be asked to carry on.' Two weeks later he rang me to say: 'They are seeing you and one other on Monday. It'll be a happy chat. You're 80 per cent there.

I arrived early at Broadcasting House on the Monday and walked round in the wet snow for fifteen minutes rehearsing my lines. The 'chat' took place in the chairman's office, just Joel Barnett and Mike Checkland with him. I talked about the need to invest in the channels and to produce more big series, about how we would make the Funding the Future savings and prepare for more independent production and, very much at the chairman's prompting, about how 'to get the full range of opinion' in our programmes. I left feeling that if they wanted me beforehand, they would not have changed their minds, and strolled down to the HMV shop to buy myself as compensation or reward CDs of *Tancredi* by Rossini, an opera we had seen in Pesaro the previous summer.

The following day I hosted an evening party for the 25th anniversary of

Jackanory in the new White City building. Philippa Giles, the producer of the much lauded *Oranges Are Not The Only Fruit*, came over to me to say: 'If it came to a vote of producers, you would win easily.' Then, just in case I started feeling pleased with myself, she turned to my wife Jane, who was looking gorgeous, and voiced what many must have thought over the years: 'How did he manage to get you?' At the General Advisory Council the next day the chairman greeted me as usual with 'Good morning, Will', Joel Barnett with 'Good luck. It's a big job,' and Sir Graham Hills, the Scottish governor, with 'Have you heard the latest Glasgow joke? A scud missile [the Gulf War was on] landed on Glasgow and did £6 million worth of improvements.'

Eventually, on the Friday, Mike Checkland told me formally that I had the job, congratulated me, informed me that the salary was £90,000 (less at the time than one of the programme heads), and handed me a sheet of paper on which was a brief description of my overall task and nine specific objectives. The BBC had got round to writing down such things but not yet caught up with the notion that they were first best discussed and agreed. Not that I could argue with any of them. At the head was 'recruit, develop, train and retain creative staff, artists and writers to produce a complementary schedule of high quality programmes on BBC1 and BBC2 across the full range of information, education and entertainment'. In second place, and indicating the anxiety about impartiality, was 'ensure that the full range of opinion and cultures in the United Kingdom is reflected in the programme schedules'. Four of the remainder were about saving money, reducing staff and contracting out. 'No fixed term,' said Mike, 'That only leads to eighteen months of speculation before it comes up. You take over at the end of April. The story that I wanted Paul to stay on is rubbish. You have the complete confidence of the board and John Birt. I did put various possibilities to the board a while back: inside or outside, move people around. They went on from there.' I thanked him. 'Look in on John,' he suggested. I did and he beamed: 'Absolutely the right appointment.'

Now I had to demonstrate that it was. Keith Samuel handled the press conference, as he had fourteen years earlier when I had become a baby executive. The papers were neither unkind nor bowled over. 'New BBC chief to wield axe', the *Daily Express*; 'BBC picks "safe" director of TV', the *Independent*; 'While he may lack the "bottom" or charisma of the most recent [predecessors], he has wider interests than any of them. Wyatt's strengths are a thoughtful intelligence and the fact that he is a good committee man', the *Observer*; 'Staff were split over the appointment. Some said he was "perfect" for the job but others dismissed him as "a grey man with a face that happens to fit"', the *Daily Mail*. The trade papers had me as 'somewhat bland, rather clever . . . quintessentially the BBC' and 'a staunch defender of public service broadcasting'. *The Times* said 'if he lacks dynamism . . . he makes up for it with intelligence, enthusiasm and realism'. The *Daily Telegraph* pleased me most. I did not mind being 'exceptionally uneccentric', as long as I was 'good-humoured, clever, straightforward, hard-working. Steely when necessary, confident without arrogance and modest without self-deprecation', and, quoting a colleague, 'he thinks very fast on his feet, is extremely intelligent and is no coward. He never chickens out of the hard decisions and doesn't mind whether you like him or not.' I have sprinkled these quotes here (I think it is a fair mix – though 'bureaucrat' was in there somewhere, too), not because they are right or wrong, but because it is interesting to know how one is perceived. Readers may have their own ideas by now, but this is how I was seen then. I recognized some of the above, not always the flattering bits, and was surprised by some, not always the unflattering bits. Thus murmured the passing throng.

Within a day or so Janet Street-Porter came to tell me, in case I did not know, 'I'm very ambitious, Will.' She was not happy under the wing of Jim Moir in light entertainment, even though Jim claimed that his first annual report on her had read: 'She is a most capable woman doing an excellent job and I would have no hesitation in breeding from her.' I had decided, anyway, that her youth programmes department should stand on its own, not least because I had it in mind for possible relocation. Derek Jameson rang: 'Jolly good, Will. Now, if you're thinking of making any changes, I think the time is right. When I stand in for Wogan, the audiences go up. I want you to know I'd be interested in doing it. See, I could plug it on my radio show in the morning.'

I needed someone to do much of the job that I had been doing and wanted a woman. Television was still a largely blokey culture and there were few women in BBC senior management. I hoped to send a signal. I talked to several likely people within and without, and asked Jane Drabble to take the role, to which she agreed. This was a big jump for her. She had been a notable *Panorama* producer and was now the highly able editor of the documentary strand *Everyman* but had not run a department. Nevertheless, I had been impressed with the drive and guile she had brought to *Everyman* and, when we were together on a management course, with her forward-looking thinking.

Paul Fox's departure did seem like the changing of the guard. Although he had only been back for three years, he had made his name in the BBC and was regarded with much affection as one of the great industry figures. He did not like the changes that were sweeping through television and thought it 'disgraceful' that Mrs Thatcher had received a delegation from independent producers. Some of his happiest times as managing director were at rehearsals for emergencies when he had been able to capture the excitement of being channel controller again or when changing schedules for real to accommodate special broadcasts during the Gulf War. He was a big man physically who could seem intimidating. His 'hrmph' of disapproval at a sloppy or self-indulgent programme would startle some producers at programme review and he was never slow to make his feelings clear. He made sure, for example, that he was prominently out of the room, in the gents, when the Dimbleby Award, named after one of Paul's heroes, Richard, was presented to John

Pilger at BAFTA. But he was the firmest of friends and the warmest of men. He enjoyed celebrating others' achievements: honours, prizes and twenty-year bonuses. Paul welcomed people's spouses as part of the family. He had been discovered by his wife Betty singing Happy Birthday to their dog Cocoa.

There was a big turn out for his final programme review, which we followed with drinks, a video and a Jane Asher cake featuring a fox jumping out of a television set. On the Friday of his last week I had a final meeting with Paul. He went over unfinished business and advised, 'As for the money, you can leave that to the finance team.' Of which, more later. That evening Mike Checkland hosted the biggest dinner I had seen in the sixth-floor suite, packed with people from around the industry, and Paul concluded his generous speech by tossing me the key to the executive lavatory before calling on everyone to toast Jane and me. He had left me my appointment card for my first day:

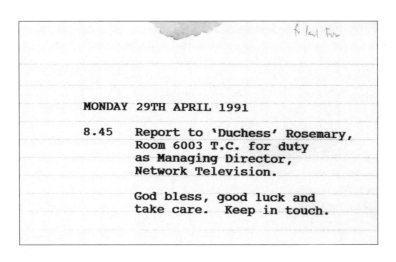

```
f. led For

MONDAY  29TH APRIL 1991

   8.45   Report to 'Duchess' Rosemary,
          Room 6003 T.C. for duty
          as Managing Director,
          Network Television.

          God bless, good luck and
          take care.  Keep in touch.
```

On Monday morning, a new treat. I was picked up in the managing director's car by Bill Ansbro, who had driven Paul, Michael Grade and Brian Wenham, and was now to drive me. I had had occasional lifts from some of the other drivers in the extensive roster. There was Roy, the acknowledged godfather, who collected cars at home (more than thirty were discovered when he died in 2002). Roy liked to tell you his stories: 'I drove Huw Wheldon to Sandringham once. He had me stop at King's Lynn to look up the other guests in *Who's Who* in the library. I asked him to find out who Charles was going to marry so I could get a good bet on. When he came out of Sandringham, he said, "Roy I raised your problem with the Queen, but she was unable to help. She doesn't mind who it is, as long as it is someone and soon."' Being driven by Roy's son, Keith, was a hair-raising experience. He was an ex-jockey with 'good contacts at the Epsom stables', though he never tipped me a winner, and appeared to believe that the 70 mile per hour limit was a minimum and applied on all roads. He collected speeding tickets as others collect beer mats. Terry, a portly fellow, was the pool driver. His hobby was fresh water fishing, for which he would rise at the crack of dawn and then sit still watching the float for six hours. It was a bit like driving really, for I do not think I ever saw Terry actually move into or out of the car; he just seemed to come with it.

Bill Ansbro was nervous on 29 April 1991 and had, he later confessed, practised three routes for the mile or so from my house to Television Centre in order to find the swiftest. Nothing was ever too much trouble for Bill. He would, and did, help anyone with a problem, especially if that problem was to do with a motor car, about which he knew everything. Bill is Irish and had begun his driving career on buses in Birmingham before moving on to BBC outside broadcast vehicles and then to driving the bosses. He was as courteous to other drivers on the road as he was to everyone he dealt with, and had an inconspicuous and highly effective way of chatting up whomever dispensed the best parking spaces or could let you through even though they should not, or knew the best route home or had the information you needed. He was teased by the other drivers for his conscientiousness but shrugged it off. They would not have dared go further, for he could have lifted any of them above his head, not that violence would cross his gentle mind. One of his great delights was that he had an identical twin brother who also worked around Shepherds Bush, so had regular stories that made him giggle of how one had been mistaken for the other.

On that first morning as we turned into Wood Lane, a thought suddenly struck: Paul had thrown me the lavatory key but I did not have the key to my office door. Would I have to spend my first half-hour as MD skulking in the executive loo? I need not have worried, for my new PA, Rosemary Haynes, the 'Duchess' to Paul, was waiting. Rosemary, always on time, always well dressed, always on the alert, had been PA to Charles Curran as DG and to Stuart Young when chairman. She knew the highways and byways of getting things done in the BBC and shifted work at astonishing speed, running rather than walking around the office when busy. She could lay down a mortar barrage of telephone calls, organize her junior, Alison, sort mail and greet visitors while her keyboard rattled accompaniment to all this as she attacked it like a woodpecker drilling a new hole. I was once to ask her apologetically if I could get a button fixed somewhere. 'Will, I've done buttons – and *much, much* more all my working life. So, don't worry about such things. In these days it's probably different. But I belong to the *OLD* school.' Rosemary was a perfectionist in the accuracy, spelling, tidiness and etiquette of anything leaving the office. She hated wasting time. On the telephone she would switch disconcertingly to a distracted 'Yes . . . yes . . . yes . . .' once the business was done. She protected me from friend and foe with the determination of an imperial bodyguard.

I held a big meeting of the senior television staff to announce appointments and lay out my stall, noting hopefully that I was taking over on the same day as did Gary Lineker as captain of England. Our aim, I said, was 'to provide for the British people the best television service in the world, entertaining, original, informative, popular, fair, accurate, setting standards in all areas of programming and to do this with efficiency, enterprise and cost effective use of the public's money'. I emphasized the increasing intensity of competition from ITV and Channel 4, and that BSkyB would eat into audience share as well as become a major player in sport. 'Change will be everywhere. It's no good thinking that if we can just get over this particular hump – whether it be a demand for savings, reaching the independent targets or the arrival of a new channel – we can all settle down. It's not going to be like that ever again. We just have to adjust and enjoy it.' I introduced Jonathan Powell, whom I had asked to lead a programme strategy team, to conduct a rolling review of all our output.

As the meeting broke up, Janet Street-Porter sought me out. 'Will, I don't think the BBC takes me seriously.'

'I've just given you your own department.'

'Yeah. But I could do a lot more.'

We were not going to resolve this then and I had to leave for lunch with the chairman who had invited me to Brookes. 'What can I give you if you could have anything you wanted?' he asked.

'We are badly under funded and can't afford a year round schedule. £100 million for BBC1 and £20 million for BBC2 is what I need.' That was not forthcoming and Dukie turned the conversation to his renewal that had just been confirmed.

'I didn't expect another five years. The Home Secretary rang up himself. It was all over in fifteen seconds. Hah.' He paused for a moment. 'My daughter said to me, "Daddy, all the BBC chairmen die in office. Now I suppose you will do the same." Terrible, these children, aren't they? Telling you the truth.' A few weeks later he caught me to report on his canteen lunch. It had, he said, confirmed his views. 'Cut the staff.' I had already, before formally taking over, had to announce more than 700 job losses to meet the independent quota. It would not be the end.

I set to work to build my new team, seeking too much consensus I feel in retrospect. The big task was, of course, getting the right programmes, and I will come to that in a while. I took over the chair at programme review and endeavoured to make it more rigorous and self-critical by nominating two programmes each week that were new or important and that people would be expected to have viewed. This enabled me to pick out people for their views, the shy and the cautious as well as the forthcoming and opinionated, to achieve a range of responses before coming to the producing department head and then the channel controller. I also invited independent producers when their programmes were on the homework list. Jane Hewland was the first. I encouraged franker minutes, but after damaging leaks of what someone said about Selina Scott, I had to have them sanitized again.

I was determined that I should have better information and data than that which was currently available. Whenever I asked for some figures of costs or programme hours or staff usage and so on, I was told that they were very difficult to collate and would take weeks. Going back more than a year was a problem because figures were gathered in different ways. I had witnessed the manic, all-hands-to-the-pump effort to pull together information for the consultants sent in to brief the government on setting the licence fee. Cliff Taylor was an heroic warrior at these times, both in getting the figures and in the battle of attrition with the consultants to force on them the interpretation we wanted. But there had to be a better way. I asked David Docherty, a bright former academic working at Broadcasting House, to come to work for me and set up a modern information system. David, who had written books about London Weekend Television and Channel 4 and been director of research at the Broadcasting Standards Council, did not take much persuading. He came and was a central player in the changes we made and success we achieved over the following years.

I wanted more and better contact with the world beyond television and began inviting the Fleet Street editors into lunch. (In the spirit of the times I ordered new menus of lighter food with fresh fruit rather than pudding, and instructed the catering staff that wine glasses should not be filled to the brim every few minutes.) They all came, and with Alan Yentob in top charm form, this definitely improved our relationships with the press. The top people had seen that we were a bright bunch, full of good intentions, not set on destroying capitalism or undermining family life. We still took a pasting from some of them, but found it much easier to get our voice heard in defence and to make the running on occasion. I brought in the Henley Forecasting Centre to present to all the programme heads a picture of what was going on in the nations their programmes were made for. I remember jaws dropping at the fact that 50 per cent of the population lived within five miles of where they were born. That was not the experience in Notting Hill, Ealing and Barnes.

I played host at the first of what was to be an annual summer party for writers. They were one of our most important constituencies and many of them felt unloved. Not that a party would put everything right, but it might help give the BBC a human face. It would also offer an opportunity for writers to buttonhole the suits. They were enjoyable occasions, each year in a different location. The Chelsea Physics Garden lives in the memory for an encounter with Keith Waterhouse. I admired Waterhouse inordinately, as good a writer of English prose as anyone alive I believed, so I sought him out. He soon became blurry and suddenly announced to us in the group round him, 'I think Keith's going home now', as he fell backwards completely unconscious. I was alarmed. He looked for all the world as if he had expired. But perhaps this was not unprecedented and, cradled in the arms of two attractive and admiring women, he happily came round.

The first thing that I looked at in the morning remained the duty log of telephone calls from the night before. It was a crude litmus test as to whether we had misjudged the mood of the audience. A dozen complaining calls (unless an obvious 'ring in') would tell you something was up; thirty or forty meant something serious. The huge numbers, 200 or 300, were for when we made short notice changes in the schedule: a sporting event over-running so the next programme to be dropped; a sport being postponed; a movie being changed. The log provided an insight into the minds of those who bothered to ring. On a natural history series: 'We've seen it so many times, hyenas being attacked by cheetahs. It's not entertainment. I would rather watch sex.' A titled woman rang about Ben Elton: 'After hosting a delightful dinner party, I do not want to hear about having sex with elephants or putting condoms in people's mouths. Your chairman will hear about this.' Mr Pratt from Bromley wanted a written apology and explanation for the use of 'prat' as a form of abuse. Sometimes it was hard to know what people were getting at: 'If Whitehouse and her ilk have their way, we shall soon be a nation of ponces and lesbians.' The small team who answered these phone lines demonstrated patience, helpfulness and an even temper. They had to suffer intemperance, banality and the ramblings of the lonely, as I discovered on the two occasions when I joined them to take calls myself.

In my second week in the job I received a visit from Michael Hodder, a fresh-faced ex-Marine officer who was on the BBC's payroll in a mysterious capacity. He blushed when I asked him the precise nature of his job. He was here to brief me on The War Book, which was kept in a combination locked safe in my outer office. In a matter-of-fact manner he took me through the alarming contents of the document. If one took it too seriously, it was enough to give one the screaming abdabs. 'State of the USSR . . . transition to war . . . food stocks run down . . . restriction of movement . . . no censorship . . . move to a single channel controlled by the BBC . . . 222 committee . . . code words . . . air attack warnings . . . no television.' What it all came down to was that BBC radio went to the bunker at Wood Norton while I remained in the smoking ruins of Television Centre.

Television had draft plans for the less apocalyptic, but more testing in broadcasting terms, eventualities of royal deaths or assassinations of prime ministers and so on. They looked incredibly restrictive and demanded all kinds of prepared programmes we did not have, so the channel controllers and I began revising and updating. At our first meeting we passed over Operation London Bridge, death of the monarch, and considered the more urgent arrangements for Operation Lion, the funeral of the Queen Mother. We went through a list of things to be discovered: whether we could have a camera on the royal car (or 'Royal Car' as it was typed), what the car's speed would be, the length of the procession and so on. Would we want an airship? Could we pool with ITN? 'One thing is certain,' I said before we started, 'It is on our watch that the Queen Mum will die, so we had better be ready.' The good woman was to spare us.

I was responsible not just for the channels and the programme makers, but for 6000 staff in the production resources and for the buildings. I began receiving the daily facilities log. It reported the security level we were at, which lights had failed and any incidents 'at the perimeter': 'Mrs X at main gate with usual array of rubbish for Terry Wogan.' Then there was 'Called to main gate where "Lord Waterstone" had been delivered in a cab. He claims to be related to the Queen and is in full regalia. He refuses to leave until he has been allowed to read the news. Police contacted. Mr Waterstone eventually removed in the van.' I said that I did not need to see this, just tell me about anything important. So I was rung on the next Christmas day to be told that a member of staff had been found dead in a lavatory in the basement, together with amphetamines and a porn mag.

I duly toured Television Centre to discover its nooks and crannies, walk over the roof and wonder at the boiler room reminiscent of an ocean liner. I supported the plans to complete the question mark shape of the original design with the stage five extension to bring videotape editing up from the basement blinking into the light of new space. I was deeply unhappy about the arrangements for our studio audiences. They had to arrive early and then queue outside in all weathers before being allowed into the studio. We were giving over 100,000 licence payers a year a good reason to moan about the BBC, and that was before they had seen the shows. It was insulting and it was unsafe. I asked Cliff Taylor what we could do in the short and the longer term. True to form, he leaped at the task and created an additional covered waiting area. We then developed plans for a new audience holding space within the new extension to Television Centre, with seating, a coffee bar and a shop. It took a while but we got there.

I spent time with the resource managers to understand their operations and how they were intending to cope with the job losses. I was still on John Birt's resources group and our recommendations were taking shape. Mike Checkland was worried. 'I can't argue with the report,' he told me, 'But I just don't believe the figures I've seen.' The figures calculated by Deloittes, implying huge over capacity, had been, and were to remain, bitterly disputed. Mike feared that John Birt would use the report to demonstrate at the joint boards conference how everything needed to be changed with the obvious implications. The conference was to be held in the week after I had taken over as MD, at the luxurious Lucknam Park Hotel in Wiltshire. It offered good food, the most comfortable of surroundings and was handy for Dukie Hussey's country home in Somerset.

By this time the whole Corporation was emitting a silent scream of pain as it waited for a decision on whether Mike Checkland would be renewed as DG, and if so, for how long, and whether John Birt would succeed him. The atmosphere was charged as the conference opened. Mike looked tense; John nervy. As was customary, the responsible cabinet minister, still the Home Secretary, Kenneth Baker was the first act on the bill. He said we had to match the ITC rules over balance and impartiality, that he sensed that many of our producers' attitudes were out of touch with the mood of the country and that we should try to find an alternative to the licence fee. 'A tough message,' thought Dukie.

The next day John Birt gave an interim report on where we had reached in the resources study. Phase one, measuring the BBC's capacity and comparing it with forecast demand two years hence, was complete. Phase two was nearly finished. This would establish where man power and facilities should be reduced and identify departments that might be moved out of London. The third phase was to introduce a market mechanism that would ensure the capacity of and demand for resources would remain in balance in future. We were confident that this would drive down unit costs, bring high utilization of people and equipment, offer greater freedom to our producers and reveal for the first time the true cost of each programme. We would save money that could be spent on more programmes.

The market system described here and above was what became Producer Choice, a name coined by the ever-artful Cliff Taylor. But the defining central principle of the system is usually missed in the arguments about Producer Choice. It was that for the first time the BBC's programme funds would flow down solely through the commissioners and the producers. The creative and editorial needs would drive the whole organization. The money would follow the programmes, the makers of which could spend it according to how they chose to create their programmes. No longer would the resource departments be funded directly. Their income would be determined by the amount of work they attracted from BBC producers.

In the discussion that followed I argued strongly for the internal market. Cliff Taylor, quick to launch on the tide, had already released producers to choose their film crews from in-house or the external market as they wished, and planned the same with editing and design shortly. The governors were warmly on side. Mike supported the market proposal, adding the mischievous suggestion that we should look at extending it to include news and current affairs, exempt in the plan, as they, too, would be commissioning independent productions.

That evening the speaker at dinner was Greg Dyke, managing director of London Weekend Television. We had consulted him for the study and he gave the same free market message to the boards. 'The change so far in the BBC looks half hearted from the outside,' he said. 'You must introduce the discipline of the market.' It was gung ho stuff. LWT had licked the unions under the threat of the franchise auctions. 'Use charter review in the same way. You gotta do it.' It was clear that we would.

Jane and I held a big lunch party at my brother's house in Oxford that weekend to celebrate our 25th wedding anniversary. It was a happy launch pad for some difficult weeks. Both Mike Checkland and John Birt were ringing me about the report. The big argument was where we should set our capacity ahead of introducing the market, and this came down to how many studios we should close and which ones, and what the scale of our outside broadcast fleet should be. I was conservative on the latter and a moderate on the former. John was steely in the group meetings. Logic said we should close two regional studios, but Mike would not buy this. At the beginning of June he rang me. 'I'm lying awake at night over this resource study. I never do that except on holiday. I can't close Birmingham *and* Manchester.'

There was still no news about whether Mike would stay on, and the draft report was due to go to the board of management. I pressed John to concentrate on where there was full agreement. He refused but did take specific points I made on the draft that I was broadly content with. At the board the market system proposal received a big tick. Mike, fighting hard now, made much of how little programme making we proposed moving out of London. Afterwards he showed me a note of the meeting that he had written before it began mentioning the news and current affairs centre at White City, the project he had previously saved from the chop. 'I think I'm going to pull that and put the money into programmes.'

When the governors took the report towards the end of June, the governors for Wales, Scotland and Northern Ireland piled in to argue for retaining the regional studios. The Edinburgh studio's usage was only 27 per cent. 'Chairman,' began Sir Graham Hills, the Scottish governor, 'I beg to point out that at my house my wife and I have a double bed. We sleep in it just eight hours a night and we are away a certain amount, so all in all its usage is about 27 per cent also. No one has ever suggested that was a reason to get rid of it.' The trade union leader, Bill Jordan, from Birmingham like Mike, was absent, but his letter defending the Birmingham studio was read to the meeting. Mike Checkland got what he wanted from the day. The proposals were agreed, except we were sent to look again at the studios and at what the regional centres of excellence should be. This was our plan that programme making for the networks in the English regions should be confined to the three main centres – Birmingham, Manchester and Bristol – each of which should have a critical mass of programme makers in one or more genre, thereby establishing clear areas of expertise.

Mike was not to get everything he wanted. 'I won't accept a year. I'd be a lame duck and I don't want five years,' he had told me. But would John leave in that case, I asked? 'Where's he going to go? He will wait.'

'I wouldn't want to see him go,' I said.

'He won't.'

On Tuesday, 2 July I knew an announcement was imminent following the governors' private dinner the evening before. I was due at a lunch Mike was hosting for the chair of the organization of Eastern European broadcasters. His PA sent a message to call in at his office on my way. When I did, Mike's face gave me the news as he opened the door of his office. It was flushed and he was bending low. It came tumbling out. 'John Birt is to be the next director-general. The board has asked me to stay on until 1 March 1993. Those I have spoken to this morning have urged me to stay on. They said it would give time for John to re-establish or build relationships and for people to work out their positions. I decided to about twenty minutes ago. I kept the chairman waiting three hours, as they told me at 9.30 this morning. I see Joel's hand in all this and in all the press stuff. And boards are influenced by what they read in the press.'

'I'm glad you're staying. Otherwise you'd have to go straightaway and that would leave a cloud over your time as DG, which would be unfair and inappropriate. We don't want another Alasdair situation. One of those was enough.'

'Come on,' said Mike. 'We'd better go to lunch.' In front of our guests and several members of the home team he sparkled. The BBC people present assumed that things had gone well for him. A classy performance.

I left the governors dining room where we had lunched and walked past the lift to the wedge shaped office of the deputy director-general. 'Congratulations, John. Well done, though this is an odd way to do it.'

'Thank you. It is.' He paused. 'I've talked to Mike about this. We've worked well as a team for nearly the whole time since I've been here. Only the past few weeks – since the television resources review and even then . . . I've done no scheming, I promise, I've not. Mike and I are quite alike in many ways. That's not something either of us would do.'

'Did you ever threaten to go?'

'No. Well, only a long time ago, when asked, in circumstances I won't reveal now, I said that I didn't want another five years as DDG. You can understand that. I don't run news and current affairs, I keep an eye on it. I work on policy, I have a certain number of tasks, but I don't have a job. But I was not threatening. It was long ago and I was answering questions.' I learned later that I was the only member of the board of management to speak to him that day.

Board of management meetings were held in a gloomy room and needed the lights switched on all year round. We sat at an oblong of baize covered tables, the DG in the centre at the north end, his back to two large doors that could be swung open to make one space with the governors' dining room next door. On his right was the deputy DG, on his left the secretary. The next Monday, Mike opened to the point: 'After last week's announcement I want to make it clear that I do not intend to be a titular DG only. I feel we should congratulate John, and,' turning to his right, 'John, I wish you well when you take over.'

'Thank you, Mike,' replied John, almost in a whisper. That was all. I learned later that Mike had asked him not to say more.

'I think we need our summer holidays,' said Mike. 'Now, let's put last week behind us.'

At lunch afterwards there was one seat too few. 'Just think what the press could do with that,' said Mike. He was in buoyant mood. 'Last week, I was visited by the ambassador for Outer Mongolia, who urged me to make a visit. "Was this the right moment?" I asked myself.'

Two days later Mike issued a formal announcement that the news and current affairs building at White City was postponed *sine die* and the money put into programmes. In happy, or unhappy, symmetry, that evening I hosted a huge party at Lime Grove to mark the closing of the studios, home of BBC current affairs since 1950. It was, according to your view, a monument to the glory days or the last chance saloon of the cowboys. Hitchcock had directed there; *The Quatermass Experiment* and *1984* went out from there; Richard Dimbleby had introduced *Panorama* there; *Tonight*, *Twenty-Four Hours* and *Nationwide* had been made there. Now it was being sold to be pulled

down to make way for houses. Vast herds of mega-fauna, among them
Alasdair Milne, Alan Whicker, Ludovic Kennedy and Frank Bough, returned
to the swamp hole for one final watering.

We faced a twenty-month period with a director-general in waiting. For
most of that time John Birt kept his powder pretty dry, but the resources
work had to be finished. The stand-off over the two big regional studios
turned to head butting by the autumn, and Margaret Salmon, the new director of personnel, sought to interpose herself between the DG and the DDG
in order to mediate. We had too many studios. If we closed Manchester and
Birmingham, where there was under usage, Mike would walk out. If we did
not close them, we would have to close two in London where most of the
work was. John was determined to achieve a unanimously accepted report:
'I don't want the board of governors to run the BBC, so we must have an
agreed position.'

This was making life hard for all around. Ron Neil, now managing director of regional broadcasting, was in despair, uncertain as to what cuts he
would have to make. Cliff Taylor was not one for agonizing. 'Mike ought to
go. I love the man. I've worked for him for twenty-four years and done his
bidding. But John is going to be DG and we've got to work for him. I hate
saying it, but Mike should go.'

It was for me to write the brief for the centres of excellence and decide
whom to move from London and to where. The BBC had an obligation to
make programmes around the country, partly to reflect regional interests in
the output, partly to be active economically away from London. Regionally
made programmes needed a sense of purpose, to be on the channels because
they provided essential genres, not to be there on sufferance. Bristol was
healthy. The natural history unit was one of the glories of the BBC, and
alongside it was a lively general features department making *Antiques Road
Show*, documentary and magazine shows. Birmingham had a drama unit,
Asian programmes and a strong hand of leisure programmes. Manchester
was the author in search of a character. It had a small sports department,
was struggling to retain its entertainment tradition and made the odd documentary. I decided to move Janet Street-Porter's youth programmes up there.
Some of the output was entertainment and I persuaded John that we could
keep many of the Manchester facilities open for her.

This would not be enough on its own to make Manchester a fully viable
centre. I needed to move another department and discussed this with the
channel controllers. It came down to one of the two smaller factual departments, science and religion. *Realpolitik* decided it. The science department
was the only one of its scale in the world. It had some outstanding producers and I did not want to risk losing them if they were forced to move.
There were good people in religion but fewer of the very top quality and the
department was less strategically important to us. If we lost people, it would
be a pity rather than a disaster. Religion it was.

I saw Janet Street-Porter first. She had a bad cold and was feeling poorly
but if it meant more output, she would be keen. 'I've got to sell it to myself

so I can sell it to the people I'd want to come with me.' She quickly embraced the proposition and the youth programmes soon had their Manchester credit at the end. How many of them were actually made in Manchester was another matter.

Stephen Whittle, the head of television religious programmes, was very upset. Stephen, round faced and bespectacled, argued in his softly spoken but insistent way against the move, his lip trembling. I said that Mike had agreed to see him if he wished. I briefed Mike, a strong Methodist who was sensitive to religious issues. 'Are you sure about this?' he asked.

'I am. I don't like having to tell Stephen to do this. He's a good man doing a good job. But if we show a chink of weakness, we'll never make anything stick again.' I persuaded Mike to fund another six *Everyman* films to help them, as a sop I suppose. The decision stood. Stephen rang me at home.

'When you took over you promised a more collaborative style of management. Now this.' His voice was breaking. 'I'm absolutely gutted.'

I anticipated trouble when we took this to the governors but it went though with minimal discussion. Mike thought we should send radio religion as well to make one bi-media department. The radio head Rev. Ernie Rae objected at a big meeting of senior managers called by Mike, pedalling hard to prove it was essential he be close to the religious leaders: 'Only last week I had a call from the Archbishop of Canterbury saying could I go and see him that very evening.' That did not wash. Manchester was as close to his ultimate boss as London.

I addressed an angry, uncertain and resentful meeting of the religious department and tried to steer their attention towards making the move a success. Jane Drabble was happily on hand to help them do so. She was ex-religion and upset by my decision but determined to do the best by her former colleagues. Worse was to come for Stephen Whittle. One bi-media department required only one head: him or Ernie Rea. The new overall boss would be Ron Neil, MD of the regions, and he, David Hatch (MD of radio), the Manchester head and I met to interview both and choose. To me, Stephen was much the stronger in both programme nous and leadership, but the other three were adamant for Ernie. I broke the news to Stephen, who has, I am glad to say, had a successful career both outside the BBC and now back within as controller, editorial policy.

Meanwhile, the charter review groups had been conducting their research and were drafting conclusions. When the chairs came together to share ideas, they were cast into gloom by the financial forecasts. The great debate was about where the BBC should place itself in the coming broadcasting department store of schedule choice and competition. Once it had been the only shop in town. It then shared premises more or less happily with ITV and later Channel 4. Now, should it move to the upper floors only, offering a limited range of the stuff commercial operators would provide only sparingly, if at all: the serious, the artistic and the educational? Or should it be on all floors, influencing quality in every department and filling the carrier bags of all customers? How should the BBC, publicly funded, differentiate itself from commercial broadcasters?

The governors' discussion of the emerging document veered worryingly towards an Oxbridge common room approach. Some of them would have liked to see the BBC as purveyors of television programmes to the quality. They were heading for what McKinsey's dubbed the Himalayan Heights option for the BBC, with only Joel Barnett, Bill Jordan and Keith Oates, finance director of Marks and Spencer, rolling up their sleeves to mix it on the terraces. Dukie was bullish, too. Looking at the forecast of declining audience share, he commented sternly, 'I'm used to looking at charts like this in the newspaper business and to seeing them turned around.'

I argued long, loud and to anyone who would listen, especially McKinsey's, that the BBC must be popular as well as distinctive for the reasons I have given above. I was responsible for producing the television section of the report with the channel controllers. I tried to make them and others worry less about what rumours said and to concentrate on our own solutions to the properly hard questions being asked of us. Alan Yentob was terrific when he got going on these issues, and we were of the same mind. Over the years to come, he was the one person in the BBC whose views about the purposes of the organization always chimed with mine and mine with his. The one difficulty was he tended to walk out of the room and fail to write anything down. We found ways of capturing it.

Nick Lovegrove was the McKinsey's man on the case. Nick, slim, red-haired and with rimless glasses, was a regular presence around the BBC for many years. He was the epitome of McKinsey's politeness, never fazed by ill-will or ignorance, always ready to press a proposal or line of questioning in his quiet, rapid way of speaking. When hearing a well-worn argument, he would give the best impression he could of patient listening, though you could almost hear the hum of his brain waiting at the traffic lights of the discussion. I was impressed with the McKinsey's people I met over the years. Only one ever stumbled badly on a task. They were all clever, courteous, personable and responsive. There was a hint of cloning about the neatness of their dress and easiness of their smiles, but I had fun as well as rigorous exchanges with many of them. You did need to know when to say 'thank you, that's enough' and finalize the work yourself. Also you had to beware being used as a laboratory for intellectual models. And they were expensive. Did we become over dependent? Probably, but McKinsey's gave a lot of value to the BBC and helped develop the Corporation's own considerable brain power.

Nick Lovegrove pressed us to define our difference from ITV (a good thing) and to identify things we would cease to do and leave to the competition (a dangerous thing). I was dead against telling the world that in time we would give up this or that kind of programme. 'It is almost impossible,' I told him, 'to proclaim a mid-distance strategy for the BBC in which we abandon things without abandoning them straightaway. If we don't put the case for wide-ranging public service strongly, we let down our true believers.'

The heavy stones on which the organization kept stubbing its toes were

Radios 1 and 2 and television entertainment. The two radio networks were deemed too similar to new commercial stations with too little BBC added value. 'I think that the radio argument will be unwinnable,' said John Birt, who was not voluble at most of these discussions, 'unless we change them significantly.' The debate about television entertainment usually came down to Saturday night shows, full of lights, noise and silly games, a family knees-up not inclined to appeal to those placing candelabra on polished walnut prior to guests arriving for dinner. I wrote to the chairman explaining some of the elements of BBC1 that would not be there if we were interested only in ratings, and that much thought was given to the appropriateness of entertainment shows. 'Jonathan Powell commissioned a programme called *Old Flames*. We transmitted a pilot and he instigated audience research that confirmed his own assessment that, while this would be a hit show, it would not develop into a show he would be proud to run on his channel. So he decided not to commission a series.' We thought *Old Flames*, a raunchier version of *Blind Date*, tacky. I suspect it would look pretty tame against much of today's output.

The good thing about these debates was that over more than a year, hundreds of the BBC's staff had argued about core purposes as well as individual programmes. It was an invigorating process. No questions were being dodged. But it did not make the job of running television any easier. Nor did the general climate. When the board of management spent a day considering the coming few years, we took a list of thirty things the BBC had to do and each put them in an order of priority. Mike Checkland put 'Introduce Producer Choice' at number twenty-seven.

Chapter thirteen
'IS THIS A NIPPLE WHICH I SEE BEFORE ME?'

The most important part of my job was, of course, the programmes. The summer of 1991 was a summer of repeats. Over the year, 30 per cent of all programme hours on the two BBC channels were repeats, as against 15 per cent on ITV. To look at the threadbare schedule now makes the blood run cold. BBC1 could only afford to run a full schedule for eight months of the year, and that summer, my first in charge of television, had no new drama or comedy on a Sunday between April and September. By July our Saturday nights were down to repeats of *Columbo* and *Casualty*. While we were running repeats of *The Two Ronnies* and *Butterflies*, ITV had *The Darling Buds of May* and *Jeeves and Wooster*. They had £300 million more to spend than BBC1 and carried twice as much new drama.

For many years BBC1 had partly compensated for this with popular American series that could run successfully in peak time, but *Cagney and Lacey* had ended in 1988, *Dynasty* in 1989 and this was the last year of the most popular of them, *Dallas*. The price of these per episode was between 5 and 10 per cent of the cost of home-made drama. There were not the new American shows that would work in peak on the main channel, and there have not been since, so the BBC could not afford to sustain that level of fiction in the schedule. ITV had added a third episode of *Coronation Street* in 1989, winning them Friday evenings. The gap between BBC1 and ITV in share had been around 11 and 12 points in the early 1980s, had been reduced to 3 by 1989 and had now widened to 8 points in the past two years.

I had asked Jonathan Powell to lead a review of programme strategy in each genre, I instituted a regular cross channel review of the schedules to ensure we made the most of our two channels' strengths, and began reading all the programme offers to the two channels. This last was not to second-guess the controllers but to enable me to review the whole picture with them and to help shape the programme departments' bids to prioritize what we most needed. My chief aims were to maintain the range of programmes in the two schedules, improve the popular drama, bring back adaptations of classic books – a traditional BBC strength that had fallen by the wayside –

and to encourage the development and commissioning of substantial and ambitious documentary series, landmarks, as we came to call them. I pressed then and did so for the rest of my time at the BBC for big events and big programmes that would leave a glow in the minds of those who saw them and would leave people saying, you hoped, thank goodness for the BBC.

With the two controllers I put together a bid for more money that, with Mike Checkland's encouragement, I pitched to the board of governors. I won nearly £40 million extra, though there was a wobbly moment when one or two of the governors thought it was for one year only. The relationship between managing director and channel controller was an interesting one. I was ultimately responsible for the health and performance of the channels and for the overall management of the programme departments, resources and support teams. The controllers worked to the managing director but it was they who shaped the schedule and commissioned the programmes. Managing directors did not traditionally interfere in this process, and I believed, and still do, in a channel being run by someone who lives and breathes its needs and who feels personally responsible for the output and editorial standards. That being said, if one did not interfere, it was occasionally necessary to intervene with a veto or a demand. Things worked best when there was mutual respect. I sought to affect the output by influence and by creating the climate for what I wanted, and later with some specific objectives. With managerial power over the producing departments, I could come at output issues from two sides. In any event, controllers often wanted advice or to refer a decision, and out of such discussions came agreed ground rules.

You never have to encourage a controller of BBC1 to be more competitive. The incumbents are acutely aware that every programme in the schedule goes head to head with ITV or, increasingly, with three terrestrial commercial channels. BBC1 controllers commission programmes, wait often a year or more until they are ready and then try to bring them to the screen with the best possible chance of finding a decent audience. It is what good programmes deserve. So the controllers look for every edge. You do sometimes have to remind them that winning a slot an evening or a week is good but not the overriding purpose for the BBC, that they need to maintain the range of programmes in the schedule and that the schedule must be demonstrably different from an ITV without ads. ITV's job is to deliver audiences to advertisers by means of programmes; BBC1's is to deliver a wide range of great programmes to audiences. The programmes are the end in themselves.

Jonathan Powell, the controller of BBC1, had been in this tough and exhausting job for three and a half years by the time I took over. He had been a hugely talented drama executive (*Tinker, Tailor, Soldier, Spy*; *Testament of Youth*; *Bleak House*, and he'd overseen the launch of *EastEnders*) who had brought ideas and energy to the channel. He was an eloquent proponent of the ambassadorial role of BBC1 for the Corporation. Jonathan was a most engaging man for most of the time but had a fierce temper when frustrated or believing he was being tricked or short-changed. He had had a famous 'fight' in the sixth-floor corridor with Ron Neil, then head of news, soon after taking over. I had seen him shouting at the head of plays and, once, in a meeting about the future schedules with me and others, his frustration boiled over and he screamed at me before walking out, only to apologize sweetly later. He came in then, as he did to most encounters, with a big, winning grin. He knew that I admired him and we got on well, but at some meetings of my senior team his body language would signal irritation in capital letters: he would sigh loudly and progress to noisy apple eating. Slowly he would subside and then join in enthusiastically. Jonathan enjoyed the mischievous try on. He would announce to news that he had no room for coverage of the party conferences, partly because he would like to begin his autumn daytime schedule earlier, partly to set a cat among the pigeons.

Jonathan Powell had developed a plan to restructure the BBC1 schedule. He wanted to end the thrice-weekly early evening *Wogan Show*, which had done long and valiant but now failing service, and replace it with what we were just allowing ourselves to call a soap. The plan would also have the successful fifty-minute drama *Casualty* go twice a week at half an hour, offering an equivalent to ITV's *The Bill*, would move *That's Life* from Sunday to Saturday and would bring *Songs of Praise*, our most visible and popular religious programme, significantly earlier on Sunday, making it late afternoon rather than early evening. I was for the *Songs of Praise* move but the chairman, director-general and deputy director-general were dead set against it, concerned about the signals it would send while the BBC was arguing for its special nature and privileges. I think we could have got away with it, though not doing so did not harm the Sunday evening audience. I backed the new soap but thought we should wait for the *Casualty* move, as that would mean in effect a third soap with *EastEnders*. In any case, the DG to be was adamant that we should not over soapify our schedule in imitation of ITV and said we could not do both. We were by then well advanced on thrice weekly, so that it was.

In August I had joined Jonathan, Mark Shivas, the head of drama, and Peter Cregeen, head of drama series, for pitches from the final two contenders for this new show. In order to fulfil the quota, we had confined the field to independents. The choice was between *Westbeach*, set in an English seaside resort, created by the writer Tony Marchant and to be produced by Alomo, and *Little England*, set among expats on the Costa del Sol, from Julia Smith, who had launched *EastEnders*, and Verity Lambert, creator of *Dr Who*, *Minder* and producer of many distinguished dramas for BBC and ITV. The latter would be difficult and expensive to set up. I questioned, too, whether viewers would identify with characters who had left Britain for the sun. Both Jonathan and I preferred *Westbeach*, which sounded funny, and we liked the seaside setting. Both needed more work, which we sent them to do.

Two months later Jonathan and the drama folk came to see me. They now all wanted *Little England*. I asked what had changed their minds. Verity Lambert, whom they admired and trusted, had convinced them of its long-term strength and the idea of including characters from other European countries as something new. I said that I would not second-guess them. I liked the other one, but if they were sure, I would back them. They were all sure. Work began on a tight timetable to get the required permissions in Spain, build the set, do the deals for staffing it locally, recruit the team and cast the parts.

Another part of Jonathan's plan was to replace some long-running successful dramas – *Howard's Way*, *All Creatures Great and Small* and *Bergerac* – before they began to go stale. The success of the new series, *Lovejoy*, starring Ian MacShane, encouraged him in this. However, other successful new series were to prove hard to find.

The overall drama boss was Mark Shivas, whose contract I renewed soon after taking over. A gentle, charming man, his credits as producer included *The Six Wives of Henry VIII*, *The Glittering Prizes*, *Telford's Change* and several good feature films. He was one of the top people in the business, though his interests were increasingly in one-off films for television and, beacon for talent that he was, he presided over rather than managed the drama empire. Too few in the department lived by the words that Dr Johnson wrote for David Garrick: 'The stage but echoes back the public voice. The drama's laws the drama's patrons give, For we that live to please, must please to live.'

Most of the talented people gravitated to the single films or serials in search of the significant, the edgy and the showy. Nothing wrong in such ambitions and terrific work turned up, *A Question of Attribution* by Alan Bennett and Anthony Minghella's *Truly Madly Deeply* in that first year, but it was also territory where if no one watched, comfort could be taken from how interesting a project it had been, how brave to have tried it. Never mind that 'brave' was sometimes code for 'getting my name in the papers at all costs'. Too often it was a culture cut off from what was going on in life elsewhere. It was not many years since one prominent producer had scheduled daily breaks for the entire crew, who had mostly hated this, to read and then discuss that day's edition of the *Daily Worker*.

There was a lack of drive and urgency in finding popular successes. Meanwhile ITV, with *Jeeves and Wooster*, *Inspector Morse*, *Poirot* and the Catherine Cookson adaptations, were stealing our clothes. I employed someone to work with Mark Shivas to bring more and better people onto the popular series. Drama was the most difficult department to manage or to deal with. A sense remained that it had the right to do as it pleased. Although it employed many freelancers and was the most ruthless in securing the craft talent it wanted from within or without the BBC, it was the most resistant to change when we introduced Producer Choice.

The serials unit was the most perplexing. It could turn out work like *House of Cards* and its sequels and the heartrending *Goodbye Cruel World*. At the same time it could disappear up its own obsessions, as with *Die*

Kinder, not the smart thriller you might hope for when you first saw that name but actually *Die Kinder*, a German title for a story about German political terrorists. Too often both here and in the single films one inferred a horror of positive characters or happy endings. Yes, the world is for many a grim place; yes, television drama should engage with this; yes, the BBC should employ writers and directors who want to explore the waterfront. But there is much else it should do as well. I used to dread being told by independent producers that the project they had on hand was 'a real BBC project'. I knew that it meant too dark, too depressing or too marginal to get away anywhere else.

Long running drama series are, apart from their own intrinsic virtues and pleasurable qualities, essential to the structure of a successful main channel schedule. The controller needs some bankers to play in runs of thirteen episodes, a quarter of a year, providing the centrepiece for an evening, attracting an audience not just to themselves, but also to the surrounding programmes. Knowing that these shows are available frees the controller to concentrate on all the other decisions of selection and placing, and provides a following wind for new shows launched off the back of them.

A promising entry was *Trainer*, set in the racing industry. The subject was absolutely to my taste and I visited the team on location at Peter Cundell's pretty stables at Compton in Berkshire. The programme was starrily cast but did not truly catch on and made it no further than a second series. *House of Eliott*, a 1920s costume drama about two attractive sisters running a London fashion house, was cleverly put together and a hit. It starred Stella Gonet and Louise Lombard, and Dukie Hussey was colour sergeant in the battalion of their fans. On a visit to the studio I learned that Stella Gonet had had her hair cut off for the part, which required a 1920s bob.

'What did you do with it?' I asked.

'My father is a keen fisherman and he made flies out of some of it.' She laughed. 'They're all called Blondie.'

Enormous care, as usual with BBC costume drama, went into the design and to good effect. Thus I was irritated in the most old bufferish way when, in a scene at a grand society dinner party, Louise Lombard, surrounded by thousands of pounds worth of accurate costumes, emphasized a point by jabbing her fork in the air across the table as if a teenager in MacDonald's. I made the point to the producer.

'Yes,' he replied. 'I noticed it, too. But it's difficult to tell someone about their table manners.'

We had three series of *House of Eliott* and made the big mistake of wrapping it when the two stars said they wanted to leave. By the time I learned of this it was too late to do what we should have done, namely to introduce new characters who could take over from them. We had too few shows with a 10 million audience to lose one.

Jonathan also commissioned *Spender*, the Jimmy Nail vehicle, a good and successful programme with a big star. It ran three years. We had *Love Hurts*, a romantic comedy series written by Laurence Marks and Maurice

Gran and starring Adam Faith and Zoe Wanamaker. This did run for the full thirteen weeks, and for three years. And there was a classy hit in *Between the Lines* from Tony Garnett, the greatest of British drama producers. Garnett had been an *enfant terrible* of BBC drama in the 1960s, making a series of brilliant left-leaning dramas, among them *Cathy Come Home*, *Days of Hope* and *Law and Order*. He had been to Hollywood in the meantime and now was back with his company World Productions. Sadly, *Between the Lines* self destructed after three series when it could have run for several years. Other hoped for bankers sank with little trace. A series about a minicab firm run by women paused at the end of every scene for the sisters to give each other warm 'we'll make it together' looks. The audience looked the other way. Popular drama was still in special needs. I began looking for a new drama head.

We had some fun and games with matters of taste in drama. Adapting the second amendment of the American constitution, the belief seemed to be that, a lightly regulated regime being necessary for the happiness of a free drama department, the right of the producers to bare bottoms shall not be infringed. Melvyn Bragg's 'bonkbuster', as the papers had it, *A Time to Dance*, was adapted as a three-parter for BBC1, featuring much full-length nudity, then a rarity. It met an entirely predictable and not unwelcome storm. *The Men's Room* featured some of the same, and then there was *Lost Language of Cranes*, a steamy homosexual story. The following year came *Lady Chatterley's Lover*, which I suppose passed as a classic adaptation on BBC1, featuring all of Joely Richardson. More press pyrotechnics and a flood of letters and phone calls. 'A scandal,' said one viewer; 'a triumph,' said a woman; 'Is this what all the fuss is about?' asked another man, 'I've seen better humps on Quasimodo.'

All these programmes had been shown to me before transmission, but I did not view individual episodes of running series, save in exceptional circumstances. Occasionally I asked: Is this a nipple which I see before me? (See overleaf.)

A programme called *Ghostwatch* was much more worrying. It had not been flagged as controversial, and after a Saturday walking in the Chilterns with Jane, I watched it on transmission. The drama was constructed as if it were a live factual programme monitoring events at haunted houses. It was set in a television studio with Michael Parkinson talking directly to viewers and to the 'participants' played by actors, and it included 'live' video coverage from the haunted premises. It broke the rules about fooling viewers. A spoof is fine, but this was an extremely convincing imitation of the sort of factual programme the BBC must be trusted for, presented by a known and respected figure. There were credits at the end and clues within that this was not what it seemed, but it was presented as if it were for real. I rang Jonathan as soon as it was over and he, too, was taken aback by the upfrontness of the imitation and by the response in calls to the duty office. At the programme review the following Wednesday the experienced and talented producer was amazed by the universal condemnation. Far worse was that an unstable young man hanged himself because, according to his parents, he was so

10 FEB 1992

BBC TELEVISION

MANAGING DIRECTOR

To: <u>Jonathan Powell</u>
     Alan Yentob

cc: Jane Drabble

<u>SEX</u>

Can you make sure that programme departments appreciate that
the sexual content of "The Men's Room", "A Time to Dance", "Lost
Language of the Cranes" is at the outside edge of what we can
transmit? I am quite happy that we have not overstepped the mark
but I do not want this level of frankness to be taken for
granted.

There was a naked breast in "Spender" the other week.
Nothing in itself perhaps but it wasn't necessary and didn't feel
right in a good popular series.

(Will Wyatt)

10th February 1992

disturbed after watching the programme. There was no way of knowing
what part the programme had played, if any, in the young man's death. The
suspicion was salutary enough.

On BBC2 Alan had brought excitement, controversy and ideas to the
channel. It was hip. I had underestimated him when he won the job; after all,
I was a disappointed runner-up. He could be forgetful. When Jane Lush, the
producer of *Film 89*, tried to persuade him that Barry Norman should go to
Los Angeles to cover the Oscars as he had the previous year, Alan was
unhappy because Barry was a BBC1 figure. Eventually, Jane Lush reluctantly abided by the decision that no one should go. On the morning after

the ceremony, as the team were editing the recording for transmission that evening, Alan called.

'Jane, how did they get on yesterday?'

'How did who get on?'

'Barry Norman and whoever went with him?'

'With him where?'

'LA for the Oscars.'

'But Alan . . .'.

Life around Alan was lively but unsettling. He would be re-writing *Radio Times* billings as the presses rolled. When he was commissioning the new logo for BBC2, the lively '2' that brands the channel to this day, Martin Lambie-Nairn, the designer, rang me: 'Will, help! Can you stop Alan trying to design the logo himself?' Yet after a row or he had messed someone about, Alan would always make amends, shamefaced and genuinely contrite. He was easy to forgive, as he was so utterly disarming. He would launch into an angry diatribe about an artist, a producer, a programme or a department, then suddenly burst out laughing at himself in mid-flow, seeing the daft side of it all.

After three and a half years in the job, he was still firing on all cylinders; indeed, for Alan there is no other way of firing. When the Royal Opera House staged Verdi's rarely seen *Stiffelio* with José Carreras back on song after leukaemia, Jane and I took Clive James and Allison Pearson to an early performance. I rang Alan to say he should see it quickly. He did, and with a typical piece of showmanship he cleared his schedule to take it live the following Saturday, creating a buzz and sense of excitement.

Alan understood talent. He spent time with them and would seduce them with his heavy charm phone calls. In many ways he was like a star himself. He could easily be destabilized. In working with him you had always to bear in mind his sensitivity about how a move would be perceived in the world at large, what its effect would be on his reputation, whether he would be seen to be rising or falling. He hated it and looked crestfallen when I had mentioned that I might want Jonathan Powell to be director of programmes, which would be senior to him. A newspaper article about 'BBC2's poor scheduling' upset him but served the purpose that several reminders had not, of stimulating him to take action about BBC2's dipping share. If share was a part of how people perceived success, he was going to win it.

When I took over, Alan was planning a season of rerun dramas directed by the inspirational Alan Clarke, among which were to be two of the greatest ever single television films: *The Firm*, about chic football hooliganism, and *Road*, the vivid, intense realization of Jim Cartwright's play. Alan also wanted to include *Scum*, the searing account of life in a brutal Borstal, banned when it was made in 1977. I viewed it, did not much like it but thought it was transmittable and worth getting out to clear the shelf marked 'banned'. I told Mike Checkland what we had in mind.

'Don't,' he replied. '*Scum*?'

'Yes.'

'Don't. I was one of the group that decided against showing it.'

'I don't like it,' I said. 'But it would be good to get rid of the ban.' I persuaded him to look at it again. He still did not want to show it. I maintained
the pressure and *Scum* went out in July 1991.

Alan's fretting was about light entertainment, or 'the slight entertainment' in Brian Wenham's phrase. As assistant MD, I had been aware that
relations between Jim Moir, the head, and the controllers were strained,
and had had Jonathan Powell in my office close to tears as he described his
need for better entertainment. Alan thought that too many of the rising talents were working with independent producers and too many of them were
with Channel 4 rather than the BBC. There is never enough good entertainment, and controllers become desperate for hit shows. To them the glass is
always half empty.

Jim Moir is a wonderful man. He is big of frame, portly would be the generous term, a devout Catholic, sharp of mind and very funny. After
university, apart from his two years in the army ('I was once a lean mean
fighting machine'), he had spent his whole career in BBC light entertainment,
with a long list of production credits, including *The Generation Game* and
The Mike Yarwood Show. Jim was always good for a funny speech and contributed greatly to the gaiety of the nation.

'How are you Jim?'

'I can tell you there are a number of balls in the air and two of them are
mine.'

At one programme review the mood grew steadily lower as programme
after programme was torn to pieces. Then the voice of rugby, Bill McLaren,
was criticized for heaping praise on every player *and* the referee. 'I think we
might invite him to this meeting,' said Jim.

He is a good writer with a light formality of style that spills over into his
speech. I had one meeting at an unhappy time for him. As we drew near the
finish of our business, Jim said, 'Now let me see. We've talked about sponsorship, about the Queen Mum's gala evening, about the head of comedy
job . . . yes, that's all. Now you were kind enough in your note to make mention of my private difficulties . . .'. On the night of the Queen Mum's gala at
the Palladium, a triumph for Jim, he confided, 'When I come back in the
next life, I want it to be as a dresser to the *corps de ballet*.'

The light entertainment department had always run on near military
lines. You worked your way up from assistant floor manager to floor manager to production assistant to director to producer. Alan Yentob and
Jonathan Powell were vexed when they heard stories that one or two bright
young people had offered ideas they wanted to produce, only to be told that
the ideas were good but, if they wanted to produce, they would have to work
up from the studio floor like anyone else. True or not, such tales were
thought to be symptomatic of problems with finding sparkling new entertainment. Controllers are like everyone else. They take what they already
have for granted, in this case some successful shows, and want more and different. In fact, 1991 was the first year of *Noel's House Party*, an inventive

Saturday night show packed with ideas and energy. It became a huge hit, won the BAFTA for best entertainment show in the face of trendier, smarter opposition and ran for ten years.

Jim was low. He knew that he was losing credibility with the controllers, who felt he was not frank with them. At the same time he felt they were capricious. When I told him he needed to bring in someone specially to develop shows for younger people for BBC2, he said he was not trusted: he had offered *Drop the Dead Donkey*, which became an award-winning Channel 4 show, only for it to be rejected. I knew that sooner or later I would have to move Jim, but first we needed a new head of comedy. Robin Nash, a big warm, cuddly bear of a man with an easy charm at work and a huge collection of Clarice Cliffe pottery at home, was leaving. He had successfully produced every kind of entertainment show and most recently the hit Carla Lane comedy *Bread*.

The relationship with the channel controllers was an issue. Since the arrival of independent producers with attractive ideas and talent signed up, the role of the controller began to change. For years the heads of the big production departments, entertainment, say, had a one-to-one relationship with the controllers who had nowhere else to go for that genre of programme. The head would largely devise or assemble the portfolio of likely programmes and would debate the priorities with the controller, who was forced to rely on him utterly. Now the top indies had direct access to the controllers. This flattered the latter and gave an inside track to the former. It also began to upset in-house producers and heads. This was at the heart of the entertainment tensions. We eventually brought over Martin Fisher from radio. It was a big leap but he was godfather to a clever hit show, *Goodnight Sweetheart*, by Laurence Marks and Maurice Gran, writers of *Birds of a Feather*. The programme, featuring Nicholas Lyndhurst, was about a man who finds a whole in a wall that takes him back to the days of World War II where he conducts an affair. 'I don't understand it,' Fisher told the writers, 'but I know that it's funny.'

'Broadcasting, having already created a wholly new vocation, will probably bring into being a new genus of comedians. It is to be hoped that the event will not be long deferred, for it is on the lighter side that the broadcasting entertainments appear at present to require most strengthening.' That was *The Times* in June 1925. We never have had and never will have enough funny people or programmes. Looking back, things were not at all bad in 1991. On BBC1 *One Foot in the Grave* had begun the year before, as had *Keeping Up Appearances* and *Waiting for God*, big successes all. New comedies that year included *2 Point 4 Children*, a show I was always fond of, and *The Brittas Empire*, which had a couple of years of huge audiences, and *Birds of a Feather* was going strong. Within a year *As Time Goes By* began, a lovely series with Judi Dench and Geoffrey Palmer that was to run for ten years. *Have I Got News For You* had just started on BBC2, along with *Bottom*, true inheritor of *The Young Ones*' crown, or bandana. A year later one of the all time great comedies appeared, *Absolutely Fabulous*, writ-

ten by Jennifer Saunders and starring her, Joanna Lumley, June Whitfield and
Julia Sawahla.

In the early autumn of 1991 David Elstein, director of programmes at
Thames Television, came to see us. I noted that his body language suggested
that he expected Thames to lose its franchise. Would we be interested in *The
Bill* and *This Is Your Life*? We would, and Jonathan Powell and I went for
a breakfast meeting at Elstein's house in Barnes. As our car slid secretively
into the drive immediately behind that of the Thames MD, Richard Dunn,
Jonathan giggled happily. 'This is just like it would be in a film.' Thames, a
big supplier of programmes to ITV as well as the broadcaster with the
London weekday licence, was developing an insurance policy. The company
would remain a producer even if it were to lose the broadcasting licence, and
was seeking to create some competition for its programmes. No deal followed the meeting but lines were open.

On 16 October we interrupted programme review to catch live the ITV
franchise announcements. Sure enough, Thames lost its licence to Carlton. A
couple of weeks later Jane and I took a shattered Richard Dunn and his wife
Jigga to a dreadful production of *Les Huguenots* at Covent Garden. Richard,
the tall, good-looking spokesman for all the ITV companies over the past
two years, was brought low by defeat. As it happened, George Russell, chair
of the ITC, which had awarded the franchises, was also at Covent Garden
that evening, studiously directing his gaze anywhere but towards Richard. In
the new year Richard, looking haggard, came back to me for a programme
deal and we bought *This Is Your Life*, a valuable early evening show that
had begun life on the BBC. 'The line is that we're not poaching it,' I told the
press office. 'It's coming home.'

The quality of the programme department heads was crucial to the success of the output. As managing director, appointing them was my
responsibility, though like all my predecessors, I did so in close collaboration
with the channel controllers, whose channels were dependent on the heads'
ability to develop and deliver good programmes. Almost as soon as I had
taken over I had to appoint a new head of music and arts. Janet Street-Porter
came to see me.

'I think I've solved your problem, Will.'

'Which problem is that, Janet?'

'I'll go for the music and arts job. But I don't want to apply unless I know
I'm going to get it. If I were turned down, I'd find that very hurtful to me.
I've never applied for a job in my life. I've always been offered jobs.'

'Ah,' I replied. 'There is no possibility of saying "yes" before the board . . .
I'd no idea you were interested. I anticipate a very strong field.'

Janet did not apply and the job went to the 33-year-old Michael Jackson,
editor of *The Late Show* and protegé of Alan Yentob.

He had come to the BBC at Alan's invitation and later told me how.
'Alan rang and asked me to have lunch with him. In those days heads of
department were powerful figures, so I went. It was an interesting lunch and
towards the end Alan said: "I'd like you to come to the BBC to be assistant

head of music and arts." This sounded good, so I said "yes". "There's just one thing," said Alan, "I have a very close friend called Leslie Megahey who is already assistant head of music and arts and I haven't mentioned this to him yet."' *The Late Show* was Michael's creation and a success. His appointment now would, I knew, alarm the older hands in music and arts, but Michael was a man to move the place forward. In my office the day after the interview I congratulated him on being the new head of department and shook his hand. 'Can that be music and arts *group?*' he immediately asked, group being a grander BBC title.

'No.' But it was a good try.

The next job up was head of features, a large factual department making *Crimewatch* and Children in Need among much else. The outstanding applicant was Mark Thompson, a year older than Jackson, editor of *Panorama* and before that of the *Nine o'Clock News*. Jane Drabble, who would be his line manager, was sceptical, and Jonathan Powell viewed him, I think, as a fifth columnist from the news and therefore suspect. We kept the candidates hanging on over Christmas, interviewed all three again and eventually I got agreement for Mark. It was a messy process that I should have managed better.

The factual departments remained in fair shape and in 1992 we found a new long-running hit in 999, a format that combined exciting tales of heroism in the emergency services with useful information on safety and first aid. The series that rightly won all the prizes that year was *Pandora's Box*, written and produced by Adam Curtis, who had been a shy, clever and funny young producer with me in Kensington House. It was wonderfully original in subject matter as well as style, on the politics of science during the Cold War. Even while I was still in docs we had begun exploring a big series telling the history of the twentieth century at the instigation of the independent producer John Gau. We could not get his proposal going but I was determined we should do such a series and asked Peter Pagnamenta to pick up the project and reinvent it, which he did. With the help of the American public television station in Boston and the BBC's commercial arm, Worldwide, Peter produced the twenty-six-part *People's Century*, the biggest BBC documentary series for thirty years.

Alan Howden was in charge of our purchases of films and American series. Alan was a skilled negotiator, an assiduous cultivator of relationships and had a phenomenal knowledge of movies. He also had good judgement about what should be transmitted when or not at all. The movies were usually offered for sale in packages: a blockbuster or a group of first-rate films in the van, pulling behind them a clutch of reasonably attractive titles and in the rear some, frankly, crap productions. A news story broke castigating the BBC for buying Martin Scorcese's *The Last Testament of Christ*, a film that had upset some with its controversial depiction of Jesus. It was acquired as part of a package. I asked Alan Howden for a tape and viewed it. The film was far better than I had expected, a serious and thought-provoking work that I felt we could and should show and I told Mike

Checkland, the director-general, as much. He was unhappy. He was a religious man, had seen the nonsense in the press and, I suspect, had the chairman hopping up and down.

'I'm going to be difficult about *Last Testament*,' he told me. 'I don't want it to go out while I'm DG. I'm sorry but I feel strongly. It's not one of our programmes. I went along with *Scum* but not this. Think how you want to play it. I can overrule you if you like.'

'No, I don't want that. But you haven't seen it. It is a good film.' Mike was adamant and I announced at the next board of governors that we had 'no plan to transmit' it. Channel 4 took it off us, so it went out.

Another difficult movie was *The Accused*, for which Jodie Foster won an Oscar as a rape victim whose attackers receive light punishment because she is deemed of poor character and who sues them to get justice. Alan Howden asked me for my view. I watched it with Jane. It was a good and powerful film but the rape was prolonged and I asked for one or two cuts. I am not sure I was right. After it had gone out I bumped into James Ferman of the British Board of Film Censors. 'Editing it may have worked for women,' he said, 'but for men, the film had to raise the old Adam and then demolish those feelings. With the cuts, I don't think it did.' I have not seen the film since, so I cannot be sure.

A comedy film came in handy when, in accordance with the eternal rhythm of the spheres, bad language again troubled some of the governors. I had inherited and retained a rule that any use of the word 'fuck' had to be approved by the managing director before transmission. Channel controllers referred the programmes to me, save when they said 'no' themselves. Sometimes I was their alibi; mostly they wanted to keep the word in. I was thought to be conservative. I do not think that I was but I had to be firm or the word would have been everywhere and the audience was not ready for that. Slowly 'fuck' has lost much of its power to shock or offend, and may one day become as enfeebled an expletive as 'bloody', a very bad word when I was a boy. But 'fuck' is still beyond the pale for many, and broadcasters must take that into account.

I have always felt that it comes down to good manners. On meeting people for the first time, even if you were regularly foul-mouthed, as I am, you would not presume to use the word until you sensed that this person or this group would not be affronted by it. You just might in some circumstances want to shock for effect but you would find a way to give warning. On television it is much the same. A late night laddish show or a tough movie is a context in which the audience might expect to hear 'fuck', the viewers being mostly those for whom it is in everyday use. Otherwise you include it sparingly and tell people before the programme starts what they are in for. I once saw an extreme solution in a Canadian documentary about a union negotiation in which obscenities flew. At the beginning of the film there was a caption about language: 'to remove would make the picture of events untrue'. Later came a superimposition: 'Warning: coarse language upcoming. Viewer discretion advised.' Then, two minutes later: 'Warning:

coarse language follows. Viewer discrimination advised.' It did everything but shout 'Duck.'

The film that helped me with the governors was *Trains, Planes and Automobiles*, in which Steve Martin, boiling with frustration at an airline ticket desk, lets rip with 'fucking' every other word. Dukie Hussey had put language on the board agenda and I did a reassuring turn about our rules, concluding with the Steve Martin clip, first unedited, at which everyone – well nearly everyone – fell about, and then edited, to make it 'fuck' free, at the same time sucking it dry of humour.

'Why are we discussing language?' asked Lord Nicholas Gordon Lennox, a wise ex-diplomat. 'Surely, there's no problem?'

'Because I asked for it,' replied a grumpy Dukie. Afterwards, Mike Checkland came over, laughing.

'The chairman didn't expect it to go like that you know.'

The time I could devote to the programme agenda was limited by the pressure of other matters. Through the second half of 1991 and all of 1992 the BBC was preparing for the introduction of Producer Choice, due to go live in April 1993. Many of us were worried at first that eighteen months was not long enough to ready the organization for such an earth-shattering change in the way it ran itself. Looking back, it was the best way: a tight deadline to concentrate the minds and force action rather than debate. Coopers and Lybrand were employed to help. A BBC-wide steering group guided the process but many of the solutions and much of the action were in television. The Corporation was divided into more than 400 business units that would trade with each other. Each had to write a business plan, an entirely new discipline that some took to and others struggled with. The principle was that the funding for the two channels should equal the full cost of all the production and resources business units in London and the regions, including charges for capital, property and overheads. The programme funding managed by the television channels would rise from £350 million to more than £800 million. All programme budgets had to be recast to include the full costs, the new budgets reconciled with all the various business planning assumptions and with the available cash. New standard contracts, financial authority levels, reporting requirements and financial systems were all being developed. It was a massive task.

There was support and training courses aplenty but it was the cultural change that people found hardest. I pushed the resource heads to think about their pricing policy, how to sell rather than apportion their services and how to build relationships with producers who, for all their protestations of undying loyalty, might turn out to be promiscuous when the day came.

In production and in commissioning we faced a 6 per cent reduction in the tariff for programmes. No one thought it possible but it was easily achieved. For the first time we had to worry seriously about the stock of programmes made but not yet transmitted and the amount of cash tied up in work in progress. Controllers had tended to be prodigal with this, commissioning to shut people up and putting on the shelf programmes they were disappointed with. One of the planners had his own vocabulary for these: 'a pleasure deferred' meant stock; 'a jewel in the crown of another season' meant stock; 'important to our Celtic chums' meant regional stock.

Fears abounded. I feared lest the creation of tariffs for each genre of programme lead to direct central control. Production departments feared that they might be revealed as too expensive and that the whole scheme was a plot to scale down in-house production and create a massive switch to independents. Resource departments also feared a plot to drive them out of business because of their heavy overheads, and close down BBC resources. An *Evening Standard* story forecast that 10,000 BBC jobs would go. Producers feared lest their favourite camera team, editor or designer leave to go freelance. The crafts teams feared for their jobs. The leftist tendency in some parts of the place believed that the BBC was introducing these 'Thatcherite' reforms merely to curry favour with a Tory government just when it was throwing off Thatcherism, that the changes were both craven and unnecessary.

The world, especially those who would make decisions about the BBC's next charter and the talent with whom we worked, was watching. John Cleese took me to lunch to ask about what the BBC was trying to do. He had an idea for a film about a zoo with a new Thatcherite boss, and the BBC seemed to be the model. Of course, many talented contributors and producers were ambivalent. They worried about the creative health of a BBC revolutionizing itself, yet liked the idea of a system that would give producers more control and choice. When I argued the case for change I pointed out to production teams that in the past the complaints I had were about the constraints now being thrown off: producers being allocated in-house crafts people they thought were unsuitable or no good, producers not being allowed to go outside for people to build the team of their choice, young women directors being patronized or humiliated by old-stager cameramen who were wished upon them.

The system, at introduction, was over-complicated with too much unnecessary internal trading, but the bigger mistake was in failing to prepare the ground enough by convincing an all too insular organization that the change was essential. It would have been impossible to whip up enthusiasm but we could have got more people on side sooner. As we pushed on, I would tell people to look at what had happened or was happening to the companies or industries their parents or partners, their siblings or friends worked in, let alone what had happened in ITV in the run-up to franchise bids. The world was a more competitive place and new systems made it possible to achieve efficiencies and drive out waste. Why should the BBC be insulated from this? How could the BBC be insulated from this? The people who paid our wages with their licence fees had every right to expect that the forces acting upon their places of work would act upon us too. What was more, there was the prospect of a big investment in programmes from the savings that would be made.

Jane Drabble found a company that had worked on the health system changes to lay on a Producer Choice business game, a two-day simulation of what life might be like when the new system was in operation. In a hotel at Bexleyheath about eighty people from across the Corporation played different roles, mostly their real life ones, as we went through two years of television at fifteen minutes a month, stopping now and then for a debrief to extract lessons. Janet Street-Porter shone as the wiz at working the system.

Throughout this I had been wrestling with the consequences of a mighty blow to the solar plexus delivered by my finance team. They had told me how managing directors were usually briefed on the television budget in the fifteen-minute car journey between Television Centre and Broadcasting House for the budget meeting with the director-general. I intended to be different. I had involved myself in the budget and felt I was well acquainted with it. Nothing had prepared me for what I was to hear that Tuesday, 19 May. I went to a memorial service for a former BBC luminary, rehearsed a presentation I was to give to the governors next day at the joint board conference, then addressed and took questions at the sports department meeting before returning to my office. Julian Ekiart, my financial controller, came to see me looking strained and, as I noted in my diary, 'gave me dreadful news about the end of the year accounts. God knows what's happened – he doesn't seem to.' We had overspent by at least £25 million.

But the full awfulness was yet to come. Julian Ekiart and his colleagues were poring over the figures, but by the first week in July it was still not clear where many of the millions had gone. I said I wanted an external investigation and called in a team from our auditors. Late in August I was on holiday driving between Suffolk and Sussex when I received a call that made me want to throw up.

'Will, we have reworked the figures.' It was the finance number two. 'The final figure is just over £38 million.' Back at work I spent a whole day going through the findings. It was an appalling mess and our systems were a shambles. I told Mike Checkland that I wanted a new financial controller straightway: John Smith, the bright young accountant who had worked on the television resources committee. He agreed. He also handed me an envelope.

'What's this?'

'It's your bonus.'

I handed it back. 'I can't take it with this financial mess.'

'But it's not your fault.'

'That's not the point.'

A couple of weeks later I had a call from the chairman. 'Will, we've all been dropped in it by our finance friends at one time or another. Don't blame yourself. I know you are having a bad time, but I want you to know that I understand these things.' That was that. It was decent of him. A few days afterwards, my bonus, a cheque for £3000, arrived in the post.

At last I learned what had happened to 'the missing millions'. The biggest error was that the budget to pay for the resources elements of education programmes had been added as intended to the channel funds but had not been removed from the education budget. Thus the money was allocated twice. Along with this was a £15 million discrepancy between the resource department budgets and what programmes had been charged, a shortfall in the savings to pay for independents and a hole in the forecast income from co-productions. Other savings offset some of this, but it netted out up to £38 million. It transpired that the crucial account-keeping for the channels was still done in a hand-written ledger. Such were the antediluvian systems that none of this was visible till the year-end.

I learned, too, that there had been a £13 million problem the previous year, sorted between television and the director-general. No one had seen fit to tell me about it and no one had investigated to discover the underlying causes. To be clear, there had been no fraud. The money had been spent on what we were supposed to spend money on, programmes, and the BBC as a whole was not overspent. But the reporting and control procedures were hopeless.

I threw myself into understanding every aspect of our finances. I would not have myself put through that again. The bustling John Smith and I drew up an action plan. We presented the full horror of what had gone wrong to all the senior people in television and John conducted a series of financial seminars with all departments.

The governors' audit committee, chaired by Joel Barnett, former Financial Secretary to the Treasury, understandably waded in. I reported on what had happened to it and to the full board. I worked out £20 million worth of pro-gramme cuts with the controllers, but that would not be all. The lead time for commissioning and making programmes meant that by September 1992, where we were, the spend for the following financial year 1993–4 was all but committed. The faults that had caused the hidden £13 million in 1991 and the £38 million in 1992 were only now being corrected. I had moved as quickly as I could, but the machine had been churning away and I was now given a forecast overspend for the year we were in of a heart-stopping £80 million.

Mike Checkland did not believe this. 'Accountants are always giving me forecasts that are wrong.' He battered away until it was reduced to £20 mil-lion and I again set about cutting our transmission plans. The BBC reports formally on the amount spent on transmitted programmes, so by holding completed programmes to the following year, we could make savings. This also reduced the need for later production spend to fill those slots. We also abandoned some of those few projects that had not yet gone into production for the current year.

All this was a big embarrassment for Mike, now into his final months in office and whose reputation was as an effective and inventive manager of money and resources. What is more, the BBC was bumping up against its government-imposed borrowing limit. With the charter debate underway, the governors would not countenance any approach to have the limit extended.

Joel Barnett was strutting his stuff now the audit committee was centre stage. He wanted a dramatic resolution to demonstrate that governors ruled OK. Ian Phillips' strained appearance showed that Joel had his scalp promised. Joel was in his element as he reported to the full board at the White City building. It was decided that there should be a press conference to accompany the BBC's statement. John Birt, now a month from taking over, wanted it to be given by Joel or me. I could not let a governor do it, so I was whisked down to Broadcasting House with our new director of corporate affairs, Pamela Taylor. She had joined a month or two earlier after the ever cheerful Howell James had left for Cable and Wireless. Pamela was taken aback as we walked into the council chamber to face an excited mob of reporters and photographers. She turned to me and said: 'Good God. Does the BBC do this to people often?' It was bloody. As always on such occasions, reporters competed with each other to sound more aggressive and self-righteous than their rivals. Faces I knew to be friendly suddenly appeared to be snarling at me. They smelled blood but found me only bruised. I went back to Television Centre to address all the senior staff there.

A week later Jonathan Powell asked to see me. He told me he was leaving and had accepted the post of head of drama at Carlton. I was not surprised and nor was Rosemary, my PA. When Jonathan had left the office I told her he was going. 'Oh, I guessed,' she said. 'I've seen that expression and the pacing up and down many times before. I knew what was up.'

Jonathan had been controller of BBC1 for five years, longer than almost all his predecessors, and it had begun to run him ragged. He was badly knocked back eighteen months earlier when his plans for a redesign of the schedule were mostly rejected. The period since had been blighted by *Eldorado*. Jonathan had asked for the start to be pulled forward in order to launch it in the soft summer period rather than against the full autumn ITV bombardment. This was tight but possible, according to the team. At first we had encouraging reports. I was buoyant about it: 'on course, high risk, exciting'. Then came stories of problems. The producer was over-working and refusing to delegate.

On 1 July we had broadcast the last of Terry Wogan's thrice weekly programmes that *Eldorado* was to replace. Terry was fed up at being taken off, but the live show had run for seven years and had been a great achievement. No one before or since has sustained that number of evening talk shows on British television, but then Terry is witty, well read and has a sharp eye for the absurdities of the world around us. At television he is a great talent; at radio, whither he was now to return to for a daily show, he is a genius.

The first episode of *Eldorado* opened with a pair of knickers being thrown from an upstairs window. For all the arguments that I could and did make about the boldness of the ambition, the innovativeness of its setting, the creative risk of including a variety of nationalities and the quality of its production team, I knew that this did not bode well. Ordure began to be poured on the show from the press, fellow broadcasters and those closer to home. 'I won't discuss it at the board of governors,' said the chairman, 'but it's sleazy.'

Jonathan conducted himself well: defending the show in public; pressing it for change in private. The casting, normally one of Julia Smith's strengths, had been poor, so characters were being written out and new ones in. I held a crisis meeting with Jonathan to question him on his remedies before he came to the board of governors, where he dealt with a storm of criticism with wit and honesty. Things were getting to him, though. The day before he told me he was leaving, he was almost in tears at a breakfast meeting with a possible new drama head: 'Mark Shivas wanted to do *Eldorado*. He should be sacked.' On top of all this, Jonathan was resisting my plans for the more formal commissioning system that I wanted under Producer Choice. So his news was not a surprise. I asked Alan Yentob to mind the shop at BBC1 as well as run BBC2 until I had found a successor.

Thus I found myself in the middle of December 1992 looking for a new controller for BBC1, reeling under the impact of 'the missing millions', waiting on a change of command at the top and hearing rumours that I was about to be sacked put to me by the press. What made it worse was that what with all this and the corporate shenanigans of the past eighteen months, I felt as though I had not been able to get properly started.

Chapter fourteen
'YOU'VE ALL BEEN TOLD TO CLEAR YOUR DESKS. TRUE?'

As the General Election of April 1992 approached, there was talk that Mike Checkland hoped that if Labour were to triumph, he might win a reprieve. I could not see how. A new government might have asked Dukie to retire gracefully but they could go no further. In any event, when the Basildon result came in – Labour had failed by 2000 votes to recapture it – I was standing next to a shocked Baroness Blackstone in the sixth-floor suite at Television Centre, and both her face and the studio pundits told me that the Tories were back.

Mike wanted to see the charter review work that he had instigated through to publication as the BBC's case for its future. Most things were agreed, though the debate about programme purposes continued. John Birt hated the term 'mainstream' to describe any part of our activities, believing that this characterized the broad current of commercial provision and that, to justify public funding, we had to distinguish ourselves from it. Saturday evening entertainment remained the arena of disagreement. It was easy to say what a BBC Saturday night show should be, and I did so: 'It should have wit and originality; when members of the public are involved they should be celebrated rather than mocked, emerge enhanced rather than diminished . . .'. The problem was finding such shows. I encouraged both controllers and planners to ignore the more theoretical messages emanating from Broadcasting House.

Still, the BBC case was coming together impressively under Howell James' skilful handling, and by May the BBC's document was well nigh ready. Many of us had been able to comment on or contribute to the draft. It was to be called Extending Choice, a cunning title, as 'choice', everyone agreed, was a jolly good thing. The document argued that while a new broadcasting market would offer a cornucopia of new channels, the BBC, far from becoming less relevant, would become more so as the guarantor of genuine choice. It identified four important tasks for the BBC: informing the national debate; expressing British culture and entertainment; creating opportunities for education; and communicating between the UK and abroad. In each, emphasis was placed on range of provision and supplying what purely commercial operations would, or might, not. Extending Choice explicitly rejected the Himalayan heights position, as I knew it would have to. To take that line would have removed from most licence payers programmes they enjoyed, pushed public service broadcasting into a cultural ghetto and limited the BBC's ability to influence the full range of programming. The document argued the case for a single organization and for the licence fee against all other funding alternatives. It promised value for money and greater accountability.

We felt that it was an impressive case and were well pleased with it. Such was the position as the boards of management and governors gathered for the third year within the honey-coloured stone of the Lucknam Park Hotel for trial by luxury, or the joint board conference as it was called. As a day visitor two years earlier, I knew it was too swish when I heard a governor complain, 'water's too warm in the pool'. This time the press had cottoned on, were kicking the BBC to pieces and staking us out. The pool was one of the reasons that Dukie liked the place. Swimming was his exercise and he was a goer, moving swiftly, like an athletic crab on his two arms and one leg from changing room to pool, then completing his lengths at surprising speed.

On the second day David Mellor, Secretary of State for National Heritage, the new sponsoring department, spoke before dinner. He was supportive, urging us to be clear about our vision, to sort out our cost structure and not to cut him off at the knees by implying that he was over-friendly to the BBC. So far, so good. Then came a blow.

'Don't publish your document before we have set out the framework. It is up to you but I advise against it. Your enemies in the Commons and the Lords will use it to mount an attack and we will have to set a framework to take account of the issues they raise.' He then turned to his permanent secretary, Hayden Phillips, 'He's my Sir Humphrey.'

'I would say, Minister,' began Phillips, as if imitating Nigel Hawthorne, 'that it would be very courageous of the BBC to *plunge* in earlier. It would certainly be a very *brave* thing to do.'

Joel Barnett pressed Mellor on this but the message was clear. Mike Checkland's face had become glum. We were geared up for the final draft in three weeks and to publish three weeks after that. This was now impossible. Would he be able to launch the BBC's case before his time was up?

A difficult period followed. The four managing directors, David Hatch, Ron Neil and John Tusa and I, met a couple of times for dinner, a sure sign we felt threatened. The BBC was three-ways dysfunctional at the top, with Hussey, Checkland and Birt manoeuvring round each other. At the Edinburgh Television Festival, Michael Grade made a crowd-pleasing attack on Hussey and Birt that hit the easy targets and ignored the real dangers facing the BBC. The *Sunday Times* tracked John Birt down to a hotel in Santa Fe. '1000s to be sacked. Eldorado to go,' ran its headline.

At the beginning of September the trade magazine *Broadcast* carried a leak of the programme material from Extending Choice. Mike Checkland was downcast. 'Who could have done it? Not for money surely?' I said they would not have got rich from *Broadcast*. I asked Keith Samuel to check on the copied pages I had given to Alan Yentob and Jonathan Powell and to David Docherty, whom I had now made head of planning and strategy. A while later Jonathan rang. He had lost a file while in Edinburgh, where he had performed valiantly following Grade's lecture. His office had just told him that it had been returned in a brown envelope postmarked Camberwell. Here he broke down sobbing. The programme section of Extending Choice was inside. 'So that's how they got it.' I told him to bear up. Only Alan, Keith and I knew about this. I did not see why it had to go further. Jonathan wanted me to tell Mike. Keith, as usual, gave good advice. 'Tell Mike. But not until he is away from Broadcasting House and the atmosphere there.' I rang Mike in his car as he was returning home from the theatre. He was reassured that the papers had not got the whole document and agreed that this would be between ourselves. I reported as much to Jonathan. 'We won't speak of it again.' I do so now because it can no longer harm anyone and the story conveys something of the feverish atmosphere of those months.

The cork could not remain in the bottle forever. I was at the Royal Television Society's conference in October when Mike gave it the necessary easing. He was interviewed by Jon Snow and was hitting balls all round the ground. John Birt was in the audience and when Snow asked him, 'Do you agree?', his reply was, 'Wholeheartedly.' Shoulder to shoulder, the BBC's top brass were marching to the broad sunlit uplands. Then Snow asked Mike about the period of dual leadership and Mike unleashed an attack on Hussey. He was too old to be leading the BBC, he said, and gave the example of the chairman asking what FM meant, 'Fuzzy Monsters?' The atmosphere was electric. Applause broke out. The reporters besieged Mike when he came off stage. Within a few days it was announced that he would stand down as director-general at Christmas rather than the following March as planned.

Mike did, however, preside over the launch of Extending Choice. On 24 November the government issued its green paper. I noted that it was 'herbivore rather than carnivore' about the BBC, and that the policy and planning department, which negotiated with government, had done a good job. Two days later the BBC pressed the button on its own communication. The day began with a big meeting of 200 senior staff in the concert hall at Broadcasting House. John Birt paid what I noted was 'a warm and heartfelt tribute to Mike Checkland and called for a standing ovation. Not a dry eye.' It was a good way to begin. At the press conference that followed I heard John speak for the first time about the BBC as a place he believed in and cared about. He was to do so many times over the coming years, though many chose not to hear.

I spent some time briefing some of our stars, among them Terry Wogan, Clive James, Esther Rantzen, David Coleman, Sue Lawley and Robert Kilroy-Silk, then had drinks with all the department heads to hear their, mostly positive, feedback. Hundreds of copies of Extending Choice were posted to people thought interested or influential, though at least one came back marked, 'Return to Sender. Unsolicited Junk Mail.'

Mike was relaxed now. His last year cannot have been as he would have wished, what with the tensions at the top, the pressures on borrowing and the overspend, but he had delivered the BBC's case for its future and it was recognized that he had started the years of necessary change. The least pompous of men, always positive, slow to chide and quick to bless, he left a wealth of friends who respected his thoughtfulness and care for people. I hosted a dinner as television's farewell. I staged a medal ceremony for him, his wife Sue and his long-time PA Elsie, and engaged Alan Opie, Susan Bullock and John Hudson from the English National Opera to sing after the meal, the first of these to perform an appropriate tribute, the largo al facto-tum from *The Barber of Seville*.

The question for me now was would I have a job? I had not covered myself in glory in my first eighteen months. I had not yet made the impact I had hoped, nor pushed through enough changes. I had tried to do too much myself without putting the right support in place. As I reflect on that period now, I am less harsh on myself than I felt at the time. I had had some successes: the first Premier League contract, of which more later; a more strategic approach to our programme plans that was to bear fruit; a start on improving the way we commissioned; and the beginnings of a modern system of management information, something else that was to prove invaluable. It had been difficult to motivate people, difficult to motivate myself at times, when the place was riven with corporate politics so that staff were looking not just over my shoulder but over the director-general's as well, searching for clues as to the next regime. All the while, we were planning the introduction of a root and branch reform of our financial and business processes. Throw in 'the missing millions' and it is evident why 1992 was a grim year for me, the least happy of the thirty-four I spent in the Corporation.

Everyone was on tenterhooks waiting to discover the new director-general's plans. At the December launch for new year programmes, the editor of *Broadcast* sought me out. 'Will, there's speculation that you will be leaving the BBC soon?' Two days later, after their Christmas lunch, the governors reassembled with John Birt for the afternoon.

'The chairman was spotted leaving the building at 5.50 p.m.,' said my PA Rosemary, who had seen a few chairmen in her time and knew when trouble was brewing. 'Unprecedented.'

Next day I saw Noel Edmunds with Alan Yentob to say, 'we love you and sign again,' which he did, before Bill drove me to Broadcasting House for my arranged meeting with John Birt. 'I sensed the sack,' I wrote in my diary, 'and Jane at home, hoping for it I think.' But no.

'I want you to be in my team, Will,' said John. 'But there is a general sense that television is the worst managed part of the BBC. You need to raise a gear.' He would outline the full plan in January.

It was not a quiet Christmas. I was on the phone a good deal to external candidates for the controllership of BBC1. At 1.20 a.m. on 23 December, Phillip Gilbert, producer of the Queen's Christmas broadcast, rang me to say that the *Sun* had the text of the already recorded message. This was usually a bland and decorous affair, but this time there was a news angle, for the Queen described the year of the Prince and Princess of Wales' separation and the Windsor fire as '*annus horribilis*'. The broadcast was recorded and distributed worldwide by the BBC under a strict embargo. It had never leaked before. At 7.00 the next morning I asked John Wilson, controller of editorial policy, to conduct an enquiry for me.

With mischief in mind Kelvin McKenzie, editor of the *Sun*, announced on the radio that he had received the tape 'thanks to a BBC employee'. I learned that tapes had gone to independent radio stations as well as overseas. The leak could have come from anywhere. I could find out no more that afternoon and belted down to the West End to buy Jane a Christmas present. At 9.20 p.m. on Christmas Eve the chairman rang me at home, ostensibly to wish Jane and me a happy Christmas, but in reality to let me know that he wanted an answer on the leak and quickly.

Wilson sent me his report four days after Christmas. It showed that 120 copies of the broadcast had been struck, seventy of them sent to commercial radio stations. There was no clue as to where the leak had come from. I put the BBC's professional investigator onto the case. After interviewing the BBC staff he was convinced they were in the clear and that the leak had come from outside, probably from an independent local radio station. I wrote to Sir Robert Fellowes, the Queen's private secretary: 'All in all, no smoking gun, no fingerprints, no significant lead.' Philip Gilbert worked to devise a simpler distribution system for the future. The Palace sued the *Sun* and won a settlement for breach of copyright.

John Birt was to lay out his plans as director-general at a big liaison meeting of senior staff in studio three at Television Centre on Monday, 11 January. He had planned his communications with typically meticulous care and was to brief the board of management individually the week before. I was called on the Thursday, my 51st birthday. In an hour and a half he explained his plans, including that resources would become a separate directorate, so no longer would I have to manage that as well as the editorial arms of television. This was not unexpected and not unwelcome. I left excited by his ideas and could see that life would be very different.

He was to see each of us again to reveal the shape of the board. His guns were spiked that Friday when Michael Grade announced that Liz Forgan was leaving her job as Channel 4's director of programmes to join the BBC. She had planned to tell her staff on Monday. John's jaw tightened with anger. 'Michael Grade doesn't stand for anything. This is what you'd expect.' I dropped in on David Hatch, as he was to be last in, and found him clearly tense about it. He said he would ring me later but did not. He left me a terse message the following morning: 'I shall be joining you on the board.'

Both within and without the organization there was the sense that an earthquake was about to strike the BBC. At 10.15 that Saturday evening Brenda Maddox rang from the *Telegraph*. 'Will, the news desk here has a line on the BBC board of management. You've all been told to clear your desks and not come in any more. True?'

'Brenda, the full story is that we've been sent to Orkney to clean up the oil slick and have signed a document forbidding us to speak to the press for three years.'

On Monday morning John met the board members together in the chairman's bare Television Centre office to tell us about the new appointments. David Hatch was red-faced but smiling and I knew at once that the message he had left had been deliberately vague. Liz Forgan was to take his job as managing director of radio; Bob Phillis, the cheery chief executive of ITN, was to be managing director of the World Service and deputy director-general; and the new job of managing director of resources was to go to Rod Lynch, a Scot with a background in BA and Forte Hotels. David was to be advisor to the director-general. I was relieved that he was still on board. He was the most supportive of colleagues, who sent warm, encouraging and funny notes at times of stress and messages of congratulation when things went right. He was good on his feet, bold in argument and unafraid to show emotion. He loved the BBC, above all BBC radio, for which he had first worked as a comedy writer and performer in *I'm Sorry I'll Read That Again*.

We trooped into the studio and John made a speech I thought well of. He had spent the previous months visiting all parts of the BBC and many outside companies, and now laid out his detailed plans of how the Corporation would meet 'its Extending Choice goals'. Most importantly, there was to be a review of programme strategy across all areas, led by Liz Forgan and Alan Yentob and involving as many people as possible. There would be an annual review of performance within each directorate before the director-general reviewed each in turn. He itemized a host of other plans. Also, over the coming year every single member of staff would be invited to a day-long series of discussions about the BBC's principles and plans, in the last hour of which the director-general and/or members of the board of management would join to take part.

The buzz afterwards was generally positive. The new world was underway. I received a number of cards and notes from friends, all of which said, in one form or another, 'Glad you are not dead.'

In strictest secrecy the new board of management convened for two days at Amberley Castle in Sussex. This had been booked in the name of a fictional company, 'Martin Gibbon Associates', so no one would know the BBC was there. The letter of instructions had a portentous tone: 'By the time you receive this letter you will know the names of the other people attending.' It ended ominously: 'The portcullis will be closed.'

Dr Warner Burke, an American organizational psychologist with whom John had been working, had been to see each of us, and Warner now led many of the discussions, gently nudging and probing us in his soft Southern accent. The exchanges were tentative at first, then more flowing. There was a hint of revivalism in the air and we all vowed that we wanted to work more collectively. John placed great emphasis on breaking down the baronial nature of the BBC. All agreed, though, when I suggested, looking round at the ancient stonework, the display of pikes on the wall and the full suit of armour in the corner of the room, that this was an odd place to pledge the end of baronial behaviour.

The dinners were full of jolly tales of days of old, we got to know Liz and Bob better and everything seemed possible. At the end of Friday's discussions we all said how well it had gone. John concluded, 'I am feeling wonderful . . . A load has been lifted from me. It has been fairly lonely . . . I have complete confidence that we can deliver what we say.'

After we next met formally, I wrote: 'Work plans for dozens of projects. Much sycophancy around. Some gushing with enthusiasm for the new world. I didn't gush but was not wholly innocent.' We felt we were off.

First I had to appoint a controller of BBC1. I informally interviewed three BBC people, two from Granada, one from Yorkshire and the chief executives of two big independent producers. With reluctance I dismissed the application from Murray the Midget of Barnum and Bailey Brothers circus ('summary of duties: making children of all ages laugh/falling over large feet/part-time cleaner of lion's cage') and that from Gary Bushell, the larky television critic of the *Sun*. I wrote to him, knowing it would be published:

> I read your application for the job of controller BBC1 with interest. I never doubted that you would have some forthright views of how it should be done. In fact your views on the desirability of celebrating British talent and the work of British authors are in tune with our Extending Choice vision, which I am sure you have seen.
>
> I am not so convinced by gunging as a management tool . . . No doubt you will continue to give us regular and robust advice.

I had not surprised myself in the interviews and came out, as I had gone in, convinced that Alan Yentob was the outstanding choice. He was the most talented commissioner in British television and an inspirational figure. He was competitive, had drive and ingenuity and believed utterly in the values and purposes of the BBC. Although Alan had talked to me about the job and had thrown himself into being temporary curator, I had to handle him carefully. I did not want him to bid and be rejected, for he was then likely to go into a tailspin. I felt that he wanted it but wanted to be asked to do it rather than be seen to declare his hand.

I briefed the new director-general on all the candidates seen and not seen, how I rated them and why I wanted Alan. John asked about one or two of the people, then agreed. I said that I only wanted to bring forward the one candidate to the governors, so there was no danger of things going wrong. John gave the chairman the headlines and I rang Dukie to ask him not to say anything at the *What The Papers Say* lunch. 'I understand what you're saying, Will. I'll tell the vice-chairman to keep his mouth shut, though I can't make any promises there.'

I told Alan that I was going with his name alone and made him promise not to wobble. I explained to the governors selection committee, comprising Dukie, Joel and Phyllis (P.D.) James, the novelist, how I had gone about the task, told them who I had seen and why Alan was the person.

'He did go a bit overboard about Mandela,' said Phyllis James referring to the Free Mandela concert that Alan had run and then repeated at Christmas early in his controllership. 'There was a lot of rather schoolboyish enthusiasm around . . . Is he alright politically? I don't mean his politics with a capital "P" of course.'

'There was a time,' said Dukie, 'when Salman Rushdie was on his channel every night.'

I said that they need not worry. Alan had matured in the job, knew what was required on BBC and had public service broadcasting in his bloodstream. They agreed to see only him. On the day he was impressive, so the governors anointed Alan, and he and I returned to a conference of television staff. I waited until the end of the morning before announcing the appointment, which was greeted with great warmth and enthusiasm.

On Saturday, 27 February I was in optimistic mood. I had the controller of BBC1 I wanted and the press had welcomed the appointment, seeing it as signalling 'a quality drive'. I had picked up my own pace, we were motoring towards the beginning of Producer Choice in good shape, we had sorted the television budget for the coming year and the board of management was still in honeymoon mode. After a walk with Jane and our little dog Becky to Chiswick House on a clear, cold morning, I watched the racing on television. Then in one of life's little ironies I viewed a future episode of *Casualty* that Alan thought might need rescheduling, unaware that it was the episode to be transmitted that evening (hospital burning down after a riot) that was a bigger problem. Oblivious, I went off with Jane to *Don Pasquale* at the English National Opera and had supper out. Things were looking good.

The following morning a thunderbolt struck the BBC. The *Independent on Sunday* ran a story that John Birt was not on the staff of the BBC but was contracted through his company, employing his wife Jane as secretary and offsetting expenses, including clothing, against tax. This was against the background of the BBC laying off staff as it reduced capacity and John's proclaimed intention for a more open, accountable and transparent BBC. He quickly volunteered to come onto the staff but there was much unhappiness within and barracking without. I saw him during the week and after our routine business I said, 'Can I offer you some advice? You need to say "sorry" to the staff.' John explained that his arrangements had not been that beneficial and that they were common, as I knew, in the commercial world where he had 'offered his services in the market place'. I believed him but said, 'The staff won't listen to all that. They just want to know that you are aware that it was a mistake.'

The next weekend the *Independent on Sunday* piled in again. I rang around my heads of departments. The messages were clear: 'anger and cynicism . . . it's a moral matter', 'double standards', 'thin credibility in any case' and 'working in the BBC is not the same as elsewhere'. My view was that the whole thing was a cock-up of the first order but that there should be no question of John resigning or being forced out, as commentators were beginning to suggest. The last thing the BBC needed was a hole at the top. I was convinced of John's diagnosis of what had to happen at the BBC and of the broad thrust of his plans. I told colleagues that if there had to be a head, it should be the chairman's. He was responsible for accepting the terms of the contract.

I had to go to Lausanne to see Juan Samaranch, president of the International Olympic Association, and missed the board of management meeting that agreed a statement of support for the director-general. A few days later we assembled at The Greenway hotel in the Cotswolds for our first off-site conference since Amberley Castle. By now John had handed all his financial affairs to the accountants Ernst and Young for independent scrutiny, and written to staff saying he very much regretting the distress he had caused. Rodney Baker-Bates, the new director of finance, appeared for the first time: a very un-BBC like figure in tweed jacket and cravat. He was to play a crucial part in the struggles and achievements of the next few years, but over tea in the drawing room of The Greenway he understandably looked not a little bemused by his new colleagues. Talk was intermittent and stilted until someone brought up the subject of what was referred to as 'the events of the last few days'. One or two expressed the view that it was behind us. I said not, that John's letter was a step on the way back but only the first on what would be a long hike. Liz Forgan and Margaret Salmon agreed and there was a lengthy open talk. John sat nervous, doodling what appeared to be Celtic patterns and then, in large decorated letters, the words 'Check Mate'. Was this for me to see, I wondered?

David Hatch came in late and with telling theatricality. 'You have to realize, John, that for many people in the BBC the director-generalship is a holy office. You may laugh [no one did] but it is like that. Mike Checkland is one of my closest friends but the first time that I spoke to him each day I called him DG.' John listened contritely. 'I've learned a lot . . . I didn't understand things.'

I said, 'The trouble is that many staff felt that you did not really like the BBC and now they believe that you never really joined it.' The dinner that followed was actually quite jolly, though John went to bed straight afterwards.

By the end of the week a number of newspapers were calling for the director-general to go. I rang around some of the governors. Keith Oates, finance director of Marks and Spencer, said there had been an occasion when John had not been able to sign across the seal of the BBC because he was not an employee. Another governor appeared to relish the thought of a putsch. 'A number of us are not happy,' he told me. 'It is no good just pointing the finger at John Birt. You'll take my meaning.' The chairman had been in Australia the while and was due back the following week.

I was invited to do some interviews that weekend. Before I accepted I asked Pamela Taylor, director of corporate affairs, if there was any more to come out about money or anything else. I had to know this if I was going to go hard. She said that she had been through this with John. There were no further revelations waiting. I did the interviews for *The World This Weekend*, BBC and ITN news and on the Monday, after Dan Maskell's memorial service, went on to *Newsnight* with Peter Preston, editor of the *Guardian*, who was calling for Hussey to resign. My line was that the board of management was solidly behind John. The next day the governors met at short notice at Television Centre. Sam Chisholm, the chief executive of BSkyB, arrived to see me at the same time, and the apparent sight of the governors and Chisholm assembling together caused some consternation.

Those who disliked the changes that John Birt had wrought in news, those who resented or feared changes to come or opposed him for other reasons, thought they smelled blood. 'The loyalty parade was nauseating,' wrote my old friend Brian Wenham to me. He and others urged us senior executives to use the leverage the moment had given us to roll back plans for change. On Oxford and Cambridge Club paper with a signature I could not decipher, a letter began: 'You are known throughout the corporation as a considerable student of form and horse-flesh. With Cheltenham about to start, what a pity that you have backed a loser already. On the way up you were able to jump the fences well but everyone knows you have been got at.' It went on: 'It's not very heartening to know that you are the biggest toady of the lot . . . [Birt's] damaged. And I would hope mortally wounded.' It was easy to shrug this off. What did get up my nose was the assumption of some friends and former colleagues that because I had been in the BBC a long time, I could not possibly agree with John Birt's plans. I must, therefore, be dissembling.

The turmoil continued. I reported on the matter to the programme review board. I said that there were some who saw no need for change at the BBC and believed that if John Birt were destabilized, it would not come about. They were wrong about that. I said that 'I understand the anger of people on contracts who have been forced into PAYE arrangements by the Inland Revenue rules and also the sadness of those who feel, as I do, that John Birt's tax arrangements were inappropriate and demonstrated a lack of understanding of BBC values. It was clearly a bad mistake, but not the mistake of a bad man. John Birt is an outstanding leader and executive and is needed.' I then invited an open discussion that would not be minuted. The views were as before.

I went straight to a quarterly meeting of the BBC's general advisory council, a large group of the fairly great and quite good, a couple of dozen or more of whom turned up to discuss the Corporation in the presence of governors and executive. Regional representatives were always disproportionately prominent. They had a day in town with flights and train fares paid by the BBC. This time the chairman of the GAC, Sir Terry Heiser, asked governors and executive to withdraw, and to my astonishment Dukie agreed. We trooped out to wait in a mixture of mirth and irritation while the GAC discussed the affair of the DG's contract for an hour and a quarter. They issued a statement that the chairman should consider his position. The eventual demise of the GAC dated from that morning.

As luck would have it, that evening was the chairman's dinner for Mike Checkland. Crowds of photographers clustered outside Broadcasting House for what should have been a quiet occasion. As we went into the council chamber, Liz Forgan asked Lady Susan Hussey, the chairman's wife, 'Now, how are we going to do this?' Sue Hussey, tall, good-looking, a long-time lady-in-waiting to the Queen, replied, 'We shall do it magnificently.' It was done well enough.

The last formal act of what the press dubbed 'Armanigate' – after the Armani suits John Birt was said to be charging to his company expenses – came the next day. Board of management members waited over an hour for the governors to debate a statement in private session. We learned that when John Birt had joined the BBC in 1987, two other members of the board had similar contracts (John Tusa and Michael Grade), that John was already being pressed to join the staff when the *Independent* story broke and that no one was resigning. When we went in I pressed the chairman as to whether he had now told the director-general to go on the staff. It was evident that negotiations were underway, and Bill Jordan put me in my place. 'This is not the board of management's statement, it is the board of governors' statement.'

So that should have been that. But it was not. The contract affair became central to the demonology of John Birt. It made it appear that he was not fully committed to the BBC, and yet I cannot believe that anyone ever worked harder for it.

Chapter fifteen
KEEPING UP APPEARANCES

The next three years were hard pounding but exhilarating. There was no ambiguity about where power lay at the top of the BBC, I no longer had the burden or distraction of managing production resources and the yellow card I had received inspired me to raise my game. I had some extraordinarily talented people working with me and I was able to bring in more.

The first task was to replace Alan Yentob as controller of BBC2. One of the former leading candidates, Peter Salmon, had just left BBC Bristol to go to Channel 4, where, as he told me later, he found that 'The people are older, they've been in jobs longer, you can't find them on Fridays and they don't leave numbers.' I talked to a number of possibles inside and outside the BBC. I had a firm idea as to who should get the job but thought that the chairman would jib at my bringing only one person forward for a second time, so produced a shortlist of three. Back in December 1980 all twelve members of the board of governors had interviewed two candidates for the controllership of BBC1 and had been unable to agree on a decision. They called both back for the same treatment after Christmas before rejecting the choice of both the managing director of television and the director-general. While that sort of madness was long gone, thank goodness, the chairman did expect to have a hand in the appointment, though both John and I believed that selecting such a crucial editorial position was the job of the relevant executive.

I briefed the chairman and the other two governors before we interviewed the three: Mark Thompson, Janet Street-Porter and Michael Jackson. Dukie was very excited by Janet but went along with what I, and John, wanted – to select Michael Jackson. I knew that Janet would be very disappointed. Friends of hers had been promoting her candidature for both controllerships in the press. This did not help anyone. It would never have influenced the choice and set up a sense of failure for Janet when someone else got the job. She was full of ideas and brilliant in one or two areas but did not carry the confidence of many of the other talented players. She was very low afterwards, partly fed up with rejection and partly in pain with a slipped disc. I had persuaded her to stay once when she had written to me with her resignation. She had been overworked then and soon bounced back. I still wanted to keep her and tried and failed to come up with another job. Janet stayed for another year, then left to berate the dreadful male suits that ran the BBC. I had a fair idea of whom she had in mind.

The quick thinking and fast moving John Smith was redesigning and rebuilding the financial systems for television. I persuaded one of the brightest people in radio, Tim Suter, to become my directorate secretary, my man of affairs if you like. My new personnel controller was Kate Smith, tough minded, wily and persistent in negotiation and always making colleagues and I think through what decisions felt or looked like from the point of view of the staff in general. She became a rock in times good and bad.

I had six programme groups: drama, entertainment, factual (which included music and arts), sport, children's and acquired, each with an editorial board that included relevant BBC regional programme makers and someone from the independent production unit. I had set up this unit to provide a route for independent producers to offer programmes without having to go through one of the in-house production departments. The departments had mostly embraced independent producers but conflicts of interest were emerging with increasing sharpness. The independents feared that their ideas would not be promoted if in-house departments had similar projects or producers idle. They were not always right about this, for departments could not resist taking good ideas into their charge, even at the expense of their own staff, but the fear was understandable. With the introduction of Producer Choice it was given a hard financial edge. The size and scope of BBC programme departments now depended entirely on their annual commissions. We reshaped the commissioning system to provide equal opportunity to different suppliers, and I issued an independents' charter proclaiming the principles and practice of how we would work with them.

In time I set up separate boards for the two arms of television, programme production and channels, in order to focus upon their different, as well as common, editorial and business needs. The production departments' big issues were in staffing, especially finding, developing and retaining talent, in quality control of productions and in being responsive to and anticipating audience and channel requirements – all this in a less benign environment than they were used to. Over the years the ITV companies had occasionally pinched people but had also developed their own. The independents supplying Channel 4 had raided in the 1980s. But now there were more and better run independent companies and they were in direct competition with the in-house producers for commissions and for talented staff. This was a severe shock to the system for BBC production units.

Equally, the job of running channels was becoming more difficult and more pressured. For a start, three developments were changing the way in which people watched television. The first of these, the video recorder, made less difference than expected when it had first been introduced. It allowed users to shift the time at which they watched programmes but it was tricky to record more than one programme at a setting ('the children are the only ones who know how to work it'), so was mainly used as a back-up tool to catch programmes that would otherwise have been missed. The other use of the machine, to play purchased or rented videos, did lead to displacement of broadcast programmes. Your schedule, especially at weekends, was now in competition not just with other broadcasters but with the movie library as well.

The second transforming piece of technology was the remote control. In the good old days in order to change channels you had to raise yourself from your chair, walk across the room, press the switch (or even turn the tuner) walk back and sit down again. These circumstances encouraged default viewing. You tended to give programmes a chance to draw you in, you would wait to see where a drama or a documentary was going before taking the decision that it was not for you, and get up to switch over. And once committed you were more likely to stick with a programme through boring bits. The remote changed all that. With the press of the button you could savour any and everything else that was on at the same time. If a programme began slowly, you could be off; if it dipped in interest, find something better. Children could happily watch two or even three programmes at once. The remote was the birth control pill of television: it encouraged promiscuity on a scale hitherto undreamed of.

The third and most significant innovation was multi-channel television via cable or satellite. By the time I took over BBC television in 1991, there were around 2 million homes with cable or satellite; by 1996, when I handed over, 5 million; and by the time I left the BBC at the end of 1999, 7.5 million. As the subscribers grew, so the new channels' share of total viewing rose from 4 per cent to 10 per cent to 14 per cent. From 1997 there was another mainstream terrestrial competitor, Channel Five, which quickly reached a 5 per cent share. All in all, a 20 per cent smaller audience for the four old channels to divide between them.

These developments enabled the long march of the audience from passive and grateful receiver to demanding and picky consumer. The producer no longer held sway. We had to think more deeply and become more inquisitive about the audience, and work harder to attract and keep the viewers' attention. The task of the BBC channels, as always, was to offer programmes of sufficient variety and popularity for every licence-paying household to find pleasure in the schedules, at the same time maintaining the range and ambition that justified public funding. This became an ever tougher challenge for the channel controllers and their teams. What is more, they had to do this while ensuring that we transmitted 25 per cent independent productions, measured by hours (monitored by the Office of Fair Trading), and a new BBC imposed target of 33 per cent of programming made outside the South East of England, measured by spend. Planning and delivering the schedule became an exercise in variable geometry.

I had put David Docherty in charge of the support to the controllers. David was a Glaswegian from an unprivileged background whose brain had brought him academic success. I once likened him to a partly trained Labrador, clever and bold enough to find and fetch anything but requiring plenty of patting. With his floppy, prematurely grey hair, his forcefulness in argument and an often presumptuous manner, he was a rich mixture and crucial to our success over those years. He swiftly won the confidence of both Alan Yentob and Michael Jackson with his energy and insights. He needed encouragement and mentoring but was passionate about the values of public service as well as being suitably competitive.

We built up a powerful team to support Alan and Michael, among them Sue Price, David Bergg (who later moved on to Channel Five, ITV and Sky), Rosemary Newell (who later followed Michael Jackson to Channel 4) and Adam MacDonald. I very nearly brought in a young woman in a hurry from Carlton called Dawn Airey. She was known as Zulu Dawn, bright, tough and glaringly ambitious, and I offered her the job of number two to David with the liklihood of more to follow. She accepted. I said to think it through because her employers would make a big play to keep her once they knew she was coming and I did not want it all to fall through at the last minute. She said she had. That would not happen. We agreed the job and title. We agreed the salary. We agreed the press release and her quotes. The night before it was to go out, she rang me. She had told the people at Carlton and, blow me down, they wanted her to stay. So, collapse of not very stout party, she was going to stay. I was furious but we strode on without her and her career seemed not to founder.

The channel teams grew their skills apace in planning the schedules and conducting their business. The whole television team began to work hard at understanding the changing lives, tastes and interests of the audience. David Docherty came from a research background, to the suspicions of old BBC types ('number-cruncher') but to the advantage of the channel controllers. Research played a greater and greater role in how we ran the television service. People misunderstood this at the time and since. It was not a matter of researching programme wants from the public and merely supplying them. As if one could. We sought to learn about the things that were important to people's lives, to find out how they used television and how they responded to what we transmitted so that we could devise, commission and make programmes that met their needs. None of this lessened the requirement for creative leaps, for programme makers' inspiration, for writers' passion or for the commissioners' or producers' intuition. It just gave you a better chance of getting it right more often, of chiming with the mood of the audience. Why would you not want to know as much as you could about the people who paid for the programmes and for whom they were intended?

One tool that had changed the way that all broadcasters worked was the arrival of overnight audience figures. Previously in the BBC we had 'the grey book', which came out on a Tuesday and carried the full weekly figures for the week that had ended ten days earlier. This meant that you had always transmitted two or even three episodes of a programme before you knew how many people had watched. When the overnights had first come in, many in the BBC thought that they were not a good idea for a public service broadcaster, that we should trust our judgement about the quality of a programme and not be rushed into an opinion based on viewing figures. Once available, there was no denying them. The overnights were brought in to the controllers as soon as they arrived, providing information that might prompt the rescheduling of a programme or a demand for more work on a series still in production. Of course, the overnights could also supply the bars of a ratings prison if you let them. From now on the question about last night's new programme was not, 'Was it any good?' but, 'How did it do?'

We planned the shape of the schedules more carefully and the channel controllers commissioned with ever more thought as to the place in the day, week and time of year that programmes would be transmitted. I did not intervene in the channel commissioning but conducted a cross-channel review after the spring editorial meetings to assess plans against our avowed strategies. I kept an eye on the two channels' schedules to spot weak nights or clashes: American movie against American movie was my *bête noir*. I also instituted a twice-yearly look at long-term plans for 'landmark' series, big documentary series or prestige dramas, to ensure that they were being commissioned and that we had them across the seasons in the years ahead.

Alan Yentob was for my money the best controller that BBC1 has ever had. He believed in the BBC's mission, he hated being beaten, he wanted the channel to be admired by people he admired and he fought for quality in every commission for every slot. He was a highly creative person who took advantage of what research and focus groups offered to make better decisions. He took a brief, he listened, he thought and was both wily and practical in how he set about his task. Though we got some more money, we were badly short to fill the schedule, and Alan, who was right on top of his budget, made sure that he spent wisely. The autumn season remained the most costly but he spread the money more evenly through the year. Where he could not find enough early evening entertainment he grew factual programmes that worked in these slots. As they were cheaper, he had more new programmes in the schedule. He was nervous of the BBC's ability to produce popular drama and was short of funds for it, so he commissioned new series in runs of six rather than the usual thirteen in order to spread his bets and give more ideas a go. He was savvy in apportioning his goodies, holding back programmes for the right moment to give the schedule an added glow.

Alan would rehearse his thinking aloud to those around him and wind himself up when his irritation broke through. Of one contributor: 'He wants a meeting, does he? He goes on about his workload to people with the most stressful jobs in television. He wants a meeting. He can have a meeting. He only wants to hear how wonderful he is and what a success his big series was. Well, it wasn't.' Once I had the whole senior team away for a conference and we had been discussing how we related to the rest of the staff. We had done some psychological profiles that suggested we were insufficiently sensitive to people's views. Too few of us truly listened to people. 'You're absolutely right,' exclaimed Alan. 'We don't listen enough to our own staff.'

Turning to me: 'I think you and I should go out and start *talking* to them.'
There was a pause, and then laughter broke out round the room, Alan joining in.

'The whole system depends upon the whim of one person,' was a
common complaint. The controllers did delegate decisions to the editors of
strands like *Horizon*, say, and would go with the advice of programme
heads whose judgement they trusted, but more and more decisions were
taken by the controller himself. This was partly, in Alan's case, a matter of
his appetite for detail and hands-on style, but also because, with the influx
of good ideas from independent producers, the channel controller was the
only person in a position to make the decisions about which project should
be chosen for which placing. Producers, understandably, just want a 'yes' or
'no' for their proposal; the channel controller rarely takes a decision in iso-
lation: for him it is which project of two or more should go ahead and how
does that affect the money available for others?

It took time – and I do not think that we ever quite got there – for the controllers to understand the pivotal nature of their roles in the new era when
business plans depended on their decisions and when production staff and
resource capacity depended on those business plans. With the help of John
Smith, the financial controller, and David Docherty, I put in place a framework that allowed the controllers the greatest possible freedom to achieve
their vision for the channel while containing the effects of their commissioning within what was manageable. With this, and with very occasional
interventions, I was able to manage the total television economy.

Michael Jackson was a quick learner on BBC2. His teacher was Alan, to
whom he was then in thrall. Michael, the first media studies graduate to
achieve high office in British television, had only ever worked on programmes as editor – not for him the long apprenticeship of researcher,
director and the like. He picked up Alan's determination to get to the bottom
of things, the obsession with the creative process of making television programmes. He thought through decisions with enormous care and would
agonize about which way he would jump. Michael was a cool customer, quietly spoken and often reticent but flashing a sharpness when disappointed by
a programme or referring to someone he considered not up to the job. He
was interested in the history of television. In his office he kept a collection of
television memorabilia: ancient Dinky toys of BBC vehicles and a Muffin the
Mule puppet.

One thing surprised me: Michael began to arrive late at meetings. I could
not believe that this was because he was disorganized. He was not. It was
either, I felt, because Alan was often late and Michael thought that this was
what you did as a channel controller or – and more likely – this was a con-
scious way of asserting himself, the last to arrive being seen to be important
and deferred to either because others had had to wait or go over things again
for his benefit. He developed some slightly self-conscious eccentricities, like
taking his shoes off and walking over the office furniture. It seemed a touch
calculated for one so self-disciplined. There was no doubt that he had been

the right choice. People liked dealing with him, for he gave them his instant and concentrated attention and was able to spell out what he wanted. And Michael had an insatiable interest in what was going on around us. Some of this came from gadfly attention to television and magazines, some from analysis, much from putting his nose to the wind. There were always little bits of paper covered with notes in his spiky hand that he would write on as you talked.

Alan's first big decision on BBC1 was *Eldorado*. The programme had improved beyond expectations and was now more than respectable, it was good. However, it was cursed by its early problems, and the perception of it as a disaster would change only slowly. It was almost inevitable that a new person in charge of the channel would scrap it. I told Alan that I would back whatever his decision was, but if he were going to cancel, it would be much easier for him if he did it quickly. He did and handled it with great skill. There had been 156 episodes, and when I was questioned about the programme by the National Heritage Select Committee in July, I told them that I was still dealing with letters from people protesting at it being taken off.

Alan and Liz Forgan were also leading the programme strategy review covering all parts of the BBC. It was a massive undertaking and, at John Birt's behest, involved much detailed audience research, from which we all learned much and which I imported into television. I was edgy about the enterprise as a whole lest it undercut what I was seeking to do. It did not, and I was much involved anyway. When Liz and Alan had more or less finished, John threw it all back at them, asking for much more work. Now things became difficult. Mark Thompson, clever, fluent and eager, was drafted in to write the document and was confident he could satisfy all parties. He giggled about it. 'I'm the Reverend Casaubon,' he said, 'writing the Key to All Mythologies.' McKinsey's were now involved, 'asking inane questions' to the anger of Alan and others.

'This girl asked me what folk music we were doing,' complained Alan. 'I said we were not doing any fucking folk music and, by and large, we won't.'

I became irritated when I learned that the work was going into organizational matters that were my responsibility and wrote to the director-general: 'The PSR is becoming ever more mysterious and is causing pain, anger and even mirth among some of our very best creative people. Yet six months ago it was engaging these people and they were energetically and eagerly involved. Something valuable seems to have turned into one more burden.' Thus when Liz suggested I join her, Alan and John for a weekend meeting on it all in March 1994, I felt obliged to go, leaving Bob Phillis to host the party I was taking to Twickenham ('Will, you're nuts,' wrote Jeffrey Archer, one of the guests). I went down to the meeting steaming and came back relatively relaxed. Liz was on the point of chucking the whole thing in and John decided enough was enough. Mark Thompson had done a brilliant job steering a way between John's demand for data (good) and precision (not possible) and Liz's resentment at the process. We resolved that it was now for television, radio and news to respond to take it on. This they did and the outcome was launched a year later in February 1995, not under Liz's proposed title 'Something in the Air' that I said sounded like a Julian Slade musical, but as the more clunking 'People and Programmes'. The exercise had been valuable in throwing up good ideas and fresh thinking and I carried it on.

The chief programme task in television was to secure more consistent performance in drama. Good programmes were made – some wonderful programmes – but there were too many that failed either creatively or to find an audience or both. The culture had to change. If a series began with disappointing audiences, people would comfort themselves with the thought 'that it will build'. When we analyzed the audience figures for popular series going back many years, we learned that series nearly always had their largest audience for the first episode, they did not 'build'. Too few dramas were set in attractive locations or had positive characters that the audience could cheer for. Writers were paid to write second drafts of scripts even if there was no intention of ever going into production, a sort of work-aid. Scripts for green-lit projects were usually ready only at the very last minute, so there could be the traditional blue arsed fly rush to get into production. 'Don't talk to me, dear. I'm busy, busy, busy. We've just got the green light and we're on location next week.' The drama group also had a senior common room, the films department, where there were people who had not worked in ages.

I brought in Charles Denton to be the new head of drama and told Mark Shivas that he could stay on to produce the single dramas for BBC2, which he was pleased to do. Charles had been a big figure in ITV, as director of programmes at Central, and had then run a sizeable independent production company. He was a lean, outdoor looking man who was fond of pink shirts. He was strong-minded, forthright, hard working and resilient. From his commercial experience he brought a demand for clarity of roles. He reorganized the drama departments, and though inclined to empire building – I had to tell him that he could not move drama lock, stock and barrel to the BBC site at Elstree – brought discipline and a sense of much needed order. He did not see himself as the editorial leader but as the chief of the tribe. One of his achievements was to bring the drama units in Belfast, Cardiff and Glasgow fully into the fold, making sure that they knew as much as anyone else about the channels' needs and that their projects had as good a chance as anyone else's. This was to pay off handsomely.

We did have *EastEnders*, both popular and of high quality. It had gone through one or two archetypal BBC drama phases with many episodes set mostly in prison and the audience drifting away, but it was now back on song. Alan with hard-headed calculation decided to build from strength and invest in a third weekly episode. The decision was taken in the summer of 1993, to come on stream the following April. On the evening of 7 April, Alan hurried into my office in a severe tizz. 'You'd better look at this,' he said, handing me cassettes of the first three episodes of the new pattern, due to air the following week. I watched them at home that night in disbelief. The storyline was a siege at the Queen Vic, way over the top in treatment, with the villains waving a shotgun around and putting it to the heads of well loved characters. The plot unfolded in a claustrophobic atmosphere of sexual threat that was unrelieved. We had been planning the move to thrice weekly for nine months and the producer, whose final three shows these were, had taken leave of his senses and landed us with programmes that could not go out in the *EastEnders* slots. I called Alan. The choice was stark. Either we played them at 9.30 p.m. after the news, whereby we look like complete idiots and irritate the show's fans, or the three episodes be edited down to two, losing the nastier sequences, and we try to pull forward the first of the following week's. Alan found a bright young producer from the show who did just that and we escaped by the skin of our teeth. The third episode was a success and within the next year the 'Sharongate' episodes achieved the highest television audience of the decade, 25.3 million.

In 1993 we had further runs of previous shows but much of the new BBC1 drama that Alan inherited moved us nowhere. *Roughnecks*, about oil workers and their families, nearly made it, and two unusual and charming series began: *Pie in the Sky* with Richard Griffiths, and *All Quiet on the Preston Front* by the talented Tim Firth, both of which did well enough and were renewed for four years. Two other shows did qualify as hits: *Crocodile Shoes*, written by and starring Jimmy Nail, and the touching and funny *Common as Muck*, well cast with Edward Woodward, Tim Healy and Roy Hudd, written by William Ivory.

Seaforth was a ten-part period saga written by Peter Ransley and starring Linus Roach and Lia Williams. It was gripping stuff and I remember Alan ringing me in high excitement from his car after seeing the first episode. But it was a very expensive show and only a modest success with the audience. To renew or not to renew, that was the question. It was, as usual, a matter of the opportunity cost: there were other attractive ideas in the queue for money. Alan wavered and with some sorrow did not recommission. A world in which the decision not to renew a drama series is front page news in a broadsheet is a world that has lost its bearings one might think. If so, the bearings went with Alan's decision over *Seaforth*.

Coverage of the media had expanded in scope and freneticsm. Newspaper writers about television had been a somewhat rare breed in the early 1970s when I first had dealings with them. The first I could remember meeting was the improbably named L. Marsland Gander of the *Telegraph*, who wore black jacket, striped trousers and a bowler hat. Only two or three papers had daily critics, of whom the one-armed Peter Black of the *Daily Mail* was the doyen. He enjoyed television, wrote beautifully and was always being asked onto discussion programmes but was no performer. When I first invited him on he replied, 'Are you sure? I've been on every programme – once.' By now in 1994 papers had TV critics, previewers, media editors, correspondents, reporters, reviewers of TV sport and more. This hot house atmosphere raised the stakes all round. It made it harder to experiment. Once upon a time you could tuck an oddball show in a quiet corner to see how it went. If it was no good, no one was hurt. Now, though, everything was previewed and reviewed, and if a well-known name was attached, probably commented on in news pages as well. The word 'flop' threatened any new departure.

It was in this climate that Keith Samuel, our head of press and publicity, earned his money. He was there at any time of day or night with a warning call or a quote. Keith caught the 6.45 a.m. from Winchester every morning and had read all the papers by the time he arrived in the office. It was the devil's own job to get him to leave the premises. I would drop into his second-floor office by the lifts at 7.30 or 8.00 p.m. to find him sorting through the foot-high piles of paper on his desk. 'Go home, Keith.'

'I'm just clearing up a few things,' he would reply, for one of his sayings was: 'I regard an in-tray as an unexploded hand grenade with the pin out.' By the time he reached home it was 10 p.m. No wonder he enjoyed his chips in the canteen at lunchtime. Keith acted not just as my eyes and ears, but also the channel controllers', protecting them from mistakes and alerting them to danger. It had been Keith who had seen the *EastEnders* siege and signalled an alarm. He was a master at helping us avoid what he called 'red-faced BBC bosses' stories and took huge pleasure in the success of colleagues. He cheered on the improving performance of our popular drama.

Part of the impetus behind this was the influence of Nick Elliott, who joined in the summer of 1994. He only stayed for nine months before being tempted back to head drama for ITV, but his clear thinking and common sense had helped. In 1995 there came a smash from Scotland, *Hamish Macbeth*, dark, funny and genuinely original. It made a star of Robert Carlyle. Quality control was improving and we had no bummers. At last there seemed to be a shared understanding between Alan's BBC1 team and drama as to what was needed. By the nature of things, not all series worked, but 1996 brought four more hits: the delightful *Ballykissangel* from BBC Northern Ireland, created by Keiran Prendiville, produced by the great Tony Garnett and starring Stephen Tompkinson and Dervla Kirwan; *Hetty Wainthrop Investigates* with Patricia Routledge; *Silent Witness* with Amanda Burton; and Colin Buchanan and Warren Clarke in *Dalziel and Pascoe*. This was more like it.

Perhaps the biggest triumph of this period was the adaptation of Jane Austen's *Pride and Prejudice*. When I had taken over in television I had urged a return to classic adaptations. The serials department under Michael Wearing was unenthusiastic. *The Secret Agent* was produced for BBC2. It was a gloomy piece that hardly registered. Then, in the teeth of opposition from some in drama, Alan, still running BBC2, commissioned a £6 million production of *Middlemarch*, adapted by the master of the craft Andrew Davies and beautifully directed by Anthony Page. This was thrown garlands by critics and public alike. Television versions of great books were back. In the same year BBC2 had *Martin Chuzzlewit*, demonstrating that each generation of actors deserves its crack at Dickens' characters, in this case including Paul Schofield, Pete Postlethwaite, Tom Wilkinson and Elizabeth Spriggs.

Pride and Prejudice was on BBC1. Alan had been emboldened by the

belief of the producer Sue Birtwistle and the fact that once again Andrew
Davies was the adapter. Alan was rewarded with a phenomenon: viewing figures, a standing ovation for the BBC from the chattering classes and press
hysteria, especially about Colin Firth, dashing and wet-shirted as Mr Darcy.
'I can't wait to see tomorrow's edition of *The Times* to find out where you've
put Mr Darcy,' wrote one woman to the newspaper. 'On Tuesday his portrait
was on the front page. Yesterday he was on horseback to illustrate an interview with Colin Firth. Today, he's on page 5 with a photograph from the
final episode. Please keep it up – it is so much more fun than the news.'

The bra company Berlei issued a press release that claimed that what
they called 'the eye-catching cleavage' of the actresses had been 'given a lift'
by their products. Not so, replied the BBC, explaining that any support for
Jennifer Ehle and the others came from the historically authentic soft corset
or, on occasion, from the empire line ties under muslin. A modern bra would
have completely ruined the line. We were a little ungallant, I felt, to give no
credit to the young women themselves.

To stimulate thinking about future adaptations I had asked David Lodge,
a professor of English, a novelist himself and a writer for television (he had
adapted *Chuzzlewit*), to give us his thoughts on which books up to the generation of Greene and Waugh might work well on television, taking into
account what had been done before. He made the important proviso that
you must have a producer enthused by an idea, and then worked his way
forward from the eighteenth century. I sent his paper to Alan, Michael
Jackson, Charles Denton and Michael Wearing, and invited David Lodge in
for dinner with us all at Television Centre to discuss it. A number of point-
ers to later projects emerged, for we discussed *Tom Jones*, *The Mill on the
Floss*, *Vanity Fair* and *Our Mutual Friend*. The one author that never
worked in adaptations, said David, was Joseph Conrad. Ah. This was unfor-
tunate. The previous week Michael Wearing had persuaded Michael Jackson
to give the go-ahead to a production of *Nostromo*, and even as we ate the
search was on for locations in Colombia. When the mini-series arrived on
screen two years later, I knew we should have held that dinner ten days
earlier.

Over the years I noticed how drama on television had its fads. Whether it
was to 'push the boundaries' or earn the badge of peer cred, there had been
a time when no programme was without an alarmingly noisy birth scene. By
the mid-1990s it was compulsory to include a scene shot in a men's urinal,
the noise of the splash amplified year by year. This was now being replaced
by the on-screen vomit, this in turn beginning as a back to the camera job
before developing into a fully frontal, mouthful of cold soup chunder. I hes-
itate to think what will follow.

For all the perversities of the serials department, we had often done well
by it. On BBC1 we had Roddy Doyle's *The Family*, epitomizing Alan's policy
of 'if we can't have good and popular, then we'll have very good'. I ought to
draw a veil over *Rhodes*. This was a pet project of Charles Denton's. At one
point, determined to get a decision on casting the lead, he thrust a piece of

Above left: WW demonstrates his winning way with writers, this time Alan Plater.

Above right: Judging an *Are You Being Served?* competition for a US station with the great David Croft, writer and producer of this show as well as *Dad's Army, Hi Di Hi,* et al.

Left: With Clive James. Was he joining or leaving?

The team running BBC
television in 1995 — about as
good as they get.
Back rows: John Smith, Keith
Samuel, Jonathan Martin, Pam
Masters, Alan Howden, Kate
Smith, Jane Drabble, Anna
Home, David Docherty, Tim
Suter. Front: David Liddiment,
Alan Yentob, WW, Michael
Jackson, Charles Denton.

Above: TV's Mr Showbiz at the BAFTA awards 1999 with, left to right: Charlie Dimmock, *EastEnders'* Barbara Windsor, Sid Owen and Steve McFadden.

Right: Sam Chisholm. 'My management style? Delegate – then interfere.'

Left: Bill Ansbro always knew the way, but this time we ended up in Tellytubbyland.

Below: The Queen visits Broadcasting House in 1997. Christopher Bland introduces her to Alasdair Milne who has just been appallingly rude to his successor as DG, Mike Checkland (centre).

Above: In the heady days of devolution the *Daily Record* hunts down the hammers of the Scots, WW, Tony Hall, Mark Byford and Michael Stevenson.

Below: For much of the1990s Ken Pyne's *Corporation Street* ran in *Private Eye*, paying homage to John Birt, Alan Yentob, WW and other BBC heroes.

At my leaving thrash with clockwise from left: David Attenborough, Chistopher Bland (Julian Wilson behind), Esther Rantzen, Peter O'Sullevan and Joan Bakewell.

Children in Need night with Jane.

paper in front of Alan on which was written 'Martin Shaw. Tick or cross.' The series did not work on any level, save scale. The next chairman was to identify one of the problems: 'No girls.' On BBC2 we had a brilliant realization of Hanif Kureishi's *The Buddha of Suburbia*. Then in 1996 came two electrifying dramas that will be remembered for years. The first was *This Life*, again from Tony Garnett's company, an of-the-moment chronicle of the turbulent lives of a group of middle-class twenty-somethings sharing a house. The subject matter – work, sex, drugs – the fluid direction and the immediacy of its attitudes brought it the intensity of following that comes from word of mouth, from being 'discovered'.

The second was produced by Michael Wearing himself. Wearing was a dashing figure, handsome with swept back white hair and a slow, deliberate way of moving. His mouth was usually signalling hints of a knowing grin, as if he and no one else knew what time the semtex was going to explode under your desk and he was not telling. He carried a permanent sense of crisis with him. He was difficult, always complaining, indecisive and undermining of anybody who might stand in his way or merely not do as he pleased. Because of this, I would often wish that he would clear off and spread mischief and misery elsewhere. But Michael had produced two of the greatest contemporary dramas seen on British television in *Edge of Darkness* and *The Boys From the Black Stuff*, and now he came up with a third, *Our Friends In The North*. In nine parts Peter Flannery's scripts followed the lives of four idealistic young friends from Newcastle over three decades of social and political change. The idea had been knocking around for many years before Michael Jackson commissioned it. I am not at all sure that I would have done but thank goodness he did. The series was a genuine television masterpiece: intelligent, emotional and humane.

The director-general was hugely admiring of it and gave a drinks party in his office for some of the production team and cast. Gina McKee, luminous as Mary in the series, was among those there. She shone equally in real life, being beautiful and with a captivatingly intimate manner. I was standing with her and another of the stars, Mark Strong, as John Birt made an elegant little speech. 'Excuse me for concentrating on Peter's script,' said John, 'but it was realized [turning his eyes to Gina McKee] so perfectly with not a single false note in any part . . .', and his eyes remained locked upon her until he finished praising 'this wonderful production'. When he had concluded, John followed his eyes and came directly over to join our little group.

'Well done,' said Gina McKee smiling at him, a delicious Durham lilt to her voice. 'That was a lovely speech.' John has a propensity to blush and he did so now, the blood rushing pink over face and scalp, naked in his admiration.

Too many of the single films we made for the two channels were slight pieces, and however good a single was, it became increasingly difficult to attract attention to them. Most, including good ones, were soon forgotten. Stars made a difference, as with Roy Clarke's *A Foreign Field*, which featured Alec Guinness, Leo McKern, Lauren Bacall and Jeanne Moreau. At a screening I gave, the invited Normandy veterans were very emotional, the Chelsea Pensioners a bit tiddly and the host in a daze after a special treat for a man of a certain age, meeting Jeanne Moreau.

We also maintained a run of studio plays under the title of Performance, produced by Simon Curtis, possibly in the death throws of a doomed genre but the means of bringing some great works to a wide audience. Among them were *Measure for Measure*, with Corin Redgrave, Tom Wilkinson and Juliet Aubrey; O'Casey's *Shadow of a Gunman* with Kenneth Branagh; Harold Pinter directing his own play *Landscape*; Michael Gambon in *The Entertainer*; John Thaw in David Hare's *Absence of War*; and John Gielgud in J.B. Priestley's *Summer Day's Dream*. Gielgud was 89 and his studio day was organized to finish at 5.00 p.m. Even so, he was tired and given a rest day. However, he turned up tired after this because he had been entertaining friends. Simon Curtis told me, 'I had to speak to him. Though it seemed odd my warning an 89-year-old about his too lively social life.'

In the spring of 1996 Charles Denton stood down after his promised three years. It had been a tough time for him but his drive and determination left BBC drama far stronger than he had found it, with a string of high quality hits and with BBC Scotland and Northern Ireland contributing valuably. An experienced producer, Ruth Caleb, took over pro tem, and before I could re-appoint, the shape of the BBC was changed again.

At the same time as I brought Charles in, I made a change at the top of BBC light entertainment. Jim Moir, a good friend, was estranged from the channel controllers, his only clients. As we must have known, and were certainly to discover, creating good entertainment shows that pleased large audiences is the triple lutz of television, and falls are common. But a change seemed essential. I knew whom I wanted to bring: David Liddiment, the rising star of Granada. He had a record of success, had good ideas and was straightforward about the negotiations. 'I won't be flirtatious with you about this,' he promised, and nor was he. I took to him and arranged for Alan Yentob and Michael Jackson to have dinner with him. They warmed to him as well. David agreed to come. He was a catch.

I thought that Jim had lots still to offer the BBC and wanted to keep him in the organization. I shared my thinking with John Birt who admired Jim and told me that he hoped to persuade Liz Forgan that Jim should be the next controller of Radio 2. In the meantime I suggested that he become number two in corporate affairs. Pamela Taylor, the director, was not making much progress. She knew what she wanted to do but could not make it happen. Jim, liked and admired throughout the BBC and yet a street fighter, would provide some know-how.

At the beginning of June 1993 I saw Jim to tell him that I wanted to replace him, 'begin a new era with a new person', as I creepily put it, but that both the DG and I wanted his talents and skills to remain in the BBC. Jim listened with a quizzical look and then thanked me, laughing at himself for doing so. 'I sympathize with you for having to steel yourself to do this as I know you will have had to,' said Jim. 'Now, Will, you say there is some flexibility over timing. Therefore can it be Christmas, when I will have completed thirty years in the light entertainment department?'

'No,' I said, 'it can't.' We talked a little of other possible jobs but I could not mention Radio 2.

'I hope that when my BBC funeral comes, so to speak,' said Jim, 'it will be an honourable one.' Emotion forced him to pause. 'I would like to go out with bayonets fixed.' Now I was nearly tearful. Half an hour later Jim's PA asked to see me, pleading for a stay of execution until Christmas. I commended her loyalty but the matter was closed. In the event, Jim was a gust of optimistic and practical air for corporate affairs and then became controller of Radio 2. There has never been a better radio network controller.

David Liddiment did not work out at the BBC. It had been a wrench for him to leave Granada, where he had grown up with people, and he had given up a great deal. I and others tried to make him welcome at Television Centre but I do not think we managed to. As head of the production department he did not have commissioning power without the agreement of the channel controller, and that frustrated him, though he knew this full well before he came. I think the BBC often finds it hard to assimilate new people. The group I now had in place running television comprised talent of the first order, but as a bunch we were probably arrogant, opinionated and full of people who never stopped talking. David had an attractive softer side to his personality but a temper that flared up now and then, notably in the midst of a performance review meeting with the controllers, John Birt and me. Suddenly berating Alan and Michael for not responding to requests and never saying thank you, David upped and walked out of the room.

At first he had appeared absolutely on top of things, but within eighteen months he felt he had lost Alan's confidence and there were rumours that he was looking round. 'My God, we don't want that,' was Alan's response, but a few months later David announced, 'Will, I'm going.'

He went back to Granada and then to be director of programmes for ITV. Frankly, when we heard he had got that job, the crucial competitive position as far as the BBC was concerned, we were pleased. But David proved us wrong, and for the first three years at least he was outstanding. ITV was his natural home, where he was a passionate advocate of its public service obligations.

We did find some of those elusive early evening shows during David's two years in the BBC. *Do The Right Thing* and *How Do They Do That?* were both respectable and popular. *This Is Your Life* finally turned up from ITV, and we won the lottery show. This last was important to us and getting it was no fluke. Alan, David and I reckoned that if it was the 'national' lottery, it ought to be on the BBC and that it would provide a reliable tent pole for Saturday evenings. We went to see the regulator to hear from his own lips how it would be decided. We engaged an industry consultant to map the competition and criteria for winning. I wrote to all bidding consortia and Alan followed up terrier-like. Thus the three of us sat preening ourselves in the audience as Noel Edmunds hosted the first draw show. A week later I arrived for lunch with David Frost to find him seated in the back seat of his Bentley parked outside the restaurant as he filled in his lottery tickets. 'For my children, dear boy, I assure you.'

We ended two near permanent fixtures in the schedule, *That's Life* and *Jim'll Fix It*. Noel Edmunds was going strongly on Saturdays, though I noted after a long meeting with him about his contract struggling over who owned which bits of the show – merchandizing rights and the like – that an aria from Handel's *Semele* came to mind, 'No. No. I'll take no less, than all in full excess.' Clive James and his producer, Richard Drewett, wanted to go independent. Alan and I went through it all with them, found a way we could make it works and agreed. Clive and Richard took us to dinner to tell us 'how gracious' we were. A few months later Alan called me when I was on holiday in Martha's Vineyard to say they had gone to ITV. Alan was beating his chest but there was no need to. We quickly discovered the bright side as we remembered how expensive their shows were and that we now had a pile of money to spend elsewhere.

The two comedy arms of light entertainment were situation comedy, from early 1995 under Geoffrey Perkins, a writer and performer himself, and comedy entertainment – sketch and panel shows – under Jon Plowman, former producer of *Wogan* and *French and Saunders*. Situation comedy is Holy Grail for broadcasters. Good ones help define a channel, create an aura of success and can be rerun often. But many are developed and few are chosen, and of them the audience chooses even fewer. Failures are inevitable. One real turkey was *Honey for Tea*, produced by star producer and one time head of comedy Gareth Gwenlan. Gareth took a four-week holiday while the series was transmitted, thus demonstrating, said Jim Moir, that the secret of comedy is timing. The other thing about comedy is that critics have no clue about it. 'It turned out to be one more comedy series bent on representing the British male as a born idiot,' had been the opinion of one of the better critics of the day on *Yes, Minister*. It would not be hard to find similar wrong-headedness about every great comedy since.

In 1993 we had *Goodnight Sweetheart* and Lenny Henry in *Chef*, and these were followed by *The Vicar of Dibley*, starring Dawn French and from the pen of the saintly Richard Curtis – saintly because of his tireless work for Comic Relief and his unfailing ability to be funny. Another hit, *The Thin Blue Line*, was written by his *Blackadder* partner, Ben Elton, and starred Rowan Atkinson. *Men Behaving Badly* was snatched by Alan Yentob from the jaws of ITV and became a huge success, making stars of Martin Clunes, Neil Morrissey and Caroline Quentin. *Harry Enfield* and *French and Saunders* moved from BBC2, and *They Think It's All Over* ran onto the field for the first time. For Christmas 1996 John Sullivan wrote a three-part *Only Fools and Horses*, back after three years away and the highest single programme audience ever. One has to forget failures in comedy and savour such successes.

At the annual party for BBC1 artistes, David Jason and others were discussing funny performers, among whom they referred to Ronnie Barker as 'the Guv'nor'. Charlie Drake evidently hated others getting laughs on his show and was universally loathed. I liked the story of the diminutive comic walking off the set and slipping his arm round a leggy blonde extra and asking, in his high voice, 'What do you say to a little fuck?' To which the girl replied, 'Hello, Little Fuck.' I hope it is true.

Perhaps the even greater glory was on BBC2, where in the space of these four years to 1996, we launched *The Smell of Reeves and Mortimer* and later *Shooting Stars*; Caroline Aherne as the wickedly subversive chat show hostess *Mrs Merton*; *The Fast Show* with Charlie Higson and the extraordinary Paul Whitehouse, likened by John Mortimer to Charles Dickens in the number and vividness of the contemporary characters he created; Steve Coogan as the odious Pauline Calf and then as the unforgettably cringe-making Alan Partridge; Armando Iannucci's *Friday Night Armistice*; and *Fantasy Football League* with Frank Skinner and David Baddiel. Perkins and Plowman had a personal hand in many of the successes on both channels.

We were running less American material partly because their series no longer worked on BBC1 as they once did, and partly because we had the money from savings for more origination. Channel controllers had always enjoyed the annual buying trip with Alan Howden to Los Angeles. They could become overexcited in the competition for any good stuff and we had at times ended up with material we could not afford to run or that had to be hidden at the midnight hour. I instituted a pre-trip review of what we had, what we needed and what was in the budget. The result was that one year the controllers returned having spent nothing – a record.

In contrast to drama and entertainment, I never jerked bolt upright in the theatre, a cold tingle down the spine, worrying about the strength of our factual programmes. They remained strong and began to please the audience in the early evening on BBC1. *Watchdog* was re-launched with Anne Robinson, a tiger on the consumer's behalf. I told her she must not wink in this programme as she had in *Points of View*, and she did not. Would I be so bold now? *Home Front*, *Changing Rooms* and *Ground Force* were all thoroughly worthwhile programmes I was proud to see doing well but whose contribution was in time discounted by imitation. *Animal Hospital*, cleverly cast with Rolf Harris as presenter, caught on immediately. The first run was live daily across a week. The camera crew would leave the hospital to follow a story. News came in that a bin liner full of hamsters had been thrown out of a window nearby. The investigator and crew went to see the neighbour who had witnessed the act, to be told that the person concerned was fed up with his kids not looking after the animals so had chucked the hamsters out to die. Reporter and crew knocked on the door of the culprit. He opened it, was taken aback by the camera and lights, then looked at the reporter and exclaimed, 'Hey! Aren't you the guy from that *Animal Hospital* programme? We've just been watching that. It's really good . . .'.

With *Children's Hospital*, *HMS Brilliant* and *Airport*, long form documentary serials (all right then, docusoaps) began to capture people in the early evening on BBC1. It was an entirely positive development that well made films about contemporary institutions should thrive in prominent positions in the schedule. They provided genuine insights into the way organizations operated and into the lives of those who worked in and used them. As with make-over shows, there was soon a glut, this time of our own making. The individual series, among them *Driving School*, *Hotel*, *Vets in Practice* and *Battersea Dogs Home*, were fine in themselves, but I have named fewer than half of them. Also, a knowingness crept in. Some of the characters played up their personas and acted cute for the camera, one or two crossing from real life to take part in other programmes as reporters or panellists.

Arts programmes were hard to create satisfactorily for BBC1. Sister Wendy conducted a popular history of art and Griff Rhys-Jones presented several runs of an inventive book programme, *Bookworm*. Alan and Michael reduced the spend on music and arts from the high water mark it had achieved when they in turn had run the department. Some reduction was in order (in 1994 there were more staff in music and arts than anywhere else save the combined drama departments) but I had to lean on them to ensure that we delivered on the public promises we had made about the output. There was no shortage and we had some impressive achievements on BBC2. *Arena* produced trilogies on Graham Greene and Peter Sellers, Neil MacGregor wrote and presented *Painting the World* and Andrew Graham-Dixon a *History of British Art*.

Every few years Melvyn Bragg would drop his handkerchief before us and we would pick it up. He had done an heroic job in sustaining ITV's arts output, and the BBC had never developed a comparable figure, someone who cut mustard in the arts and who was an easy broadcaster. Back in 1988 Alan Yentob had been considering Melvyn to edit and present what was to become *The Late Show*. He was evidently keen to do it but he could not come free straightaway and the editor's job went to Michael Jackson. On one or two other occasions Melvyn fluttered his eyelashes at us, then John Birt rang me to say Melvyn did want to come to the BBC, was content to work in the arts department and was 'not interested in money'. Meetings followed. Alan Yentob put to me a plan of work he had agreed with Melvyn including programmes for both BBC1 and BBC2. We allocated the money. Only Melvyn decided to remain at LWT. Was I unduly cynical to view Melvyn's dalliances with us as not unconnected to his negotiations with ITV?

The big projects came as hoped for. *People's Century* transmitted in three separate runs, the first programme included only people born in 1900 or earlier, among them a 110-year-old man who had stormed the Winter Palace ('little opposition'). The natural history department delivered *Life in the Freezer* and David Attenborough's *Private Life of Plants*. We had *The Gulf War*, *Death of Yugoslavia* and a season of programmes on Northern Ireland, *25 Bloody Years*. Jana Bennett was the new head of science and brought energy, and a stream of projects began production: *The Human Body*, *Walking With Dinosaurs* and, my personal favourite, *Earth Story*, a six-part account of the geology of our planet presented by Aubrey Manning. Nothing was better than the *Horizon* programme 'Fermat's Last Theorem' in my all-time top ten documentaries. I have seen it three times. Each time I think I can understand it while watching; each time I have a lump in my throat at its denouement.

We commemorated the 50th anniversaries of D-Day, VE and VJ with seasons of programmes and triumphant outside broadcast coverage of the events, many of which had been helped into existence or shaped by Philip Gilbert and his team. A memorable image was the sight of Major John Howard being pushed across Pegasus Bridge in a wheelchair at the head of the marching veterans. Richard Holmes began his splendid *War Walks* series. *Timewatch*, under Laurence Rees, regularly made headlines.

Michael Jackson told me that someone had come up with the idea that we make a history of Britain. I was determined that we should find a way to do so, even though, unlike with most other grand projects, co-production funds were unlikely. In July 1995 I played host at a lunch and informal half-day seminar in the upstairs room at Orsino's in Holland Park. Janice Hadlow, the executive producer, gathered the participants: Neal Ascherson, David Cannadine, Linda Colley, Peter Marshall, Miri Rubin, Raphael Samuel and David Starkey. Brian Walden took the chair. I explained that we wanted to hear their thoughts on what we might do, what pitfalls to avoid and how such a history might be structured. It was fascinating and, naturally, inconclusive, but provided ideas for Janice and her team. They eventually made the inspired choice of Simon Schama to write and present. I made sure that the project remained alive through changes of controller, and with the help of Jane Drabble, by then director of education, who invested heavily in the series as an educational resource, made sure that the project went ahead, co-production or no.

We had a good head of children's programmes in Anna Home and much excellent programming, but families with young children were leading the take up of cable and satellite, and the new dedicated children's channels were beginning to make an impact. We had children's programmes for two hours in the afternoon and on Saturday morning and children had to find them there. Nickelodeon and others ran only children's programmes; children knew that programmes for them were always available. In time we knew we had to have our own children's channels. In the meantime we played to our strengths and made more children's drama, including *Just William* and *The Borrowers* on Sundays, and *The Demon Headmaster* and *The Queen's Nose* in the week. We introduced a block of rerun children's programmes on BBC2 in the early morning, discovering that the previous day's *Blue Peter* could win a larger audience than *The Big Breakfast*. Thirdly, Anna developed a new pre-school series that she was confident would be a winner. She showed me the drawings of the odd creatures with TV screens in their stomachs that were to launch in 1997 as *Teletubbies*.

In this second term, as it were, of my running television we did a good job. We had reduced repeats in peak hours by half, to just 11 per cent. We had closed the gap between BBC1 and ITV from 7 per cent to 1.6 per cent and between the two BBC channels and ITV and Channel 4 combined to less that 1 per cent. More than 94 per cent of the population tuned into BBC television each week. And the programmes had got better. There is always an element of luck in awards but bad programmes do not win them, and we won record numbers of the ones that mattered. In 1994 we won three Prix Italia and in New York five International Emmys. No other broadcaster had ever won so many at one time. The morning after the Emmy news, the DG rang my office to say he was coming down to Television Centre. The attendees at programme review were taken aback as John arrived at the end, made a generous little speech congratulating everyone, me especially, then called for a round of applause after presenting me with a magnum of champagne. Shucks. It was a kindly act.

Formal awards ceremonies were not always as gratifying. I witnessed two embarrassing evenings at the Writers' Guild Awards. At one, Andrew Davies shouted 'Get off, fatty', at David Mellor whose jokey speech was falling flat, oblivious to the fact that Mellor had just bravely defended the BBC in the face of baying hecklers at the Tory conference. The next year John Osborne was given a lifetime achievement award. He was clearly not well and his acceptance speech was halting, with long silences. As Osborne struggled, Barry Took stood up and strode out announcing loudly, 'I'm going for a pee.' Alan Bleasdale leapt to his feet and shouted, 'This is the greatest writer of the century,' and went to help Osborne away from the microphone, not, I sensed, what Osborne yet wanted. Spotting a moment of drama, two others present, producer Linda Agran and writer Lynda La Plante, now rose and moved importantly to the stage to assist. Suddenly John Osborne was no longer the hero and centre of attention but rather the medical orderlies Bleasdale, Agran and La Plante. Thespians move in many ways their limelight to achieve.

Alan Bennett was not one for such occasions. He declined my invitation to join us at the BAFTA awards, saying that he would have to give a bigger performance responding to the result of the writer's award than any of the actors had to getting nominated – and you did not get paid for it. I made a wonderful fool of myself one year. *Absolutely Fabulous* was up for a shelf-full of awards and I had the stars at my table, among them Julia Sawalha, whom I had of course seen in the show but had never met. I was at the table promptly looking out for my guests and I spotted this one walking along the raised walkway and beckoned vigorously. She looked a little surprised but came towards me and stepped down to the table. Will 'Mr Showbiz' Wyatt greeted her warmly with a broad grin and a kiss on each cheek, before glimpsing someone who looked much more like the woman in *Ab Fab* over her shoulder, indeed the real Julia Sawalha. I was sure I had seen the woman I was embracing before. I had. It was Helena Bonham-Carter, whom I now pretended to be a great chum before allowing her on her way. I expect you get used to being grabbed by tubby old fellows in the film business, but I thought that Miss Bonham-Carter behaved amazingly well in the circumstances.

Chapter sixteen
THREE HANDSHAKES WITH DES

I had been managing director of television for about a year when I received a tip that another company was interested in Desmond Lynam. He did not seem unhappy and was well within contract, but it was sensible to move quickly. Des was the face of BBC sport, a hugely accomplished broadcaster whose relaxed demeanour and laconic wit created a unique style. 'Hey! Shouldn't you be at work?' were his opening words for the coverage of an England World Cup match that kicked off on a weekday morning. He played off the events around him rather than hyping them. Coming out of synchronized swimming at the Olympic Games: 'All look alike, don't they? The Stepford Wives in water.' At another Olympics: 'Going down to the pub is not yet an Olympic Sport. Beach volleyball is.'

I asked Des to come to see me, offered him an immediate pay increase and a contract for four more years to take us past the 1996 Olympics. 'You've got a deal,' he replied and shook hands. That was that. We chatted. He told me of walking out onto Fulham's pitch with Jimmy Hill, once a player and now chairman there. The crowd chanted, 'Jimmy Hill's a wanker, Jimmy Hill's a wanker.' 'See?' said Jimmy. 'They still shout for me.'

This was a decade that changed forever the coverage of sport on television, and gave us at the BBC a gruelling time. The BBC had had so much sport for so long. ITV had always been interested in football and at the beginning of the 1990s had eighteen live matches from the then first division and access to big international championships shared with the BBC. It had the Rugby World Cup, boxing and domestic athletics but had passed racing to Channel 4. Elsewhere it had retrenched and had decided that its coverage of the 1988 Seoul Olympics, again shared with the BBC, would be its last. Channel 4, with a remit to be different, had opted for minority sports. Basketball flopped, Sumo wrestling was a curio and American Football gave the new channel a cult success for several years. Apart from this, the BBC carried pretty well everything else.

Things changed. In the middle of the decade ITV decided to boost its sports portfolio and invested heavily to win exclusive contracts. Channel 4 built up its racing brand and began to look at mainstream sports. BSkyB, with some football inherited from its takeover of BSB, made sport the chief driver of its subscription services and would pay accordingly. With the exception of the growth of live league soccer matches, if these players were to acquire major sporting events for their services, there was only one place they could come from. We would have to defend on every front against rivals who would go in hard and dig deep to pick off individual territories. In 1987 the BBC had transmitted 64 per cent of all hours of televised sport. By 1991 Sky Sports 1, 2 and 3 had launched and the BBC's share in hours was 17 per cent, falling to 9 per cent in 1997. Our intention was that where necessary we would be able to retreat in good order to prepared strongholds. What we could not know then was that while our income was to rise by around 3 per cent per year, the price of the top sporting events was to rise by 30 per cent per year.

Head of sport was Jonathan Martin. He had joined the BBC as a general trainee and had spent almost all his career in television sport. He was both a strategist and tactician, thought hard and long-term about our contracts and prepared meticulously for negotiations. A slight, wiry man, he was as precise in his thinking as he was about the neat way he rolled up the sleeves of his shirt in summer. Jonathan was a worrier. Was an issue raised on a contract a ploy to get out of it? Was a competitor nuzzling up to one of our rights holders? He worried about the output, watching everything, and was swiftly on the phone if he saw something sloppy. 'I'm a BBC guy. I believe in the place,' he told me after an approach from elsewhere. He was the loyalist of colleagues: tough in debate within, a superb ambassador for the BBC without. His own favourite sports were skiing and Formula One, but always his top priority for the BBC was football.

We were facing a big test. Football was planning a 'super league' that would offer many more live matches to television. We wanted to be part of a new football era. We would have liked some live games but realized that the cost was likely to be prohibitive. Our aim was to secure Saturday night highlights and bring back *Match of the Day*, our emblematic Saturday night soccer programme that had been off the screen for several years. Late in 1991 Greg Dyke, managing director of LWT, came to see me looking for a deal. ITV would bid high for the live games, we could have the highlights. I listened, said that we might be interested but could make no commitments, as bidding was some way off.

A couple of months later Sam Chisholm, the boss of BSkyB, came on a similar errand. Sam was a tough and wily New Zealander who had worked in Australia for Kerry Packer and was now managing Rupert Murdoch's big satellite TV investment. He was short, solid, bull-necked with square shoulders from which his arms hung loose. Sam liked to show what a brute he was: 'My management style? Delegate, then interfere.' He would begin a telephone conversation: 'My Lord Wyatt [it was usually this or 'My dear Wyatt'], I want you to know that I rule with a whim of iron.' Bob Phillis had told me how when he was running ITN Sam had rung to suggest that they should be working on things together and ought to meet to brainstorm some ideas. Sam arrived for the meeting and as they all sat down at the table, he kicked off, 'Now I said we should do some brainstorming. You've got the brains and I'll do the fucking storming.' With the BBC Sam held a grudge that he never forgot. He had agreed that Sue Barker, who had been under contract to Sky, could work for the BBC at Wimbledon. At the end of this stint Jonathan Martin established with Sue that her contract with Sky had lapsed and offered her one with the BBC, which she accepted. Thereafter Sam would only refer to Jonathan as 'that little shit, Martin', refusing to deal with him and urging me to sack him.

In March 1992 Jonathan Martin and I went to see Graham Kelly and Glen Kirton of the Football Association and Rick Parry who was to be chief executive of the new league. We told them that we were happy to work alongside Sky, ITV or anyone else. They, in turn, presented a united front and gave us a clear indication that their preferred outcome, money allowing, was that Sky have the live league games and many more of them and that we have *Match of the Day* and retain live FA Cup matches. They liked the combination of subscription and free to air and they had not enjoyed the relationship with ITV. Work it out with Sky, they said. I asked Jonathan to check with Kelly alone that this was truly what he wanted. We did not want to gain the Premier League, as it was to be called, at the expense of losing what we already had, the Cup. Our risk all along was that we bid alongside Sky and win the league, only for ITV to come piling in to take the Cup away from us. I briefed Mike Checkland, who was still director-general, and he said to go ahead. So, Jonathan and I sat down with Sam and his people to thrash out a bid for the new league. I had to posture, 'We've got other ways of getting this,' when Sam said we should pay £10 million a year. I believed that they needed us and we said £3 million. By the following day we had fixed the sums and made an agreement that neither would withdraw from the linked bids for league and Cup until the deal was lost. This meant we could not offer ourselves alongside ITV as well. In return Sky would support only our bid for the FA Cup.

We went together to Lancaster Gate to present our bids. Glen Kirton ran the meeting and gave nothing away. Sam's hands were trembling as he read out from his sheet of paper. We spoke from ours. I worried now lest Sky renege or that Graham Kelly of the FA and Rick Parry of the new league might not stay shoulder to shoulder. After three weeks an anxious Sam rang: 'The silence is *deafening*.' Then a flurry of activity. ITV upped their bid; Sky upped theirs and we put a little more in ours. It was now ITV against Sky, mano a mano, for the live rights. Sam rang again on the day of decision, Monday, 18 May. Would we put in more for *Match of the Day*? The answer was no. At the post Sky pipped ITV to subsequent cries of 'foul' over whether all was fair. We had a highlights deal that gave us the first television showing of all the Saturday games. Next we had to keep the FA Cup from an ITV that was both angry and had money to spare.

Sam now tried to link our bids for the Cup to Sky winning access to other BBC programmes, calling Murdoch in the middle of the meeting to emphasize the significance of this move. Not on. Together our bids totalled £50 million. Jonathan confessed to me that this was the time he had a sleepless night, for if he had misread the signals or been misled by the FA as to their accepting that our bids for league and Cup were inextricably linked, we would now find out. This time at Lancaster Gate only Glen Kirton sat at the head of the T-shaped table. He said for the figures to be comparable to the Premier League deal, £75 million was what he was looking for. That evening I asked Mike Checkland for extra money so we could demonstrate our keenness to the FA and encourage Sky to keep pumping. His reply was £3 million over the five years. When we sat down with Sam the following morning, we got the total of the bids up to £68 million, but he had brought a lawyer with him and tried to spring a new coverage agreement on us. I waved it away. For once Sky seemed under briefed as they scribbled figures on a fax they had sent to Murdoch. Neither Sam nor his lawyer understood the football end of things, and when someone mentioned 'the draw', Sam, very much on edge, snapped, 'When do they play that?'

That evening, when we went down to the FA with the new figures, again it was Glen Kirton alone. He opened by saying, 'ITV has guaranteed to top any bid you make. But we are committed to reaching an agreement with you.' After hearing our new offer he said, 'This could give me difficulties.' The meeting broke up and Jonathan and I gathered with Sam and his people on the pavement outside. Jonathan said we needed to close or this could unravel, with ITV winding up the papers to put the screws on the FA. I said we should go back in. We would find an extra £2 million in the final year; Sam agreed the same. That made a total of £72 million. We returned and put this to Glen and asked for an answer there and then. He said he would have to ring Graham Kelly who was in Sweden. We waited while he tried and failed to reach him. Glen said he would call Jonathan with the answer later. 'What do you think?' I asked.

'I think you'll be OK,' Glen replied.

I went off to Covent Garden where I missed the curtain up and was shown to an empty box to watch the first act of a splendid performance of *I Puritani*. I rang home in the interval but there was no message. As we left the opera house, I rang Jonathan from the car. 'We've got it,' he said. There was a huge thunderstorm that night as a long spell of fine weather broke. It echoed the reaction of ITV.

We completed the formalities. Jonathan had the pleasure of pointing out to Sam, who had been frosty with him throughout, that he had added up the figures wrongly in the Sky letter and was offering £1 million too much. Greg Dyke, after the first of what was to be for him three unsuccessful bids for the Premier League, briefed the press for ITV: the BBC had helped Murdoch, who was a danger to all we held dear; we should have helped ITV, who were our blood brothers. Then and later the cry from many in ITV was that we could have killed off Sky, who would not have won had we refused to work with them. I pointed out in the press and on conference panels that my job was not to use licence payers' money to damage or support anyone's business but to secure the best value for the BBC services. We had got exactly what we wanted. It is true that this football deal was the bedrock of BSkyB's success, but the FA had shown us a signpost to the football portfolio we sought. We had followed it successfully and not without risk.

The relationship with Sky worked well enough. Sam Chisholm was often on the phone. 'Can you do me a favour, my dear Wyatt?'

'What is it, Sam?'

'Selina Scott. She's always complaining about how the lighting makes her look. Can you give me the name of a lighting man who could help?' I tried to help. He twice asked me to work for him as his number two. 'How much do you earn?'

'Between 140 and 150.'

'I could pay you 200, at least.' I think he liked the notion of winkling someone half-decent out of the BBC. I was not seriously tempted and told him that working for him might be a lot of fun but also a nightmare. He took some handling. I once heard him taking a call from another company, expecting a complaint. I could just about make out the other end of the conversation.

'Hello, Mr Chisholm?'

'Yes.'

'I'm the chief executive of X Television . . .'. He was interrupted by Sam moving to the centre of the ring.

'Not for very much longer from what I've heard, my friend.'

When Richard Dunn joined Sky he gave me an insight into Sam's managerial techniques. Richard was allocated a big office close to Sam, who urged him to do it up just as he wanted. A few weeks later, when the office was finished to Richard's satisfaction, Sam came in. 'Richard, I've just hired a new finance director. I need him near me so I've told him that he can have your office.'

'Oh,' said Richard, 'OK. It's a pity. I have just finished having it decorated but if that's what you want, I'll go along with it.' Richard waited to be told when he should move out but heard nothing more. After a couple of months, he approached Sam. 'My office, Sam. When do you want it for the new guy? Nothing's happened.'

'Your office?' asked Sam. 'Aaw, that was nothing. Just didn't want you to feel too secure.'

Sam also liked to offer largesse. When he heard that I was taking Jane to Australia and that we were going to spend a few days on the Barrier Reef, he asked where we were staying. 'Dunk Island,' I told him. Sam made a face.

'No, no. I've met Mrs Wyatt and Dunk is not the right place for her. Look, Rupert has a terrific resort, Hayman Island, and we'd be happy to put you and Mrs Wyatt up there for a while.' I thanked him but said I did not think that would be wise.

Match of the Day was a big success and gave us an important football presence for forty weeks a year. Thus when the Premier League contract came up again in 1996, this had replaced the Cup as our first priority, although we hoped to retain both. We had just taken a double blow to the solar plexus. ITV had beefed up their interest in sport and were on the hunt. What was more, they had swallowed their pride and were prepared to work with Sky. They were after the FA Cup and England home matches and were willing to share live coverage with Sky as we had. Consequently Sam began lording it: 'I want to be in a position to direct the traffic.' He rang from Australia, a bit pissed. 'I'm bored with subsidizing BBC sport. I haven't dealt you out of the game . . . yet. [Chuckle]. ITV have put a proposition to us. I've not said "yes" and I've not said "no".'

'What are you going to do?'

'*That* depends on Jonathan Martin's behaviour. It doesn't look good for you. Everyone wants to slit Martin's throat.'

It was not Sky but the FA that would decide. But Jonathan and I had to construct a bid for the Cup bearing in mind that the Premiership contract was soon to follow and we were determined to retain it. We had a finite sum for football and so we were compelled to submit an FA Cup offer that we feared would lose and it did. We heard on 30 November 1995, a black day. 'The worst is not so long as we can say, "This is the worst."' But it was not.

A few days later I was on my way to the press launch of our winter programmes when Jonathan called me in the car. 'Will, a devastating blow. I've just had a call from Bernie Ecclestone to say that ITV have the Grand Prix contract from '97. It's a five-year deal at nearly nine times what we are paying. Bernie said he had had to promise not to come back to me. In any case, he said, either we could never afford to compete or I had been cheating him all these years.' Jonathan had loved and cherished Formula One, and much of its success on British television had been due to him. Ecclestone was a personal friend. We had been planning a substantially increased offer to renew but could never have reached the figure in question. When the press launch was over I went down to sport's fifth-floor offices at Television Centre to tell Jonathan not to blame himself and that we all had huge confidence in him. Brian Barwick, his number two, said that only the day before, Jonathan had come into his office to say that Ecclestone's office had left a message apologizing for not being at Sports Review of the Year, the annual programme for which the top stars, executives and administrators in British sport formed the studio audience, and had added, 'Good manners from a good mate.' Interestingly, Ecclestone came back to us in 1999 in the midst of negotiating renewal with ITV, offering to renege on them if we matched their offer. We could not and, in any event, Formula One was no longer a priority.

When the Premier League contract came up for renewal, we had to win. Rick Parry had investigated the possibility of running the league's own operation with the BBC producing the pictures that the league would sell on wholesale. He had hoped, too, for a consortium using digital transmission, which would provide some opposition to Sky, but it was too early to make that fly. I saw Rick in my office to get a bead on what we would need to pay to renew *Match of the Day*. He returned to hear from Jonathan and me what we would offer: just over three times what we had been paying. 'You're in the right ball park,' said Rick.

'I should hope that we're on the centre spot with a bid like that,' I returned. The normally impassive Rick was smiling when he left and, as with all negotiations where you are successful, I wondered if I should have shaved off £1 million from each year of the contract. We secured a five-year renewal.

That summer, 1996, our sports and outside broadcast teams co-hosted with ITV the European football championships, doing a terrific job. At the England v Scotland match at Wembley I went round the media centre and then, as I stood in the tunnel shortly before the teams went onto the field, was charmed to hear the supporters from the land of Shakespeare welcoming their team: 'We're English. We're barmy. We're off our fucking heads.' Later that summer, at the Olympics in Atlanta, foreign television journalists were to wonder why a number of British TV colleagues were dressed in T-shirts announcing 'Official ITV Tosser.' The answer went back to Euro 96 when Paul Gascoigne would give a television interview to BBC and ITV, but only one. They would have to pool it and decide among themselves who conducted it. The BBC producer met his ITV equivalent about this and asked him: 'Any questions for Gazza?'

'I don't know what you're on about. We haven't decided who is doing the interview yet,' said the ITV man.

'Yes we have. We tossed and you lost.'

'Well,' said the ITV man pompously, 'you didn't toss with me my friend. And I'm the official ITV tosser around here.'

With *Match of the Day* renewed and the end of Euro 96, at which the BBC coverage had drawn a big majority of viewers, it was time for a second handshake with Des Lynam. He had had a 'drop dead' offer from a competitor. He described what happened to a journalist: 'Will Wyatt invited me to his office. He said, "Your contract's very near renewal. I hear hints that there are other offers around. I want to underline how important you are to the BBC, how important sport is to the BBC and I want to do that by suggesting that you sign a new four-year contract at this price." I shook him by the hand, said thank you very much, that'll do for me. It took thirty seconds.' It was a big hike.

Big hikes were required wherever we looked in sport. In the glory days the price of sport rights had been artificially low, owing to the limited nature of the competition for them. Even as late as 1991, sport provided half the total audience for BBC2 for one-seventh of the channel's cost. As director-general, John Birt took a long-term view of sport as he did of every other aspect of the BBC and asked for a review of our strategy and future prices. Sport as the potent driver of subscriptions to multi-channel television had changed the economics. Because it was the engine of their entire business, rights to live sports were more valuable to BSkyB than they were to the BBC or even to the advertiser-funded ITV. Over and above generating subscriptions, big one-off sports events were tailor-made for pay-per-view television. Half a million homes paying £10 for a boxing match put it beyond reach for a sensible terrestrial television bid. The logical outcome would be that live sport would be sucked away from free to air broadcasters, save for rights holders wishing to retain a free to air broadcast window for reasons of marketing or profile or legislation ensuring certain events must be universally available. Certainly the cost of rights was likely to spiral out of the BBC's reach.

We reviewed our priorities and made the best estimate we could of the increased spend needed to keep us on the pitch and in reasonable fitness. We ran a five-year rolling budget for sports rights. For each event in each sport we allocated either the contracted sum for each year or an estimate of what would be required under a successful contract renewal. Five years allowed the inclusion of the big irregular events like the World Cup and Olympics, which were on a four-year cycle. The BBC's income rose by the retail price index each year; the sports team believed that we required RPI+7.4 per cent compound to hold on to our portfolio. John Birt agreed the money, a significant shift of resources especially as costs were being driven down elsewhere in the output. But it was nowhere near enough. We had underestimated. Between 1990 and 1997 contracts were to rise by between 10 and 25 per cent per annum. From being one of the cheapest genres in cost per viewer hour, sport became much more expensive, with *Match of the Day* and Five Nations rugby more expensive than drama series, comedy, music and arts and political programmes.

As part of our prioritization, we pulled out of boxing. The competition of pay-per-view made us bantams to their cruiser-weights. Moreover, four separate world champions at each weight, to feed the commercial vanities of American television, confused the public. The sport was increasingly under question on health grounds and looked ever more tacky. You could also spend a fortune on a fight that lasted only a few minutes. What is more, our great boxing commentator and a superb all-rounder, Harry Carpenter, had retired. I hosted a dinner to thank him and celebrate his career, which had begun, he reminded us, with a boxing commentary at Hoxton Baths in 1949. When the speeches ended, Harry asked Frank Bruno, who was sitting across the table from him, whether he fancied being Mike Tyson's first opponent when he came out of gaol, where he was nearing the end of his sentence for rape. 'I wouldn't mind being his first opponent, 'Arry,' replied Frank. 'But I wouldn't want to be his first date.'

The next chairman of the BBC, Christopher Bland, was also concerned by the unbridgeable gap opening between what the BBC could afford out of an RPI based income and the ever rising price of sport. He and John Birt pressed me for a new sports strategy, 'anticipating the inevitable' in television and optimizing our position in radio and on-line. I had a struggle with John over this. Papers were batted back and forth in a gruelling game of our own and we had some scratchy meetings. I could not argue about the long-term logic of the market but there were other forces at work. I believed that most rights holders would continue to want a shop window of some sort for their sport on free to air television and that the cost of rights was on an S curve, which would flatten out. That flattening might not be far away and so we might not have to go on stoking the boiler to the same extent for long. For both reasons we should try to remain a major player. Apart from anything else, there was a public expectation that sport was something the licence fee brought. If we were forced out of big time live sport, that was one thing. Volunteering ourselves out would look like betrayal.

I was all for beefing up sports news, Radio 5 Live and the internet. Indeed, I had been intrigued by some research in Canada that the network most valued for sport was one that had no rights but offered a top class sports news service. But no amount of ancillary activity would make licence payers forgive us if we folded our tent at Wimbledon, St Andrews, Aintree, Augusta, Murrayfield and so on. I won the argument for continued funding at the same RPI+7.4 per cent level, and the cunning John Smith, by now director of finance and sympathetic to my case, took the base year as 1998, a heavy one for payments, thus adding £40 million over the funding cycle

A central part of our strategy, and one that John Birt pressed hard personally, was to win the case for the government retaining a list of top sports events that should always be available for everyone via free to air broadcasting. I believed the social and political case for this: that the great events should be accessible via television to all children, to older and poorer people who could not afford subscription TV and to those who drop in for the big days that help pull the nation together. Of course, it helped us by reducing competition to just ITV and Channel 4. There had been such a list for years but Sky and others were pressing to put an end to it. I fought hard on this. We were helped by a big political mistake that Sky made in 1995 when they refused any terrestrial access to highlights of the Ryder Cup golf. David Elstein sustained a lengthy public and private correspondence with me about this, claiming that the BBC had not asked for highlights. But we had seen their contract, which 'for the avoidance of doubt' specifically stipulated that there would be none. The ensuing row about the absence of any coverage from most people's televisions was the trigger for our successful campaign over the listed events.

Denis Howell, once minister for sport and latterly a shrewd and skilful parliamentarian in the upper house, played a blinder on this when the Broadcasting Bill came to the Lords. Michael Cocks, a fellow peer who became vice-chairman of the BBC after Joel Barnett, had been Labour Chief Whip when Callaghan's government had a majority of one and knew a thing or two about operating in the Palace of Westminster. His view when we discussed the chances of Howell getting an amendment passed to protect the list was, 'Denis Howell made it rain to end the drought when we were in government. He is not to be underestimated.' He was right, for Howell made it rain again.

Two years later the new Labour government set up a group to advise on the list of sporting 'crown jewels'. Some thought this might be the opportunity to discard events from the list. We intended otherwise. The BBC's policy and planning unit began its campaign. I briefed all our sports presenters on the case for strengthening the list. We carried the argument to government, party conferences, MPs, journalists and anyone who would listen and 'got a result'. In June 1998 Chris Smith, Secretary of State for Culture, Media and Sport, announced that he was *adding* to the list the European Football Championship finals, the Rugby League Challenge Cup final and the Rugby World Cup final, as well as crucial qualifying matches for the World Cup and European Championship tournaments. He retained The Olympics, World Cup finals, FA Cup final, Scottish FA Cup final, Grand National, Derby and Wimbledon finals and introduced a new category of events, the highlights or delayed coverage of which had to be on free to air.

Through the BBC's membership of the European Broadcasting Union (ITV and Channel 4 were also members) we secured some of our most valuable rights through Europe-wide agreements, chiefly the Olympics, World Athletic Championships, European Football Championships and, until the end of the decade, the World Cup. The deals tended to be long term and very good value. When the Olympics contract was looming at the turn of the year 1995–6, Rupert Murdoch's News Corporation mounted a bid for the world rights. Juan Samaranch, the long serving president of the International Olympic Committee, liked dealing with the EBU, for he could be sure the games would be available free to air to all Europeans. But both the length and breadth of EBU contracts were under challenge. Sam Chisholm came on to do his bit with the usual mixture of threat and enticement: 'The EBU – it's all over. You can stay with them if you like. It isn't going to be the EBU that gets the games. I gave our presentation – hundreds of pages long. We've done a lot of work on this. The price will make people gasp. There are other complications you guys haven't thought about.' Samaranch, he said, was trying to control the whole thing 'from the grave' by making the deal very long term. 'Well, it won't work. In any case, there are European Commission problems with these contracts. They're illegal. Give this some thought. It doesn't break you getting in. Rather you than ITV. I only go to ITV when you turn me down.' He ended on a conspiratorial note. 'I'm the post box for a lot of secret interests on this.'

Jonathan and I kept close to the EBU negotiating team. We remained confident and two weeks later the EBU secured the rights to the games for 2000, 2004 and 2008, with an offer that was one-third less than Murdoch's. 'BBC Win Olympics War' and 'Snub For Murdoch' were among the gratifying headlines.

I had visited our team at the Albertville Winter Olympics and had been staggered by the scale of the CBS presence providing coverage for the USA: 1400 people, 140 drivers, four different sets in a huge studio and a music suite. At Barcelona for the summer games it was NBC but on comparable scale: 2000 people, its own commissary and security. These looked like the final extravagances of mighty empires. Barcelona was wonderful but hot. The BBC camera people covering the tennis for the pooled host production worked in the baking sun, wet towels round their heads, one and a half hours on and three-quarters off. The highlight for me was sitting next to

David Coleman, right on the finish line thanks to the BBC team's wheeling and dealing, as he commentated on Linford Christie's 100-metre victory. I was in the same position four years later in Atlanta when Christie was disqualified and jogged along the track in what he obviously thought was the noble champion's farewell, but was much to the irritation of the crowd waiting to celebrate a new champion.

Rugby Union had always been a very BBC sport but by 1994 the home unions let us know that they were open to competition for the Five Nations tournament. The sports department prepared with some care for our presentation at Television Centre but we got off to a shaky start when, after I had met the twenty or so blazered middle-aged men off their coach, I led them round the circular corridor to the newly dedicated sports studio, nearly losing them in an audience of old ladies on their way to a comedy recording. Sky were after some of the action and Sam took me to lunch at Harry's Bar. There was some talk of whether he should have offered me a job, then: 'How about if I offered you a deal on the rugby on condition that you sack that little shit Martin?'

'You know that I wouldn't do that.'

'If you'd have said yes, I would have said you were just the guy to work for Rupert.'

We waited on the rugby decision and even John Birt was fretting. 'The chairman will be furious if we don't keep this and he'll blame me and you.' Well, we did, and Jonathan had skilfully recommended an offer that did not outbid the competition from ITV but secured the contract.

It was a three-year deal but, as always, we felt that no sooner had a negotiation been concluded than we had to plan for next time. The England camp was now puffed up with arrogance, announcing that as England was the best team, the English union would decide the Five Nations contract. Scotland, Wales and Ireland were not happy and asked me if the Five Nations could be listed to keep it off Sky. Tony Hallett, the secretary of the English union, invited Jonathan and me to lunch at a little restaurant in Kew. Hallett was friendly and voluble and ordered two bottles of red wine, of which Jonathan and I between us drank perhaps two thirds of a bottle. Hallett's message to us was that there was no hurry about the contract and he would be in touch to tell us when we should make our offer. The following week he announced a unilateral five-year deal with Sky. I have cheered Scotland, Wales or Ireland ever since. All was not lost, however, for Jonathan struck a good deal with the other three home nations for all their home matches, including those against England, in all eight of the ten games per season.

We mostly had a warm relationship with the Rugby League authorities. They moved their league to summer and on to Sky but the Challenge Cup remained a BBC1 fixture. The final was always a happy day out, and on the eve we entertained the league bosses and the chairs of the two finalists to lunch on the sixth floor of Television Centre. There would always be a few words from Tom Mitchell, a Cumbrian, the rosy cheeked, white-bearded guru of rugby league, a man of indeterminate age, mysterious occupation and great warmth.

The year of the England rugby loss, 1996, had otherwise gone well, with the Olympics deal, a second Premier League contract, a listed events success and Des Lynam's renewal all in the bag, as well as victory in a tough battle to keep the Open Golf championship. Each year in December the championship committee held a meeting in London and in the evening they and the BBC took it in turns to host the other for dinner at Television Centre or Brown's Hotel, followed by a game of indoor golf, played for the Cotton Bowl, a trophy donated by Bill Cotton. The game would vary. One year the club constructed a board with assorted holes through which one had to chip; on another the BBC made a mini-replica of the final hole at St Andrews. These were happy occasions but would not have helped if the BBC golf team had not stayed close all year round to the Royal and Ancient's committee – the Open is run by the St Andrews private club – going out of their way to help the club, introduce new ideas and listen to its views on the coverage (that was not the case with all BBC contracts). It stood us in good stead in 1996 when Michael Grade at Channel 4 tried hard and bid high for the Open. Mark McCormack, the all powerful sports agent, was advising both Channel 4 and the R and A, yet we retained the event with the lower offer. This was a telling victory and a big boost to morale in the sports department.

My own preferred sport was horse racing, in which Channel 4 had managed to give us a bloody nose. The three-day Cheltenham Festival is the championship meet of jump racing and the BBC covered it. In 1990 I had been a guest in the BBC party along with another racing fan, Cliff Taylor, with whom I spent much of the afternoon. 'I feel lucky,' he had said at lunch and, after the fifth of the six races, had won £250 and was still in the placepot, for which you pick a horse in each race to be in the first three. For this many people do complicated permutations, spreading their chances of winning by nominating a number of horses in each race. Cliff had simply picked one horse per race for a single one pound bet.

'How much would you sell the ticket for?' I asked, not altogether seriously.

'Honestly, Will, I wouldn't sell it for £1000. I've never had the placepot up. I've often been near and I want to collect.' In the thirty or more runner final race his selection was placed and I went with him to the Tote counter in our marquee to pick up his winnings. We waited then the screen flashed: 'Placepot win: '£22,203'. It had been a day of large fields and outsiders winning. Cliff put a hand on the counter to steady himself. 'I don't believe it,' he said. But it was right: the all-time record placepot pay-out. The two women behind the counter were trembling.

'I've never had to pay out so much,' said one. 'Here, have £200 in cash while the manager comes.' Cliff began to consider aloud what he might do with the money. After five or ten minutes the manager, a grumpy little fellow, arrived. Had we been in the USA, the Tote would have seized this opportunity to promote its wares. There would have been a congratulatory smile, a magnum of champagne, a ceremonial presentation, complete with leggy blondes, in front of the grandstand. Not here.

'Who is it?' asked the manager in resentful tone.

'It's this man,' said one of the Tote assistants, pointing to Cliff. 'And do you know what he's going to do with it? Give it to his daughters to buy a flat.'

'I don't care who he gives it to,' said the Tote's Mr Misery, examining the ticket and then writing the cheque as if it were his own money for a surprise tax demand. Not that he or anyone else could dent Cliff's smile. The following day the placepot paid £200.

In 1994 Channel 4 came steaming after the contract for Cheltenham. We offered what the course said it was looking for, only to be told that Channel 4 had offered 30 per cent more. We upped our bid to top that; they doubled our offer. I called a halt. We could not defend every redoubt if the enemy was determined. We made sure that we did retain Aintree and Ascot through the decade.

The Grand National at Aintree was regularly one of the biggest sporting audiences of the year and a wonderful event that pulled in many non-racing fans for a once-yearly bet and the nation's day at the races. I took a party each year and in 1993 had a group of writers and artistes, all of whom were afterwards able to say, 'I was there,' of the day the Grand National was abandoned after two false starts. Peter O'Sullevan, who called fifty Grand Nationals for the BBC, conducted an impeccable commentary on the race between those horses that set off whilst at the same time telling viewers that this was a contest that would not count, displaying broadcasting skills, journalism, experience and authority combined as in no other.

Martell, the sponsor of the Grand National, once flew Desmond Lynam and Peter O'Sullevan down to Cognac for the weekend. The entertainment included a splendid dinner and they were shown all the mysteries of making cognac: the cultivation of the vines, the distillation, the cellars and the cooperage. At the last, tough, hard muscled men sweated and strained to swing the red hot steel in an arc that could be wound round the shaped oak staves and shrunk into place, creating a sturdy barrel. It looked, Des Lynam told me, to be skilled, dangerous and exhausting work. On the flight home the British Airways crew, recognizing the two television stars, invited them up to the cockpit, where the pilots showed them how a computer programme controlled the navigation and speed of the plane. When they were back in their seat, Des and Peter discussed what they had seen. 'You know,' said Des, 'I reckon that with a lesson or two I could fly one of these. It doesn't look that difficult.'

'Yes,' said Peter in his most thoughtful drawl. 'I reckon I could too.' There was a long pause before he added: 'I'll tell you one thing, though. I could *never* make one of those fucking barrels.'

In 1997 Peter O'Sullevan retired at the age of 79, 'before I outstay my welcome'. He had become synonymous with his sport on television. His voice was the most beautiful and distinctive instrument for broadcasting, 'velvet smooth', 'honeyed, gravelled', 'timed at 240 words per minute', according to different tributes. The description I liked best wrote of 'the blue-bottle like hum of his commentary'. I had always relished his characteristic conclusion to a race: 'No doubt about the winner . . .'. In one anthology of the turf a fellow journalist, tasked with describing the epic Cheltenham Gold Cup between Arkle and Mill House, simply quoted verbatim Peter's television commentary. The live, extempore words became the well-turned prose that captured the excitement and story of the race. He was as well turned in person: ram-rod straight, well-dressed and with impeccable manners.

I went to Newbury for his final commentary, which was on the Hennessy Gold Cup, where, happily, his own horse won the following race. This time he did not have to commentate on it as he had, with flawless self-control, when his horses had won big races at Cheltenham and Haydock. The previous week some friends had thrown a retirement lunch in his honour in a private room at Le Gavroche, in which Peter had generously included me in the twenty guests. Lester Piggott, Brough Scott and John Oaksey were among the other friends and racing luminaries present and the guest of honour was the Queen Mother. I sat next to Katie Boyle, like Peter a great supporter of animal charities, and who used to live in the same block of flats as the O'Sullevans, with whom she shared great friendship and great rows. After one of the latter, Katie Boyle had run round to the O'Sullevans, the argument still running through her mind. Peter's wife Pat had opened the door and Katie Boyle began talking fast until Pat interrupted her: 'Do you realize that you are stark naked?' And so she was. After the pudding Peter relinquished his seat next to the Queen Mother to allow J.P. McManus, legendary Irish owner and gambler, to take his place. They appeared to get along like a house on fire. When the guest of honour left sometime after 3.00 p.m., with a wave to all and a parting thought, 'I think that we should make this an annual occasion', a thrilled J.P. reported, 'I've found another punter who can get on for me.' A punter of his renown often needed to place bets through others so that bookmakers would not refuse the wager.

Peter was replaced by Jim McGrath while Clare Balding became the new face of BBC racing with the departure of Julian Wilson. Julian was another serious punter, though watching him on the few occasions that I knew he had had a decent bet made it look like a wearing occupation. He gave little away, but with his drawn face pale and brow furrowed he would slip silently away at the end of the race, leaving one none the wiser but fearing the worst. With Willie Carson already part of the team as well, the whole coverage of racing was given a make-over, giving it a more friendly and modern feel while shedding none of the expertise. Some of the improvements should have come earlier.

The BBC sports producers had been bold and innovative in a number of areas, for example the technically brilliant and journalistically savvy rerun of the Grand National from a variety of camera angles, the first mini-cams on Grand Prix cars and the remotely controlled mini-cams on board the boat race crews. But there was also a conservatism. I could remember the debate about whether to shoot cricket from behind the bowler's arm at each end or whether this contravened the 'natural' way of watching cricket from one position. The sports team had always been clever at choosing music, not just for the regular output (*Match of the Day*, cricket, *Ski Sunday*), but also for the big events: 'Nessun Dorma' for World Cup soccer in Italy and 'Ode to Joy' for the European soccer championships, though the latter, would you believe it, was accused by some asinine Tories of being 'politically biased' in favour of Europe. At the same time the BBC producers had not been so smart in updating coverage of every sport each year.

This was a problem with cricket and the lack of new ideas in our coverage was a factor in our losing the contract. Cricket was a troublesome sport to schedule. It was on all day – unless it rained; test matches were scheduled to last five days but rarely did; you never knew for sure when the day's play would end. However, it was England's summer game and important to us. For years no other broadcaster was interested, and there had even been a time when the BBC had paid *less* to renew the contract than it had been paying previously. By the beginning of the 1990s Sky had the World Cup and was chasing the tests. We renewed the test cricket and NatWest knock-out cup contract in 1991 and again in 1994. The NatWest games ended within the day and could build to big audiences. Dukie Hussey had insisted on a box at Lords in order to entertain more people, and I usually took it for the NatWest Final, enjoying one of the great days of cricket there in 1993. Among the guests were Stephen Fry, who revealed a vast knowledge of the game, John Sullivan, author of *Only Fools and Horses*, Simon Gray, writer of many single dramas for us, Mike Checkland and David Hare, not only a great playwright, but a lifelong Sussex fan. David wore his father's Sussex member's tie and shone with pleasure as Sussex batted first and accumulated the record score for a one-day innings of 321. As Warwickshire began their chase, his face smiled, frowned and then crumbled, for they matched Sussex' scoring and won off the final ball, thus two record-breaking innings were played in the same day.

We had a slightly scratchy relationship with the cricket authorities, who believed that we did not cherish their sport and, to be fair, we did probably take it for granted. I put to them the idea of a cricket channel, which we would run in a joint venture and which could include cricket from around the world. We could not find a way of bringing it to air without Sky, to whom it would be a threat. There were other skirmishes with them. Geoff Boycott learned the hard way that you don't monkey with BSkyB. He was working for both of us but they wanted him exclusively. Their carrot was the offer of a big fee; their sticks – with Sky there would be more than one – were the threats to banish him from the air and have the *Sun* drop his column if he refused exclusivity. He came to see me and I agreed to pay him a bit more to help. Sam Chisholm was soon on the phone. 'Will, I just want you to know that I've no interest in Geoff Boycott. He's overrated so we do not want him. You have my *word* on that. So don't let him use us to push up the price to you.'

Jonathan Martin retired in 1998. He had been in combat at the top level for nearly twenty years. We had shared some lousy moments and some great moments, and I would miss his canniness and unstinting support. We were different in many ways but he was one of those I would have trusted with my life. His replacement was Mike Miller, the energetic and straightforward head of sport at Channel 4. Mike had a dreadful baptism. Within a month or so we had to make our presentation and offer for the next cricket contract. We did this on the day before we celebrated the 40th anniversary of *Grandstand*, the Saturday afternoon sports show, at an Ascot jump meeting (at which I stole away from my guests for ten minutes to find a bookmaker's screen where I watched a horse I had a share in win at distant Bangor). To Mike's surprise, for there was no thought at all of cricket at Channel 4 just a month earlier, we heard that Channel 4 was bidding seriously for the Tests. Lord Maclaurin had invited me for a drink a couple of months before when all his concern had been whether we might walk away from cricket, and I had detected no other terrestrial interest. It was quickly evident that the rumours were true. Channel 4 came from nowhere and promised money, marketing and more excitement and passion in cricket coverage. It was music to the English Cricket Board's ear and they awarded them the contract.

We conducted a breast beating post mortem. Money had been a big factor but that was not all. The ECB had believed we had been arrogant and negative and that cricket was no longer a priority for the BBC. Soon afterwards Maclaurin invited me to lunch at the House of Lords. He asked whether we might have avoided the loss had he and I stayed closer together. I said that we had had several telephone conversations over the crucial days but that had not helped us. We could have found a bit more money. I told him that I thought it was a three-way cock-up. We should not have lost the contract, cricket was not a good fit for Channel 4 and the channel was the wrong home for cricket. I have now reversed my opinion on all three. Channel 4 has done a first-rate job in livening coverage and explaining the game; cricket seems to have brought the advertising the channel wanted and the BBC has not missed it. This last has been aided by the fact that cricket is a declining sport and England is no longer much good at it. The future will be interesting. I do not see the BBC returning to cricket, and changes of regime at the top of Channel 4 could bring changes of strategy. It was the marketing chief there who dreamed up the cricket bid and he has gone.

It would have been unthinkable not to have retained Wimbledon, and we did three times in the 1990s. ITV had been keen once but now our negotiations with the All England Club were directed to preventing it trying to stir up the market and to maintain five year rather than shorter term contracts. The club in turn, under the shrewd chairmanship of John Curry, sought a price that reflected the increasing value of sport to television. Wimbledon provided an example of the BBC as a good and attentive partner. Our producers and engineers provided much help to the club in the planning of their new media centre and number one court, and did all they could to deliver a high quality service to the contracted overseas broadcasters. A perk for me was an invitation to the royal box on men's final day, when the club extended this treat to those who helped put on their show: home and foreign broadcasters, Chief of Defence Staff (who supplied the stewards) and the Commissioner of the Metropolitan Police (provider of security).

The year of the third Wimbledon renewal, 1999, brought the climax of two legal challenges, in one of which I was on the offensive, in the other, the defensive. The former was the Monopolies and Mergers Commission inquiry into the proposed BSkyB takeover of Manchester United. I gave evidence opposing this on the grounds that if Sky owned the most powerful club in the Premier league, it would have an unfair advantage in influencing the outcome of future broadcasting arrangements. Even if Sky were not on the actual negotiating team, it would be bound to have a say in and full knowledge of the league's strategy. Many others challenged and the merger was not allowed. My memory of giving evidence is of waiting in the lobby with Mike Miller and the economic adviser who had written our submission. I asked Mike what it was that David Elstein, now running Channel Five, might have rung me about.

'Probably football,' said Mike. 'How we should try to keep out of each other's way next year in bidding for clubs in Europe.'

'Ah yes, that would make sense,' I replied.

'Sh! Sh!' whispered our economic adviser urgently. 'Not here. Not *here*.'

The other case was in the Restrictive Practices Court, defending the Premier League contract against the ill-advised challenge of John Bridgeman, Director-General of Fair Trading, who contended that the collective selling of the matches was illegal. Our defence was that each match only had meaning as part of the overall league programme and that to sell matches or clubs separately would lead to chaos and confusion for the consumer. There was an argument our chairman Christopher Bland leant towards, that if the wholesale selling of the league collapsed, the BBC might be able to pick up some live matches. This was true in theory but we had little alternative but to defend our contract. Not to have done so would have betrayed our partners, the Premier League, and hobbled us when it came to renewal after, as I believed almost certain, the league won its case.

When I gave evidence I was surprised both by the relative informality of the proceedings and the scale of the operation. In the huge oblong room at 81 Chancery Lane there were some benches on the left where the public and waiting witnesses could sit, and halfway down the same side the judges, three of them, sat in high backed chairs on a raised podium, before them a long desk. A narrow passage separated this podium from the ranks of lawyers who were arranged in four booths, each surrounded by piles of documents on tables. The first group of lawyers on the right were the BBC's: Christopher Carr QC with a junior and half a dozen or more solicitors from our retained firm and in-house; then came similar teams from Sky, the Premier League and finally the Director-General of Fair Trading, thirty or more in all, and with them the near audible whirr of school fees being generated and Tuscan farmhouses being earned. In the far corner on the left was the witness stand where I was cross-examined for two and a half hours before lunch, shut away with some sandwiches, then for another hour afterwards. Several hundred ring back folders of documents were on hand. 'Mr Wyatt, would you look at document bundle 73? If you would care to turn to page 234,' and so it went on. In all honesty I do not believe Bridgeman's QC managed to land a blow. Unlike some of the prosecution witnesses, I was well prepared and had the arguments in my head.

The trial lasted four months and called seventy witnesses. The verdict was due on a day when I was a guest of the course at the Goodwood summer meeting. I arranged to call in to hear the announcement. If we won, then Niall Sloane, editor of *Match of the Day*, could do the interviews; if we lost, I would dash back to handle the flak and media post mortems. My racing was safe. The court, in its judgement, commended my 'wholly credible and frank series of answers', and found in favour of the clubs selling collectively, held that the arrangements encouraged competition in the television industry and that the revenues from selling rights exclusively enabled the clubs to invest in stadia and players. It was an embarrassing defeat for Bridgeman, the first time that the OFT had lost court, and the whole thing was a massive waste of public money.

The following Monday came the third handshake with Des Lynam. Soon after I had arrived at my office in Broadcasting House on a hot, sticky morning, I had a message that Des wanted to come and see me. This was unusual. I rang Bob Shennan, the head of sports production. 'Do you know what this is about?'

'No.'

'Could it be to do with his private life again?' Des had been caught playing away by a red top.

'Not that I know of,' said Bob.

'Can it be about his contract?'

'You've talked to him about that. So have I. It's on course. You've got me worried now.'

At 9.45 a.m. when I ushered someone else out of my office, Des was looking edgy in my outer office. He came in and got straight to the point. 'Will, in the all time list of difficult conversations, this is definitely in the top five. I'm quitting. I'm going to ITV to front their live football. You've got to understand, it's irreversible. I couldn't have come to your office this morning if there had been any doubt because I wouldn't have been able to face you. I'm very, very sorry because we're friends. You've always been great to me and I didn't think this would ever happen but it has. You know I wanted to work less. I'm getting stale on *Match of the Day*, same old routine. I love doing Wimbledon but I'm only a Wimbledon presenter for two weeks a year. I don't feel I'm as sharp as I was. The BBC hasn't got much live football to speak of, and ITV have offered me sixteen days of it. I think it's the right move for me now.'

'Is it definitely irreversible?'

'Yes. We're looking at the legalities. You may want to make me stay at home for a bit. I'm very, very sorry, but that's it.'

'When will it be announced?'

'This afternoon. I'll call the football team as soon as I leave here.'

'It's a hell of a week, Des. We get the results of the licence fee review on Thursday. We celebrated saving *Match of the Day* last week.'

'I know,' he said. 'It just fell that way. I hope that we stay friends. You've always been absolutely straight and fair with me.' We shook hands.

I got onto the lawyers and said to wield the big stick. We were as difficult as we could be to demonstrate that a contract is a contract, keeping Des at home for a while and extracting some money from ITV. But that was not really the point. The following morning the *Sun* announced a 'Where's the new Des?' competition. Gary Lineker was our answer and Bob Shennan signed him for five years. ITV were after John Motson and Alan Hansen as well. Motty re-signed for us. Our sports team asked if I would see Alan with them. I was a huge fan of his, not just as a football analyst. He had a natural grace and decency in person. A year or so earlier I had arranged a dinner for my history master from school, inviting some others he had taught, mostly headmasters or deputy heads, and all came. The master and his wife stayed with us and the next morning I took him, at his request, on a tour of Television Centre. His mind was as sharp as ever but he had had a stroke that had severely slowed his speech. He had also been for many years head of Blue Coats School, Liverpool and knew all about the football heroes of the city. As we were leaving the Centre, he spotted Alan Hansen coming in for *Match of the Day*. Alan came over and I introduced them. There was every reason for Hansen simply to say hello and go to work, but that was not the man. He chatted away about Liverpool and football and more for ten minutes while I had to nip off to take a call. Many far less talented and far less busy would not have bothered.

The meeting was in my office on the day of the eclipse, which I watched with Jane in Regent's Park on the way back from seeing an architect who was designing an extension to our house.

Alan arrived charming and charismatic as ever. ITV had made him a big offer and was pressing. I had arranged for Greg Dyke, the DG-to-be, to call him and confirm that he would try for more live football and that he was confident of retaining *Match of the Day* and I now laid out our plans and ambitions. Bob Shennan took him through the money on offer. 'I'll let you know in a couple of days,' said Alan. 'Is that OK?' It was, and so was his answer. Although we were knocked back by the loss of Des Lynam, it soon seemed like a blessing in disguise, for the new football line-up, with Gary Lineker as anchor, had a fresher look that the audience as well as the press appeared to recognize. After I had left, the BBC, in the process of regaining the FA Cup, lost *Match of the Day* to ITV, so Des found himself back on that particular treadmill. In 2002 he fronted the World Cup coverage for ITV as he had for the BBC, but the new squad won the BBC's customary audience victory by an even larger margin than four years earlier. As Jim Moir was fond of saying, thus nature balances herself.

Greg Dyke was keen to talk about sport when he arrived at the BBC. I explained how we were working to improve our coverage, introduce new ideas, market our sports brand better and be more attentive and strategic in our relations with the sports bodies. I told him what we would do with a bit more money and what with a lot of extra money. 'What do you mean a lot extra?' he asked.

'£65 million a year.'

'Oh. That's impossible. What do you mean by a bit extra? About ten?'

'£20 or £30 million,' I said. He pulled a face.

Looking back, I regret that any of the events had to go, but the one I can blame myself for was the cricket. That should have been spottable and stoppable. Apart from that, we did a good job. The other few events lost could only have been kept with a lot more money and, even if it was there, would it have been right to draw down from other BBC programming in order to prevent sport going, as it mostly did, to other free to air broadcasters? We could not chase the market in every sport. Nor could we beat off targeted and determined raids. In just under ten years the television spend on sport had gone from £50 million to £150 million per year, almost as much as on all hours of factual programming. There had to be a point at which it was more sensible to spend on BBC made drama, documentaries and entertainment. Even so, at the end of this time the BBC still had a raft of top class sport. If a new broadcaster came on the scene with such a list of events, jaws would drop in admiration. We were, of course, judged not on this but by what we had had in the easy years. Still, the press was slowly coming to understand the realities. Our more integrated approach across television, radio and on-line and a sense of freshness in the coverage was beginning to make an impact. For all that I had had to conduct a sometimes orderly retreat, we had some significant victories in a world without certainties, among them the continuing and extended list of events that could not go to pay TV, *Match of the Day*, the Masters, the Open, the return of athletics, Wimbledon and the longest ever Olympic contract, which ensured that Britain's eleven golds at Sydney were seen on BBC1.

Personally, I had been privileged with some unforgettable memories: the Olympic men's 100 metres, sitting next to Bobby Robson as England played Holland in a World Cup qualifier and he forecast only too accurately what the Dutch might do, in the BBC's box watching Generous winning the King George at Ascot by six lengths, Dettori's Ascot seven-timer, Agassi's five set victory at Wimbledon, and taking each of my daughters and then my Dad to the Cup Final.

Chapter seventeen
'THE CAPSULES WERE MEANT FOR YOU'

John Birt was chastened by Armanigate but neither he nor the rest of us on the board of management allowed it divert us from the long march on which we had set out. John had fired an arrow to the future of the BBC, describing a broad arc over the questions, challenges and competition that we faced, to where the organization would not merely survive – something not to be taken for granted – but thrive: well-run, creative, well-funded and in touch with the world around it. Some could not see the need for this; some thought it ludicrously ambitious; some doomed to failure. John's plan was radical, his mind determined and his approach Cromwellian.

Everything was directed towards ensuring the long-term strength of the BBC: improving its services in breadth and quality, preserving its independence and justifying public funding. The BBC needed to lay out the case for its existence with a clear mission and strategy and had done so in the Extending Choice document, which now became the mantra. We attacked costs through the market system, examined every corner of the organization with a view to reform, modernized the conduct of business and sought to demonstrate greater accountability. Because John forced the BBC to articulate its role, question its shibboleths and argue for its privileged position, many thought he did not like the place. He had not when he first arrived, but as director-general he came to identify with its history, future and value to the world. By pressing everyone in the BBC to think about its role and reasons for being, he was not attacking but training the limbs and strengthening the sinews in readiness for the real attacks. Of course, this was uncomfortable. It had to be. John's style did nothing to mitigate the discomfort. Personally he was always kind and thoughtful. But with business, he was formal, unwilling to try to charm, to compromise or to lift his foot now and then. I am sure this was a deliberate strategy. He believed, I think, that he was the rock against the chiding flood: if he relaxed for a moment or made concessions, all would revert.

Such were the extent of the changes underway that there was genuine and understandable worry that programmes would suffer and that, in improving cost consciousness, efficiency and managerial skills, we would destroy valuable aspects of the culture. This was the fear of some former BBC bosses still

hoping for a coup and, more importantly, of many of the staff. While the
rhetoric of Extending Choice always, and genuinely, put programme quality
first, I guess it did not feel like that in many parts of the Corporation where
jobs were going and budgets reduced. In fact, as I said in a previous chapter,
I am certain that programme quality improved over these years, not always
in spite of, and often because of, the changes in culture that we were pushing through.

The board of management, now with the added bonhomie of Bob Phillis
as deputy DG and managing director of the World Service, was committed
to the task. I could never quite bring myself to refer as some did to 'the new
BBC' and 'the old BBC', though I was signed up to the idea. At our quarterly
away days the chief complaint was about 'the load', which now included
reviews of commercial policy and press and PR, a commitment to introduce
the Cadbury code of corporate governance and a staff survey. Warner Burke,
our facilitator, continued to attend but said less and less, calling into question, I suggested, his cost per word. There came a time after a year or two
when he interviewed each of us about what changes we would like in the
way the board was run. That was the last we saw of him.

The board meetings themselves were fortnightly, formal, accompanied by
thick papers and followed by a buffet lunch. Occasionally we had a guest.
Colin Marshall, chief executive of the then riding high British Airways, came
and John Birt asked him how long he thought it took to change the culture
in a large organization. 'Oh, about twenty-five years I would say,' replied
Marshall, to John's consternation. 'It doesn't completely change until there
is no one remaining from the old days.'

Tensions arose from the people surrounding John. They did his bidding in
demanding ever more information and erred on the side of excess. Some on
his staff did him no favours by the haughty tone they adopted. In response
to a query about a BBC statistic that was inaccurate, a note claimed that it
was accurate 'because it was first used by John Birt in public in January
1993'. Eventually Liz Forgan and I took John to dinner to moan about 'the
army of spooks round the back of us'. The second-guessing, we said, had to
stop.

'We need data,' replied John. 'When I came here and asked for basic
data, we had none. I agree that this must be done in a collaborative way.' Liz
pressed on and John did take notice, especially when she ended a sentence,
'. . . or I leave.'

On editorial matters he was very proper and helpful. He expected consultation over any strategic changes to the schedule and I would alert him
about highly controversial programmes. Otherwise he rarely rang and confined himself to sending me handwritten notes, 'inky blues', on matters of
taste or programme quality or to congratulate. Occasionally he suggested
ideas (see opposite).

John enjoyed talking programmes but did not second-guess plans or commissions. Alan Yentob was canny at heading off concerns by getting in first:
'I know you're not going to like this, John, but I've agreed Jim Davidson for

Will

A

Mr. Blobby. series   ?
                  ___

John

The Generation Game. I've discussed it with Will. It has to be an entertainer who can carry the show. I'll keep an eye on it.'

An important part of the new order was an annual performance review. Managers at several different levels reviewed the year's progress against objectives and overall performance, culminating with the director-general's review of each directorate. The reviews were fuelled by a mass of data, in television's case about, say, audiences for each genre, hit dramas launched, prizes won, costs per hour, achievement of budgets, range of programmes in peak and so on. It became a bit of an industry, such was John's demand for data and such was the universal determination never knowingly to deliver too little of what had been asked for. One thing about the BBC was that people's pride and commitment meant that whether or not each unit thought something was a good idea or however much they complained about a task, they were damn well going to do it better than anywhere else in the Corporation. Consequently the performance review packs, groaned about as they were, arrived thick in size and designed with care and attention.

The reviews may have been over elaborate and the objective setting over the top (twenty-four set for television in the first year), but this new discipline was invaluable in helping all parts of the BBC to face up to problems, understand what was happening and plan action. Debates became much more open and less defensive. It was no use saying what a good year entertainment had had if the charts demonstrated that you had failed to introduce any successful comedies, or claiming that a channel's arts coverage was blooming when the data showed no big series and a decline in hours. The television review lasted three days and John Birt was never happier than when spending the best part of a morning discussing the strengths and weaknesses of drama. I remember these meetings as nearly always being positive and enjoyable occasions, often with much good humour.

Producer Choice began to demonstrate its effectiveness at driving down costs. (It produced savings of around £50 million in the first year, and together with a reduction in overheads, there was nearly £80 million more for programmes.) The new system required hard work and new skills in the television production departments. Before she was promoted to director of education, Jane Drabble helped them learn to make proper forecasts, strengthen their financial abilities and understand their cost structures. The risk for the departments was in not securing enough commissions, so I conducted a formal review of each department's business quarterly and monitored the evolving channel plans in order to manage the effects of them and spot problems.

Without a commercial bottom line it was hard for staff, feeling the effects of rapid change, to understand the full significance of it all. Just as producers were freed from having to use in-house resources, so BBC facilities were now open to business from outside. There was anger among production staff the day that an ITV show with Philip Schofield, who had just left the BBC, was produced in TC1, Television Centre's biggest entertainment studio. In the same way, the sports department fought and failed to prevent ITV hiring the BBC's outside broadcast fleet 'selling Spitfires to the Luftwaffe' in Jonathan Martin's phrase. In fact, there was to be little ITV use of BBC resources.

The Producer Choice system was to bring huge benefits but in its first form was too complicated, with 485 business units and, in the first two years, a third of all transactions for less than £100. These were changed in time, but John Birt was firm on the rules and loath to relax them or intervene. He wanted the invisible hand to do its work. Nevertheless, I encouraged bulk deals for OBs for sport and for studios for entertainment. I instituted meetings with the new MD of resources, Rod Lynch, a tough Scottish manager from the airline business, in order to share information and help his people. For it was resources that took the hard hits, the job losses, from Producer Choice. Capacity remained high and more closures were necessary. A few producers, including some vociferous about saving the BBC in-house resources, acted capriciously once given the choice of studios, OB vans, editors and camera crews elsewhere. 'Playing shops' was the term the frustrated resource managers used. Most producers who went outside did so for particular talent or for price. BBC prices were uncompetitive because of the overhead. In time it became evident that in capital intensive resources – studios, OBs – a restructured in-house operation could compete; in film shooting and editing and in make-up a cottage industry would have the advantage.

The chairman, Dukie Hussey, thought he should say something about the effects of Producer Choice in his speech to local dignitaries on the evening before a governors meeting in Birmingham. Jim Moir, now in corporate affairs, read it and suggested he change 'a lot of suffering' to 'a lot of pain'. 'Good idea,' said Dukie. What came out at dinner was 'a lot of pain *and* suffering'. By the time he spoke to staff the following lunchtime, it was 'a lot of pain *and* suffering *and* grief'.

'Thank God he's not staying for tea,' said Jim.

Dukie had his speeches typed on pieces of card. Because of his leg, he had to support himself with one hand – on his stick or a chair-back – as he spoke, and the other would chuck each card carelessly away as he finished with it. At a similar regional dinner in Bradford there was a splendid moment when, unseen by Dukie, one of these cards looped slowly to land and fix itself in the gap between the Lord Mayor of Bradford's spectacles and his cheek. His worship removed it in a manner as off-hand as he was able to contrive.

I had first hand evidence of the unhappiness that was around. I returned to the office from a brief trip abroad to find a typed missive from Rosemary in my waiting papers:

> Will
> Last week an envelope arrived for you with an anonymous note and two capsules. The note was not abusive but the capsules were meant for you.
>   I immediately gave it to the Investigator.

The Investigator, said Rosemary, had passed it all to the police, who were instructed to say nothing to journalists. When I got into the office I asked Rosemary about this. She came in with her assistant, Alison, to explain that there had been other threats but they had not appeared serious and the two of them had thought it best not to bother me. This one looked different. I never discovered what the capsules contained.

We needed the savings that were being made. As part of the licence fee settlement, the government set the BBC efficiency targets and required us to reduce our borrowings, now bumping hard against the £200 million limit, to zero by 1996. Rodney Baker-Bates, the new director of finance, worried away to plot our route to safety. Rodney's appearance, with fob watch and the air of one who might have stepped out of a P.G. Wodehouse novel, belied his guile. The borrowings target gave us tough cash problems and 'cash, cash, cash' was Rodney's refrain. 'I'm not a white knight you know,' he told us at one of his first board of management meetings, knowing full well we hoped he was. Shaking his head, he added, 'I've been looking at the balance sheet.' He adopted the tactic of frightening the life out us, aware that 'the miserable have no other medicine but only hope', then producing his cunning plan that had us shouting his name in acclamation. Well, almost. 'I should warn you . . .' he liked to begin. Then a glimmer: 'I've been in this position before' or 'This is exactly what happened at the Midland Bank', whence he had come to us. He gave the governors confidence. Dukie declared that he was 'hoping for some wizard wheeze to get out of this'.

Rodney had his surprises, too. Like John Birt, he was brought up in Liverpool. 'My father had five children, none of which he could figure for being less intelligent than he was. He dumped us all on relatives. He'd travelled in Russia and noticed that even after the revolution, people still ate in restaurants. He was determined that we each have a second string to our bow should the revolution come to Britain, so one of my brothers is a good chef and I'm a paid up member of the bartenders' union.' Of somewhere he had worked, he said that you could only be sacked for 'gross moral turpitude'.

'What is that exactly, Rodney?' someone asked.

'What you do with your hands,' he replied.

'Your hands?'

'You know. In the till, up the skirt or down the trousers.'

It was a struggle to reduce the borrowings. The governors, strengthened by the wisdom and experience of the banker Sir David Scholey, a real heavyweight, recognized that we needed more flexibility but were rightly adamant that we stick to our undertaking and not bid for relief. In the spring of 1995 we were scraping against the wall and introduced plans to lease IT terminals, push independent productions off balance sheet, defer capital spend and drive down stock and work in progress still further. In television we had pressure on cash to pay for sports rights, films, independents and outside resources. Rodney raised the alarm and one Friday evening he, John Birt, Bob Phillis, John Smith, David Docherty and I sat from 6.00 until nearly midnight going through every element of spend, Bob phoning home every hour or so to explain to his dinner guests that he would be with them soon. The conclusion was that we were doing exactly what was expected of us in the new world. If we were not to go back on our policies, the only thing I could do to help the cash position was to put a brake on commissioning.

This was blown out of proportion into 'a commissioning moratorium', and a great harum-scarum began with stories of 'a mountain' of sub-standard programmes that we would now have to transmit. That weekend I dashed to the airwaves and the press and wrote to staff to explain that 99 per cent of yet untransmitted programmes already had places in the schedule, that I was taking out only 2 per cent of spend (£20 million) and this was partly because we had a high number of long-term projects in production. These tied up money and would occupy transmission slots for which we would not need to commission other shorter lead-time programmes. We had been and remained on budget. The weekend was memorable for other reasons. On the Sunday, driving to an off-site planning meeting with the channel controllers, I made a diversion to view a house that Jane and my daughter Rozzy had seen and liked. We had been looking at houses in Oxfordshire and surrounds for a year or more. It was not a particularly attractive house but a good size and all the rooms looked out onto open countryside. I liked it too, and that summer we moved our home there, sold our house in Bedford Park and bought a flat nearby.

In retrospect I am not sure how genuine the cash crisis was. Rodney Baker-Bates continued to complain that he had to predict the cash flow over twenty-four months to an accuracy of 0.001 per cent. The budget remained tight and I had an unhelpful spat about it with the director-general, prompting a typically kindly hand-written note from David Hatch, still adviser to the DG:

> It is vital that the television MD and the director-general see things similarly or there are soon ructions up and down the system. Between ourselves, I'm concerned that your excellent relationship with John – you've turned him these last three years from a sceptic into a fan – is now hitting choppy waters. It's the budget of course that's doing this. By now you should know that once he has made up his mind it is unalterable and has to be lived with. You have to catch him while he is still thinking.
>
> If you are going to protest because you feel you owe it to your troops, then my advice is do it privately. I see a small fire and I don't want it to become a conflagration.
>
> Cluck. Cluck.
>
> Mother Hen.

In television we brought programme prices down by 24 per cent in four years, putting more new programmes into the schedule. The BBC as a whole made savings of 21 per cent, overachieving the government's target of 17 per cent. We were demonstrating strong financial management, a critical step in creating the right climate for both licence fee settlement and renewal of the charter.

I had another eye over my shoulder to check on sloppiness on the money front. When I saw or spoke to my Dad each week, he had often given me names of those he thought I should sack from the screen, usually because he took them to be Communists. He had recently switched his attention to profligacy and overmanning. 'I've been looking in the *Radio Times*. *Coronation Street* has got twelve people in it. *EastEnders* has thirty. What's all that then?'

David Hatch gave his name to the 'Hatch targets', the one-third of production for the networks that now had to be made outside of London and the South East. There had long been frustration in the regional centres about access to BBC1 and BBC2. They felt that the London departments and now the independents were closer both physically and emotionally to the channel controllers. With one or two exceptions, they were right. The controllers believed that the quality threshold was often lower in the regional centres and were prone to make encouraging noises that were not wholly genuine. When the figures for spend in the regions were calculated, they were embarrassingly low, both for editorial and political reasons, hence the targets. 'Quotas' being a bad word, the national governors always said that they did not want quotas, but of course they did and that was what they got. I was not enthusiastic, as they took work away from my London departments, but the argument for more regional production was irrefutable. Fortunately, John Birt was as determined as I was that the one third was enough and a maximum, so that we could maintain critical mass in the creative heartland of BBC television: the London production departments. As it was, I had to manage the effect of moving £34 million worth of production a year away from them.

There had always been a pork barrel aspect to the national regions' relationship with London. The doomed General Advisory Council took up their tune and was unhappy when an analysis showed that if you compared the BBC investment in different regions and the value of the schedules provided to them with the licence fee income collected from each region, then Scotland, Wales and Northern Ireland were net recipients and the North, the Midlands and the South of England were net losers. Sometimes the national regional controllers had other things than investment to worry about. As one said to me once, I won't say when, 'You can't have a governor bonking your staff. Two of them!'

David Hatch decided to leave. He was upset when Radio 5, which he had started, was to be 'bulldozed' and relaunched as Radio 5 Live, a new continuous news and sport network. 'Everything one builds, one's successors tear down,' he said. 'It's not something to regret, it is just a fact of the transient nature of all management decisions and of life itself.' He felt he was, in effect, on the backbenches as advisor to the director-general, was young enough to do other jobs and went to be chairman of the National Consumer Council. I lost a big-hearted man as a colleague but not as a friend.

In the continuing atmosphere of turmoil in the Corporation, I spent a lot of time talking and listening to staff and explaining that changes were necessary to ensure the long-term health of the BBC. With the ever-willing Keith Samuel, I had earlier started both a Ceefax information service for television staff and a regular newsletter. Encouragingly, a survey showed that both had gained in usage and credibility. I held seminars for television staff and took part nearly weekly in the Extending Choice workshops at the BBC conference centre in Marylebone High Street. These happened daily for nearly two years and every member of the BBC staff was invited. A presentation about the changing broadcasting world and the BBC's place in it was followed by a chance to debate issues with colleagues from other parts of the BBC and then put ideas and questions to two members of the board of management. I nearly always went along eagerly, ready to listen and persuade, but sometimes the participants' level of resentment and unwillingness to look beyond their own corridor left one down and drained. Most sessions were fine. People were willing to listen and debate, if not agree. Some, when the participants were optimistic and open, were positively uplifting. And we heard first-hand of things that needed fixing, not least horror stories of how some short-term contracts were managed. As time went on, the level of debate improved noticeably. Complaints about the manning level on a shift gave way to questions about how the BBC could earn more money, examples of small Producer Choice sillinesses were replaced by views on programme policy, and elegies about the way things used to be by thoughts on the strengths and weaknesses of competitors. My message always was that the past was not wicked, that's how things were then, but life had moved on and the BBC had to as well.

We still had plenty to do to convince the world in general that the BBC was sorting itself out sensibly. I was particularly concerned about our direct interactions with the public. I asked Nicholas Moss who handled policy issues for me to draft a guide to expected behaviour – common politeness really. Apart from the title we gave it, which sounded like the staff manual for a chain of old-fashioned shoe shops, Courtesy and Care, it was excellent and was welcomed in most departments. Off the back of it Nicholas set up a simple routine of spotting phone calls that warranted a reply and urged producers to call back to answer questions and explain themselves, which many did. I had occasion to admonish Noel Edmunds for slagging off other BBC programmes. He was suitably contrite, so I seized the opportunity to persuade him to present a video for our studio audiences, welcoming them and telling them about the BBC.

I began regular open house drinks parties to bring in people from a wider range of organizations and backgrounds to meet our producers. I wrote to the invited producers saying that these occasions were not for them to talk to each other but to the guests and that they should identify those with whom it would be most useful to strike up a relationship.

I also found opportunities to ask back members of the old guard so they would still feel part of the family, even if unhappy about what the new generation were doing with the inheritance. Over the years I kept my friendships with Brian Wenham, Bill Cotton and Paul Fox, even though they were often vociferous critics. At times almost any rumour would be believed. Another hero of former days once wrote to me: 'I overheard someone suggesting that a deliberate attempt was being made to reduce the BBC's effectiveness in order to achieve privatization in some form or other with big pay-offs for the executives! Very far fetched I am sure, but it did make me ponder.'

To mark the 30th birthday of BBC2 I brought all eight controllers together. For the retirement of Sally Price, once our waitress in the canteen, then catering manager for the sixth-floor suite at Television Centre, I, or rather Sally, lured Dukie Hussey and Alasdair Milne into the same room for the first time since the dark deed had been done.

The director-general continued the seminars for selected groups, the least successful being one with writers, at which Ben Elton was heroic in his support, standing up to the gathering (a sheaf? a galley?) of fellow writers. One of those present wrote an account noting, 'Mr Wyatt whose eyes tend to glint in the manner of light coming off a scalpel'. I was rather chuffed to be thought of as such a ruthless toughie. But had it occurred to him, I wondered, that it might just have been the light on my new glasses? After a morning with backbench Tories, the MPs gave us a round of applause. I said to Bob Phillis, 'For God's sake, don't let any of the staff find out about this or they will think that we have gone completely belly up.'

These were days of seminars, speeches, interviews, workshops, staff meetings and more. Whilst I enjoyed the argument and putting a case for the BBC in which I passionately believed, there were times when I began to bore myself or slipped onto auto-pilot, listening to my voice as if to a stranger, wondering if it made sense, inventing a life together with the pretty girl at the back, planning my work for the evening or, better by far, the next holiday.

I tried not to do that when on the air. Mark Tully, correspondent in Delhi and a BBC legend but fallible like us all, gave a speech at the Radio Academy. It was the year of the Birt contract mess and the introduction of Producer Choice and he made merry with them, voicing, no doubt, the thoughts of staff who were worried or angry. But the speech was all about the entrails of the BBC and took no account of the 25 per cent independent quota or any other aspect of the changing world outside. The Corporation was for Mark, it seemed, an island entire unto itself. I went on *Newsnight* to debate with him and boxed at least a draw I thought.

Soon afterwards Denis Potter, first in the pantheon of television dramatists, gave the McTaggart Lecture at the Edinburgh Television festival. Funny and eloquent as always, he spoke of the demoralization and bitterness among the BBC staff he had been working with on his latest series, and attacked changes at the BBC in general and Birt and Hussey by name, in what was in large part a plea for a return to the days of yore. He reserved special hatred for the market mechanisms, regardless of the fact that he now worked through an independent production company that was taking advantage of that market and was presumably set up to exploit his leverage in securing deals and choosing talent.

I took part in a one hour Channel 4 debate with Potter, another writer, Michael Eaton, who did not get much of a look in, and an audience. Potter was not a well man, his psoriasis-affected hands were both gloved, and in a deft move seconds before the recording began, he apologized to the audience for feeling ill, capturing for himself a wave of sympathy. What could I do in response? Say I had a bit of a headache? In the programme while Potter was cast as both suffering soothsayer and writer-hero, I managed to avoid being BBC villain, scoring some points with a combination of righteous indignation and sweet reasonableness, even winning a round of applause. I had to admire Potter's technique: much sighing, mouthing to himself and looking around in exasperation while I spoke. He had, after all, been a leading light in the union at Oxford. Halfway through, a black writer spoke from the floor and this was followed by exchanges between me and others about how to increase the number of black voices in television. For several minutes the spotlight fell not at all upon Potter and this was clearly not to his liking. Eventually he could contain himself no longer and swung the beam back by interrupting me with a non sequitur: 'Do you think that John Birt should have been at my lecture?' Afterwards I was disappointed. I had admired Potter's work since his first television plays and now I had met him and did not like him. It was not the matter of his views but the way he behaved.

The tide was by no means all one way. At Edinburgh, Bob Phillis with warmth and bluster and Mark Thompson with cleverness and humour won the debate on a motion about the BBC.

At the Select Committee for Heritage, John Birt, Bob Phillis, I and others raised our standard, and neither the chairman, Gerald Kaufman, nor any of his fellows shot any holes in it. We held a Brussels week to lobby and show off. I hosted a screening of Roger Michell's brilliant film of *Persuasion*. We held a public meeting for Brits in Europe and, as I listened to demands for more coverage of European goings on, I found myself doodling the schedule they appeared to be asking for: '6 p.m. Brussels This Week. 6.30. Strasbourg Last Week. 7.00. Frankfurt Update. 7.30. MEP's Hour. 8.30. Delors: Man of Destiny (epic drama) 9.00. Brittan: Man of Legend (comedy). 10.00. Food and Drink – The Chancellor Kohl Story. 10.30. Moules et Frites. Nick Owen and Ann Diamond's nightly look around the exciting Brussels scene.'

If I had any doubt about the importance of the long fight to preserve the BBC's strength and independence from politicization, I received a reminder at the Prix Italia when I met the secretary-general of RAI, the Italian state broadcaster. He was pretty cool when I asked about the recent changes at RAI. With a change of government, the news chiefs and the three channel controllers had all been swiftly replaced. Where had the new people come from, I asked. 'They were with Berlusconi,' he replied.

The Prix Italia in Rome brought simultaneous honour and embarrassment. Jane and I debated whether to join the arranged visit to Castelgandolfo, where we were told the Pope would be glimpsed. At the last minute we decided to go. As we arrived and entered the courtyard, I flinched. I wore a suit to work and was rarely without a tie when there was any possibility of having to be on parade. I had taken this to be an excursion and was wearing a grey buttoned polo shirt and a very blue summer jacket. However, this was not an excursion but a parade. The Prix's Italian president in immaculate suit of the deepest midnight blue signalled Jane and me to seats in the front row of chairs. On either side were other delegation heads in suits fresh from tailor or dry cleaner. Out front was the major domo in white tie and tails and gold chain of office, whose assistants in mushroom coloured morning suits were looking at me disapprovingly, I was sure, and worse, sniggering. At length, the Pope emerged and sat on a chair under the porch, flanked by a cardinal and a monsignor. He was handed a three-page speech. General niceties, then: 'You have power in your hands . . . Do not let market values alone determine what you do.' Applause. He was led over to be introduced to the front row. As I shook his soft smooth hand, he seemed hazy about it all. The Prix president was in a nervous muddle, introducing one man as someone's wife. Only when he was about to return inside did he brighten, going to the microphone, tapping it and on hearing the click of liveness, he smiled and with a wave said, 'Thank you for the visit.' As we left through the gate, we were greeted by the next house, a group of brown habited Capuchin monks, singing and clapping to a Spanish hymn in excited expectation.

The BBC was not driven by market values alone, so it sounded as if His Holiness was rooting for us. Could we get the government and enough of the nation to do so too? Peter Brooke, the clubby, genial new Secretary of State, came to address the 1993 joint board conference. Hayden Phillips, still permanent secretary, accompanied his boss's speech with a gallery of commentating expressions: eyebrows up – 'you're surprised?'; eyebrows down – 'serious point'; eyes firmly down – 'very serious point'; eyes rolled from side to side – 'I hope you are all listening'; eyes to ceiling – 'oh my goodness'; sucking a sweet face – 'he has to say this'; firm smile – 'well he is a politician'; and mouth in croquet hoop – 'we are being very firm about this'.

Brooke's passage about the BBC needing to be more accountable received the full croquet hoop. So we would have to produce better annual reports, introduce more consultation with the public and make the governors' oversight of the BBC clearer in both definition and practise. The twelve governors constitutionally *are* the BBC. Their role is an ambivalent one in that they face both ways. On the one hand they represent the public in overseeing the running of the BBC: setting or agreeing its strategy, ensuring proper use of the public's money, guaranteeing standards, adjudicating on complaints, reviewing performance and appointing the director-general. On the other they constitute the BBC: defending its independence, arguing its case, appointing many of the leading executives and supporting its activities.

This second role was more evident to the world at large than the former, but it was the former, the quasi-regulatory role, that had to be developed, made visible and shown to work. The secretary to the board, Michael Stevenson, made most of the running on this, coming up with ideas such as governors' seminars to consult on the output, a governors' complaints committee and a fair trading committee, and then persuading the chairman to take them up. The governors knew that they should concentrate on the wood rather than the trees but found it hard to stand back. At the same time they did not want to read piles of documents. Like most boards, they wanted shorter papers with more detail. Being involved was more fun than regulating.

Making appointments was a test case. My own view was that the governors should appoint only the director-general and possibly the director of finance. Once they start appointing others they have too great an interest in everything going well. They should remain eagle-eyed about performance and disinterested as to individuals, holding the DG to account for the quality of his executives. You cannot appoint or have a hand in appointing thirty-four people, as governors did in 1993, and expect to be taken seriously as a regulator. By the end of the decade, governors were involved in fewer appointments but still too many.

The board of governors had once met fortnightly for half a day with the director-general present throughout and other members of the board of management waiting outside to be summoned in, or not. No wonder relations had deteriorated. When Dukie Hussey arrived he applied some sensible old-fashioned man management by having all the board of management present throughout and seating them alternately with governors. From the summer of 1992, as an earnest of the governors' intent to be more strategic and less concerned with detail, the meetings went monthly. Most were held in the council chamber at Broadcasting House, with occasional forays to Television Centre, Bush House and White City and an annual visit to a region. The governors usually had dinner together the evening before and held a private session, mostly with the director-general present, immediately before the meeting proper.

I first attended deputizing for Paul Fox in 1990. In those days there was a lengthy discussion about individual programmes, and Bill Jordan hammered a documentary that had questioned the conviction of the man in jail for the murder of PC Blakelock at Broadwater Farm. Bill, a short, fit-looking Brummie whose boyish face made him appear younger than his years, was a union leader and spoke as if for the Police Federation: the police needed protection and Blakelock's family and friends deserved justice. Bill, a skilled orator, had an emphatic way of putting his arguments that made him sound as if he were angry. I defended the programme and thereafter we were always on good terms. He was a public figure with a big job but quite without self-importance. He once sat in reception for an hour and a half when there was a mix-up about where he should be and made no fuss.

Bill was one of the governors that the others listened to. He was all for strong management. From when he had first joined in the 1980s, he had reminded both staff and other governors that the BBC should think how it looked to those outside where jobs were going. When the leaks and complaints about re-organization were at their height, he took a phlegmatic view: 'There are worse things than being shaken up.' He once launched into a speech about the danger to trade caused by a documentary critical of Hirohito and Dukie shut him up with, 'They've got a lot to answer for.' Yet when a *Panorama* was withdrawn, Bill was forceful in his condemnation: 'The editors should have said, "I know this programme is imperfect but I'm not going to prejudice the standing and reputation of the BBC by pulling it."' He was a populist who understood that the BBC had to please the generality of the nation, and his views on this stretched beyond entertainment and drama to news: 'The overthrow of some tin-pot dictator may be of interest to the chattering classes, but most people would rather watch something about this country.' A convinced European, Bill often urged for more and more sympathetic coverage of Europe. Some other governors joined him in this. Indeed, it was the one cause where over the years I spotted encouragement – pressure would be too strong a word – from governors for the BBC to take a particular line. I believed that BBC news did underplay the Eurosceptic arguments, but not, I think, because of governor pressure.

My earliest contact with governors had been when I was running documentary features, and it had mostly been about editorial matters. Lucy Faulkner, the attractive and friendly Northern Ireland governor, had pressed for more programmes about normal life in the province. Sir John Boyd, the trade union governor before Bill Jordan, cut a Neanderthal figure, suspicious and censorious. 'The governors should see more programmes before they go out,' he told us when he came to lunch and would not hear of the objections. Sitting next to him at dinner once, I came within a second or two of thumping him. He was famously reputed to have attacked the immorality of Dennis Potter's *The Singing Detective*, objecting especially to the scene when the boy protagonist glimpses his mother with her lover, thundering, 'It was perfectly clear that the woman was having an organism [*sic*].'

By the time I was managing director of television, there was a better group. The chairman had said to me soon after he had joined, 'When I took this job, to your surprise, ha ha, and mine, I looked up the list of people who had been governors of the BBC. Some pretty impressive names. I then looked at the present governors and they didn't stand comparison. Thought I'd do something about that.' Even so, I had to bite my lip at times. 'There are a great number of amateur dramatic companies in Britain,' suggested a governor helpfully in a discussion about our drama. 'I'm sure that some of them would do well on TV,' he continued, adding a clincher: 'And they'd be cheap.' At one intense meeting the chairman was pushing for agreement on a matter of great importance. A note was passed halfway round the table to me. I presumed it was from the DG urging me to make a telling intervention. But no. When I opened it, I saw it was from one of the governors. It read, 'Do we check when people who ring into programmes say they are "vicars"? I heard a so-called vicar standing up for lesbians on a programme the other day and could hardly believe my ears.'

Governors sometimes sought help with their other responsibilities. John Roberts, former vice-chancellor of Southampton University, was also on the board of the British Council and was asked by a contact at the National Theatre of Bratislava if we could help them. They were mounting a production of *Sheherazade* and in that poor, war-torn city were short of costumes. Could the BBC supply outfits for six soldiers and two eunuchs? I inquired of the drama department. The department's letter to Bratislava would have confirmed to the *Daily Mail*, had the paper seen it, all their suspicions about the BBC. The drama folk were sorry but they did not hold as many costumes as they once had and were thus unable to offer soldiers' uniforms. However, this being BBC drama, they could lay on a couple of eunuchs.

Like most such boards, each generation of governors liked to feel that things were different now, prone to pat themselves on the back, compare the present favourably with the past and say things like, 'I'm pleased there were no leaks, something that wouldn't have happened a few years ago.' Governors from the business world brought invaluable expertise and experience but it was usually necessary for the executive to teach them gently what it was right or possible for the BBC to do. 'Why don't we buy a business in the USA?' asked one. By and large it was the executive, and in particular the board secretaries, who carried the flame of understanding of what public service broadcasting was. The better governors were quick learners, of course, and held us to account when our actions or plans belied our rhetoric.

New governors had a tendency to go around falling in love with bits of the BBC, especially local radio. One or two were endlessly visiting and reporting back to the board in a 'what I did in the holidays' kind of way. When two new governors, the conductor Jane Glover and Shahwar Sadeque, came on an introductory tour of Television Centre, they were led into a videotape editing suite to find a man asleep on the floor before smoke from a small fire caused by a contractor forced evacuation of the whole area. I investigated. The man on the floor was on his lunch hour, his records show he had a bad back and the suite was out of use on maintenance. But who would believe it?

Someone unlikely to do a lot of falling in love was the new vice-chairman, Michael Cocks. On his first visit to television he mumbled grudgingly, 'I suppose I'd better watch a programme or two.' Lord Cocks' defining experiences had been two: as Labour chief whip with an infinitesimal majority under Callaghan, and being deselected as MP by the hard left in the 1980s. Few conversations with him were without reference to one or the other. When hearing of his appointment to the BBC, a friend high up in new Labour rang: 'It's a disaster. He's sexist, racist, a misogynist, awful.' But that was not how I found him.

He was a tall, bluff looking man with a clipped grey moustache. He said little at board meetings, save on political matters, where he was the Eurosceptic voice: 'Why don't we report European political scandals and corruption? Because there's a conspiracy of the chattering classes to keep it off.' His great value to the BBC was his parliamentary intelligence and know-how. New Labour made him angry or amused. 'The government seeks younger people, women and ethnic minorities for governors. So where do they advertise? The appointments section of *The Times*. Ha!' Later and when Chris Smith was Secretary of State, there was a discussion at the board about government relations, followed by one about BBC buildings. The new idea was to have desks and terminals but without allotted places, staff sitting wherever was free at the time. 'This is what you might call hot-bunking, vice-chairman, is it not?' asked the chairman Sir Christopher Bland. Cocks began chuckling.

'I'd better not say what that calls to mind, chairman, especially after our previous discussion about the secretary of state.' Bigger, deeper chuckle. He made other references to such nautical matters: 'I remember Chamberlain's speech at the declaration of war. The destroyer was at sea and the captain assembled the crew to hear it. At the end, they all cried in unison, "Arse legal." When you are at sea and threatened by torpedoes, things become different.' Loud guffaw.

As chairman, Dukie Hussey used to try to fix discussions beforehand. He would get on the phone to fellow governors, especially his trusties, to choreograph the contributions. Phyllis James was intensely loyal to Dukie, though not blindly so. At one meeting Dukie turned to Tony Hall, the MD of News, and said, 'Well, the election will put you and your people under a lot of pressure. Still, I'm sure you will come out of it with your reputation intact.'

I was sitting next to Phyllis who leaned over and whispered. 'Just the sort of comment to get someone looking in the sit vac column.' Her mind was sharp and appropriately forensic when questioning the executive, but she was also great for cheering you up. In meetings she usually had pen to paper and I liked sitting by her to see what she was doing: doodling an elaborate monogram or writing long-hand prose that I was never quite able to make out.

Lord Nicholas Gordon Lennox, former ambassador in Madrid, was a loyal supporter of the chairman but independent minded on many matters and always sensitive both to the difficulties the executive faced and to the morale of the BBC staff.

Sir Kenneth Bloomfield, the Northern Irish governor, was tough and clever. His contributions were lengthy but always thoughtful and well turned. He had been the senior civil servant in the province and the IRA had blown up his house in 1987. 'I put my views on one side when I joined the BBC,' he said in correct civil service style. On our coverage he was supportive: 'It's difficult to be objective about an organization that has tried to murder you personally, but we have good procedures in place and senior people with good judgement.' When there was a moment during Armanigate where Dukie Hussey looked vulnerable, I sensed that Ken was positioning himself as the person to take over. He missed little, was strong on governance issues and nearly always had a new joke or suitable quotation to hand. He was a great supporter of Children in Need and became chair of the trustees.

I have mentioned Sir David Scholey, probably the most impressive governor of my time. Apart from his expertise in money and business, he was a realist about the BBC. When ITV were whingeing about our lottery contract and some governors were wobbling, David, competitive and strong-minded, helped swing others round. He often gave you a hard time but it was always with intelligence and for a good reason.

The quality of debate around the board of governors table improved greatly over the decade. At the outset the executives tended to boast about what their troops had achieved, and the governors either cheered or picked it over. You had to be prepared to answer for the output or finances but it tended to scattergun scrutiny. By 1999 business was much better structured, the major items were taken early and returned to, we provided clearer and better argued papers and there was a more ordered and rigorous sense of governance.

There were stumbles along the way. A memorable board meeting in Birmingham in 1994 collapsed into nearly complete chaos. The first paper was on fair trading, itemizing the BBC rules and establishing the governors as the regulator. A deal had been more or less stitched up with government that if the BBC could demonstrate this governors' scrutiny, the White Paper on the future of the organization would be OK on this point. 'I'm not a regulator,' said Janet Cohen, a banker, upsetting the applecart. 'No one told me I was going to be a regulator. That's not for me . . .'. Dukie Hussey was unhappy too. He had signed up to a paper entitled 'Accountable BBC' that laid out the stand back, keep out of the engine-room approach, but every time he saw it manifesting itself, he was brought up short. Michael Cocks bluntly pointed out the politics of the situation: there was no option. The same meeting took a paper on ethics.

'Why are we having this?' asked the chairman.

'Because the board asked for it,' explained Patricia Hodgson.

'Oh well,' said Dukie, 'I'm not sure that we need it.' A look of thunder crossed the director-general's face. A later item was about providing help to the South African Broadcasting Corporation.

'Send them the flipping ethics paper,' muttered Lord Cocks.

Things were moving in the right direction. At the joint board conference that May, John kicked off with a ninety-minute review of the year, presenting an impressive catalogue of achievements on the programme front and across the board, heaping praise on us, his colleagues. The discussions were much more focused. Gwyn Jones, the governor for Wales, was good on these occasions. He was younger than other governors, a confident, main chancing, self-made businessman, who arrived with a copy of last year's minutes, to which he referred. 'How will I know if you've done a good job?' was his favourite question. What was more, he listened to Radio 1 and watched popular television.

The conference was upbeat. 'How do we know the culture has changed?' asked David Hatch at his last such gathering. 'Well, television is under spent, that's how we know the culture has changed.'

When the White Paper on the future of the BBC was published two months later, it was game, set and match for us. The clear statements of editorial purpose, the financial reforms, the moves on accountability, not to mention the skilled political manoeuvring of Patricia Hodgson and her team, had won the day. That evening the director-general, beaming with pleasure, opened champagne for the board of management and radio and television controllers. The next day's broadsheet front pages all carried the same message, in effect: 'Birt triumphs.' I wrote to television staff to thank them for all they had done.

It was not John Birt's way to sit back. We now set to work on developing a ten-year strategy for each arm of the BBC. It forced us to think hard about the likely effects of the new technologies, the long-term strategies of

commercial players at home and abroad and what the desired position for
the BBC should be. The work was invigorating, liberating and fun. It was to
provide the basis for a hugely successful strategy for the world of digital
broadcasting. We argued through the options for the BBC: whether to
remain a broadcaster and producer, whether to add more channels and, if so,
commercial or publicly funded or both, and who were suitable or possible
partners. The overall aim was to understand as best we could how broadcasting would develop and then how to carry the BBC's values, its
universality of access and its scale of influence into that future world.

Since its introduction, television had been distributed by analogue transmission, a signal that was a continuous wave bringing picture and sound.
Digital transmission sent a coded stream of data. This occupied less spectrum and would make possible far more channels. It offered better quality
sound and pictures and would also enable widescreen transmission, interactive services and programmes on demand. We had many demonstrations.
We set up a multimedia centre for staff to learn about the internet and inter-
activity and ran a programme of seminars to introduce people to digital
technology. John Birt used to complain that 'no BBC engineer ever showed
me something that someone else had not showed me first', so he brought in
technology expertise from outside. John travelled to Silicon Valley in 1997
and what he learned drove some of our thinking. We thought about the
implications of widescreen television, near video on demand, video on
demand and electronic programme guides, which would become the front
door for television in multi-channel homes. We learned about 'intelligent
appliances' ('Am I one?' I doodled). Rodney Baker-Bates installed a working model of a video on demand system. Pressed by the director-general, we
began to explore what was happening on the internet and debated a BBC
strategy for it.

Before we had finished this work, the strains were showing at the top. The
chairman and director-general were at odds. It seemed to be about who
should take the credit for the BBC's widely acknowledged success. This only
rarely surfaced in my sight, though the 1995 joint board conference revealed
the depth of it. The three days were mostly very positive. The governors
praised the programme performance and much else. One of them, Janet
Cohen, a banker and writer who found it difficult to remain silent for long,
did go off the rails in the session with Stephen Dorrell, the secretary of state,
declaring airily, 'We take the independent producers to the cleaners.' We did
not, and had we, this was not the place to say so. I grabbed her afterwards
and told her what was what.

Several governors raised the subject of bureaucracy, about which they
read in the newspapers and had heard members of staff complain. 'If you are
getting so much right,' said Gwyn Jones, 'where's the feelgood factor for the
staff?' When the governors retired for a private session, John Birt made his
feelings clear: 'Fuck 'em.' The Mexican standoff came to a head on the final
morning of the conference. John seized an opportunity for a cadenza, summing up at length and stealing Dukie's show. The themes he emphasized

were that we must keep Television Centre and Broadcasting House strong, in other words thus far and no further in regional expansion, that we should take note of the governors' (and his own) concern about distinctiveness in our programmes and the new technologies. When Dukie's turn came, he got his own back. His three headlines were to improve staff morale, reduce bureaucracy and cut down on consultants. The director-general listened with a distant expression and left peremptorily at the end.

We finished our ten-year work. David Docherty and I led it for television and proposed a growth strategy. We identified four aims: 'to remain the most watched broadcaster in the UK; make distinctive contribution to British creative, cultural, educational and political life; provide significant value in entertainment, information and knowledge building [the new words for education] to every licence fee payer; and build a distinctive platform from which to be a winner in the multimedia war.' The power and influence of the main channels would inevitably decline in the long term as more and more channels were launched. For the foreseeable future, though, the broad main channels would remain dominant.

We proposed to launch extra public service channels, so that as the audience fragmented to more specialist services, we would have some of our own ready to greet them in that new universe of choice. We would make more use of our programmes across different services and in supplying commercial partners. UK Gold had launched back in 1992 with a supply deal for BBC programmes. The channel controllers and I had first been cautious about releasing shows and insisted on a variety of restrictions to give BBC1 and 2 first choice of reruns. As time went on, we became relaxed about the commercial usage of our programmes, for it seemed not to affect their potency on the main channels. In anticipation of the new technologies, we were already producing nearly all drama and some comedy in a widescreen format

After debate, the BBC decided that we should be distribution neutral, i.e. we make sure that BBC services are available on all platforms of distribution. We were about to leave the analogue era, when anyone with a television set could receive over the air signals from land-based, terrestrial transmitters. The multi-channel cable and satellite services were add-ons. In the coming digital era people would receive all their television by one technology only, be that cable, satellite or digital terrestrial (DTT). If BBC services were not carried by an operator, that operator's customers would be deprived of them. The 'neutrality' policy meant that we would not favour one form of distribution over the others. In truth, we did favour DTT over the others, because it offered the best chance of direct access to licence payers. On cable and satellite we had to go through the electronic programme guide of the platform operator, who had his own channels to promote in competition, BSkyB especially. The government was pressing for DTT so that one day the analogue signals could be switched off and the spectrum space sold.

The result of all this work was put to the governors on October 1995 at a special day and a half meeting. We were in the run-up to the decision on the next BBC charter, *Pride and Prejudice* was triumphing on BBC1 and there was a feeling about that we were on song. The governors were pleasingly excited by the proposals. Although the overwhelming importance of ensuring strong television services screamed out of the work, they were more excited by the opportunities for news, regions and education than maintaining our competitive strength. Still, they enthusiastically waved the starter's flag, 'These are not options but imperatives,' said one. 'Get going,' said another.

Sure enough, in February the government granted a new ten-year charter. In the face of an unprecedentedly competitive broadcasting ecology, in a world of market forces and after seventeen years of a Conservative government that had made privatization its abiding theme, the BBC had emerged undiminished in size and scope and with a fair wind. The new charter came into effect on 1 May and a week later the director-general launched Extending Choice in the Digital World, the BBC's strategy for the next ten years.

Onwards and upwards then, but not for all. At long last the final part of the Television Centre question mark, Stage VI, was completed. It provided my longed-for audience area, the 'Foyer' as we called it, but the main use was to be for news, bringing radio and television news together under a bi-media flag, as in the regions. Radio did not like this. It feared that losing the live news programmes would change the culture in its home, Broadcasting House, for the worse, 'tearing its heart out,' cried the more emotional. Liz Forgan, the managing director, fought this, lost and decided to leave. This was a pity. I felt that she had never quite settled in the BBC and had been exasperated at times, but she backed the changes wholeheartedly, was an eloquent advocate for the Corporation and, as a colleague, was always good for a giggle.

At the same time John Birt was lavishing care and attention on Broadcasting House, part of a plan to preserve and celebrate the BBC's heritage. He had the art deco concert hall and reception restored and brought forth from the BBC's archive some drawings and engravings commissioned for the *Radio Times* from artists like Charles Tunnicliffe, Eric Fraser, Val Biro, even Jean Cocteau.

Another who was off was Dukie Hussey after ten years as chairman. He had seen several big things very clearly: that he had to change the top management, make sure that the news and current affairs was trustworthy, reduce the cock-ups and get the finances under control. He had done so. He had been a brick at phoning or dropping a note of congratulations on a sporting contract won, a brilliant programme or an awards triumph. Dukie was also a great turner upper. There was almost no BBC occasion too humble or too much trouble for him, and often his wife Sue, to grace cheerfully, however tedious some must have been. Noblesse truly obliged. People all around the Corporation noticed, were grateful and warmed to this. It was not easy for him with his artificial leg. He would have to lean on a stool at a spot near the door and many times, I am sure, found it both tiring and painful, not that he would show it. Lady Susan had a matter-of-fact, tell-you-anything style, usually with a serene smile, that came, I guessed, with being daughter of an earl. 'Poor old boy fell over in Belfast last night and his leg fell off. Tore his trousers, otherwise he was unhurt.'

Dukie Hussey also had his own memorable way with words. Once, when the board discussed a decision that would need careful handling, he concluded: 'Agog trod delicately. That was my father's favourite expression.'

'Chairman,' said Lord Nicholas Gordon Lennox, 'Agog was then torn to pieces.'

'Ah,' said Dukie. 'Well, we'll jolly well tread carefully anyway.'

After a detailed discussion of fair trading rules, Dukie wrapped up with: 'Good. Well, you have our support.' He paused. 'Rather more support than understanding at the moment.'

At another meeting the announcement of the names of three new governors was brought in to him. Of one of the names, he said, 'We don't know who he is. We think he's a member of the MCC. We like that.'

I gave a farewell dinner at Television Centre for the chairman and his wife, inviting my direction team and people who reflected his particular interests: viewers' champions Anne Robinson, Esther Rantzen and Sue Lawley; the face of Children in Need, Terry Wogan; Sue Barker and Desmond Lynam from sport; Stella Gonet from *House of Eliott* (Louise Lombard sent him a card); Pauline Quirke from *Birds of a Feather*; and Sue Birtwistle, who produced *Pride and Prejudice*. It was a jolly evening. Sue Hussey told our table, 'I don't like seeing people with their clothes off on television. Most people aren't very nice with their clothes off. If I were to stand naked at the foot of the old fellow's bed, he wouldn't take his nose out of the *Spectator*. Have no effect.'

'What do you do then,' asked Alan Yentob, 'to have some effect?'

'Aah! Take his leg off. He can't get out of bed then.'

At the end of dinner I proposed a toast. 'Relationships with chairmen are complicated. The constitutional gap can't and shouldn't be wished away. But human qualities shine and make a bridge. In Jung Chang's great book *Wild Swans* she tells how she and fellow pupils were compelled to chant: "Mother is close. Father is close. But neither is as close as Chairman Mao." We're British, Dukie, and don't go in for that sort of thing. But we have all felt the warmth of your affection for the BBC, your determination that it shall thrive and your guts in carrying out the job.' I summoned in some members of the Scot Guards band (I could not get the Grenadiers) who entered playing the 'Grenadier's Lament' and left with the *Match of the Day* theme. We gave the Husseys a framed photo of the house in Oxfordshire in which they had met.

Dukie had brought his last governors' meeting to an end at exactly 1.00 with a brief word of congratulations to all. He asked if there was any other business. John Birt – with whom, I was to learn much later, he had not been on speaking terms for a year – said he wished to say something.

'When I first saw Dukie in his flat in 1986, he said three things,' said

John. 'The BBC was inward looking and he was going to open the doors and windows. There was editorial anarchy. It was bloated and inefficient.' He had, said John, achieved all he set out to do. What was more, 'He has taken an indecent enjoyment at the battle.'

Dukie was completely choked and fighting back the tears. 'This is unusual for me. I'm the only thing standing between you all and a glass of champagne. Ha!' He turned to John. 'I remember the occasion. I remember you taking down notes. I thought, "Christ."'

Chapter eighteen
'OBSERVERS HAVE FREQUENTLY PREDICTED HIS DEMISE, BUT . . .'

'I want to end this but I see that two governors have a finger up.'

'I'm sorry not to be more amenable, chairman,' said Sir Kenneth Bloomfield, 'but I'm not sure whether you would prefer two governors each with one finger raised or one governor with two.'

This was one of the first board of governors meetings taken by the new chairman, Sir Christopher Bland. Oddly, for a man who came with the reputation of something of a bully, he lost his way somewhat in several early meetings, summing up, then having to allow further contributions. Unlike Dukie, he did not choreograph meetings beforehand but encouraged an open exchange and relied on his wits and personality to shape a conclusion. When scratchy, he would rough people up. Ken Bloomfield, who spoke in well-formed paragraphs, was on the receiving end again. 'What is your suggested point?'

'I have several general points, chairman.'

'I don't want generalizations, I want specific suggestions.' Ken shrugged his shoulders.

The governors showed off madly to the new chairman, competing in the firmness of their personal smack of governance. Bland established himself, had there been any doubt, by the way he dealt with the BBC's auditors, KPMG, when they appeared to report on the published accounts. Two men from the company were led into the meeting. Bland eyed them fiercely. 'Isn't Sheila Masters the partner on this account?' he barked.

'We're jointly partners,' came the meek reply. 'She's at a company conference.'

'Tell her I expect her here,' snapped the chairman. 'While I also congratulate her on her damehood, I would have wished to do so in person.'

Sir Christopher was chairman of the National Freight Corporation and formerly of London Weekend Television, where he had been John Birt's boss. He had a forceful and self-confident manner, a pleased with himself smile and a voice that demanded attention. His knowledge of the broadcasting business and commercial skills came to the BBC at a time when they were invaluable. His ultra competitiveness, as I later learned at first hand, stretched beyond broadcasting to tennis and boule. He was well read, funny and an impressive public speaker. He came to the point. 'If you have to sack everyone, do so,' he said to a senior executive at the joint conference. 'We have agreed to support you.'

'Internal markets need policing,' he told the director-general after a discussion about why it cost more to hire a CD from the BBC library than to buy it. 'Fix it.'

'We're fixing it.'

'It's taking time.' A year into mission, he was exasperated at the gloom still around. 'We lack collective exhilaration. It has been a superb year by all tangible measurements, tell people to look at the facts. They look awfully good. Enjoy it.'

Among new governors was Sir Richard Eyre, director of the National Theatre. He became one of the most important voices on the board, though an early exchange with the chairman revealed Sir Christopher's view of how the board should work.

'I'm a spokesman for the creative community . . .' began Richard.

'No you're not,' corrected the chairman. 'No more than any other governor. You're not a trade union leader.'

But Richard was such a voice, articulating the thoughts that others failed to. 'What is the BBC that people feel they are working for?' he asked in a discussion of morale.

'It's good on money,' he said of one paper on programmes. 'Nothing about art.'

He was not soppy about money but complained of what he called the 'obsession with the syntax of the market'. When news and current affairs presenters sounded off about a reorganization in news, he enjoyed the chance to observe: 'The theatre is as nothing to journalists in self-regard and vanity.'

Two other significant voices followed him onto the board, Baroness (Barbara) Young, chairman of English Nature and another Labour supporter, and Pauline Neville-Jones, former deputy Under Secretary of State at the Foreign and Commonwealth Office.

I had someone new in my office, Sally MacDougall, who had taken over from Rosemary Haynes as my PA. Sally, a warm and friendly person, had once been PA to Alan Yentob and was therefore assumed to be able to cope with anything. She was sweet-natured, hard working and a worrier. We got on from the start. Rosemary, mentor and helper (sometimes a touch fearsomely) to all the senior PAs in television, had talent spotted for me. We saw Rosemary off in style and I toasted her fondly: 'ferociously hard-working, brave in the face of adversity, private or professional, determined to do the highest quality work, fiercely loyal to the BBC, ears shut at the right moment (language) and her standards of English could usefully be taken up by the Secretary of State for Education. Such women ran the empire.'

As Sir Christopher Bland arrived in the spring of 1996, network television's fortune was on an upward path and we were graced if not with wreaths of victory, then at least with the big silly grins of those feeling that all was going swimmingly. Alan Yentob, Michael Jackson, David Docherty and I thought we had got it cracked. In drama we had followed *Pride and Prejudice* with *Hamish Macbeth*, *Ballykissangel*, *Hetty Wainthrop Investigates*, *Silent Witness* and *Dalziel and Pascoe* running on BBC1. In five years we had closed the gap between the two BBC channels and the two commercial channels from 8 per cent to 0.8 per cent. BBC1 had lost only half a point in that time, ITV seven points. The important reach figure for BBC television, how many people tuned in each week, remained high, at over 94 per cent. Even the press was noticing: 'its best competitive performance against ITV for seven years,' said *The Times*. 'In audience figures and critical acclaim BBC television is riding higher than it has been for years,' added the London *Evening Standard*. We had transformed the way we ran the place, introduced a culture of trying to understand the audience, reduced costs and were experimenting with new technologies to find new ways of programme making. Each day we cried: 'Welcome, welcome glorious morn.'

One morn it was all to be different. When John Birt had taken over as director-general, he had considered dividing the BBC into its producing and broadcasting functions but said it was too big a step at the time. I was running television in a way that recognized the differences of these two separate tasks. Thus I was not too surprised when one of the governors said knowingly to me, 'I should take this broadcasting job if I were you.' I *was* surprised when on 5 June, John told me the extent of what he wanted me to do for a three-year term in a restructured BBC. I had assumed I would take responsibility for the existing and new television channels and the radio networks. He showed me the new structure and I saw that to this was added both regional broadcasting and education. I was to be dubbed chief executive, broadcast. Bob Phillis remained as deputy DG and in charge of all the BBC's commercial activities, but had only been told about the reorganization the night before. The radio and television production departments and the network production units in England were to be brought together as BBC production, with Ron Neil on a two-year term as chief executive and Alan Yentob, as director of programmes, his number two.

I had had several conversations with John Birt about who should succeed Alan Yentob in running BBC1 when the time came, and we had agreed that Michael Jackson should move from BBC2. The new organization chart reflected this, but Michael was also to be director of television, his place on BBC2 to be filled. Matthew Bannister, who as controller of Radio 1 had bravely and cleverly turned the station from Smashy and Nicey's saloon bar into the home of cutting edge pop, was to be director of radio reporting to me. Alan was not happy, fearing it looked as though he had been pushed sideways. I was sad not to have him alongside me still, but thought his appointment would be a wonderful signal to people in our in-house production that the BBC was committed to its long-term strength. After many conversations his role was sorted out to his satisfaction. His apparent reluctance, however, made the job look less important and sent some wrong signals to staff.

All this must sound pretty small beer to those who have worked in companies taken over, merged, moved or shut down. No jobs were going, no new owners blundering about, no one having to move house 300 miles. This was, though, an earthquake in the BBC, and the press reflected that. I enjoyed the *Guardian*, which had me as 'a quiet and determined operator' and added, 'Observers have frequently predicted his demise, but he has confounded his critics and led a BBC TV ratings renaissance.' So much for observers.

The BBC never truly settled into the new structures, and when Greg Dyke arrived, he was to restructure again, abolishing the 'broadcast' and 'production' directorates, though maintaining the underlying business relationships. Was John Birt's restructuring the right thing to do? I thought so at the time, and we were beginning to make it work when I tip-toed away. It was certainly logical. The money flowed down through the channels and networks both before and after the change (as it largely still does), and the new structure was the organizational manifestation of that. That there are two distinct jobs had become ever more evident since the arrival of the independent producers. The broadcasting job was to understand the changing lives of the audience, how they used the media, what they needed from them, and to understand producers and how they work, then to put these understandings together in commissioning programmes to satisfy the full range of audience needs. The idea behind creating the broadcast directorate was to bring together and grow the expertise in audience knowledge, commissioning and scheduling and to take advantage of the full clout of the BBC across all its services. Our job was, I said, 'to make a difference to people's lives – making life better for everyone through broadcasting and all we did to support it'. Highfalutin, but I meant it. We had to make sure that every household had value for its licence fee through television or radio or, in time, the internet, or a combination of all three.

The job of BBC production was to attract, retain and inspire programme-making talents, to grow their skills, to understand the needs of the channels and networks, and of their audiences – all this in order to invent, develop and create the best programmes. The chief problem with the reorganization was that once in existence, BBC broadcast was seen to be bigger and more powerful than anyone had expected, creating an imbalance in the BBC. The result of this was that other parts of the organization tried to claw back what they could. This wasted much energy and time on all sides.

A second big problem was the closeness with which John Birt had guarded his plans. The consequent surprise at their announcement did create a sense of impetus and excitement, but it was an odd way to do it and robbed us fatally of proper preparation. It was true that the change of reporting lines was set four months hence and the whole plan would only go live with the next budget the following April, but once the announcement had been made, both Ron Neil and I had to build our teams, get around to meet our new staff, explain how things would work and try to create an *esprit de corps*. Defining who you are, of course, also means defining who you are not. Although we were determined to work as partners, we had to stake out territory and remove fudges in our respective responsibilities. I am sure that I for one, in marking my boundaries, left an unpleasant smell or two.

Had a small group of us been able to sort this out quietly before the announcement, we would have avoided much angst and wheel spin. We could have resolved some of the business issues that were left dangling. I had thought a lot about the problems BBC production departments faced with competition from the independents. One of their frustrations was that indies could offer programmes to any broadcaster, while they had only one buyer, albeit two channels. A year or two earlier I had worked through the arguments as to whether or not BBC producers could offer to ITV, Channel 4 or Sky. It did not take long to see that this could unleash a free for all in which the BBC's commissioners' closeness to in-house production would be eroded, the independent quota might be raised to 50 per cent and the BBC face calls to divest itself of production. Instead, I had asked an economic consultancy to identify any overseas markets BBC producers could target. It would be hard for competitors to argue against 'exporting for Britain', and this could offer a route to growth. I was digesting the results when the re-structuring happened.

As is the way of things, the new people in Ron Neil's team did not to want to know how we had operated the production departments in television, and were starting afresh. They ran a doomed campaign to be able to work for ITV and others. They had an additional load in that BBC production was now tasked with making a profit. This in turn worked against sensible collaboration, and it took us two years to get round to sharing information on costs and prices. Ron and his people worked under the apparently threatening cloud of what had happened to BBC Resources. Production departments had watched with dismay as work had gone outside and job cuts followed. Would this now happen to them? Was this a step to privatization? The clear answer was 'no' to both questions, but all this contributed to something of a victim culture. Ron, who was bold with his troops, would let his hair down to me: 'All our income depends on you,' was his refrain. 'And we depend on you for the vast majority of our programmes,' was my reply.

In television I had been able to sit across the flow of business between production departments and the channels. This gave some confidence to production heads when times were sticky. I could manage the economy in the long-term interests of the BBC, the talent base on which it depended and its retention of valuable rights. Without oversight from the DG, everything came down to gruelling negotiation.

While some of the production heads let their shoulders droop, there was some strutting by people in broadcast. Commissioning arms tend to what I would call 'jobswank'. It happens in other organizations – talk to some who have dealt with Channel 4 editors – it had happened in television and I could not eradicate it. It is at its unlovliest with the newly appointed, who suddenly have a say over the work, even the careers, of others. This can go to their heads. Some are even under the delusion that they have immediately become more talented than they were. Others merely lose their manners, act bossy, keep people waiting and make them jump through more hoops than are necessary.

Ron and I swore eternal brotherhood and worked hard to create a collaborative climate between our people. Our relationship helped sort many difficulties. We saw each other regularly in each other's office as well as when colleagues on what was now called the executive committee. At the first meeting I looked round and had a shock. At 54, I was the oldest person.

Michael Jackson, at 38, was the youngest director of television. His move left a gap running BBC2. I wanted Mark Thompson, head of factual programmes. At first he was sensitive to the risk of being seen to bid and fail, but then made a big pitch. He was buzzing with ideas. John agreed to the appointment and, for the first time, no governor was involved in choosing a channel controller.

Mark was recognized as a rising star who had done a number of big jobs in a short time. He had great intellectual energy and would immerse himself in a new post, thinking it through then leaping in to action. He had a mischievous literalism. As head of factual he decided to 'market test' the value of the commercial rights to his programmes because the rules said he could, only to have BBC Worldwide, the Corporation's commercial arm, put up the highest offer. Mark had a journalist's sceptical sense of humour and was funny about bosses, the party line and the sacred text of Extending Choice, his shoulders heaving with mirth. He would argue against anything for the fun of it. He was a practising Catholic with a young family. He liked to cook – I have eaten his home-made pasta – and took his summer holiday in Maine where his American wife's family had a summer place. Above all, Mark had immense self-confidence. A few weeks after he had been in the job and was already making a stream of decisions, Michael Jackson said to me in wonderment, 'Mark is the most self-confident person I have ever known.' Michael was an agonizer, going over and over a problem, testing his ideas on others. Mark just thought about something, then acted.

That autumn I had to give a couple of lectures at what turned out to be a very busy time. The first, the televised Huw Wheldon lecture for the Royal Television Society, was on the role of the presenter. I had one or two things to say, notably on the need for television not to be afraid of using big figures, included lots of clips and made it passably entertaining. The highlight for me was a congratulatory note from Sam Mendes. The second was much trickier. Jana Bennett, the energetic head of science, persuaded me to give a Royal Institution Friday Evening Discourse on the history of television. It would, she said, be good for the BBC's credibility in the scientific world and help her ambitious plans for the department. As she described it, I had a moral duty to agree. It naturally appealed to my vanity to show off in the footsteps of Faraday and a host of Nobel Prize winners. There was, however, one snag, and a big one. I knew nothing about the scientific history of television. I should not worry about that, said Jana. She would ask Caroline van den

Brul, one of her very best people, to draft the lecture and help me complete it. So she did, and I added some stuff about the future impact of the new digital technology.

Caroline was in truth the writer/producer. We also found some good clips and she arranged for some ancient television artefacts to be on hand for me to point to – I could not demonstrate anything as proper scientists did. As the day approached, my anxiety was increased when the full ritual of the occasion was explained. It was a black tie job. First there was a dinner with the Director of the Royal Institution, Professor Day, in his dining room. Then I was taken downstairs through the throng of guests and locked, as was the custom, in the small lecturer's room, until ushered out just before 9.00 p.m. and led to wait outside the imposing doors of the lovely Faraday Lecture Room. By now I felt like a complete fraud. The attendants wearing ceremonial sashes pressed their ears to the doors to hear the ping of the clock within striking nine. The door was flung open and I had to begin lecturing immediately ('under no circumstances do you say "good evening" or "ladies and gentlemen"'). The aim was to come to an elegant conclusion precisely as the clock struck ten. I had worked out some signals and possible cuts with Caroline, but a video clip failed to run as expected near the end and I finished twenty seconds early. Fortunately, the tradition was no questions, so the cigarette paper-thin veneer of my knowledge may well have been spotted but was not punctured in public. As tradition dictated, I was led back to the tiny lecturer's room where Professor Day joined me for a restorative Scotch.

The new director of regional broadcasting reporting to me was Mark Byford, who as I explained in the first chapter I was to support as candidate for DG. Under Mark's hard driving, the BBC's regional news half hours improved in content and production, overtook ITV and became the most watched news programmes in the United Kingdom. Local radio, in many ways the unsung heroes of the BBC, was doing well. When I visited stations I was always struck by the commitment and hard work of the staff, as well as the importance to the BBC of their closeness to the people they served. They were run on a shoestring. With the demands of sport, more new television programmes and the planned new services, local radio was not then a priority for more investment. However, we did spend on an imaginative rebranding of local radio that combined an attractive overall look with genuine individuality for each station.

I did two other things to help. I came up with the idea for and funded a big millennium project for local radio, *The Century Speaks*. Under the steering of Michael Stevenson, now number two to Mark Byford, the BBC gathered a group of historians to identify sixteen themes of life in the twentieth century, then each of the forty local radio stations made their own programmes on these themes and transmitted them at the same time. The resulting 6000 hours of tape were handed over to the National Sound Archive at the British Library as a resource for scholars, and a selection of the 640 programmes was broadcast on Radio 4. The other thing I did was to recommend to Greg Dyke when he took over that he get around the local radio stations as one of his first acts. He did, and fell for them.

The BBC in Scotland, Wales and Northern Ireland had had a special status, with their own controllers and broadcasting councils. It was instructive to visit the three nations in turn, as I did when reviewing their performance each year. The Scottish team, under the correct, experienced and politically sophisticated John McCormick, exuded a proud, cool, stand-offish atmosphere, as if to ask: 'Why are you here?' One or two of the Scottish executives, as they greeted us imperialists from the south, would look as though they had just received the casualty figures from Culloden.

In Wales, where the dapper, wheeling-dealing Geraint Talfan Davies was controller, the atmosphere was relaxed, blokey and rhetorical. We had a bit of a scene there with Tony Dignum, my new finance director, who had come straight from working for the no-nonsense Stanley Kalms at Dixons and was unused to BBC niceties. Tony built a strong team in finance and was famous for his very un-BBC style of management, 'Just fucking do it' being his favoured mode of persuasion. At the performance review meeting in Cardiff, the manager of Radio Cymru explained that teaching the Welsh language in schools was adding to the potential audience, hitherto biased towards rural areas. 'Ah, I see,' exclaimed Tony. 'Two groups: children and the peasants in the hills.' The management of BBC Wales reeled visibly.

BBC Northern Ireland was a place everyone liked to visit. For all the horrors they reported on and the pressures they were under, the people there were always welcoming. Led by the clever and bustling Pat Loughrey, the management team exuded genuine warmth. They felt the furthest away from the BBC's metropolitan power base and were alive to any clues as to how they could do more and better. In drama they shone.

After just a year of the new BBC structure, the job of chief executive Channel 4 fell vacant. Michael Jackson was the leading candidate. He had been part of the group that had lobbied to bring Channel 4 into existence, and when they offered him the job, I knew he would go. He wrestled with the decision for a month. 'What I do at the moment is utterly fascinating and I haven't been doing it very long. And I've got the people around me. On the other hand, I have a sentimental attachment to Channel 4.' The day after the 1997 General Election, he told me he had accepted.

I saw some tears from his immediate team at this news. Michael was a big loss. Although he had shied away from matters managerial and was quickly bored with money issues, he hoovered up data and information. He admired John Birt and had learned the value of research and of thinking widely and long term, indeed, he was probably more analytical than creative. I cannot say I ever really got to know him, for he was a cool customer, but I was fond of him and he wrote me a kind and touching note as he left.

The good news was that I was able to bring Alan back as director of television. He and I had to find a new controller for BBC1. We felt it would be too disruptive to move Mark Thompson so soon, not that he was keen. We interviewed and agreed on Peter Salmon, now director of programmes at

Granada. Peter had been brought up in the BBC before getting experience in commercial television. He had a down to earth, friendly and informal style, had proved himself something of an impresario and was at home with tough editorial decisions. I asked David Docherty, who had been the brainbox at my side, to be Alan's deputy, responsible for our developing new services, of which he was the chief architect. To replace him as director of strategy, I brought in Robin Foster, who had been the brainbox at John Birt and Patricia Hodgson's side in the corporate centre. Whereas David had been noisy, mercurial and clever, Robin was quiet, calm and clever. He shifted work in industrial quantities, told me when I was wrong and was a kindly and utterly trustworthy colleague.

I had moved my office from Television Centre to the modern extension at the back of Broadcasting House. My plan was to bring the entire senior team of broadcast, including the television commissioners, together at BH. I thought that having all the service chiefs together would create a pan BBC view of our programming and combine our considerable firepower. It was a logical but emotionally wrong idea, and thankfully I was unable to bring it off. It would have increased the paranoia in the production departments dangerously.

Where I was successful through the new structure was in bringing the regions and education into the heart of our radio and television services. I held regular gatherings of all the senior people together and they began to understand what the full impact of the BBC as a broadcaster could be. This became a catalyst for thinking about cross BBC projects, like the Computers Don't Bite campaign from education, and for cross fertilization, for example local radio developing a music policy with the help of Radio 2

Education, which now reported to me, brought some problems. Jane Drabble, the director, was doing good work. She was rigorous in defining the educational purpose and target audience for programmes, and with her editorial skills she beefed up the programme standards. She had a bright team working on how education could use the new digital technology. They came up with an exam revision service, Bitesize, which was seized on by pupils in huge numbers, as well as the Computers Don't Bite and Webwise (how to use the internet) campaigns. Two things combined to give Jane a hard time: the BBC-wide work on digital services, which necessarily had to encompass education, and the election of the Labour government with its 'education, education, education' agenda. The latter was a help, too, but the DG and governors were anxious about the BBC getting it right, including our contribution to the University for Industry. This was one of the governments big ideas but a big empty idea. No wonder Jane found it hard to identify the precise nature of the BBC's relationship with it.

Jane liked to have a clear responsibility and be allowed to get on with it, but this was hard to achieve when the BBC was still finding its way to a digital strategy. It was even harder when various bits of the corporate centre of the BBC were badmouthing and whispering about education within and without the organization. At one or two moments there was barefaced betrayal.

Under the education banner, the policy and planning empire produced papers; then, when the director-general did not like them, joined in his criticism, leaving Jane to take the rap. I had had enough, took over leadership of the education strategy myself and told Jane that I would make it my business that we get this agreed together, and we did. Jane negotiated the BBC's fourth agreement with the Open University, creating a much more collaborative relationship, so that the BBC and the OU commissioned jointly and we provided a peak time showcase for their best programmes. She also launched important campaigns for literacy and numeracy, absolutely synchronous to government educational objectives.

After the performance review of 1999, John Birt generously conceded that Jane had achieved a lot and that I had been right to fight for her in the face of his and some governors' pressure eighteen months previously. When she retired in the summer of that year, the canny, cool, politically adept Michael Stevenson took over. Greg Dyke's first speech after appointment, which was sold as a signifier of his priorities, was based on that education strategy.

Education had done much to professionalize its marketing and this discipline was now given some priority in the BBC. That it required attention was brought home by a television promotion for BBC local radio I saw in East Anglia. Shots of upland villages were accompanied by a Yorkshireman's voice intoning: 'Local Radio. Radio with nowt taken out.' Then a caption: 'Radio Norfolk'. John Birt brought over a French guru who fired everyone up and we then reviewed everything we did in that area. I had made a modest start in network television, when we learned some unpalatable truths. Our research showed that the public perceived us as 'national', 'trustworthy' and 'staid': while the first two were good, the last had to be changed. Internal research revealed, bizarrely, that many producers dissociated themselves from the name 'BBC'. They believed that 'it brought nothing' and was 'nothing to do with me'. This was both dangerous and daft. When they rang to ask permission to film or invited guests to take part in programmes, why did they believe that people agreed? Because they were wonderful human beings?

Sue Farr became my director of marketing. She was tall, blonde, impossibly glamorous yet with a dogged Yorkshire-bred practicality. Her background was in advertising and ITV, and when she came to the BBC a former colleague said, 'She's brilliant, but I never thought the BBC would take any one who looked like her – save on the screen.' Her nickname, I learned, was 'Crystal', as from *Dynasty*. Sue was tenacious and had done a spectacular job marketing the radio networks, breaking down a culture that saw the competition as the next-door BBC network rather than commercial radio. She worked like a terrier, attracted highly talented staff around her and raised the professionalism of what we did. She launched successful new campaigns, for *EastEnders* and for sport among others, and developed an approval rating to be the gold standard of the public's view of the BBC. But it was not as easy as that. A turf war with the corporate centre sapped her, my and many others' strength.

The pity was that the drive led by John Birt did raise understanding of marketing disciplines and appreciation of what it could do. David Docherty came up with a clever idea to look at the population as 100 tribes defined by age, life stage, background and interests. We pushed this until it became over-scientific, but the insights did inspire new thinking about programmes and how to win the attention and loyalty of groups semi-detached from the BBC. The force of argument and body of skill that Sue brought to bear began to win the day as to who should run the show. John Birt and I agreed we would reduce the number of messages, prioritize ruthlessly according to overall BBC strategy and invest more heavily in the campaigns we mounted. I felt that I had helped begin the transformation of the BBC's marketing but it had been a Sisyphean labour.

While still running television, I had asked a small company to interview some artistes and agents about how we handled the talent we worked with. I knew that things were wrong and the horror stories in the report illustrated just how wrong: confusion over who did what, lack of response favourable or otherwise after a programme, calls not returned, people kept waiting, stars competed for by different bits of the BBC and so on. There was good, too, but overall the report was damning. It was also personalized, so I shared it only with Angie Stephenson, who had taken over as directorate secretary, and I *think* I had each of the few copies destroyed. Angie, who was completing an MBA, did her dissertation on talent costs. When she had completed her study I asked her to take on this as a project with David Docherty and to commission the same company to conduct some more wide-ranging work that we could use as a basis for action. On-screen talent costs were rising and taking a larger share of programme budgets. By 1996 independent producers accounted for more than a third of the hours and more than 42 per cent of the spend in drama and entertainment.

The second report made it clear that we needed a systematic approach to talent management. Some of the production heads were suspicious. Was this the mighty broadcast division muscling in on their territory? They were the talent handlers for the BBC, thank you very much. Eventually everyone came to appreciate that only a joint approach would work. All this would help in-house production. We set up a group of senior players to oversee the work and I had Angie appointed as the BBC's first talent executive to drive it. To work alongside me in her place, I chose the cheerful and strong-minded Sylvia Hines, a former education producer. Sylvia not only worked hard and effectively, she also acted as surrogate conscience and carer for others, covering my blind side.

One of the often-voiced fears at the time of the reorganization was that radio might lose out. I was a television person, and 'fortress radio' would no longer have a separate voice at the top table. It was a fair concern, but it did not happen. Mind you, when I called a meeting of the radio bosses the day after the restructuring, I arrived late and am reminded that my first words to them were, 'Who is going to leak the fact I couldn't find my way to the managing director of radio's office?' Surprisingly, no one did. Matthew Bannister, the new director, was a radio person through and through and had been a broadcaster himself. His achievement at Radio 1 demonstrated that he was at the top of the radio game and resilient. He was articulate and persuasive, had a good voice, a florid expression and presence. His mind was made up quickly and he was inclined to charge ahead, occasionally knocking things over.

Radio 1 was in good shape. The changes had inevitably lost it listeners, but it was blossoming now as the first choice station of young people and the shop window for new pop talent. Jim Moir was beginning to reshape Radio 2. 'Don't talk to me about breaking new bands, Radio 2's got a search party out for Glenn Miller,' was how he described the relative positioning of these two networks. But Jim realized that the Radio 2 audience was dying off and he had to bring in a new generation, the not quite middle-aged. As a natural and experienced impresario, Jim persuaded Steve Wright, Jonathan Ross, Mark Lamarr, Paul Jones and Bob Harris to join the network that was to become the number one in the nation. One day, he said, even the *Jimmy Young Show* would come to an end, and by 1999 he had a plan.

The first thing that Matthew Bannister and I had to do in the summer of 1996 was to appoint a new controller of Radio 4 to replace the genial Michael Green, who was retiring after ten years in the job. We interviewed together and chose James Boyle, a quietly spoken Scot who had wide experience in the BBC and who had calmly and single-mindedly transformed BBC Radio Scotland. In doing so he had faced and coped with noisy opposition, coming through triumphantly. James and his small team immersed themselves in a programme of research and face to face discussions with groups of listeners, special interest groups and producers, BBC and independent. They then began a piece by piece deconstruction and reassembly of the Radio 4 schedule. All the evidence showed that there were many people who dipped into Radio 4 but did not stay long, either because they were unsure of what was on when or because the shape of their lives forced them to switch off and do something else. The new schedule was designed to fit more easily with the rhythm of listeners' days and evenings and to have a more understandable overall shape.

When James and Matthew first brought it to me, they explained that the dramatic extent of the changes was necessary because the move of any one programme implied other moves – you just could not do it a piece at a time. In discussion James agreed to go back on one or two of his proposals, but after a couple of further meetings, Matthew and I bought his proposition. While the shape of the schedule would change, the seriousness, the richness and the mix would remain constant. John Birt was taken aback a little by the radical nature of the changes but he agreed to endorse it, given Matthew Bannister's and my support, and the governors went along with it too when James Boyle gave them a persuasive presentation.

James now implemented a meticulous communication plan and began the countdown to launch. There were a few bumps along the way. He had appointed a team of commissioning editors, all experienced producers, but the selection process and the tough negotiation that went with it was new to radio, which had dodged the main thrust of Producer Choice. The commissioning was also carried out, I came to realize, in rather a po-faced 'we are the masters now' manner. 'Jobswank' again. When the schedule went live in April 1998, we knew there would be some noise, but not the Yakudo drumming that broke out. James had made some mistakes that I should have spotted. For one, he had created more places for intelligent entertainment but the supply of good entertainment was not available in sufficient quantity. The press was hysterical, with every snippet of half-truth inflated into evidence of 'dumbing down' and columnist after columnist harrumphing away. It was knee-jerk stuff. We should, though, have managed things better. The schedule did not bring in the lighter Radio 4 listeners as James had hoped, but was a better schedule for the times. The main blocks of it – the longer *Today*, the extra *Archers*, *Broadcasting House* on Sunday morning, *Home Truths* on Saturday mornings, late night comedy and so on – remain.

The most significant mistake, and one we had to go back on, was in planning to abolish *Yesterday in Parliament*, albeit that there were to be other new parliamentary programmes. This would not be a mistake with the audience, who mostly choose to switch off or over when it came on. It was a mistake in terms of the BBC's declared role, as the Speaker of the House of Commons, Betty Boothroyd, and some other powerful parliamentarians were not slow to tell us. When Matthew and I went before the select committee on the regulation of broadcasting, Gerald Kaufman, the chairman, seized the opportunity to grandstand on this. He pressed me that the BBC should not make a change on parliamentary coverage until his committee had reported. I said we had been consulting for seven months, had made contact with more than 300 MPs, spoken to more than 100 and held meetings in the House to hear and explain.

Kaufman then inflated himself like a puffing frog: 'This is the Select Committee of the House of Commons. This is not an informal group or one-to-one consultation over lunches or drinks or in some other way. This is the Select Committee on Culture and Sport of the House of Commons whose duty it is to make report to the House of Commons. What I am asking really is simply and clearly will you withhold any changes in your parliamentary coverage until this Committee has reported?' I said that it would be a matter for the BBC's chairman, not for me. Well, the chairman and the governors rightly pressed us to revise our plans. Michael Cocks advised us that, 'I have no interest in this because nothing that I have ever said in either house has been deemed worthy of inclusion.'

'Aaah!' chorused the rest of the board. A neat solution emerged, by which *Yesterday in Parliament* would be lengthened and kept at the same time but on long wave only. Radio 4 was transmitted on both long wave and medium wave, and was split in this way on other occasions. It was a row we could have done without.

Radio 3's audience would never be large. I remember one former controller, Stephen Hearst, telling me that when he was appointed, another candidate, when asked what audience the network should aim for, said this was a matter of no concern: Radio 3 had not been created with the audience in mind and should not be. Stephen said, 'My reply was that it should aim for a minimum audience. "What was that?" they asked. I said, "50,000 seeking to be 100,000." They took that to be encouraging.' He burst out laughing. In 1996 Radio 3 was reaching 2 million people a week. I was frustrated that it was not more. I was a keen listener myself and it irritated me to read that Classic FM was thought to be 'best' for classical music. It was not. It was very good at what it did and had found and filled a real hole in the market. I visited the station soon after I became responsible for radio. It was well run, seemed a pleasant place to work and relied almost wholly on recorded music, with just 1 per cent live. Radio 3's policy was for at least 50 per cent of the music it played to be live or specially recorded. It employed orchestras, staged concerts, hired musicians, commissioned new work and relayed concerts from around the United Kingdom. When I went round Radio 3 it was a bit church-like in atmosphere, but the people loved and knew music. The network was more serious in intent and played more complete works. It was the best for classical music.

The controller, the ever buoyant Nicholas Kenyon, a man forever amused by the antics of the world, had tried various ways of bringing in new audiences. Paul Gambuccini, a good broadcaster but American and best known for playing pop, had aroused the ire of the aficionados. Fitting the repertoire to the moment was sometimes a problem. Driving in one Monday morning I went apoplectic when a searching piece of solo organ was played at 6.45 a.m. I rang when I reached work. 'Think about the lives of the poor buggers listening,' was the gist of my comment. Others were even more difficult to please. Nick showed me a letter he had received: 'I am a seventy-three-year-old pensioner and I love to listen to some nice restful classical music any time of the day. I live alone and it gets me through the day.' Aah, how nice, one thought. It continued: 'But when some of the fucking rubbish you put on the air comes out of the box, I go hairless and the air is blue, believe me. I say aloud, what kind of a fucking idiot is putting this shit on and it is shit.'

In the opposite corner were those who resisted what they saw as an over-eagerness to please the passing trade. At a Prom, Gerald Kaufman wagged his finger. 'If I hear Gershwin or Appalachian Spring once more this year, I shall probably start proceedings.'

'Gerald,' I replied, 'you must remember there is always someone hearing it for the first time.'

'Yes. Probably the presenter.'

I dread to think what he would have thought of an idea I put to Nick Kenyon that in the pauses between movements of complete works, the announcer should quickly identify the work and movement to come. It would avoid some of those irritating Radio 3 silences that are such a nuisance when you are trying to tune in and provide a genuine service to listeners who do not know or have not heard what they are listening to. After all, between movements in the concert hall everyone looks at the programme to see what the next movement is, and people whisper, 'Isn't it lovely, darling?' or 'If that bastard behind clears his throat again, I'll clock him one.' When I put my suggestion to Nick and his team, they smiled as if I had told them I was Napoleon.

Nick Kenyon kicked off a two-year festival of twentieth-century music to lead up to the millennium, and in 1998 he stood down from Radio 3 to take on responsibility for all the BBC's millennium programming as well as running the annual Proms. It was vital to have the right replacement. Matthew Bannister led the search. I consulted in the musical world to ask if there was anyone we should approach who had not already applied.

It came down to three strong candidates: John Evans, head of music on Radio 3; Roger Lewis, once head of music for Radio 1 and now with Decca; and Roger Wright, head of BBC orchestras and formerly with Deutsche Gramophon. After the interviews, Matthew Bannister favoured Lewis, more of a modern radio executive in Matthew's own mould. I thought he was thin on the cultural role of the network and did not want another Radio 4 on my hands. I wanted to see both again. I said to Matthew, 'If Radio 3 does not get any more listeners, it is a pity. If we fuck up its credibility, it is a disaster.' The second interview showed Roger Wright to be the perfect choice: authoritative and personable, with strong ideas on the network as a cultural patron, bubbling with thoughts about music policy and good on money. He had spent his professional life in classical music and, as a nine-year-old boy, had sent in a record request to Radio 3. Now he could play it.

The following morning I bumped into Sir Christopher Bland and told him who we had chosen and rang John Birt. Terms were agreed with Roger Wright over the weekend, as the *Sunday Times* ran a story that Lewis had got the job. I had summoned a press conference for the Monday. Within seconds of our announcement, Roger Lewis was named as the new boss of Classic FM, with the spin that he had been offered and 'turned down' Radio 3. What happened, I believe, was that when Lewis was called back by Matthew, he thought he was the only one in the frame, and briefed to that effect. I wrote to the press to put the record straight: 'The post was offered to and accepted by Roger Wright, our first and only choice. I wish Mr Lewis well at Classic FM and believe that both radio stations have made the right choice.'

Some, John Tusa for one, could only see the tussle over this appointment in terms of 'Birtian' or 'non Birtian' candidates. Slipping into the accustomed past vindictive tense, he produced a stew of gossip, fact and twaddle in the *Evening Standard*. I must have wanted, he guessed, 'someone who was not an out-and-out Birtian'. He probably intended this as a compliment. But I had no such litmus paper, had no discussion with John Birt about the candidates and just wanted the best possible person.

Shortly afterwards, Matthew Bannister was selected to take over from

Ron Neil as chief executive of production. Ron went in a cloud of fond tributes, climaxing in an executive committee lunch cooked by Gary Rhodes,
with his wife Isobel and him as guests of honour, and a party at the Reform
club at which he was presented with a pair of Darcey Bussell's dancing
shoes.

It did not take long to find the new radio director. Jenny Abramsky was
running the radio and television continuous news services, having launched
Radio 5 Live and been editor of *Today* on Radio 4. She was a force of
nature and a champion for radio. Jenny was short, with bobbed dark hair
and a smile that charmed or challenged. To Jenny the world was full of
crises and she was going to sort them. She was demanding, let nothing go
unquestioned and was a joy to work with. A typical note from her might
read: 'It is utterly unacceptable for radio to be sidelined in this way. Who
from radio is on this task force? I cannot accept this in any circumstances.
Love Jenny.' Her personal warmth and knowledge of the radio culture
helped her heal some of the wounds left by the Radio 4 commissioning
process.

For all the turbulence that the restructuring caused, I could not detect a
creative hiatus on television. However, the BBC1 share, having held steady
and then risen, fell back. No wonder, for in the space of twelve months, four
separate pairs of hands were on the BBC1 tiller: Michael Jackson's until he
left, Mark Thomson's pro tem, Alan Yentob's when he arrived as director of
television, until Peter Salmon's took over.

Anxieties remained about drama, and the governors discussed a paper,
described by Richard Eyre as, 'Awful. Like reading Mr Men books. I'm
nervous talking about hit rates.' There, I could not agree. It was difficult,
however, to disagree with his continuation: 'We should be talking about
creative freedom and confidence', as long it was for the right people. Over
the next three years the record was mixed for new shows. The good ones
returned. David Renwick, the writer of *One Foot in the Grave*, came up with
the charming and characterful *Jonathan Creek*; Jimmy McGovern wrote
two heart-wrenching series of *The Lakes*; Kay Mellor wrote *Playing the
Field*, an ensemble series about the lives of a team of women footballers;
Debbie Horsfield gave us the funny and affecting *Sex, Chips and Rock 'n'
Roll*; and Lucy Gannon came up with the story for *Hope and Glory*, which
had Lenny Henry as the headmaster of a comprehensive school – all programmes to be proud of.

Two single dramas that stand comparison with the greats of any era went
out in 1999: *Warriors*, Peter Kosminsky's powerful film about British soldiers peace-keeping in Bosnia, and the bittersweet *A Rather English
Marriage*, which starred Albert Finney, Tom Courteney and Joanna Lumley.
The flow of classic adaptations continued with *Tom Jones*, *Vanity Fair* and
Wives and Daughters on BBC1. On BBC2 *Our Mutual Friend* and *Great
Expectations* offered wonderful Dickensian opportunities to David
Morrissey, Timothy Spall, Peter Vaughan, Charlotte Rampling, Justine
Waddell and Bernard Hill among many others. Also on BBC2 we had Alan

Bennett's *Talking Heads* and Stephen Poliakoff's *Shooting the Past*, atmospheric, funny and resonant.

Alan Yentob wanted to introduce a fourth episode of *EastEnders*, and having told people not to consider it for the past three years, I was now convinced. It was high quality work, a nest for new writing, directing and performing talent, and would provide a launch pad for another evening's output. As Alan put it, 'It's good. Let's build on it.' I put it to John Birt that we no longer had an aspiration for a new three-parter as previously and that ITV had a third *Emmerdale*, so our schedule would remain quite different from theirs. He did not want it. 'BBC1 – unlike ITV – needs to be marked by innovation and variety, and a fourth *EastEnders* would be more of the same.' It would, he said, look like a competitive move just when we were emphasizing the BBC's unique public purposes, would send the wrong signals in the coming licence fee review and, in any case, he had publicly criticized ITV for exploiting *Coronation Street* in this way. This last was the clincher. On the other points I sympathized with the line of argument but thought that he was wrong. We could have managed it with the soap in such strong form.

We did move *Panorama* to 10.00 p.m. The governors were nervous, but I promised a review after a year and it showed that the *Panorama* audience had not been harmed, the Monday evening news held up better than on other nights and the overall Monday share went up a bit. The move also made it much harder for ITV to launch new drama. This had been a soft slot for them to target, and they had managed to establish a number of dramas they could then move elsewhere in the schedule.

It was still hard to find popular entertainment successes. A long slate of new comedies were launched in 1997, none of which made it, but the following year Victoria Wood created and starred in *Dinner Ladies*, an instant classic, and Michael Parkinson returned with his talk show. The great flowering of comedy continued on BBC2. Caroline Aherne wrote and performed in the wonderful *The Royle Family*. I remember Geoffrey Perkins warning me, 'It's a bit of a risk. Absolutely nothing happens.' It was such an audience success that Alan quickly transferred it to BBC1. *Goodness Gracious Me*, *Operation Good Guys*, *Gimme, Gimme, Gimme, People Like Us* and *The League of Gentleman*, a work of comedy genius, all arrived within two years.

The big documentary series were coming through. Michael Palin completed *Full Circle*, around the Pacific, David Attenborough authored a work of love in *The Life of Birds*, Laurence Rees produced the brilliant *The Nazis – A Warning From History* and Tim Haines and John Lynch delivered *Walking with Dinosaurs*. Two important territories were revisited in fresh and audience-involving ways: Robert Thirkell with new business programmes in *Back to the Floor, Trouble at the Top* and then *Blood on the Carpet*, and the *Meet the Ancestors* team reinvented archaeology programmes.

Mark Thompson enjoyed his controllership of BBC2 and had an instinct as to where the channel should be that coincided with mine. He recognized what had to be rebalanced, not least bringing some more classical music back to the channel. I wanted to cement the BBC's relationship with the Royal Opera House and went to see Sir Colin Southgate, the chairman, to propose a BBC-wide contract and to make sure that it was the BBC that covered the re-opening. We televised both the disappointing opening gala, at which the ballet had made an imaginative effort and the opera merely booked a few stars who sang only German works, and the opening production of *Falstaff* with Bryn Terfel. It took a while, but a contract across television, Radio 3 and some children's programmes was eventually signed.

Some editorial issues still came my way. American movies came in packages under deals with different studios or producers, in one of which was *Pulp Fiction*. I agreed it for transmission having seen it in the cinema. The governors, unusually, raised it for debate. Several thought the transmission a mistake. Of those in favour, Ken Bloomfield 'hated it but it was right to show it', and the chairman had expected not to approve but changed his mind. I have seen the film again since and would not change my mind, but it is a nasty if clever piece of work.

The ugliest problem by far was when *The Vanessa Show*, a daytime discussion programme, was revealed to have hired participants from an agency – fake guests in other words. Matthew Bannister and I instituted an inquiry to get to the bottom of it. Not pretty. I told the governors that I felt our standards had slipped and that our programmes had drifted with the tide as Jerry Springer and others had come in to pollute the water. The agenda had widened in our programmes too, and had led to exhibitionism and vulgarity. The genre of programme was a useful one, but our programmes should seek enlightenment rather than conflict. The chairman said that hiring Vanessa was a reflex action, nicking one of their's (she had been on ITV), and that scheduling the show back-to-back with Kilroy was 'grotesque'.

I talked to Alan Yentob and Peter Salmon. It would be comforting and convenient, I said, to believe that this was just a matter of one rogue programme team, but I didn't think that was the case. We should look more closely at the underlying pressures on programme makers. Were they being given the right signals about what was expected? Did they know what the BBC wanted from these programmes? Or was the dialogue all about ratings?

All in all, though, we were not doing a bad job. At my last BAFTA in 1999, the BBC won twenty-one out of twenty-nine awards, including all the drama prizes. I was heartened when at one governors meeting Richard Eyre made an eloquent and generous speech about the output. He reminded me that before he became a governor, he had spoken at a conference, prophesying the BBC's descent into 'the boggy marsh' rather than the Himalayan heights, and the following day I had sent him a framed page of that day's *Radio Times*, demonstrating that there was no evidence for this. Richard went on: 'I worked in the BBC twenty years ago, but we must avoid the "when we" approach. *This*,' he said, 'is a golden age of the BBC.' The drama was better than when he was working here, the place was better managed, more efficient and offered a better service of programmes to the public. 'I will continue to criticize the management but this has to be said.'

With Mark Thompson off to the regions, we needed a new controller for BBC2. Alan and I interviewed a number of strong contenders, all from within the BBC, and in a close run contest appointed Jane Root, head of independent commissions. She was a quiet, determined person who had run a successful independent company before joining the BBC eighteen months earlier. Since her arrival she had made a big impact through her strategic thinking, organizational talents and editorial sharpness. Jane was the first ever woman channel controller. It had taken time, but I had watched a cadre of talented women rise through the BBC as producers, editors and heads of departments, confident that they would go all the way to controller and beyond.

In the previous year, 1997, two of Jane Root's predecessors and two good friends of mine, Brian Wenham and Graeme MacDonald, had died. Brian succumbed to the long expected fatal heart attack in May, having a drink with his wife Liz in the bar of the Old Vic theatre in London before a performance. Graeme faded away in September after a long illness.

There were memorial services as for many others over the years. I awarded highest marks at such occasions to those orators who kept themselves out of their remarks, concentrating on him or her we had come to remember and celebrate. I gave starred firsts for anyone who accomplished the task without use of the first person pronoun. Alan Bennett on the drama producer Innes Lloyd set the standard: funny, warm, elegantly composed and about Innes. At Graeme's, I fear, the address consisted mainly of a list of BBC dramas of the 1960s and 1970s, with credits, the overall implication being 'weren't *we* marvellous'. But this was show business and I heard worse. At the service for Cynthia Felgate, children's programmes producer, a presenter stood to introduce some music and went into an address that might have been entitled 'my life in television': 'And then I wanted to . . . I then tried something different . . .'.

I had my own near disaster at the memorial service for Geoff Hamilton, who for seventeen years was the much-loved presenter of *Gardener's World*. I arrived at St John's Wood Church, where Roger Cary, expert organizer of memorial services, handed me the service sheet at the door. I glanced at it and saw 'The Living Garden by Geoff Hamilton. Read by Will Wyatt.' I froze. This was the first I knew that I was to read. No one had a copy of the reading, so Roger hailed a taxi and sent his assistant back to the BBC shop to get a copy of the book. The vicar and choir now arrived at the west door. 'There's a bit of a cock-up, vicar,' I said. 'No reading.'

'We can't wait any longer,' he replied. 'We must start now.' He thought for a minute. 'I've got something you can read. But I'll need it back. Here, we must go. Walk with me.'

To Vivaldi's *Gloria*, I processed up the aisle with him and the choir, as if this were all part of my usual grand style at memorial services, and took my place in the front stall. During the first hymn, 'Praise my Soul the King of Heaven', the vicar with bows to the altar and a sense of ceremonial purpose, made his way over to me and handed me the order of service from another memorial service. He pointed to a reading from *The Gardener* by Rabidranath Tagore. I studied the verse carefully through the next part of the service, rehearsing the lines, and when it came to my contribution I did well enough. As we all sang 'To Be a Pilgrim', the vicar made another crab-like ceremonial move to retrieve the sheet of paper, for it contained a prayer he was to read at the end of the service. I was host at a buffet lunch afterwards and talked to the pleasant Mrs Hamilton. 'That was a very nice reading you gave,' she said. 'Only I thought it was to be a piece by Geoff.'

'Mm. Last minute change of plan,' I replied.

Chapter nineteen
WHITE CITY HERALD
EXTRAORDINARY

Death would have his days in 1997, the last day of August above all. I was woken by a telephone call at 1.10 a.m. Sandy Maier of the presentation department told me in a deliberately clear and steady voice that there was a story running that Princess Diana had been injured in a car crash in Paris. My first thought was that it was a hoax, but Sandy said Sky was carrying it on air. In a number of calls over the next three hours the story became clearer. On television the unwavering shot of the crushed Mercedes in the tunnel suggested the worst. Nicholas Witchell, who was with Robin Cook in the Far East, reported that the Foreign Secretary had been informed the Princess had died. Alan Yentob was away, so I rang Mark Thompson and agreed with him and then Tony Hall of news that we bring the networks together and run news until lunchtime. BBC1 would probably need to stick with the story all day. Early next morning I drove fast down the M40 to London, telephoning on the way.

In the years of making plans for disasters and royal deaths there was always the thought that we might not be dealing with the peaceful death of the elderly Queen Mother, but a sudden death in a public place. So it was. Media journalists became very excited when they heard of BBC rehearsals for such events. They loved stories that we intended to turn the channels over to public mourning for days on end. In truth, the draft plans were only a possible framework to be changed in the light of the mood of the time. We had to make sure we had suitable programmes and procedures for as and when.

The same journalists were equally excited when they discovered – it had been no secret – that the BBC had a 'royal liaison officer'. Indeed we had, and in 1987 it was me. I was, as one writer put it, 'a kind of White City Herald Extraordinary'. The incumbent served as a highish level channel for regular contacts between the BBC and Buckingham Palace and a conduit for programme requests: permission to film, invitations to take part, use of stills and archive film and the like. Bill Cotton had rung to ask if I would take over from Cliff Morgan, who was retiring, and in a moment of flattered weakness I had agreed. It was weakness not because I was a republican (we would end up with Richard Branson or Ken Livingstone as president, no thank you), but because I knew that I was unlikely to devote proper time to it.

There was in place the most dedicated of full-time assistants in Jane Astell, who marshalled and handled the day-to-day requests from across the Corporation, of which there were a surprising number. Jane was assiduous to the point of obsession. Her office on the top floor of Kensington House above the entrance was crammed with correspondence and cuttings from *Radio Times*. She would deal with producers in a stern, almost regal manner, and track down attempts to bypass her, as the Special Branch would a spy. No detail was too small, no check too much trouble, no double check too onerous. Jane was utterly dedicated, worked all kinds of hours and lived for her job. On hearing that I was to take over from Cliff, she brought me my personal store of 'BBC Royal Liaison Officer' writing paper, custom ordered, expensively embossed in period type and bearing no sign of anything so ungentlemanly as a contemporary BBC logo.

In truth, I saw the role as a bit of a chore but one that might help me secure exclusive access for documentaries of one sort or another. I doubt if I disguised my lack of conscientiousness. When I came to meet Sir Robert Fellowes, the Queen's deputy private secretary at that time, he greeted me with, 'How nice to meet you . . . at last.'

I had had dealings with the Palace before, but they now became more regular. I had also been to Clarence House on a memorable occasion with Ludovic Kennedy. Ludo wanted to press the case for interviewing the Queen Mother, if not for transmission, then for posterity. We met Sir Martin Gilliatt, her private secretary for thirty years by then, and gave him lunch at the Stafford Hotel, where he was evidently a favourite. Gilliatt, a splendidly eccentric old cove, tall and fit at 72, was an 'angel' and backed theatrical ventures, among them *Les Miserables* and Rowan Atkinson, whom he had persuaded to do a cabaret for a party given by the Queen Mother. 'I told him,' said Gilliatt, '"Nothing about bums or cocks or anything." To which he replied, "What on earth does that leave?"' Throughout the meal, Sir Martin kept reaching out to touch my hand to emphasize a point or reassure me. There were many points of emphasis and regular need for reassurance, much to the amusement of Ludo, who cackled with laughter all the way back in the car. The Queen Mother kept her peace.

Robin Janvrin was press secretary at Buckingham Palace, a friendly ex-submariner and diplomat with whom I established an easy relationship. Robin was without airs, direct in his views and keen to modernize. He invited me to lunch with him at the Palace. We had drinks with the equerries, elaborately polite young officers on secondment. They wore dark blue suits to a man and from tight collars sprouted very scrubbed pink faces with self-deprecating grins. At the same time they had an air of not being displeased with themselves and where they had fetched up in life. Lunch was from hot chafing dishes, and I sat at one of the three large circular tables next to Robin and one of his colleagues, Ken Scott. He was a former ambassador to

Yugoslavia, an engaging man whose craggy face and bushy eyebrows gave him the look of a Polar explorer.

Robin and I would meet for routine business, to discuss possible funeral routes, in what circumstances it was sensible or essential for a royal presence at disasters, to negotiate the terms on which the Palace would encourage people to be interviewed for an obituary of the Queen and why BBC news chose to ignore or rarely feature the royals, unlike ITN.

Mostly, I did not become closely involved with programmes featuring royals. The Duke of Edinburgh gave the Dimbleby Lecture, sending Paul Fox off for a snooze halfway through. 'Duke in Audience Coma Shock' was my diary note. Jane and I were invited to a 70th birthday thrash for the Duke, 1500 people in a huge, warehouse like tent at Windsor. It was an odd occasion and one that raised the question: is the Duke liked? He said little and not very well, and the best speaker was Prince Edward. The memory of a hokey, self-conscious Roger Moore and Michael Caine double act was happily swept away by some good fireworks and a truly class act, the guards beating the retreat.

The Prince of Wales made a controversial documentary about architecture. A little while afterwards he kindly came as guest of honour at a small dinner to mark the retirement of Christopher Martin, who had produced the film. He enjoyed a stiff Martini – six parts gin to one part Martini – and helped make it a companionable and happy evening for Christopher. The Prince had come from launching his institute of architecture, and over dinner he offered his thoughts on Richard Rogers, James Stirling and other modernists: 'Where do they live? In St Leonard's Terrace or similar. Where do they holiday? In beautiful Tuscan hill towns.'

When his youngest brother came to Television Centre to present an award, we avoided by a whisker what could have been a nasty incident. MC Hammer, the rap artist, was to receive an award and arrived with his bodyguards, from all accounts an intimidating bunch. They carried canes, quite possibly swordsticks, and alarmed the programme team that met them. MC, his aide announced, wanted to meet Prince Edward. Could the Prince come to his dressing room? It was not quite like that, the BBC people explained. In that case MC would go see the Prince. The royal bodyguards had no intention of allowing the heavies anywhere near their care. To make matters worse, that morning's *News of the World* had run a front-page story that one of MC Hammer's guards had been accused of gang rape in the past. A photo opportunity as HRH shakes hands with rape accused was something else to avoid. The chief detective, all of six foot six, reported these exchanges to me. I was led up to the studio to present an award at the same moment that Prince Edward was being taken to make up by the floor manager, so five or six of us strode along the basement corridor just as MC Hammer and his entourage, one of whom dwarfed even the chief detective, strode purposefully in the opposite direction in search of an encounter with HRH. Fortunately, they did not twig who it was they were passing until we were out of site round the curve of the corridor. Two minutes earlier and they would have invaded the green room to confront the pride of Scotland Yard.

In my esteemed capacity as royal liaison I was invited to a small lunch with the Queen and the Duke of Edinburgh at Buckingham Palace. It was brilliantly organized. The eight guests were all given a drink and then arranged in a semi-circle to be introduced. I then found myself with the Duke and the commander of the Queen's Flight, and there was mention of a current series about BA. 'I can't imagine why anyone would ever allow television people to make a film about them,' said the Duke, clearly hoping to bruise. I rose to the challenge and mentioned series that the subjects had been very happy with. The Duke was unimpressed. At table, with the Queen's Flight chap and a lady-in-waiting, there were a dozen in all. Her Majesty, I was pleased to see, ate a decent lunch though refused pudding. We were served good Moselle and claret, then a '55 port that no one touched. The lady-in-waiting next to me kept an eye open for the moment that the home team, taking a cue from the Queen, all moved as one to talk to the person on the other side.

Suddenly we were all on our feet and being led to a drawing room, the Queen leading the way, followed by four corgis, to each of whom she gave a piece of biscuit. I and two others now had our share of time with her. There had been a recent spate of dog biting children stories that exercised her. 'People seem to have the wrong dogs these days: all these rottweilers. My daughter has just got a bull terrier. Dotty.' She pointed to the corgis at her feet. 'These would attack children if you let them loose in a playground. They're cattle dogs.' The Duke appeared again, complaining about the BBC not covering the world carriage driving championships when they were held at Windsor 'That's why this pay television is a good thing,' he went on, warming to his theme. 'People can pay for what they want to see. I'm sure that people would pay to see their favourite sport covered.' Again, I came back vainly. At 3.00 p.m. the royal couple said goodbye.

I had noticed as we rose from the table a fellow guest taking a menu from its silver holder and slipping it into her bag. Now, as we were leaving, each of us was presented with a list of guests and a menu. I winced with embarrassment on my fellow guest's behalf, but she cheerfully laughed and confessed to her crime. I went back to the office and later rang my Mum to whom I had promised an early report. 'We were waiting.' She listened to my account and awarded the Queen her ultimate accolade for anyone famous: she was very 'natural'.

Early in 1991 I took my successor as royal liaison, Jim Moir, to meet Charles Anson, who had recently taken over as press secretary from Robin Janvrin, now the assistant private secretary to the Queen. Charles, another ex-diplomat, had come from the city. He was even smoother than Robin and so polite he found it hard to bring a telephone call to an end, but he had some of the thuggish qualities that all press officers require. It was with Charles and Robert Fellowes that I discussed who should take over producing the Christmas broadcast from David Attenborough. It was to be Philip Gilbert, but I remember the lunch at the Carlton Club because Robert suddenly became anxious, having left his coat on the fender by the front door. 'I hope it's still there,' he said.

'It should be safe enough here,' I replied, gesturing to our surroundings, the temple of the Tory establishment.

'Not a bit of it,' said a worried Queen's private secretary. 'A member lost two coats in a week here. Taken. Can't trust anyone here.'

While Robin Janvrin was still handling press matters, I had suggested to him several times that we make a documentary portrait of the Queen to mark the 40th anniversary of her accession. It would only be worth doing, I said, if there were special and unprecedented access. In May 1990 Robin came to see me urgently. He was excited and told me that the Queen would take part in such a programme. This was terrific news, I said. Robin warned that they, the Palace, would have to choose the producer. I said that could not be. I was aware that the producer would have to be someone the Queen was comfortable with or we would get nowhere. I would bring two people to see him and his colleagues, but I would tell him which I intended to put onto the project. Trust me, I asked.

I knew it would have to be a man from earlier conversations about possible producers for the Christmas broadcast. I had Eddie Mirzoeff in mind. His films always had warmth and humour, he would fight, charm and scheme to secure access and he could handle himself anywhere. He wanted to do it. On the day I was to take him to the Palace for the first time, I had forgotten to confirm the date with his assistant. 'Shall we go?' I asked, as we concluded a lunch meeting with a group of producers.

'Go?' asked Eddie

'Yes. To the Palace. I've got a car waiting.' Consternation from Eddie as he walked up and down, for he was dressed in jeans and T-shirt. In the event we went via his house, where he donned a dark suit and his Queen's College, Oxford tie. At the meeting were Bill Heseltine, just about to hand over to Robert Fellowes as private secretary, Robert, Robin Janvrin, Charles Anson and Ken Scott. I began with a list of Eddie's programmes and prizes, saying that I would spare his blushes by not naming them all. 'I'm not sure that a blush would be visible under that tan,' quipped Heseltine, for Eddie was nut coloured after two weeks in Italy. The meeting went well. Next we had to meet the Queen, for her to see the cut of Eddie's jib and for us, if not actually to pitch the programme idea to her, then to explain how we saw it and what we would want in the filming.

The meeting was on 2 August 1990, the day Iraq invaded Kuwait and a day when the temperature in London was in the mid-nineties. I took Eddie to lunch at Joe's Café then on to the Palace. We waited in the lobby inside the door at the far right of the façade, before Robert Fellowes and Charles Anson took us upstairs past white-jacketed footmen and corgis slumped in the heat to a small waiting room. We were quickly summoned into a large drawing room. We bowed on entering as instructed, and the Queen, who was looking out of the window at the far end, came over and waved us to sit down. She sat to the left of the fireplace, a small table between her and Eddie, and I next to Eddie. Robert and Charles took the sofa opposite. The Queen was in a magenta and blue patterned dress with an oval brooch, sapphires surrounded by diamonds. She was about to sit for her portrait with the painter we had seen downstairs, his long grey painter's hair falling over the collar of a brand new grey flannel suit, purchased for the job I guessed, and accompanied by a female assistant who held his palette and mahl stick.

No sooner had we sat down than Robert Fellowes announced, 'Mr Mirzoeff will now give you an outline of the programme.' We were under the impression that this was a getting to know you session and had had no warning of this. Eddie, who was concentrating on exuding a demeanour that proclaimed, 'I am relaxed, I am not overawed, I am not nervous', was taken aback. After a surprised pause he did well, and between us we outlined our ideas. All the while I was trying to take in the room: vases of white and yellow flowers; a wonderful Canaletto over the Queen's left shoulder, another to the right; glancing down I saw on the small table close by a small Fabergé golden temple housing a golden bird. After a while the Queen flashed her smile and began thinking of things we ought to film, which I took, rightly as it turned out, to be a good sign. 'It's not a job, it's a life,' she said, adding how difficult it would be to separate work from personal life. She gave some examples of matters that came to her. 'The Maoris and the Red Indians, because they always dealt with Queen Victoria, always approach me. When I have to pass them on to the appropriate government department, they don't really like it very much.'

The Queen was into the swing of things by now, and when Eddie suggested something, she leapt on it, saying to Robert Fellowes, 'That would help explain where the money is spent.' She turned to Eddie and me: 'People write, they did this week, and say they can't think where all the money is spent. They don't realize that everything has to be kept up, the pictures and so on.' We got a distinct steer that other members of the family were not keen on the programme and would not be in it but that the Queen would do what we wanted, within reason. Philip Bonham-Carter, the camera man, and Peter Edwards, sound recordist, who had filmed the Christmas broadcasts and other royal appearances for some time, were, said the Queen, 'quite good at it (not getting in the way) now'.

She asked Eddie if he had made other films about people. He was momentarily stumped before choosing the film he had made about Scotland Yard. We wanted to film an overseas visit. 'One disappeared in a puff of smoke this morning [Kuwait],' said the Queen. When Robert or Charles put something to her, she made a point of including Eddie and me, especially when she was amused. 'The press seem surprised that we don't go and lie on a beach in Florida,' she said with a laugh. 'They think we're eccentric not to and to go to Scotland instead. They don't realize that you want to go if you've got a property.' Mention of the press reminded her: 'Did you see what Anne Robinson said today? "I have never liked Queen Elizabeth, she's just an actress." Why say that now, after all this time?' She looked puzzled. 'Why not just . . .?' Her voice trailed away.

After about 25 minutes the conversation came to a natural end. We stood up and went out, pausing to bow as we did so. Eddie let out a sigh of relief, but he had talked interestingly and cleverly about how he worked, and I was sure all was well. We went out into the blistering sun and back in a car, debriefing ourselves. Not long after I was back in my office, Charles rang. The film was on. I called Eddie with the news. I could feel his glow warm the phone at my end.

The relationship between the BBC and the Palace was generally good. I guess that each party thought it was to a degree 'special'. In the BBC the knee was perhaps too ready to bend. Indeed, in the late 1960s a young features reporter setting off on her first overseas story was instructed to take a black arm band 'in case the Queen Mother dies'. This 'specialness' went no further than that each party might favour the other in minor matters. In greater matters the Palace had to be even handed between the BBC and ITV, say in granting exclusivity for a programme or series. As the BBC's royal contact, I had seen it as my job to land a big win when it was our turn.

The Palace knew that both the BBC and ITV would cover the major state occasions but that the BBC, the national broadcaster as we sometimes called ourselves, would feel obliged to carry more of the second tier occasions. The attitude of the BBC in return varied according to which part of the BBC they were dealing with. News and current affairs retained a proper distance and rightly did not shirk from critical inquiry. The outside broadcast department were positively chummy and needed to be, for they depended on good relationships to secure information, good camera positions and early warnings. Their job was to cover ceremonies as expertly as possible, not to investigate or hold to account. Between these two fell most of the features and documentaries. Some of these were journalistic in tone or intent, many merely wanted permission to film on, say, royal land. A number operated on less defined ground. They sought to give a true and rounded picture, yet were largely or wholly dependent on the Palace for their access to pictures or people. This relationship was similar to that with many other institutions we filmed, save that the stakes appeared higher and the tendency to cringe greater. We were dealing with the head of state.

We thrashed out a contract for our magnum opus over the next month or two as Eddie planned his filming. It was a pity he had to miss the gala television show for the Queen Mother's 90th birthday with Placido Domingo offering 'You Arrr My Harrrt's Delight', and the Queen wiping away tears of laughter at Stephen Fry. 'She had to redo her face in the interval,' said Susan Hussey, who was on duty as lady-in-waiting.

There were many minor and some serious spats when filming started. When Eddie pressed to film the changeover of prime ministers on Mrs Thatcher's resignation, the Queen was content but Mrs Thatcher said no. Many other things Eddie wanted were refused by the Palace. He was on the phone to me daily. He was allowed to film a Privy Council but was asked to go out of the room and return to film brief item by brief item of a fifteen-minute meeting. Eventually he went straight over to the Queen: 'I can't go on like this. It's nonsense', and won his point. I went to see Robert Fellowes on his behalf. 'The one way for this film to be a disaster, Robert, is not that there will be something seriously embarrassing or hurtful to the Queen – we're not going to do that – but if it is bland and boring.' Robert, sharp and clued up behind his patrician exterior, nodded. In the meanwhile Eddie had brought on board Tony Jay, co-author of *Yes Minister*, to write the commentary, and Catrine Clay as assistant producer – both masterstrokes. Catrine, sophisticated, beautiful and with a journalist's nose, massaged egos and charmed open hitherto closed doors.

Eddie was getting on famously with the Queen and was invited to lunch at Sandringham. He was shown into the saloon and offered a drink by a footman. He was dithering, wondering if he should have alcohol before lunch, when a voice behind him said, 'Vodka. Very healthy, vodka and tonic.' It was the Queen Mother. The footman said: 'I think sir will be having a vodka and tonic.' With Glenn Miller playing in the background, the Queen Mum was doing a vast 2000-piece jigsaw puzzle with no picture to work from. 'That looks terribly difficult,' said Eddie.

'It's much more difficult than the one we did yesterday,' was the reply. The family evidently belonged to a club that circulated huge jigsaws. At lunch Eddie was seated between the Queen and her mother. The talk was of Barnes, where Eddie lived, John Betjeman, with whom he had made programmes, and President Reagan.

Eddie was gloomy about the material he was getting but I saw some of the rushes and was optimistic. He was even able to persuade the Queen to record some audio comments, the nearest she had ever come to an interview. He was able to lay these over picture sequences like a royal commentary. Later I went to viewings of the rough-cut as Eddie and his editor, Alan Lygo, shaped what became a remarkable film, full of events and incidents never seen before, made with insight and much humour. Alan Lygo began the whole endeavour as a convinced republican and ended a royalist.

The chairman, Dukie Hussey, was much interested in progress and reported to me: 'The leading character regards this as very much her film. There have been one or two ructions about it – nothing to do with us. Family matters.' Eddie had tested the film on Sue Hussey to anticipate royal reactions. Dukie wanted to come to the screening we were to give privately to the Queen just before Christmas 1991. I told him that would be unwise. What if there were to be a row? 'I'll go by precedent,' said Dukie.

We held the screening at the headquarters of the British Academy of Film and Television Arts in Piccadilly. I met the Queen and the Duke of Edinburgh and took them up to the small theatre that seats about twenty people. They sat in the centre of the front row, Eddie on her right, I next to Eddie. Behind were Robert Fellowes, Charles Anson and one or two others from the Palace, and members of the production team. The deal was that if there was material they were unhappy with, we would listen to their views and consider whether to act on them. There had already been wrestles with Charles Anson, Eddie conceding one or two points, standing firm on others. The film was now pretty well finished, though Eddie would lean over to read the commentary into the Queen's ear, which he did, occasionally missing the cue and having to gabble it to catch up.

We had been warned that the Duke was an unguided missile on this project and would be the problem if there was to be one. We knew it would be all right when after a few minutes the Duke laughed at one of the early funny moments, and thereafter both he and his wife chuckled away. 'Lucky I was watching the right channel,' she said when a shot of her watching BBC news appeared. Afterwards the Queen was in bubbling form and stayed for tea with the production team. As I took her down in the lift, she reflected, 'It was surprising what they found interesting.' The following day came a request for one or two more shots of the Duke, if that was possible.

We held a big launch party for the film, *Elizabeth R*. The enthusiasm of the invited audience was palpable and Robert Fellowes was relieved and aglow. When the film went out at the beginning of February 1992, the television audience was just shy of 18 million, a record for a factual programme. The critics were full of praise. It was a win all round. For the Queen it was almost the last good thing that happened in what was to be her *'annus horribilis'*. That she recognized the success was clear at a gala performance of *Don Giovanni* we televised from Covent Garden the following month. At the reception afterwards she broke into the broadest of smiles the moment that she spotted Eddie as we were led through the throng to be presented. She had now seen the finished version with commentary. 'Did you enjoy the final version of the film, Mam?' I asked. I need not have asked.

The Queen gave a party for all connected with the production. It was a rotten day for her, as that morning the story had broken that Andrew and Fergie were to part, but she stayed well over an hour and talked to all. 'Many people have written to complain that veal was on the menu at the banquet,' she said to me. In reply I described the snake-eating scene from Michael Palin's *Around the World in 80 Days*, evoking a laugh. She admitted that she had been anxious about the wild track recording for voice over. '"What are they going to do with it?" I asked myself.'

Sue Hussey was beaming. This had been good for the Queen and good for the BBC. 'Mind you,' she said, 'people seem to be amazed that the Queen calls her mother "Mummy".'

Two years later, at the height of controversy about the changes we were making in the BBC, the chairman was worried about the Prince of Wales. Dukie thought that HRH had been 'got at' by Dickie Attenborough and just might sound off in public about us. He arranged to take Bob Phillis, Liz Forgan and me to lunch at Highgrove to clear the air. We went in mid-July and were shown into the comfortable country house drawing room, hung with Hanoverian portraits and, on an easel, one of Prince Charles. A waiter, a Royal Naval steward I thought, in navy blue uniform with collar badge, brought in a tray of drinks, Pimms and orange juice. Charles soon came in brown and healthy-looking, immaculate in a sand-coloured summer suit, blue and white small check shirt, striped tie and yellow paisley patterned handkerchief in top pocket.

He was relaxed and we soon fell to talking about the BBC and continued in more detail over an excellent lunch of vegetable tartlet, halibut with vegetables from the kitchen garden and home-bottled pear tart. Our host passed on pudding and wine. He was well briefed, and Dukie's assessment of his views was borne out. He hated the idea of performance related pay: 'I can't see how it works unless you're making widgets.' His view of Mrs Thatcher's reforms shone through in references to 'tearing the heart out of places', the BBC obviously a candidate. The BBC's value was, he said, 'providing a sense of continuity and stability when so many other things are being uprooted'. He listened in return as Bob, Liz and I each talked about the BBC's purposes, programmes and the changing world of broadcasting. He was particularly attentive when I described the strength of Rupert Murdoch's hold on customer management and access to satellite services. No love lost there, I could see.

The Prince said he had enjoyed our adaptation of *Middlemarch*, though when I said proudly that the audience figures had totalled 7 million across its two showings, he was surprised that it had not been more and a massive ratings winner. 'I tried to get my two sons to watch Ken Branagh's *Henry V* but the only bits they like are when Bardolph is hanged and when the Duke of York is killed with a mass of spears.' I asked which classics he would choose to adapt. 'Oh, Hardy,' he replied instantly.

'Which?'

'*The Mayor of Casterbridge.*' I promised him the tapes of the version the BBC had done starring Alan Bates.

As we concluded on the BBC, Prince Charles came out with a warm endorsement of the Corporation, if not everything we were doing. 'I'm so glad the White Paper has supported you. If anything happened to the BBC, I don't know where I'd go to live.' A welcome sentiment, if oddly put by the future King of England. On several occasions when I met him in later years he returned to this theme. 'I hope the BBC is alright?'

'It's in pretty good shape. It has to change to survive.'

'I really care about the BBC. Aren't you becoming more commercial? There's such a thing as principles.'

'Yes. We'll stay true to them.'

'Isn't it obsessed with efficiency? Efficiency often means losing the human dimension.'

We finished lunch at 2.30 and as we were going out, the Prince muttered something about the garden. 'Yes, please,' said Dukie.

'One never knows whether people are interested,' replied Charles, who then spent an hour and a quarter giving us a tour: the thyme walk he had planted himself, the terrace, herbaceous borders, the meadow, woodland glades with statuary and the magnificent walled kitchen garden with different lavenders, herb garden, apple tunnels and smaller tunnels of sweet peas and red and white beans. As we went through the Strawberry Hill Gothic gate, which led to the kitchen garden, we had a vista stretching down to a classical statue at the end, a huntress with arrows and a hound. Without thinking further, I piped up brightly like an eager schoolboy: 'Oh, is that Diana?'

'Well spotted,' was the reply he chose to give me of all those he might have had in mind.

The chairman thought it had all gone well. He was proud as a peacock when three days later the Queen came to a Prom at the Royal Albert Hall, her first visit as Queen. When introduced beforehand I asked her if she had ever been previously. She had been brought once as a child, was the reply. It had been *Tristan and Isolde* and they had never come again. The Queen appeared touched and surprised when spontaneous applause from the entire hall greeted her arrival, and again her return after the interval and when she left. The Duke of Edinburgh was true to form. When I was introduced he grumbled, 'Oh, why has everyone lost his or her sense of humour on television. There's nothing funny any more. Same everywhere else. There used to be *Punch*, which was very amusing, but that's all gone.'

'Have you seen a programme, Sir, called *One Foot In The Grave*?' I asked.

'No. I don't watch much television.'

'Well, it's a comedy about a miserable old man at odds with the modern world.' I knew what I was saying.

'Ha. Sounds like me.'

The nadir in the BBC's relations with Buckingham Palace was the *Panorama* interview with Princess Diana. This was a coup by BBC news: a journalistic scoop, an important contribution to a big story and riveting television. It was arranged, shot and edited under the strictest secrecy. I was not directly involved, though Tony Hall, director of news, came to tell me about it once it was in the can. He dealt with the director-general on handling it, though I was aware that the chairman, married to a lady-in-waiting to the Queen, was only to be told at the last minute. The Princess wanted to tell the Queen herself. This was hard on Dukie, but the right call.

I did not need to and did not ask to know what was in the interview: the fewer who did, the better. I was in New York when it went out, and Sally, my PA, rang me every few minutes during transmission to give me the dope. Both Dukie and the Palace were incandescent: Dukie because he had been kept in the dark and because he disapproved of it; the Palace because they hated the very idea of the interview, as well as its content. They felt they had been made to look foolish in not knowing. They felt betrayed that the BBC, of all people, had done this. But the BBC, of course, is so many things: helpful chaps rigging lights in Westminster Abbey for a big do; the attentive Jane Astell sorting out all the irritating requests to film; that nice, polite Jim Moir and Will Wyatt we have lunch with; dear old Dukie, almost part of the family; John Birt who takes us seriously when we phone; the royal correspondents who we see all the time – and also the nosy, inquiring, difficult journalists who treat us no differently from any others.

If there ever had been anything 'special' in the relationship between the BBC and the royal household, there was no more. Early in 1996 Robert Fellowes asked if I would come to see him and Charles Anson 'about the Queen's Christmas broadcast'. The arrangements for this had always been that the BBC produced it on behalf of the Palace for distribution to all other broadcasters. We sat at the round table in the press secretary's office where I had sat to negotiate contributions to obits, had first suggested the idea for *Elizabeth R* to Robin Janvrin and had discussed producers for previous Christmas broadcasts. Robert was just back from a children's party and looked a bit dishevelled. Charles Anson sat boot-faced. 'There is a question in our minds,' began Robert, 'as to whether Buckingham Palace is inextricably linked to the BBC. The programme has changed. Ten years ago there were no interviews. It has developed into something more complicated.'

'The BBC has done us proud,' said Robert, who I felt was co-driver to Charles in this conversation, 'But we feel it is time to test the market, as it were.' In short, they wanted to have ITN and the BBC produce the broadcast alternately for three years at a time. Would we be interested 'in a half share'?

'I see, Robert,' I said. 'Your motto here is "don't get mad, get even".'

'No, no, Will,' protested Robert. 'We've been talking about this for more than a year.' There was more in this vein, concluding with the curtain line that is not in the script for the rest of us: 'It's the Queen's decision.' It was a slap in the face but there is always a bright side. The broadcast was costly. There would be some extra money for something else.

When I arrived at Television Centre on the morning of Princess Diana's death, Mark Thompson and his team were reshaping the schedule. We did several more versions during the day. At 10.00 and again at 2.00 and at 5.00 there was a big meeting to co-ordinate coverage and schedules in Tony Hall's office, which John Birt sat in on. Everyone worked quickly and decisively together. People knew what to do and had the ability to do it. All round the BBC, producers and programme heads reviewed their scheduled programmes for the week ahead to assess their suitability. Sensibilities change at such times, though you can be over cautious, as I saw in one briefing note: 'Travel Show for Monday is having one small edit to remove a reference to a Scottish festival which is a favourite of the Queen's.'

We kept the news on BBC1 and 2 until mid-afternoon, when BBC2 ran a mix of the planned programmes from both channels. I should have released BBC2 earlier in retrospect. With great enterprise the Songs of Praise team arranged a special programme from St Paul's. This gave us a nervous but ultimately magical moment. The service could not begin before 6.30 p.m., so it ran through until 7.00, when Diana's body was due to arrive at Northholt. The aircraft came into view a little before 7.00 and the network cut away in picture to capture a wonderfully moving and unplanned shot of the plane with its mortal cargo landing and taxiing as the great Welsh hymn 'Blaenwern' swelled from St Paul's.

Did we overdo the coverage? Research afterwards had 42 per cent of the population thinking there had been too much. But there were developments and reactions throughout the day. It was a hard story to go away from. The day ended with Ron Neil, Alan Yentob (back from Venice), and I sharing a bottle of wine and discussing how best to handle the losing candidates for the controllership of BBC1. We were about to announce Peter Salmon's appointment and Alan was to call the others that evening. One of them, Steve Hewlett, editor of *Panorama*, had said during the day what many were thinking: 'She'd still be alive, I bet, if she had her Scotland Yard driver.'

The following week was in many ways extraordinarily enjoyable. Ron Neil, Tony Hall and I began regular morning and evening meetings about each day's schedule, production arrangements and plans for the funeral coverage. It was like being a producer again. All rivalries and negotiating were pushed aside in the interest of getting the output right, the whole of the BBC working to one end. Black humour soon surfaced. The outside broadcast producers wanted to know at what speed the funeral hearse would travel: five miles per hour, ten miles per hour or, as news suggested, 120 miles per hour (the alleged speed of the crashed Mercedes). At one meeting we learned that Elton John would be performing at the funeral. 'That means at least one queen will be crying in the Abbey,' said Tony Hall.

On the Tuesday evening Jane and I went for a walk through Kensington Gardens to sense the atmosphere. Hundred of people were out, mostly young. It was noticeable that there was no noisy, attention-seeking blubbing. People were quiet, the tears silent and private. We were staggered by the amount of flowers but this was to be only the start. Those who accused television of whipping all this up missed the point. People began laying flowers, this was reported in all the media and then others had the idea of doing the same. For some there was clearly a genuine sadness – I'm not sure it is grief for someone you have never met; for some, yes, it was a way of being in on it all; for others, like us, it was out of curiosity. I rang my daughters, Hannah and Rozzy, to tell them to go: it was something to see.

The continued absence from London of the royal family prompted a wave of anti-Windsor feeling. It looked as though half the nation was in the capital laying flowers and paying their respects while the in-laws remained in Scotland. The outside broadcast teams were working round the clock both to cover the various ceremonies of the week and to plan the funeral coverage for the Saturday. Philip Gilbert, in charge for the BBC, displayed all week the cool of Wellington before Waterloo, even when the Queen returned to London on the Friday and he had to divert himself, asked for by name, to produce her live broadcast address; even as the Royal parks were still at Friday lunchtime refusing to allow cameras in Hyde Park to cover the now extended processional route. We learned that neither the chairman nor the director-general had been invited to the Abbey. Newspaper editors had been. The BBC's punishment continued. In the end Jim Moir was invited as our royal point man and went.

I did an interview for Radio 5 Live about our radio and television plans for the day. As I went to the studio, I remembered the classic BBC gaffe made by a senior executive drafted in to assist with the radio commentary on the funeral of George VI. At one moment he had told the listening nation: 'And now the main body of the procession is coming into view.' I told myself to avoid all mention of processions and bodies of any kind. Luckily, no one I know heard the interview – or no one told me they heard it. For, sure enough, my mind tripped over the wire it had set for itself and I heard myself saying, as if from afar, 'our coverage of the main body of the procession . . .'.

On the morning of the funeral Tony Hall, Alan Yentob and I gathered early in Tony's office. We had three big TV sets carrying the output from the BBC, ITV and Sky. I had suggested that the three of us watch together so that any messages, information or comments we wanted to pass on would come from one source down one telephone line in order to keep communication clear and simple. We had a direct line to Ron Neil, who was with Philip Gilbert in the big mobile control room that was running the outside broadcast operation from near the Abbey. In this way Ron could decide if and when to pass on advice, requests or instructions. This worked. We were able to tell the production team what ITV and Sky were doing, we called for more faces in the crowd and so on.

Throughout the day I kept a note of which station captured telling shots first or had something the others missed. Our coverage was definitely strongest over the whole day. It was first by far with a close-up of the card with the young princes' flowers, the only one to catch the Queen bowing as the coffin passed the side gate of Buckingham Palace, and much more. Its chief failing was that the director had an elegant plot for the service and stuck to it. Well-planned shots of the stained glass windows and the choir would have been perfect in the ordinary run of things, but this was extraordinary. The crowd outside became part of the service, singing, praying and weeping in their thousands along the route and in Hyde Park, where they watched on huge screens.

Tony, Alan and I became agitated, as we were not getting the flavour of what was happening outside, and Alan, who was our chief man on the telephone, asked several times for the director to cut to the exterior scenes. We had a few and asked for more. Alan put down the telephone and turned to the rest of us in the room, 'There's a row.' He looked sheepish. 'The director is going to walk out of the scanner.' He became firm: 'Well, too bad.' Alan paused and a cloud passed over his face. He picked up the phone again and said, 'Ron, tell them they are doing very well . . .'. By the time that applause from outside greeted Earl Spencer's appalling address, the director had picked up a rhythm that balanced the internal ceremony with the external emotion.

Even as we debated shots, mood and commentary, our eyes moistened. We fell silent at times during the service. When we came off the air, there were drinks for those of the production team in the building. As Bill drove me back to Oxfordshire, I began thinking for the first time about what had happened rather than what we should do about it.

A fortnight later the Proms ended with two highly charged concerts. On the penultimate night I took a small party to a performance of Verdi's *Requiem*. Sir George Solti was to have conducted and had wished to dedicate the performance to Princess Diana, but he, too, had died suddenly. Sir Colin Davis took his place. The hall brimmed with emotion, and at the end Davis held the silence. And held it. The audience seemed not even to blink. On the last night Nicholas Kenyon, in charge of the Proms, again struck the right note, adding Copland's *Fanfare For the Common Man* and Holst's 'Jupiter' ('I Vow To Thee My Country'). 'Jerusalem' was sung as never before, some voices around breaking with emotion.

I was interviewed for Radio 4's complaints programme *Feedback*. Many listeners thought that the BBC had gone overboard in its coverage of the death and funeral and I answered up and explained why we had done what we did. At least, I thought I had explained, but Miles Kington in his column in *The Times* printed a transcript of what I had said. It was complete gob-bledegook. Thoughts began to shape themselves and suddenly disappear; I began sentences that stopped, slid sideways and became other sentences; I flitted from half-made point to half-arsed conclusion. I laughed. It was a fair cop. I wrote to Kington: 'Dear Miles Kington, Um ... er ... Ouch! But touched to note that you are still transcribing all my interviews. Do keep up this valuable work. Yours ramblingly, Will Wyatt.'

He replied, saying that he had never had a response from Birt, Hussey, Bland, Yentob, Kenyon or any other BBC person he had given a poke. This, I think, was meant to pat me on the head for almost qualifying as a member of the human race. He said he liked the way that BBC titles gave no clue as to what people actually did. 'I am glad to see that your opaque title of CE of British Broadcast carries on that proud tradition. Carry on whatever you do.'

The coda to Princess Diana's death came in two short parts. We put much effort into improving our obituaries, and Alan Yentob and I persuaded Eddie Mirzoeff to oversee some new productions, one a beautiful film about the Queen Mother by Jonathan Gili, which has now been transmitted. The second part was an invitation for John Birt, Ron Neil and me to go to lunch at the Palace with Robert Fellowes, Robin Janvrin, Geoff Crawford, the new press secretary, and Mary Francis, assistant private secretary. They were ago-nizing over how the institution of monarchy looked in the modern world. Their constituency was the entire population, they said, as ours was all licence payers. We discussed the causes the royals supported. 'The problem is pro-tecting the environment one day and blasting birds out of the sky or hunting the next,' said one. 'The family's lifestyle is less and less like anyone else's,' said another. 'Not even the aristocracy live in the old way on great estates.'

They were most interested in ideas for William and Harry. 'Do the boys support football teams?' I asked. 'If so, they should be seen to. And not in the directors' box. Their dress will be important – it can be inclusive or exclusive. No ties and keep them away from their father's tailor.' A few weeks later, John Birt's PA rang with a message to look in a couple of that day's papers. I did. There was a picture of Princes William and Harry at a football match.

Chapter twenty
'How can you do all this without stock options?'

M y last three years in the BBC were dominated by three themes: the contest to be the next director-general, of which enough; launching new services; and the campaign to secure funding for our digital plans. The rhythm of life was also interrupted by a distracting motif on the bagpipes.

In the multi-channel world we needed to provide new channels ourselves. The BBC branded and publicly funded channels were the more important, but we had to make better use of our programmes to earn extra revenue and demonstrate that the BBC could act entrepreneurially in the interests of licence payers. We did this with two partnerships.

The first, led by Bob Phillis, was with Flextech, a company that ran a small stable of channels for cable and satellite distribution. Flextech and BBC Worldwide, our commercial arm, established a new company called UKTV. This would take over the existing UK Gold channel, add a second and launch new channels that my team devised. One ran leisure programmes, UK Style; one documentaries, UK Horizons; and the third, comedy and music aimed at a young audience, UK Play. The negotiations were slow. The BBC was new to this, and we had to protect both our financial position and our existing and planned publicly funded services. As insurance, we put in many caveats to ensure that these could rerun any programmes they wanted. In the event this was never a problem. After many panics and alarms, the BBC and Flextech signed in March 1997.

The beauty of this deal was that the BBC owned half of the new company and had guaranteed programme sales to the channels, bringing in revenue from the outset. What was more, David Docherty, who ran the teams scheduling public service channels, would be in charge of the UKTV schedules. This gave us confidence that we could protect BBC values in this adventure. The new company also paid the BBC to manage the play out. The partnership worked. The channels found their markets, UK Gold transforming itself from a very-old-programmes channel to become the cable and satellite channel with the biggest audience after Sky One. The value of the BBC's equity grew as the channels prospered.

The second big deal was with Discovery, the American cable channel whose brand had become a hallmark of intelligent, worthwhile programming. This partnership had three arms to it. The most controversial within the BBC was a co-production agreement that gave Discovery an exclusive first option to co-produce all the BBC's in-house factual production, notably from our powerful science, history and natural history units, in return for a guaranteed investment over a ten-year period. Some producers were unhappy. They had co-production arrangements with American public television stations, the cable network A&E and others. But the overall guaranteed sum was an improvement on current income and the partnership had a strategic value to the BBC. Ways were found to keep American public television in the picture. The second arm was for the BBC and Discovery to launch jointly-owned channels in new territories. Again, it was programming that the BBC brought to the party. In return we had a half ownership of all the new channels and the already successful Animal Planet. The third arm was for Discovery to fund the launch in the USA of a BBC branded and operated channel, BBC America. This had been a long-time ambition, a chance to put out BBC programmes under the BBC flag. My broadcast division was to run it, and we appointed Paul Lee, an ex-music and arts producer who had worked on our UKTV team. He was based in the Discovery building just outside Washington, DC. Paul was an energetic and inventive self-starter who immersed himself in the American cable television market and did wonders with his small team, launching in March 1998. I felt he was a bit isolated and could do with some local wisdom other than that from Discovery executives. I asked Mike Dann, who had spent over twenty years in American cable after running CBS in the 1960s, if he would help as a part-time adviser. Mike was well into his seventies but full of ideas and knowledge about US television. He and Paul happily hit it off. Fours years on, BBC America is in 30 million cable households.

Meanwhile, at home we developed a public service proposition for the digital world. We had to launch digital versions of BBC1 and 2, to decide upon and launch new public service digital channels, and build our internet site. This was an expedition that brought together many parts of the BBC. Policy and planning were responsible for negotiating distribution and for providing the director-general with a master plan. My division was responsible for developing the channel ideas and schedules, for launching and running them on air and for the internet sites other than news. BBC technology provided expertise, as did BBC resources, which carried out the installations.

I cannot pretend that the joint work was always easy. This was a huge play for the BBC. We had a self-imposed limit, endorsed by governors, of not more than 10 per cent of the licence spent on digital services. That was £200 million or so, and the director-general wanted tight control. Consequently there were too many moments when one policy officer jumped right over another policy officer's back. Good people became frustrated at the double-checking. This was the moment, too, when the small team around the director-general exhibited some of the characteristics of a medieval court, summoning people, refusing to speak to PAs and issuing pompous notes.

In broadcast we began a huge logistical and planning operation, led by Sue Price, an ex-BBC1 planner. The deadline was tight, as we had to have our services ready to roll when Sky launched its digital satellite platform. Digitizing BBC1 and 2 was far more complicated than might first appear. There were myriad technical decisions and many a mini-crisis. We had to resolve how best to handle widescreen pictures on ordinary sets and the usual 4:3 pictures on widescreen sets; we had to find a way to deliver our regional services.

The first new service was News 24, a round-the-clock news and current affairs channel that began on cable in November 1997. It was an important move for the BBC. In multi-channel homes people now expected to find news when they wanted it, not having to wait until 6.00 or 9.00 p.m. The audience for the big bulletins was falling and would fall further. News was a core service for the BBC and we had to provide it to the public in the new ways as well as the old. Another proposal was for a parliamentary channel. 'Is this part of a please and appease strategy?' asked Richard Eyre at a governors meeting. 'We have mixed motives,' was Christopher Bland's reply.

We had a new general channel to plan, the first of our digital services, and developed a mixed service that would run complementary programmes to BBC1 and 2. We had little money for new productions and would have to rely largely on our archive and repeats of recent shows. For this reason we retreated from our first name for the new channel, BBC3, as we felt that with such little investment, it would not bear comparison with the main channels. We settled on BBC Choice. It was vital to get it up and running to occupy the territory while we had a fair wind from the secretary of state. We could change it once it was there. Sky and the BBC signed a deal for carriage of our digital services in June 1998 and Choice was launched that October.

We quickly realized that the channel's proposition was too blurry for the multi-channel environment. A well-known and well-funded channel like BBC2 could appeal to different groups at different times, and audiences would find the programmes they liked because the channel was a regular part of viewing habits. Launching into the multi-channel cacophony required a clear proposition targeted at a defined audience. So Choice was reshaped to attract an audience of young adults otherwise elusive to the BBC. It is now properly funded and has become BBC3.

A second new service was to be dedicated to education. BBC Worldwide had wanted the 'learning' service to be commercial, but we had argued that away. The budget was again tiny. The educational priority was to reach young people who had finished formal education and ought to be lured back to vocational and basic skills courses or into higher education. The channel was planned to appeal to them. It launched in May 1999 as BBC Knowledge, with some superb graphics and a bright and breezy style. We got it wrong. It was hard to reach that target audience. At the same time, passing digital viewers who liked the sound of BBC Knowledge and paused to sample it did not expect noisy young people shouting and laughing. What sounded like an upmarket BBC channel appeared to be just the opposite: a yob in nob's clothing. Therefore we redefined the educational purpose to include the sort of improving and informative programmes – science, history and arts – that the audience expected.

The big disappointment for me was that we failed to start a children's channel. Children in multi-channel homes (families with young children were the leaders in taking up multi-channel television) gobbled up the output of the dedicated commercial services like Nickleodeon, Cartoon Network and Disney. BBC children's programmes were good and popular but they were only on for short periods in the general schedule. If we did not want a generation of children growing up to whom the BBC was peripheral, we needed to have a children's channel, or rather two, for younger and for older children.

John Birt was leading us in a massive programme of work to create a complete BBC proposition for the digital future – in television, radio and the internet. This was visionary stuff, forcing us to think deeply about our entire *raison d'être*, how digital technology might change lives and businesses, what the BBC could and should do and how it should do it. This put us ahead of the pack and was critical in persuading government that we had a crucial role in the digital world. John being John, however, would not countenance further launches until we understood the full picture. Thus when David Docherty and I presented a proposal for a children's channel, aimed at two to seven year olds and running mainly British programmes, he refused to approve it. It was not the money, for we could start it cheaply, but he deemed it 'tactical, not strategic'. I argued that whatever else we did, it was inconceivable that we not provide a children's channel. As elsewhere, we should move, occupy the ground and then improve and refine. No dice.

We had plans for digital radio. The BBC had been paying out to build the transmission infrastructure for this for several years. The sets, we were told, would 'be in the shops by Christmas'. Christmases came and went. I was a sceptic, as was the chairman: 'Potty. I don't believe our own people.' But Jenny Abramsky, passionate in her ambitions for radio, roused to action by the PR of the commercial competition, planned a portfolio of new networks and threatened disaster if we did not cough up and get to work.

The internet was probably the most exciting of all the new ventures because it was an entirely new medium. The BBC's first websites had sprung up here and there. Education began some online pilots. Enterprising producers created pioneering sites alongside their programmes. This was the ad hoc activity of enthusiasts. Few had the time, resources or inclination to maintain the sites, so many soon became out of date, floating like old playbills in cyberspace. BBC Worldwide had also done some work. We thus had expertise and enthusiasm to draw on when we began the big push.

It took a while for most of us to appreciate how different the internet was from radio, television and the press. Like many, we saw it first as a promotional tool. We assumed, too, that we would merely translate the broadcast experience to the Net. By exploring and visiting successful sites, I and others came to understand the individuality of the experience. For the BBC it offered the chance to provide far greater depth of information and a richer experience to licence payers. We could extend our relationship with them and provide greater accountability. Viewers and listeners could be in direct contact with programme makers.

I was excited. I went to Silicon Valley with Robin Foster to visit Yahoo and others, where they talked about the 'old days', meaning two years ago. I returned evangelized. I had a speech that said we were in Hollywood in 1910, at the beginnings of the telephone and the invention of printing all at the same time. There was, I would proclaim, a creative and technological gold rush. I was lucky that I did not have money to invest. But people were taking to the internet at an accelerating rate. Users in Britain grew from 4.5 million to 6 million in the first quarter of 1998 alone.

BBC news had begun an embryonic on-line service that with investment and talented leadership improved by leaps and bounds. The difficulty for my colleagues and me, responsible for building the rest of the BBC's internet presence, was that news saw no reason why they should speak to, let alone share information or collaborate with, other parts of the BBC. The idea of reciprocal links between the news and other BBC sites was anathema to them. We achieved them in the end, but only after eye-gauging, ear-biting struggles at the front line.

The education team developed a particularly strong offering and spread their know-how generously. By the autumn of 1998 we had a slate of sites, among them science, children and leisure. We added others, redesigned the home page several times and built in more opportunity for users to personalize what they accessed. Information about usage was crude. We knew only the number of page 'hits', and longed for knowledge of how many different people had visited sites, how long they had spent there, where they had come from and where they moved on to. Still, by the only universal currency, the hits, the BBC was the most used site in Europe

John Birt had engaged an American technology expert, Craig Fields, who flew over each month to advise us. Craig, whose slight frame and edgy manner suggested ferocious internal energy, was a top-level adviser to the Pentagon. He gave you his assessments, good or bad, full in the face. He pressed for action. Soon after Craig's arrival I noticed that for John, 'strategies' were out and 'plans' were in. In November 1998 Craig told the board of governors, 'I was wrong when I came here. I said, "How can you do all this without stock options?" But there are enough people who are interested in public service and who want to be where you can do leading edge, innovative work. The BBC is ahead of Time Warner, NBC, Disney and others in this. But it is so easy to slip behind.' That autumn, 5 October to be precise, marked a small turning point in Britain's digital journey. The director-general ceased sending his famous hand-written notes, the 'inky blues', and henceforth communicated by e-mail.

Towards the end of 1997 I had asked Pam Masters, who managed the presentation of all our services, to consider how we should play out television services in the long-term. I said that I was neutral as to whether it all came out of a black box in the Hebrides or remained in Television Centre (neither the likely answer), but we should scope our needs. In 1993 we had been running two channels out of Television Centre; by 1998 it was ten; the following year it would be fourteen. I chaired the study to work this through that concluded we should have a new play-out centre on the spare land at the BBC's White City site. Pam began planning.

The master plan for the BBC's digital future – dubbed the 'Hever vision' after two conferences at Hever Castle in Kent – came together at a conference at Wood Norton in November 1999. The proposals had the stamp of realism and creative conviction that was essential for their success. This was in large part because Robin Foster, David Docherty and I had fully engaged Alan Yentob and the channel controllers in the development process. This prevented any sense of abstract and centre driven concepts. John Birt was rightly proud of where we were. 'This is going to be one of the most historic and important conferences in the history of the BBC as we decide what we are going to do in the future.' He was hoping, I thought, to lay down the tracks on which the BBC would run for years after he had moved on. Greg Dyke had been appointed and was present. Around the table many were wondering if this meeting really would decide things or whether the new man would concrete over the rails as soon as he had the chance. The more John sought to make the occasion definitive, the more I sensed colleagues holding themselves back a touch. The broad strategy, however, and many of the individual plans were kept to. The tracks remain and are in use.

Would we have enough money to do any of this? In 1997 we had secured a modest boost to our income when, after we exceeded our savings targets and received a warm endorsement from the government's consultants, Virginia Bottomley won a helpful five-year deal. Even so, we were stretched. I found myself torn between the obvious under-funding of BBC1 and the requirements for our new plans. Should I fight for more money for existing channels? An impassioned turn in front of governors could swing some, I reckoned. Yet there was only a finite sum and I was short of funds for the new digital projects. We had a head of steam behind these and I was convinced that we should move as quickly as we could while the climate was benign and most of our commercial competitors well off the pace. John Smith, director of finance, brought a little more cash to the pot with a blitz on licence fee evaders. A letter to every Metropolitan Police station, enquiring if they had a television licence, produced a sudden and noticeable increase in new licences in London.

The new Labour government made encouraging noises about the importance of 'the creative industries', saw the BBC as a big player in these (and a net exporter), backed digital broadcasting and wanted the benefits of the new technology made available to all. So far so good. The new administration was as keen on better accountability by the BBC as their predecessors.

One of our responses was to sharpen up the annual report. From 1997 it was to include details of executive pay. The press had some fun, of course. So did my 89-year-old Dad. 'I thought you would have been kidnapped by now,' he said when I rang him the Sunday after the report came out. 'The woman I see over at the pub in Woodstock said, "I know what your son earns." I told her I only had bread and jam.' The report was also to be more critical, to the scepticism of Michael Cocks, the vice-chairman, who warned: 'The only people who go through this in detail are those who wish us ill.' I suggested that we put an extra £3 million in the marketing budget to counteract the bad publicity the report would bring.

If we wished to win the funding argument next time round, we had to take the message out and about. I did my share, helped until he retired in 1998 by Keith Samuel, comrade in arms off and on for over twenty years. Keith knew not just the foibles and obsessions of the media journalists, but also the internal politics of every newspaper. He was a good jazz trombonist, and at his farewell party he and his band made the council chamber jump. In his place as controller of press and publicity I took on Sally Osman from Channel Five. She was quickly on top of things and fun to work with.

My share of getting the message out included a new chore: regular duty at the party conferences. I had spoken at fringe meetings before but had otherwise mostly managed to avoid the conferences. I was with Michael Cocks on this: 'Attendance at the TUC or party conferences,' he said, 'could be used as an alternative sentence at our magistrates courts.' I respect many politicians and liked a lot of those I came across, but party conferences brought some odd encounters. I remember playing host at a dinner at the 1997 Labour conference in Brighton. Baroness Hollis, whom I had not met before, arrived first, a tall, good-looking woman who reminded me of Marti Caine. She was obviously clever and outlined sensible ideas about reforming the benefits system. She then began telling me about her children: 'They're both in their twenties, doing PhDs. They were with us last weekend. They were such fun. They are clever, funny, stylish . . .'. Just in case I thought this meant they merely wore designer T-shirts, she added, 'intellectually stylish'. This appeared to be the moment at which I was expected to award her a prize of some sort, but I was too busy musing on 'intellectually stylish'. I still am. The only thing that was quite clear was that this was something *I* was not. Not that the BBC always put its best foot forward at conferences. I recall an occasion when it took seven members of the BBC executive committee to entertain nine Labour MPs at lunch.

Politicians were more fun at the races. At the 1996 Grand National, John Prescott talked non-stop over lunch about his nerves when standing in for the leader of the opposition at Prime Minister's questions: memorizing questions and follow-ups, being cheered on by his own side, whose support quickly ebbed if he did badly, trying not to mispronounce. 'Heseltine has lost it. He shakes and holds the book very firmly to steady himself. I needle away. "Shaking today I see. You're rattled then." I don't think it's an illness. I don't think I'd do it if it were.' At the same occasion Peter Kilfoyle, a local

MP, drank brandy all afternoon until blurting out: 'Tell that Lord Cocks that I think he's a bastard.'

'He would take that as a compliment,' I said.

'I know he would.'

Robin Cook came with his son to one of my favourite racing days, the King George VI and Queen Elizabeth Stakes, at Ascot in July. He had not long become Foreign Secretary and had just spent the weekend at Chevening for the first time. 'I asked if there were foxes there. "Oh, no, sir. We shoot the foxes, as they prey on the pheasant." I said, "Pheasant? Do we have pheasant?" "Yes, sir. We raise about 3000 every year for shooting." "I see. Who shoots the pheasant?" "The trustees, sir." I was beginning to understand what the purpose of the whole enterprise was.' No talk with a politician was complete without their complaints about news. Michael Howard, as minister, had explained: 'You deliberately put the good news way down the bulletin and the bad news at the top.' Oh, that was what we were doing.

The council of Equity asked me to talk to them about the BBC's plans. Tony Robinson had a drink with me the week before to warn that I might well be torn to pieces. But no. All the questions had been organized beforehand and most people read them out. The most passionate contribution was from a former member of the BBC radio repertory company, who had a splendidly projected voice of the old radio school and enunciated every syllable and consonant. A nice chap – 'I work as Rhubarb the Clown' – asked why circuses were not on television any more. Far from tearing me apart, they were the very soul of old-fashioned politeness, even applauding me at the end of my short speech and again when I left.

When Bob Phillis left to go to the Guardian Media Group in 1997, I took over from him as the BBC's person at the European Broadcasting Union and became vice-president. I think John Birt thought it a waste of time. I disagreed with him for two reasons. Firstly, the EBU was listened to as the voice of European public service broadcasters and I wanted to influence its policies and actions. Secondly, I felt there was – I hope this does not sound too pompous – an element of *noblesse oblige*. Most of the other organizations looked to the BBC for a lead in many areas and craved the BBC's wholehearted participation in the EBU. We could not claim to be the pre-eminent publicly funded broadcaster and ignore colleagues in the rest of Europe. I made some good friends there. Albert Scharf, the president from Bavaria, was a reassuring presence, a learned, multi-lingual lawyer with an old-fashioned formality. When he came as a guest to hear the Vienna Philharmonic at the Proms, he was the only person of the 5000 in the hall who declined to take off his jacket on one of the hottest evenings of the year.

I was not proselytizing on behalf of the BBC, merely serving as ambassador, when Jane and I were invited to the Lord Mayor's banquet in 1997. I had donned the white tie of full evening dress to go some years before, but that was on my own and in a distant corner. The new government had made one or two gestures in the direction of less formality on this sort of occasion.

Gordon Brown did not like wearing a dinner jacket, we were told, and there was speculation as to what Tony Blair would wear at this, his first Lord Mayor's do as Prime Minister. When the week arrived I looked in my diary, where Sally had noted 'B/T' for black tie. Aah, I thought, a new Labour compromise between ordinary suit and a full white tie job. Bill dropped us off at the Guildhall and we joined the queue waiting to be announced. 'Do you notice anything about the men in front?' I asked Jane.

'They are all wearing white tie,' she replied.

'And I'm not. No going back though.' At the entrance to the Old Library, the major domo took our invitation card (and looked me up and down, I fancied) and announced us. The form is you walk the length of the room between the tiered rows of already arrived guests who politely applaud. There was not another black tie to be seen. I listened hard for any hint of satirical clapping. As the Lord Mayor greeted us with a smile, I said, 'Sorry about the rig. A bit new Labour I'm afraid.' When the Prime Minister arrived, he was resplendent in white tie and tails, and at the outset of his speech he made a joke about the speculation as to how he would dress. I forced a thin smile.

The BBC governors were happy with the successes achieved and swept along with the excitements of the neon-lit Valhalla that was promised by the new technology. At the same time, with the ground of internal reforms largely won, they showed signs of nervousness as the accelerator of change remained pressed hard to the floor. They had toughed out the difficult years but were now listening more closely to external comments. John Birt was passionate about improving the BBC's accommodation. 'Our staff work in slums,' was his refrain. All BBC buildings, he believed, should provide modern and flexible accommodation and be as open as possible to the public. We reviewed our existing buildings. Broadcasting House was sacrosanct. John was uncertain about Television Centre. I said that it was 'a heritage site for British entertainment'. In Scotland we needed a replacement for the existing, inflexible building, and identified a site at Pacific Quay. Plans emerged for a news building in central London, a Norman Foster reworking of Bush House.

The governors were cautious when 'the property vision' came forward. The chairman would take some shifting on the news plans. The combination of a new vision and Norman Foster, he said, meant that you could double any figure we had yet seen. On the overall policy, voices around the table warned, 'this is more change' and 'this is top down'. The governors were becoming impatient that problems with the internal market were not yet fixed.

They showed how effective they could be over *Yesterday in Parliament* and *Vanessa*. They pressed for and approved new guidelines about the portrayal of real people in drama. When they were insistent on change, we had to make it. They showed up well again in the budget debate in the spring of 1999. The budget proposed an extra £30 million for further digital developments. They argued the case and refused this, electing to put more money into BBC1. John Birt was down afterwards, while the rest of the executive said, 'Wasn't that a good discussion?' It was exactly what the governors were for, especially as the £30 million had only been flourished at the last moment and we had not had a chance to discuss it at the executive committee.

In 1998 there was a debate that might well have split the board of governors in twain. The government's plans for devolution – a parliament in Scotland, an assembly in Wales – released separatist ambitions that had long lain dormant, or at least out of sight of London. There were implications for the BBC. We had to plan proper coverage of these new democratic institutions. We would have to respond to the heady atmosphere being generated in Scotland and, in the least favourite phrase of Geraint Talfan Davies, BBC controller, Wales, 'to a lesser extent in Wales'. Whatever was good for Scotland and Wales would have to be nearly as good for Northern Ireland.

It all came down to the six o'clock news. BBC Scotland proposed that it produce its own to offer 'a Scottish perspective' on the UK and the world. This raised a matter of high principle in BBC terms. It is the *British* Broadcasting Corporation and the main national news bulletins, a core service, are transmitted to all corners of the kingdom. For BBC Scotland to produce its own would entail Scotland not taking the BBC's national six o'clock news.

This first came to the board of governors at the 1998 joint conference. Norman Drummond, the Scottish governor, declared his hand early: 'Doing nothing is not an option.' A Scottish six would 'cheer the staff, satisfy the Broadcasting Council for Scotland and head off the Nationalists'. The council was a BBC body chaired by the Scottish governor, with advisory rather than regulatory responsibilities. Ken Bloomfield, Northern Ireland, and Roger Jones, Wales, made their bids too. The director-general pointed to the considerable costs involved and to the political implications of the BBC appearing to take a lead in devolution. I knew that John had cleared this BBC position with Downing Street. Three significant governors piled in against: Pauline-Neville Jones, 'This could result in the break up of the BBC'; Bill Jordan, 'Is it sensible to parochialize flagships?'; and David Scholey, 'We should not be one inch ahead of the government and the BBC charter.' The battle lines were drawn.

Christopher Bland played a blinder throughout the whole saga. He gave everyone space and time. There were many other aspects to the plans that Mark Byford, director of regions, had drafted. Other money was allocated, but the six o'clock was the prize the Scots wanted. The legislation had reserved responsibility for broadcasting to the government in London rather than cede it to the Scottish parliament, something the Scots were to challenge fiercely. The chairman told governors they should not lobby each other on the six, though the staff of BBC Scotland were obviously hard at work lobbying press and politicians. John Birt asked me to instruct John McCormick, controller Scotland, that he should not do so. McCormick was in a spot. The chattering classes of Scotland and many of the BBC staff looked to him to raise the Saltire on their behalf. At the same time he was a senior and trusted servant of the BBC.

For the Scottish council, this was their hour. A place in history beckoned; the dinner parties of the New Town urged them on. Tony Hall, chief executive news, and I went up to meet them. 'All hell will break loose . . . This will not do . . .' they cried. Horses came no higher. The fieriest spirit was an unlikely Braveheart, a testy, red-faced and red-haired professor. We promised to take their views into account Unfortunately, two days later news published a grand programme strategy review that took it for granted that there would be no Scottish six o'clock news. So when the board of governors travelled to Scotland two weeks later, the council approached their session with the board with dirks sharpened. Christopher kicked off the meeting with an apology for the 'PR cock-up'. Some of the council members made their case well, though towards the end the hot headed professor lectured us on how important the Canadian angle on the world was to the people of Scotland. The meeting ended acrimoniously. One governor accused the council of 'flag-waving by accent', provoking a 'Let me tell you, Jimmy' response.

With news we went over the plans and forged a new shape for the six o'clock news, making the regional half-hour integral and planning a justifiably more prominent place for Scotland, Wales and Northern Ireland in the coverage. When it came to the decision-making meeting of the board, Christopher chaired it brilliantly. We played in the new scheme for the six, which was welcomed. Norman Drummond had one final go. 'If we had listened to the colonies, there would have been no Boston tea party.' He warned that the professor would resign from the council. 'He can only resign once,' said Christopher. Richard Eyre sided with Drummond, quoting Lenin: 'Common sense is always the view of the ruling party', and warned, 'This will detonate an explosion in Scotland.' The chairman finally called for a vote, which went seven and a half to four and a half for the UK-wide six o'clock news.

The full package of changes brought £10 million a year and fifty jobs to BBC Scotland. I told John McCormick and wrote to confirm: 'You will tell your senior staff . . . that there should be no more campaigning on the six o'clock news. To do so is to breach our impartiality guidelines as well as contractual obligations . . . the polls make it clear that there is no overwhelming mandate for change on this matter and it is both wrong and dangerous for BBC staff to strike attitudes in public about this.' Interestingly, when the elections took place for the Scottish parliament only 55 per cent of the population turned up to vote.

For all the external attacks on the governors as a mechanism for regulating the BBC, for all the ambiguities about their role, they have one huge virtue: they consider the activities and performance of the BBC only in the interests of the public it serves. If OfCom or any single regulator held full sway, it would trade off the BBC's interests against the commercial interests of other players in the market. The BBC is not any other player. While Parliament wills that the BBC be funded by the licence fee to serve the entire public, it is wholly sensible for the interpretation of that remit to be sepa-rated from what suits or does not suit commercial broadcasters. Like others, the BBC is bound by the competition laws and, unlike others, it has to have new activities approved by the secretary of state.

Through much of 1999 a panel under Gavyn Davies of Goldman Sachs was deliberating on the funding requirements of the BBC in order to recom-mend the level of the next licence settlement. We were more than hopeful that we would be funded to unleash our plans. We were confident, even arrogant. As the secretary of state was about to arrive by helicopter at the joint governor-management board, Christopher Bland said to us all, 'I think that he's a little afraid of us, but we'll make him welcome.' On one of the panel's visits to the BBC they were given a demo of how the internet would develop. As he spoke to them, John Birt was flying, assured of our thinking and persuasive in his arguments. When Davies reported in August, he gave the BBC a huge tick of financial confidence and proposed a special digital licence fee that would bring in extra revenue as digital take-up grew. The sums mentioned, however, were disastrously low. John Birt led a polite but firm response to the effect of 'thank you but this will not do'.

John's tactics here were bold. He was ultimately rewarded early in the new year, after I had left, with a five-year licence fee of 1.5 per cent above the retail price index. This would have been undreamed of a dozen years earlier. It was a magnificent result and a fitting reward for an extraordinary term as director-general.

Chapter twenty-one
CLOSEDOWN

Soon after Greg Dyke had been appointed as the new director-general in the summer of 1999, John Birt gave the New Statesman Lecture. A dinner followed, and as this broke up, I spotted Greg leaving with a little entourage of BBC executives. They were hanging on to the coat tails of the new man and laughing rather more than was strictly necessary. It is the way of things.

Soon Greg, who was to join officially in November, began popping up here and there, finding out about his new domain. Colleagues began to drop his name nonchalantly into the conversation: 'I had a drink with Greg' or 'I've spoken to Greg.' They were saying to others and themselves, 'It's going to be alright for me. Really, it is.' As the new man let slip hints of his thinking – more money for sport, more for local radio – he left little pools of turbulence in his wake. At a seminar for news, Nicholas Witchell asked of John Birt, 'Will news be as safe in the new regime as it has been . . .'. He trailed away, searching for the right way to put it.

'As under me?' asked John, he and the whole room laughing.

When Margaret Salmon, director of personnel, came on the chairman's behalf to ask if I would stay on for a year or so, I said no. I had nothing but warm feelings about the BBC and I liked Greg, but I did not want to be the last lord standing from when the old king was alive. Moreover, I had agreed to become chair of the governors of the London Institute, a consortium of five of London's colleges of art, design and communications, where I had been a governor for a while. I was considering other offers and my daughter Rozzy had just announced that a grandchild was in the offing. I was ready to go.

The knowledge that I was heading for the check-out began to colour my attitude to familiar tasks. I became more impatient with the piles of papers for my weekend reading. At the English national forum in Manchester – a gathering of the chairs of all the regional advisory committees – instead of enjoying this sort of debate as usual, I began feeling grumpy. When an old friend, Gillian Reynolds, the critic and broadcaster, gave a funny and pertinent talk to all of us there, I reverted to metropolitan type, wondering why Liverpudlians talk as if being born there was the equivalent of the Order of Merit but none of them ever seemed to live there.

However, I also savoured with pleasure things I knew I was experiencing for the last time in the BBC. Among these were visits to Cardiff and Belfast, where I had an expert briefing on the political situation and visited the bright new call centre. At the end of November, Jane and I were at Television Centre for Children in Need, as I had been for nineteen successive years, save for the night that my mother had died. In the early years I always stayed until the show came off the air at 2.00 a.m. That was no longer part of my role, but I always enjoyed the atmosphere and on the night made silly bids at the auction, successful in one, outbid by the chairman in the other. The last big sporting occasion I went to was the Rugby World Cup Final at the new Millennium stadium in Cardiff, where Australia beat France. I took my brother and we sat with Greg and his son Joe, a sharp lad, who when his father returned home after an early visit to the BBC and said, 'I met 250 people yesterday,' had challenged him immediately: 'Name one of them.'

However much I enjoyed life in the beeb and however hard I was working, I had made sure that I kept some balance in my life. I took my holidays with Jane, usually Cumbria in the spring and France, Italy or the United States in the summer. I tried to be home for family birthdays, preferably to take Jane, Hannah and Rozzy to the theatre. When running documentary features, I served as a judge for the Olivier theatre awards; as managing director of television, I was a judge for their opera awards. I played occasional Friday morning tennis in the 1980s and cricket for the Mis-hits until the mid-1990s. I stopped before I became a makeweight.

Living near work until 1995 had helped. I could be home in a trice or pop in of an evening for a recording or on Christmas morning with chocolates for reception, the presentation and weather teams. For most of the 1990s I worked all day Sunday and watched cassettes late into midweek evenings or on Saturday mornings. Some Saturdays I was too knackered to do anything but put on a CD – Bach cantatas at the most stressful times – and try to find my way back to the light. On the other hand, when travelling in this country or abroad, I would manipulate my schedule to find an hour or two for art galleries or interesting buildings. I went racing when I could. I had been in one syndicate owning a couple of two-year-olds trained by Toby Balding, and had now joined another to share a jumper trained by the welcoming Paul Webber. I wanted more of all this.

I intended to continue to work, but in new pastures. I was offered a well-paid part-time job in the broadcasting industry but turned it down. It was too much like the more tedious side of what I had been doing. I took over as chairman of the London Institute, and past and future came together when I went to the Central St Martin's graduate show for the MA in Fine Art and found several of the cast of *EastEnders* in a room full of portraits of themselves. I was able to tell Pam St Clement, Pat Butcher in the programme, that I had just bought three ceramic busts of her done by another student: one to give her, one for the producer and one for me.

I expected no withdrawal symptoms at disengaging from the on-line steering group, the digital steering group, the marketing steering group, the financial systems steering group, the efficiency review, the rights strategy group, the Discovery working group, the UKTV board, the broadcast steering group, the presentation project and many more. Nor would I miss the documents, of which there was always one more iteration, the iterations of which there is always a next, the circles that were always virtuous, the 'issues' that were always 'key' and came in 'sets'. It would be a relief not to be working in television so that at parties people would not keep telling me that they had no television or 'we don't watch much television', as if they expected me to burst into tears at this news. I would no longer have to mask a smirk when a few moments later they began asking or complaining about various programmes that they had by some magic seen.

When Greg Dyke joined officially, I proposed that my team report to him from then on. It seemed sensible for him to get to know them and for them to forge a relationship with him. We all met together. His first headlines to the group were that he wanted to 'reduce the aggro round the place', that it all felt very metropolitan, that it was mad that our studios were empty with work going outside and that the BBC was 'very process driven – I like to work by instinct'. To all this there was much nodding and agreeing. Alan Yentob said to him, 'Your message will be . . .'. Laughter as Greg looked amused. Alan tried once again: 'Well I'm sure your message will be . . .'. More laughter, Alan joining in. 'Will it be . . .?'

I had moved into a large open plan office and was a convert to this way of working. Greg came for a chat and looked around with apparent approval, though complaining that on the DG's floor, 'They've given me a smaller desk that I had when I joined LWT as a researcher.' Then and on other occasions he asked me lots of questions and appeared to listen intently but never took a note. I knew that John Birt, sceptical as I was that Greg appreciated the scope of what he had taken on, was deliberately involving him in the more tedious aspects of running the BBC, such as the World Service funding, Brussels issues and so on, in order to help him see the whole picture.

In the final months some other farewells contributed to my twilight mood. Jana Bennett, by now director of programmes in the production directorate, left to accept an offer to work for Discovery in the USA. Jana was American and this was a great opportunity. She said some kind words about colleagues at her farewell drinks and concluded with a paean of praise for John Birt, 'a great DG'.

Others left not the BBC but this life. Tony Isaacs, editor of *The World About Us* in documentary feature days, was buried at Golders Green Crematorium on a grey August day. I was reminded of how I had once sent him a telegram to some distant spot reading: 'Come home immediately.' Friends recalled how his famously bad back so often necessitated extra days away. He had once tried to persuade the departmental manager that the most cost-effective way of getting to Germany was via Israel, with a stopover. Frank Gillard, former head of radio and friend from programme-making days in the 1970s, died. At the 30th birthday of local radio, which was his inspiration, I had seen him give a spontaneous speech about its beginnings, which for its attack, construction and liveliness would have been a triumph for a man half his 89 years. Jennifer Patterson, one of the *Two Fat Ladies*, died. I went to the funeral at Brompton Oratory. The congregation for the stratospherically high Catholic mass was an eclectic mix. The family were very smart in black, elsewhere were business suits, jeans and a man in pink trousers. Next to me a chap was going solo in a rite all his own. He was always first to stand and first to kneel, adding a lot of special individual kneeling, often with highly choreographed crossings of himself. At the 'mea culpa' bit he hammered himself noisily on the chest. Quite a turn. Jennifer Patterson's coffin was borne out very slowly and splendidly, her motorcycle helmet carried before. The memorial service for Jill Dando in All Souls Langham Place was of a very different order. It featured a kitsch modern anthem and a deeply embarrassing contribution from Cliff Richard. John Birt spoke admirably about Jill, passing with an A-grade for avoiding any use of the word 'I', save in a brief aside.

Ludovic Kennedy was still very much with us and I gave a small dinner for his 80th birthday, to which came Robert Kee and Sir Robin Day along with all his and Moira's children and other friends. Ludo recalled distant cavalier days when a crew of seventeen travelled to Germany for two days to film an interview with the German president that was so boring not a frame reached the screen.

Wistful goodbyes and birthdays apart, I still had masses on my plate. Apart from everything else, millennium matters were approaching their climax. Two years before, I had assembled a group to devise and pull together all our programming for 2000 and put Nicholas Kenyon, an impresario, at the helm. We planned programmes to look back, to celebrate the turn of the year and to look forward. Radio and television came up with many good ideas. At the centre of it all was to be the coverage from the Dome, which in turn was the chief part of the BBC's contribution to a 28-hour continuous broadcast from around the globe, masterminded from Television Centre. It took months to negotiate what was to happen and what we could cover, in part because BSkyB was a sponsor of the Dome and wanted its return. Alan Yentob was on the so-called 'litmus group' assessing ideas for the Dome, as well as responsible for our television plans. As usual, Alan had lots of ideas. At one programme discussion he was carried away: 'Yes, what we want at midnight on the 31st is David Attenborough live at the North Pole.'

'Alan,' interrupted Alistair Fothergill, head of natural history, 'I think you'll find that at midnight on the 31st David will want to be at home in Richmond.'

I had established a group to set a strategy for the BBC's wonderful archives, which contained 50,000 feet of files, 3 million photographs and 1.5 million film and video items. I was able to move things to the point where we secured funding to preserve material that existed only on obsolete and deteriorating tape, planned the digitization of both sound and video, reviewed criteria for selecting and retaining material, and sought to encourage greater use by programme makers. When I left, the head of the archives gave me facsimiles of Brian Jones' hand-written letter asking for an audition for the 'Rollin' Stones' with their 'authentic Chicago rhythm and blues sound', and George Bernard Shaw's letter urging the BBC to commission Elgar's Third Symphony.

I was a big fan of the comedy *Operation Good Guys*, a cod documentary series about the police. For the third series the producer asked me to play myself interrupting a recording in a supposed BBC studio and then being hustled off the premises by one of the cast dressed as a policeman dressed in turn as a snowball. This did not go on long enough for me. I was hungry for more scenes but the producer, with the audience in mind, offered none.

I had to think about the futures of three people I saw everyday and who managed much of my life for me. Sally, my PA, was going to get married and was thinking of moving to work for the BBC in her native Scotland. Sylvia Hines was my company secretary, as it were, and would have no obvious job. But she was able and the first person I had seen disagreeing with Greg, telling him what needed to be done. 'Did I come over as a bad-tempered harridan?' she asked me afterwards. No, like someone who knew her stuff. Bill Ansbro, my driver, might be out of a job. At my first meeting with Greg Dyke I had said, 'You should know that I have got the best driver. Ask around, you will hear the same. Make sure you get him.' The next thing I heard was that the transport unit would not allow Bill to have a trial for the new DG because 'he is working for you, so he's not free'. With some irritation I pointed out that he would be out of a job in a month or so, and that if it would help, I would surrender him right away. Meanwhile, Jane was working on Greg's partner, Sue. Bill had his trial and Greg chose him.

The Birt era was coming to an end. At the Royal Television Society conference in Cambridge, the most important industry gathering, John was interviewed for an hour. He was reflective, generous about his colleagues and twice emphasized how much change had started under Mike Checkland as DG. Back at the office I could tell the sun was setting when John was heard in meetings saying, 'I'm a bit process lost' and 'We seem to have too many meetings discussing the same paper.' I even heard Patricia Hodgson, very much the tough policeman when it came to protecting the BBC from over commercialism, say, 'Worldwide is clearly too constrained.' John was determined that we all help Greg in every possible way, but things were drifting away from him. Several times he rang me beginning, 'Another disappointment', as Greg's plans took shape. One or two of the people close to John, as if in occupied France in 1945, were desperately trying to find out what was happening and hoping not to hear the sound of approaching hair clippers.

By November, Sir Thomas Wyatt's words rang true for me: 'They fly from me that sometime did me seek.' I was history. At a joint broadcast and production day at Lord's cricket ground I had flu, was groggy, lost my voice and had to retire from the crease. I could see that there was nothing I could do anyway. Everyone was retreating to prepared positions, production colleagues playing a dead bat in the hope of future change.

I had had a wonderful voyage but was now looking forward to disembarking. I was also aware that the culture had changed and the language had changed. In business papers 'detail' had become 'granularity' and 'neutral' had become 'vanilla', a slur on a flavour if ever there was one. On the air, 'literally' now meant metaphorically, 'invariably' meant sometimes and, of a programme, 'live', heaven help us, now meant 'recorded', albeit in front of an audience. BBC correspondents threw prepositions up to land where they would – 'the idea *to* open free speech,' 'causing injury *of* many others,' 'the attack *against* Clinton,' and 'oblivious *about*'; or land not at all – 'the crowds protesting the decision'. Pronunciation notes on the wall of the newsroom were clearly a thing of the past, for all stresses had been reversed: 'r'cess' was 'reecess', d'spute' was 'disspute', 'St James' was 'Saynt James', whereas '*West*minster' was now West*min*ster, '*h*ospital' was ' hospitoow' and 'Sainsburys' was 'Sainsburees'. This was not where I came in. I was becoming a crusty.

I had always felt that television should take note of Charles Dickens' introduction to the first issue of his magazine *Household Words* in 1850: 'We have considered what an ambition it is to be admitted into many homes with affection and confidence; to be regarded as a friend by children and old people . . . and to be associated with the harmless laughter and the gentle tears of many hearths. We know the great responsibility of such a privilege.' I think that the BBC could still nail this above its door, but it now sounds almost absurdly old-fashioned. The laughter on the air is not always so harmless. The new humour that would recoil in horror at mother-in-law jokes is happy to be cruel about people's physical appearance. The divide between private and public jokes is being torn down, as is that between public and private behaviour. Switch between digital channels at 10.30 of an evening and you will see at holiday resort after holiday resort young people throwing up and dropping their trousers.

By 1999 we were in a world where Channel 4 ran a series in which contestants identified their partner in a line up of people who revealed only their private parts. It did not lift the heart. As for common politeness and respect for the audience, fewer seemed to notice or care. In an early Graham Norton show he interviewed a member of the public on a live link to her line-dancing club. The woman had difficulty in hearing a question because of a technical glitch. Norton turned to the camera and studio audience and sniggered, 'Deaf cow.' Norton is a star and highly sought after.

The lessons I had learned over the years were many and disparate, among them that it was essential to trust the talent. But it is not always enough, *pace Eldorado*; research does help even the best people. Beware when someone tells you, 'I'm not going anywhere', for they may well be. Do not hope for the day when 'morale is at an all-time high' and bosses are carried round the courtyard of Television Centre of a Friday afternoon on the shoulders of the joyful staff; it may never come. When someone comes into you office and begins, 'You know me, Will, I have never been concerned with money . . .', he or she is about to ask for a pay rise. And the day of the speech *does* come round.

Earlier in the year, as we had debated our ideas for new services around the baize-covered tables in the Tudor Suite at Hever Castle, I had had mixed emotions. I was excited by the scope and ambition of the plans. This was the right road ahead for the BBC and I was proud to have played a part in draw-ing the map. Yet I left the conference feeling that the task of delivering all the propositions was beyond the ability of the BBC as it then was. It would require a profound change to achieve a much more collaborative culture. At the last gathering of the top thirty or so people in my division, I asked each of them to say what they wanted the new DG to do. 'More money for sport', 'invest in local radio', 'get moving on digital radio' and 'reduce the demand for information' were among the varying replies. They then asked me what I would do first if taking over. I said that I would take my senior team to learn from whichever companies we could identify around the world that had built success on a collaborative and creative culture, then use the lessons to transform the BBC.

Yet I was leaving a BBC in rude health. The hard won licence fee increase that was about to be awarded would make this health even ruder. We had 45 per cent of the public's listening and viewing with around 30 per cent of the broadcasting revenues. There were fewer bum programmes than in times past. I noted some pleasing parallels between the year I moved into television and the year I was going – 1968 was the first year of colour, promising 'the dawn of a new era'; 1999 was the first year of digital, promising the same. In 1968 the BBC won the Prix Italia for drama and the Golden Rose of Montreux for comedy; in 1999 it did the same with *Shooting the Past* and *The League of Gentlemen*. In 1968 the Postmaster General (then the respon-sible minister) authorized an increase of broadcasting hours from 50 to 53½ per week on BBC1 and from 30 to 32½ on BBC2; in 1999 the Secretary of State for Culture, Media and Sport had just authorized the BBC's digital services. In both years a new director-general was about to take over.

In 1968 you might think that the BBC had been at the height of its power. It was the only radio broadcaster and had two of the only three television channels. Fifteen million households could receive three channels and the average viewing of BBC television was 6.8 hours per head per week. Yet in 1999, when 24 million homes had at least four channels and a third of homes had access to dozens more, the BBC's average weekly viewing per head had not merely held up but risen – by four hours. On radio, where it now faced competition national and local, BBC listening had risen by two hours. The BBC had more services of course, but this command of the audi-ence is not what anyone had anticipated. As I write, commercial media companies have been hard hit over the past three years. The BBC, with a licence fee increase and rising revenues, looks even more powerful than in 1968, stretching across television, radio and its superb internet services.

The pressure on the Corporation now is to remain part of everyone's daily existence in a way that enhances the quality of life in the United Kingdom. There have been some wobbles in recent years, as in the past. As broadcasting services of all kinds become more particular and more targeted and as taste and consumption fragments, the question for the BBC is whether it can remain in touch with the whole population. That means with the broadening and, to my eye, coarser taste of many of the young, at the same time as it keeps an arm round the elderly and a warm relationship with the middle classes. It will be more difficult than ever, especially with bruised competitors discarding commercial swagger in favour of shouts to the ref.

Greg Dyke had a strong inheritance with money to spend and has done some excellent things in his first three years. He has made some good appointments, has cheered people up, raised the standing of local radio and put himself around. I get the sense that he is fun to work for. He is also striving to build the modern collaborative culture in the BBC that I sensed was essential to achieve its ambitions – a big prize if he can pull it off. He scored high marks all round for agreeing swift action to move the news to ten o'clock, taking advantage of his honeymoon period with the governors. He has made much of the BBC's sport, and while there may not be more of it (*Match of the Day* was lost in 2000 – he will want to get it back), the message is strong and the output looks confident. Greg also found a way to keep digital terrestrial television alive when ITV Digital collapsed, by launching Freeview, which is going well, and pulled off a coup in bypassing Sky encryption for BBC channels on digital satellite.

The two big question marks are over the output and the future. The big messages about the output have been wrong and the rhetoric lacking in what makes the BBC different. Television has appeared too keen on figures alone. You never ever have to encourage channel controllers to be more competitive. Once they sit in those chairs, they start to fight for every half share point; the job of those managing them is to remind them, push them and at times make them do all the other things that a BBC schedule has to, and do them prominently. Beating ITV must have been fun – and I did cheer – but it is *not the point*. No need to do it again as long you stay in touch and are competitive when you need to be.

The BBC's charter expires in 2006 and the campaign for its renewal looks to have started late. The trick with political campaigns is to set the agenda. That means being sure of your own vision, thinking through all possible challenges and arguing on your terms. So far it is the BBC's enemies who have been making the moves, and the play is all in the BBC's half. There will be a new charter and the BBC will remain a mighty broadcaster, but there are many who want it less mighty than it has been. This is the agenda of those who want the BBC entirely regulated by OfCom. It will be hard to move out of defence and chase them off. But Greg is a charismatic chief and a powerful advocate and I hope to see him prevail. As to my fears about the politicization of the BBC, it is far too early to judge. Greg Dyke has spoken up strongly for the independence of the

BBC's journalism, as I would have expected him to. It is interesting, though, how often the press refers to the Labour sympathies of both chairman and DG.

As I said to Greg Dyke when he arrived, by far the greatest pleasure of working in the BBC is the people you work with. I had colleagues I admired, whose company I looked forward to when I got up in the morning, who made me laugh and whose talent, energy and commitment brought the best out in me. It was also true that the very institution itself was something I was proud to work for. It was big, it was cumbersome, it could be maddeningly perverse and arrogant at times and you felt that you were working and managing in a goldfish bowl, but this was because it was the public's money you were handling and because the public cared about what the BBC did and how it did it. This sense of public ownership brought a unique relationship with the audience. The BBC has one purpose only: to provide programmes and services for the public. It was a great idea that became – and remains – a great reality.

On the final working morning of my time in the BBC I visited a live programme from the Floral Hall of the Royal Opera House, one result of the negotiations I had instigated. Ballet and opera on BBC1 in the morning felt like a bit of a triumph. Jane Lush, once my PA and now in charge of daytime programming, was there, as was the producer, Frances Whitaker, a colleague from my first days in television. As Jim Moir was fond of saying, 'Thus nature balances itself.'

There were parties, of course. John Motson took a box for a gang of us at Newbury Races. My team in broadcast gave me a jolly dinner, complete with a hilarious quiz. They took my book on B. Traven as the model and conducted 'The search for the real Alan [my baptismal name] Wyatt.' John Birt had begun a tradition that a BBC star chef cooked the annual executive committee lunch. This year it was Jamie Oliver. Jane was invited and John made a blush-making speech about me. I wrote to thank him.

> Thank you so much for that very happy lunch on Monday. It was exactly right in tone and style. I know that Jane loved it – albeit feeling below par – and for me to have Jane there to share the pleasure (and hear the praise) was the most special part. Thank you, too, for the presents.
>
> Your own words were generous in the extreme. I am glad that you sent me the notes – that was a kind thought – although I shall wait a while before I look at them. Too much of all this may not be good for one.
>
> I glowed, of course, at your praise. We work in different ways and that has meant that there has not always been a complete fit with frustrations on both sides. But these have been secondary to the main business in our working together.
>
> I have always been clear about the huge strengths that you have brought to the BBC, strengths that I could not have

supplied and which I know has brought the best out of me. My strengths were different and I think complemented yours well.

In any event, it has worked well overall. I suspect that the past years will look even more extraordinary in retrospect – the scale of the task, the risks, the competition, the pressure, the opposition, the workload and the breadth of change. Thank you for making me part of that.

I go with our services looking good and I feel surprisingly unsentimental and unemotional. There has not been much time for that as until last week I was working still at full steam. I wish there was a clean and simple hand over to be effected but there is not so I have tried to ensure that the stride of the place does not falter.

Good luck in your own final months.

Finally I was given a huge party in studio six at Television Centre. The guests covered all my years in the BBC, 'The Night of the Living Dead', as Desmond Wilcox dubbed it. The centrepiece was *This Is Your Life*, conducted by Terry Wogan with contributions from Joan Bakewell, Bob Robinson, Bill Cotton, Paul Fox, Peter O'Sullevan, Alan Yentob and John Birt. In response I tried to make them laugh. I had had thirty-four happy years; I was now happy to go. Since I had first heard it, I had liked an Australian expression that all people in big jobs should bear in mind and I reminded guests of that evening: 'Today's roosters; tomorrow's feather dusters.' My feathers, I said, were falling as I spoke. When I looked back on it all, I found it impossible to conjure up great emotions or find an epic story. Rather, I told them, I was reminded of an exchange in *Waiting for Godot*. Vladimir says to Estragon: 'Well that passed the time.' Estragon replies: 'It would have passed in any case.'

TV Version: Fade to Black.

Radio Version: The Shipping Forecast followed by National Anthem.

JOBS AND PEOPLE

Year	W. Wyatt	Director-General	MD Television	Dep. MDTV or Dir. Progs	CBBC1	
1965	Sub-editor in radio news	H. Greene				
1966	(marries Jane)					
1967	(Hannah born)				P. Fox	
1968	TV Presentation	C. Curran				
1969			H. Wheldon	Attenborough		
1970	(Rozzy born)					
1971	To *Late Night Line Up*; (moves to Oxon)					
1972						
1973				A. Milne		
1974	Exec. Prod.				B. Cowgill	
1975						
1976	(moves to London)		I. Trethowan			
1977	Asst Hd, Pres. Progs	I. Trethowan	A. Milne	R. Scott	B. Cotton	
1978						
1979						
1980	Traven book published					

CBBC2	Chairman/ other	Programmes		Year
Attenborough		24 Hours, Tomorrow's World		1965
		Cathy Come Home Softly, Softly		1966
	C. Hill C'man	Forsyte Saga, Wimbledon in colour		1967
				1968
R. Scott		BBC1 in colour, Civilisation	Moon landing	1969
		Six Wives of Henry VIII		1970
		Two Ronnies, Film 71, Old Grey Whistle Test	Radio licence fee abolished O.U. broadcasts	1971
	(Attenborough left)	Mastermind, A. Cooke's America		1972
	M. Swann C'man	That's Life, Last of the Summer Wine, Ascent of Man		1973
A. Singer			Ceefax	1974
		Fawlty Towers, The Good Life		1975
		I, Claudius, When the Boat Comes In		1976
			Annan Report	1977
B. Wenham	(Singer – MD Radio)	Pennies From Heaven, All Creatures Great and Small		1978
		Life on Earth, Antiques Roadshow		1979
	G. Howard C'man	Newsnight, Children in Need, Yes, Minister		1980

Year	W. Wyatt	Director-General	MD Television	Dep. MDTV or Dir. Progs	CBBC1	
1981	Hd Doc. Features				A. Hart	
1982		A. Milne	A. Singer			
1983	Ch. Violence guidelines			B. Wenham		
1984			B. Cotton		M. Grade	
1985						
1986						
1987	Violence g'lines. Fail to become CBBC1, CBBC2 or Chief Exec C4	M. Check-land			J. Powell	
1988	Asst MD Tel		P. Fox			
1989						
1990						
1991	MD Tel		W. Wyatt		(Powell left in Dec)	

CBBC2	Chairman/ other	Programmes		Year
		Forty Minutes, Only Fools and Horses, Bergerac	Broadcasting Complaints Commission	1981
		Boys From the Blackstuff	Channel 4	1982
G. MacDonald	<u>S. Young</u> C'man	Breakfast Time, Blackadder		1983
		Crimewatch UK, All Our Working Lives	Jewel in the Crown	1984
	(M. Checkland Dep. DG)	EastEnders, Live Aid, Real Lives, Comrades		1985
	<u>M. Hussey</u> C'man (Wenham MD Radio)	Casualty, The Singing Detective, The Monocled Mutineer, Childwatch	Peacock Report, 25% independent quota announced	1986
A. Yentob	(J. Birt Dep. DG) (Wenham left)	Kilroy	Licence fee to be pegged to RPI	1987
		Tumbledown, See For Yourself	Broadcasting Standards Council	1988
		Around the World in 80 Days, The Late Show, Birds of a Feather	Sky launched	1989
		Have I Got News for You, One Foot in the Grave, Keeping Up Appearances, House of Cards, Oranges Are Not the Only Fruit	Funding the Future report; Sky becomes BSkyB; Broadcasting Bill published; Mrs Thatcher resigns	1990
	Hussey reapptd	Noel's House Party, Spender	Lime Grove closed; Television Resources review; ITV franchises awarded	1991

Year	W. Wyatt	Director-General	MD Television	Dep. MDTV or Dir. Progs	CBBC1	
1992					A. Yentob	
1993		J. Birt				
1994						
1995	(Moves to Oxfordshire)					
REORG	Chief Exec. Broadcast	Director-General	Director Television	Chief Exec. Production	CBBC1	
1996	W. Wyatt	J. Birt (re apptd for 4 years)	M. Jackson	R. Neil	M. Jackson	
1997			A. Yentob		P. Salmon	
1998						
1999	Retires 31 Dec	(Greg Dyke appointed)		M. Bannister		

CBBC2	Chairman/ other	Programmes		Year
M. Jackson		*Elizabeth R, Absolutely Fabulous, Between the Lines, Eldorado, Pandora's Box*	Premier League deal; Major wins Election; Green Paper on BBC; TV overspend revealed; Extending Choice pub.	1992
	(L. Forgan MD Radio) (B. Phillis Dep. DG)	*Goodnight Sweetheart, Buddha of Suburbia, The Wrong Trousers*	Producer Choice begins; 'Armanigate'	1993
		Middlemarch, Martin Chuzzlewit, Vicar of Dibley, Men Behaving Badly, Knowing Me Knowing You, The Fast Show	White Paper on the BBC; D-Day anniversary	1994
		Diana interview, Pride and Prejudice, People's Century, Death of Yugoslavia, 'Fermat's Last Theorem'	World War II anniversaries; Premiership renewed; FA Cup and Formula One lost	1995
CBBC2				
M. Thompson	C. Bland C'man (L. Forgan left; M. Bannister Dir. Radio)	*Our Friends in the North, Ballykissangel, Dalziel and Pascoe, Only Fools* returns, *This Life*	Extending Choice in the Digital Age; BBC Charter renewed; Olympics deal	1996
	(B. Phillis & M. Jackson left)	*Nazis – A Warning From History, Jonathan Creek, The Provos*	Flextech & Discovery deals; launch of News24 & BBC Online; Blair wins Election; Channel 5	1997
J. Root		*Vanity Fair, Life of Birds, Human Body, Our Mutual Friend, Royle Family, Talking Heads 2*	BBC America launched; BBC Choice launched on digital	1998
	J. Abramsky Dir. Radio)	*Wives and Daughters, Walking With Dinosaurs, Shooting the Past, League of Gentlemen*	BBC Knowledge launched; Wimbledon renewed; Des Lynam goes	1999

RATINGS

Share across TV channels, 1986-2001

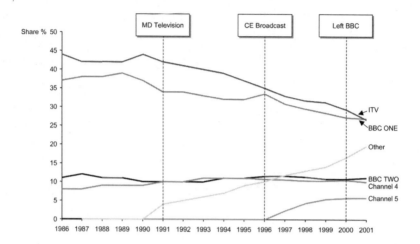

Difference in share

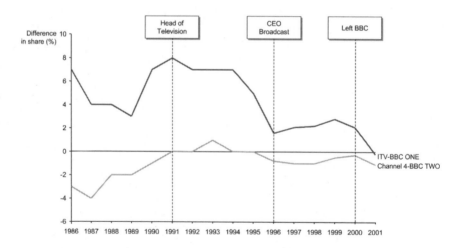

Difference in share: (ITV plus Channel 4) - (BBC ONE plus TWO)

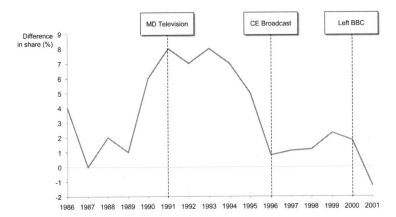

INDEX